Busks, Basques and Brush-Braid

Busks, Basques and Brush-Braid

*British dressmaking in the
18th and 19th centuries*

Pam Inder

BLOOMSBURY VISUAL ARTS
LONDON • NEW YORK • OXFORD • NEW DELHI • SYDNEY

BLOOMSBURY VISUAL ARTS
Bloomsbury Publishing Plc
50 Bedford Square, London, WC1B 3DP, UK
1385 Broadway, New York, NY 10018, USA
29 Earlsfort Terrace, Dublin 2, Ireland

BLOOMSBURY, BLOOMSBURY VISUAL ARTS and the Diana
logo are trademarks of Bloomsbury Publishing Plc

First published in Great Britain 2020
Paperback edition first published 2022

Copyright © Pam Inder, 2020

Pam Inder has asserted her right under the Copyright, Designs
and Patents Act, 1988, to be identified as Author of this work.

For legal purposes the Acknowledgements on p. xi constitute
an extension of this copyright page.

Cover image: Sleeve of an 18th century dress, Leicestershire Museums
Collections (565.1977). Photograph © Pamela Inder.

All rights reserved. No part of this publication may be reproduced or transmitted in
any form or by any means, electronic or mechanical, including photocopying, recording,
or any information storage or retrieval system, without prior permission in writing
from the publishers.

Bloomsbury Publishing Plc does not have any control over, or responsibility for,
any third-party websites referred to or in this book. All internet addresses given
in this book were correct at the time of going to press. The author and publisher
regret any inconvenience caused if addresses have changed or sites have
ceased to exist, but can accept no responsibility for any such changes.

A catalogue record for this book is available from the British Library.

A catalog record for this book is available from the Library of Congress.

ISBN: HB: 978-1-3500-6089-0
       PB: 978-1-3502-4283-8
       ePDF: 978-1-3500-6090-6
       eBook: 978-1-3500-6091-3

Typeset by Integra Software Services Pvt. Ltd.

To find out more about our authors and books visit www.bloomsbury.com
and sign up for our newsletters.

Contents

List of illustrations	vi
Sources of illustrations	x
Acknowledgements	xi
Introduction	1

Part One The development of the dressmaking trade

1	'About suppressing the women mantua-makers'	11
2	'The art and mystery of mantua-making'	25
3	'I bought me a gowne'	49
4	'Undeviating endeavours to please'	85
5	'At short notice … and at most economic charges'	115
6	The watershed of the 1870s	139
7	Winners and losers	169

Part Two Dressmakers in fact and fiction

8	Dressmakers in fiction	195
9	Dressmakers in fact	213
10	Ladies and their dressmakers	229

Conclusion	261
Notes	273
Bibliography	287
Index	300

List of illustrations

Colour Plates

I *The Vyner Family* by John Michael Wright, *c.* 1673.
II Samples of printed calico and ribbon sent to Lady Winn at Nostell Priory in Yorkshire by Mrs Charlton, her London dressmaker.
III The Shrewsbury mantua, 1708–9.
IV Details of the construction and stitching of the mantua.
V 1770s dress of striped silk brocade with elaborate garniture.
VI Detail of a printed muslin dress of 1835 showing the 'diamond' back and huge sleeves which were a feature of the period.
VII Detail of a dress purple ribbed silk made by Adderly's department store, Leicester, *c.* 1895.
VIII *The Song of the Shirt* by John Thomas Peele, 1849.

Black-and-white illustrations

1	Madame Mason's bill, 1692–3.	12
2	Page from *The Workwoman's Guide*, 1838.	13
3	Detail of a nineteenth-century chemise showing the use of an oblong for the sleeve and a folded square for the underarm gusset.	14
4	A French tailor measuring a lady customer, *Gallerie des Modes*, 1778.	23
5	French fashion plate of the 1880s showing a cap decorated with enormous feathers.	28
6	Fashion plate of 1774 showing fashionable ladies in the Assembly Rooms at Weymouth.	31
7	Trade card for Mary and Ann Hogarth's ready-made 'frock shop'.	42
8	Trade card for Martha Cole and Martha Houghton, drapers.	49
9	Draper's shop from *The Book of Trades*, 1818.	50
10	Bill from Susan and Elizabeth Neale, New Bond Street, 1767.	53
11	Mantua-maker's workshop from *Diderot's Encyclopaedia*, 1751–80.	56
12	Flier for Thomas Lomas, draper of Leicester.	69

List of Illustrations

13 Thomas Moxon had premises on Leicester High Street between the late 1820s and the early 1860s. — 81
14 A-L Fashion plates showing the development of fashion in the nineteenth century. — 87
15 Chaffards' former shop on the corner of Castle Street and Princes Street, Edinburgh. — 100
16 Elizabeth Chaffard, 1865–6. — 105
17 Mrs Pattinson's shop on the corner of High Street and Upper Brook Street, Ulverston. — 108
18 The Debtors' Prison in York. — 131
19 Advertisement for Thomas' sewing machines, 1850s. — 140
20 Advertisement for Elias Howe's sewing machine, 1871. — 140
21 Wanzer plaiting (or kilting) machine. — 143
22 Fashion plate from *Le Moniteur de la Mode* of September 1880. — 143
23 Advertisement for the French Bust Company on Tottenham Court Road from *The Draper's Record*, 1895. — 144
24 *Punch* cartoon, 18 November 1893. — 145
25 Dressmaker's workroom from *The Book of Trades*, 1818. — 147
26 Give-away tissue paper pattern from the *Allgemeine Muster-Zeitung* for 1852. — 148
27 Rebecca Thomas's shop on The Promenade, Cheltenham. — 151
28 Caley's of Windsor letterhead, 1846. — 153
29 Lucks of Darlington shop front after the renovation work of 1870. — 156
30 This used to be called 'Bondgate House' and was tenanted by Dodds of Alnwick from the 1880s. — 159
31 Flier from Lindop's of Chester announcing the arrival of Miss Pinch from Redferns. — 163
32 Advertising calendar for Bainbridges of Newcastle, 1868. — 164
33 Madame Clapham's staff in 1908. — 175
34 Advertisement for Samuel Miller's and Marie Schild's publications. — 180
35 The 'Dreadnought' pattern-drafting template. — 185
36 *Punch* cartoon, 26 February 1876. — 186
37 A dressmaker and her assistant from the *Gallerie des Modes*, 1778. — 196
38 *The Seamstress*, watercolour sketch by Richard Redgrave. — 202
39 *Adversity* by Thomas Benjamin Kennington, 1891. — 203
40 Illustration from *The Seamstress or the White Slave of England* by G.M.W. Reynolds, 1853. — 206
41 Advertisement for 'The Period' sewing machine, 1870. — 211

42	Mrs Priscilla Bark, milliner in Leicester, 1870s.	223
43	Eliza Spurrett, *c.* 1855.	240
44	Charlotte Hill, her husband (seated centre left), sons and grandchildren, early 1870s.	244
45	Susanna Ingleby in the widow's weeds made for her by Mrs Dinsdale in 1873.	254
46	Susanna Ingleby with her brother and nephew.	256
47	Cover of the first – and only – issue of *The Sempstress*, dated October 1855.	263

Newspaper advertisements

1	*The Times,* 13 April 1799.	4
2	*Jackson's Oxford Journal,* 5 August 1786.	32
3	*The Newcastle Weekly Courant,* 13 November 1779.	39
4	*The Public Advertiser,* 12 May 1778.	41
5	*The Ipswich Journal,* 23 July 1796.	41
6	*The Bath Chronicle,* 15 February 1780.	41
7	*Jackson's Oxford Journal,* 14 April 1798.	43
8	*The Derby Mercury,* 7 May 1789.	54
9	*The Norfolk Chronicle,* 29 May 1790.	55
10	*The Bath Chronicle,* 12 December 1799.	55
11	*The Times,* 20 September 1780.	70
12	*The Bath Chronicle,* 7 December 1780.	77
13	*The Leeds Intelligencer,* 23 April 1782.	84
14	*Leicester Chronicle,* 11 October 1845.	222
15	*Leicester Chronicle,* 19 May 1827.	239

Figures

1	Map of the UK showing county boundaries as they were in the 1850s.	8
2	Social status of dressmakers in Leicester, Ulverston and Sidmouth, 1841, 1861 and 1881.	218
3	Ages of dressmakers in Leicester, 1841 and 1861.	220
4	Ages of dressmakers in Ulverston, 1841 and 1861.	220
5	Ages of dressmakers in Sidmouth, 1841 and 1861.	220

Tables

1	Relative numbers of girls and boys apprenticed by the tailors' guild in York 1702–10 and 1720–28.	19
2	Table of eighteenth-century garment prices.	61
3	Table of eighteenth-century fabric prices per yard.	71
4	Mantua-makers in the *Universal British Directory* 1791–5.	83
5	Nineteenth-century fabric prices.	122
6	Transactions 1803–4, the McCleod sisters.	124
7	Transactions arranged by month.	126
8	Transactions 1873–83, Miss Clarke of Guildford.	127
9	Mrs Pattinson's accounts for 1897.	129
10	Transactions 1827–8, Binningtons of York.	130
11	Transactions 1844–5, George Nicholson of York.	132
12	Transactions 1876–84, Dodds of Alnwick.	161
13	Population, dressmakers and firms in Leicester, Ulverston and Sidmouth, 1841, 1861 and 1881.	217
14	Arabella Calley's expenditure on dress, 1779–89.	232
15	Eliza Spurrett's dress purchases, 1817–35.	237
16	Eliza Spurrett's annual expenditure, 1817–35.	238

Sources of illustrations

Colour plates: I, National Portrait Gallery, London; II West Yorkshire Archive Service, Wakefield, WYW 1352/3/4/6/8; III and IV, Shropshire Council, Shropshire Museums; V, VI and VII Leicestershire County Council Museums Resource Centre; VIII Albany Institute of History and Art, NY (Daderot, Wikimedia Commons).

Black-and-white plates: 1, by courtesy of the County Archivist, West Sussex Record Office; 5, 6, 8, 14G, 14J and 37, Victoria and Albert Museum; 10, Cambridge County Record Office; 12, 13, 41 and 42, Leicestershire and Rutland County Record Office; 14 A, C and E, Wikimedia, Los Angeles County Museum of Art; 14 B, D, I, K and L, Wikimedia; 14 F and H, Wikimedia, Cooper Hewitt Collection; 15, Valerie Hawkins; 16, National Library of Scotland; 18, Mango salsa, Creative Commons; 21, Norfolk Museums Service (Norwich Castle Museum and Art Gallery); 26, courtesy of Northamptonshire Archive Service; 27, Cheltenham Local and Family History Library; 28 and 32, The John Lewis Partnership Archive; 29, by permission of Durham County Record Office; 31, by permission of Cheshire Archives and Local Studies; 33, Wilberforce House Museum, Hull Museums; 38, courtesy of De Montfort University Library Special Collections; 43, Shropshire Archives (SA 4173/5); 44 and 45, private family collections; 46, The British Library Board.

Acknowledgements

I would like to thank the staff of all the record offices, archives, libraries and museums – too many to name – and David Parkinson of the Incorporated Trades of Aberdeen, who have all assisted me with my research. I would also like to thank my PhD supervisors, Dr Margaret Scott and Professor Janet Myles, formerly of De Montfort University, Leicester, without whose support and encouragement this work would never have been started; Professor Keith Snell of the Department of English Local History at Leicester University who taught me all I know about doing research; my editor Frances Arnold; and my friends – Valerie and David Morley, Christine and Michael Endacott and Valerie Hawkins – for their hospitality while I was working on this book. Finally, I would like to thank my husband for his support and my sons Matthew and John for looking after him, as well as the cats and the house, while I was away from home 'doing research' for weeks at a time.

Introduction

Making an elaborate dress that fits and flatters the wearer, working from an illustration and adapting it according to the instructions of the customer (paper patterns as we know them did not become generally available until the 1870s), requires manual dexterity, taste and understanding of materials on a par with those of a potter, silversmith, woodworker or glass-blower. It also required confidence and courage to cut a garment from fabric that often cost more per yard than the dressmaker would be paid for making the entire garment – yet we seldom know the names of the women who made dresses, even those working in elite establishments for an upper-class clientele.

For much of my working life I was a curator of applied arts in English provincial museums – Birmingham, Exeter and Leicester – all of which have large collections of dress. I became aware that when I put on a display of ceramics or silver, furniture or glass, the labels I wrote attributed artefacts to their maker, but labels for items in a display of dress were purely descriptive – 'Blue silk day dress, c.1862' – or described the *wearer* – 'Wedding dress of ivory satin, worn by Mary Smith at St Margaret's Church, Leicester in February 1877'.

I wanted to learn more about the sort of people who made the many garments that had passed through my hands, and so, quite late in my career, I decided to do a PhD on women working in the dressmaking trade in the nineteenth century. My choice of period was informed by the fact that the majority of dresses in the collections I had curated dated from the nineteenth century; I was also aware that the Children's Employment Commission had reported at length on the dressmaking trade in the 1840s and 1860s; and, naively, I assumed that a reasonable number of nineteenth-century business records would also survive. I had not read *Why Dressmaking Does Not Pay*. It was written by an anonymous author, 'Scissors', and published in 1895: 'Many dressmakers keep no book' she wrote, and I found, to my cost, that she was right. Back in the 1990s when I began my research, record office catalogues were not online and my starting point was the National Register of Archives. When asked for details of nineteenth-century dressmakers' records they could provide me with just three references. It was not a propitious start. A search on the keyword 'dressmaker' on their site today would throw up over 1,400 entries, though, to be fair, most of them would not be sets of business records. In fact, from the tens of thousands of women who set up as dressmakers in Britain in the course of the nineteenth century, barely fifty usable sets of records survive.

While my work on the nineteenth century produced some interesting findings – notably what I describe in Chapter 6 as 'the watershed of the 1870s' – I soon saw that to create a proper history of dressmaking I would need to go much further back in time, to the end of the seventeenth century when women 'mantua-makers' gradually began to infiltrate what had previously been the male-dominated tailoring trade. The purpose of this book, therefore, is to extend my original study and trace the development of dressmaking by women from the 1670s to the end of the 'long nineteenth century' in or around 1914. Nonetheless, the nineteenth century occupies more of this book than do the preceding centuries because this reflects the way the trade developed. Only a handful of women became mantua-makers before 1700, and as we shall see, those who did risked the wrath of their local tailors' guilds. Numbers increased as the eighteenth century progressed, but throughout the century there were far fewer mantua-makers than there were tailors. Norwich, still a prosperous city in the eighteenth century and with a population of around 35,000, had only five mantua-makers in 1783, for example, while just ten served Manchester's 80,000-plus inhabitants in 1788. At the same period Norwich had twenty-nine tailors and Manchester had forty-four.[1] It was the nineteenth century that saw the great expansion of the trade, of developments (notably the sewing machine and paper patterns) that served it, of enquiries into conditions and of outrage at what these unearthed. I therefore make no apology for this apparent imbalance.

Furthermore, if nineteenth-century records of the trade are thin on the ground, those for the preceding centuries are virtually non-existent. Of course, some early dressmakers were illiterate, and no doubt there were many others like Ann Okely in Bedford. Ann's son, Francis, wrote that his milliner mother's 'real knowledge of Accounts was very scanty to the last'. Ann died in 1766. She never kept records nor did a stocktake, but she was of 'a most obliging turn' and knew what her customers wanted; to her family's surprise she became 'one of the most Considerable Traders' in her home town.[2] Girls seldom learned more than simple arithmetic, so it is hardly surprising that many businesswomen like Ann kept inadequate records; it is actually much more surprising that any of their businesses were successful. Another aim of this study, therefore, is to learn more about some of these individuals.

This shortage of records seems to have deterred other authors and very little has been published on the dressmaking trade. There are histories of major fashion houses and a handful of short papers on aspects of the trade, a range of books about women and work in general but virtually nothing on the dressmaking trade per se. This accounts for the comparatively few references to recent material in this text. Of necessity, therefore, I have drawn on a wide range of primary sources – guild records, bills, ladies' personal account books, apprenticeship indentures, inventories, wills, settlement examinations, the reports of court cases, newspaper advertisements, directories, census returns, journals, letters, diaries, novels and paintings. Much of this material has not previously been published. The result is rather like a jigsaw with a lot of the pieces missing – or rather a mosaic, as the surviving pieces do not all fit neatly together – but it is a first attempt to create a coherent history of the British dressmaking trade and I rely heavily on case studies, even though some of them are of relatively insignificant establishments. Where few records survive, those that do are important. I have examined these survivals in considerable depth and I realize that in some cases the level of detail I provide may seem overwhelming; I apologize for this but believe it to be a useful antidote to the shortage of such information elsewhere in the literature on dress history.

Both Ivy Pinchbeck and Alice Clark, practitioners of 'women's history' long before the subject was officially acknowledged, recognized the importance of millinery and dressmaking as skilled trades for women – 'among all business women the milliners ranked first in importance.'[3] Beverley Lemire, in the introduction to *Dress, Culture and Commerce* (1997), remarks on the absence of a study of these trades. Another function of this work, therefore, is to begin to fill a gap in our knowledge and to better understand dressmakers' role in the business world.

This is a history of women, but whether it is 'feminist history' is more open to question. At some points the history of the dressmaking trade intersects neatly with feminist historical theory – the attempts by the men of some tailors' guilds to prevent women encroaching on their trade are a clear example of the patriarchy attempting to suppress women workers. Similarly, the idea of certain skills being essentially female, that it was 'natural' for women to sew, cook, care for children and do housework – the so-called 'separate spheres' theory of women's role – can be applied to the dressmaking trade. Charles Bray in 1857[4] wrote:

She has her sphere; let her work be found in it. If she feed us, clothe us, bring us into the world, educate us, nurse us and make a home what it ought to be, this is her work; and if it be done properly, surely she will have enough to do.

On the one hand, dressmaking was an acceptable occupation because it was apparently an extension of domestic skills, particularly for those women working on a relatively small scale from their own homes; on the other, any involvement of women in commerce was troubling, and as a result many dressmakers took pains to create establishments that appeared to be an extension of the home and 'deliberately cultivated non-business-like behaviour' and insisted on the respectability of their employees[5] as the following advertisement implies:

> WANTED immediately, a PERSON of respect-
> ability, who is Mistress of FANCY DRESS and
> MANTUA-MAKING, and who can finish in an elegant stile.
> Also wanted, an Apprentice of respectable connections. Ap-
> ply at No. 70, St James's-street.

1. *The Times*, 13 April 1799.

However, the suggestion that this meant fewer women set up in business in the nineteenth century simply does not hold water where dressmaking and millinery are concerned; the numbers of such establishments mushroomed.

The fact that the dressmaker's apprentice became a symbol of downtrodden womanhood cannot be laid at the feet of the patriarchy. Women workers were exploited by their mistresses, and both mistresses and their employees were exploited by their female customers, with the result that by the 1840s dressmakers were seen as a uniquely deprived group: 'There is no class of young people in this country, living by their labour, whose happiness, health and lives, are so unscrupulously sacrificed as those of the young dressmakers.'[6] True, dressmakers operated within the male-dominated capitalist system, but women proved to be just as capable of being exploitative of their workforce as any man when their profits and reputations were at stake.

There are many misunderstandings about the position of women in business. For widows or unmarried women over the age of twenty-one, there were in fact no legal problems about running a business – though if a father interfered in his adult daughter's affairs, that daughter would probably have considered it her duty to obey him. But legally, adult single women had control of their own money. For married women the problems were greater. In law they could not own property, make contracts, sue or be sued, and they needed their husbands' authorization for such basic transactions as renting property or opening a bank account. However, the principle of women as 'feme sole traders', defined in *Black's Law Dictionary* of 1891 as 'a married woman, who, by the custom of London [*and elsewhere*], trades on her own account, independently of her husband; so called because, with respect to her trading, she is the same as a feme sole' continued to be recognized up to the 1880s. Nicola Phillips has examined the legal position of women in business in some detail[7] and makes it clear that 'feme couvert' (i.e. married women) and 'feme sole' were 'highly contingent categories rather than concrete determinants of women's trading status' – in other words, a woman's marital status was not necessarily important. Phillips gives numerous examples of the elasticity of the law respecting women's business activities and concludes that a woman's reputation in business was what actually mattered. Indeed, as Jennifer Aniston and Paolo di Martino have shown,[8] up to the Bankruptcy Act of 1880, being a 'feme couvert' could be a positive advantage; married women could manipulate their status to protect not only their own, but their husbands' businesses, from bankruptcy.

Certainly, despite their lack of political and legal status, a great many women managed to trade perfectly successfully, and married women whose husbands were prepared to support them had no particular problems in establishing a business. Numerous married dressmakers mentioned later in this book had no apparent problems in managing their affairs. Doubtless there were men who did not wish their wives to work – though few husbands in the social bracket from which most dressmakers came could have afforded to deny their wives' earning potential. There were also, no doubt, idle husbands who lived off their wives' earnings, and men who drank and gambled their wives' profits away, but there is nothing to suggest that these men were in the majority.

There is another myth about dressmakers that also needs to be examined. There is a belief that needlewomen of all kinds were downtrodden, underprivileged and often immoral, with the result that some feminist historians have come to see needlework itself as a symbol of women's subservience.[9] This is not entirely inaccurate but it is over-simplistic. The needle trades covered a wide range of occupations within which there was a definite hierarchy; milliners and dressmakers were at the top, ranked by the class of firm that employed them. The various grades of seamstress were at the bottom, arranged by how much they were paid and how they were employed; working for a shop was preferable to working for a manufacturer and working directly for a client was better than either. There was some mobility, mostly downward, within the trades. A girl who had trained as a dressmaker would have been able to work as a seamstress but few seamstresses would have been able to get jobs as dressmakers. It is with women at the upper end of the hierarchy, those who made complete garments to order for individual customers, that we are concerned here, and the evidence is that many of these women were highly respectable; the idea of dressmakers' immorality was a masculine construct that had little or no basis in fact.

At this point it might be useful to add some notes on money, measurement, places and terminology.

Prices are given in 'old money' – pounds (£), shillings (s) and pence (d). There were twenty shillings in a pound and twelve pence in a shilling; there were also halfpennies (½d) and farthings (¼d) and guineas (£1.1s.0d). Sometimes sums were rendered in shillings only, rather than pounds and shillings (e.g. 42s.0d = £2.2s.0d). Where currency other than English is referenced (e.g. Scots or French), the contemporary English equivalent will be given in the text. Converting money to its present-day value is fairly meaningless because relative prices have changed so much. What is important is the differentials – when a dressmaker's assistant was earning £4.00 a year (or about 1s.6d a week) for example, a customer able to spend over a pound on a single dress must have seemed like a creature from another planet.

Most British readers are still familiar with the Imperial measurement system of yards, feet and inches. There were three feet in a yard (91.44 cm) and twelve inches (12 × 2.54 cm) in a foot (30.5 cm). There were also ells. The English ell was usually forty-five inches while the Scottish one was usually thirty-seven inches, but it was a measure that varied from place to place and country to country.[10]

I apologize in advance to non-UK readers for referencing so many small, obscure places – it was most inconsiderate of so many people living in such places to involve themselves with the dressmaking trade! I have perhaps also included a disproportionate number of references to my home town of Leicester, not because it was particularly important but because I know it well, and it is, in many ways, a typical provincial English city. I have tried to locate places that are likely to be unfamiliar to many readers by identifying them with their UK county or city, e.g. 'Howick, Northumberland' or 'London's Regent Street' and I include a map showing the UK counties as they were in the mid-nineteenth century [Figure 1]. Where a street, district or parish is *not* so identified, it will be a part of London, e.g. 'St Martins-in-the-Fields'. Finally, let me add that unfamiliarity with British geography should not make a great deal of difference to understanding the picture I present – in this context *what* happened is nearly always more important than *where* it happened.

The terminology I use may also be confusing – again, I apologize. To clarify. Up to the early 1800s the women who made women's dresses were called 'mantua-makers', from the mantua, a new fashion which arrived in Britain in the mid-1670s. The name probably derived from 'manteau', the French for 'coat'; as like coats, mantuas were open down the front. Indeed, in early documents the word is often spelt 'manto' or 'manty'. The term 'mantua-maker' persisted throughout the eighteenth century, though on bills the garments they made were usually called 'gowns' or 'sacks', but in the early 1800s the makers of women's dresses began to style themselves 'dressmakers'. However, confusingly, in nineteenth-century trades directories they usually appear under 'M' for 'Milliners and Dressmakers'. Milliners sold fabric and trimmings and made up accessories like ruffles and handkerchiefs, caps and bonnets and the occasional garment. The two trades were closely interlinked and many firms provided both services. Some milliners specialized in making and trimming caps and bonnets, but until the late nineteenth century the name did not necessarily denote someone who only dealt in headgear. To muddy the waters still further, drapers, haberdashers and mercers sold fabrics and many of the same items as the milliners and often had on their staff women who could make up items to order: the smaller the town, the greater the cross-over between the trades. I shall therefore try to use the various terms in the ways my subjects would probably have used them themselves.

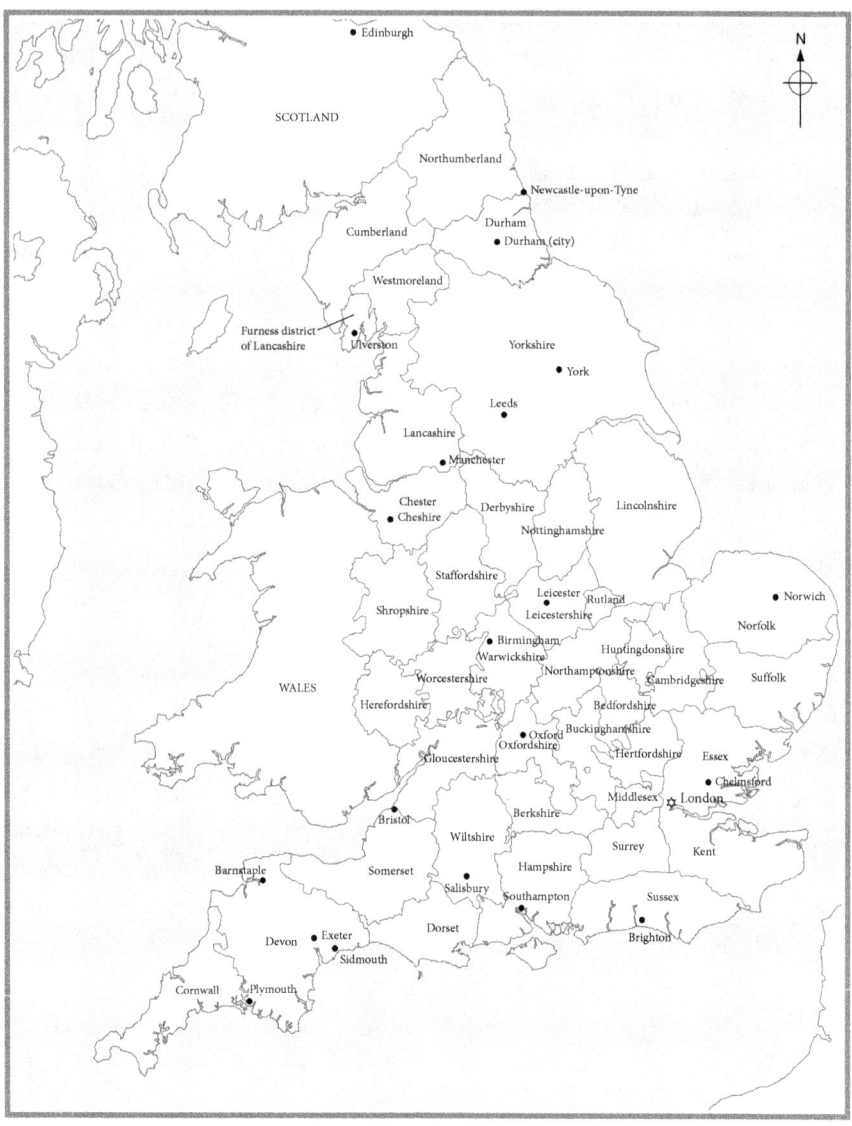

Figure 1 Map of the UK showing county boundaries as they were in the 1850s. They were redrawn in the 1970s.

Part One

The development of the dressmaking trade

1

'About suppressing the women mantua-makers'

In March 1706 in Durham, Isobel Wood gave evidence before the tailors' guild on behalf of her mantua-maker daughter, Elizabeth Browne. 'Mantoes is a forreigne invencion,' said Isobel, 'and brought from beyond sea, and not used in England till about the year 167?' – Isobel could not remember the precise date. She had been in service with Mr Hope, one of the Clerks of the Spicery to Charles II, and remembered 'the Duchess of Mazarene, who came from beyond sea that yeare, and brought the garb of Mantoes with her'. Hortense Mancini, Duchess of Mazarin, came to England in 1675 after the death of her protector, the Duke of Savoy, and within a year she had become one of Charles II's mistresses. Isobel remembered Mrs Hope 'had her first Mantoe made by a Frenchman'.[1] It seems likely, therefore, that Elizabeth Browne learnt about mantuas and how to make them from her mother.

It would appear the mantua was known in England before 1675, however. A portrait of Sir Robert Vyner, later Lord Mayor of London, with his wife, son and stepdaughter, shows Lady Vyner wearing a pale blue silk mantua over a decorated corset and a pink striped and brocaded petticoat.[2] Lady Vyner died in 1674 so the portrait probably dates from 1673. It is a strange picture, in that while the two children are dressed in their silken best, the girl wearing lace and pearls, the little boy in a coat ornamented with gold braid and knots of yellow ribbon, their parents are in expensively casual undress. Sir Robert wears a banyan (a type of housecoat for men, often made, like Sir Robert's, of a rich fabric) but sports a formal full-bottomed wig, while Lady Vyner wears pearls and sparkly earrings with her mantua and has had her hair elaborately coiffed. [Colour Plate I] The fashion spread rapidly. In the late 1670s, for example, Katherine Stewkley wrote from rural Cheshire to her cousin Penelope, in London: 'Pray send me now word what is worn about the neck with a manto, I know they do not generally wear anything, but all people are not able to go bare-necked this winter.'[3]

Randle Holme mentions mantuas in *The Academy of Armory* printed in 1688: 'There is a kind of loose Garment without, and Stiffe Bodies under them and was a great fashion for women about the year 1676. Some called them Mantuas.' These early mantuas seem to have been something like a kaftan or dressing gown, a T-shaped garment, the sleeves cut in one with the bodice, shorter at the front than at the back and open at the front, worn over a skirt or 'petticoat'. The garment wrapped around the body at the front and fastened with pins (if it fastened at all) and was often pleated and/or looped up at the back. The key thing about early mantuas, however, was that they were not fitted and would not have been difficult to make.

Corsets – Holme's 'stiffe bodies' – were worn underneath giving the conical body-shape that was fashionable throughout the seventeenth and eighteenth centuries, and where the corset was on show it was sometimes trimmed or covered to match the mantua. In 1692, for example 'Madame Mason' in Chichester (Sussex) acquired a mantua made of 'strip't silk' for 4s.0d and a pair of stays covered in matching striped silk for £1.5s.0d.[4] [Plate 1] In Berkshire, Lady Judith Alexander[5] favoured black and silver as a colour scheme, and in 1691 she had a black 'anterine'[6] mantua made for 6s.0d., black petticoats trimmed

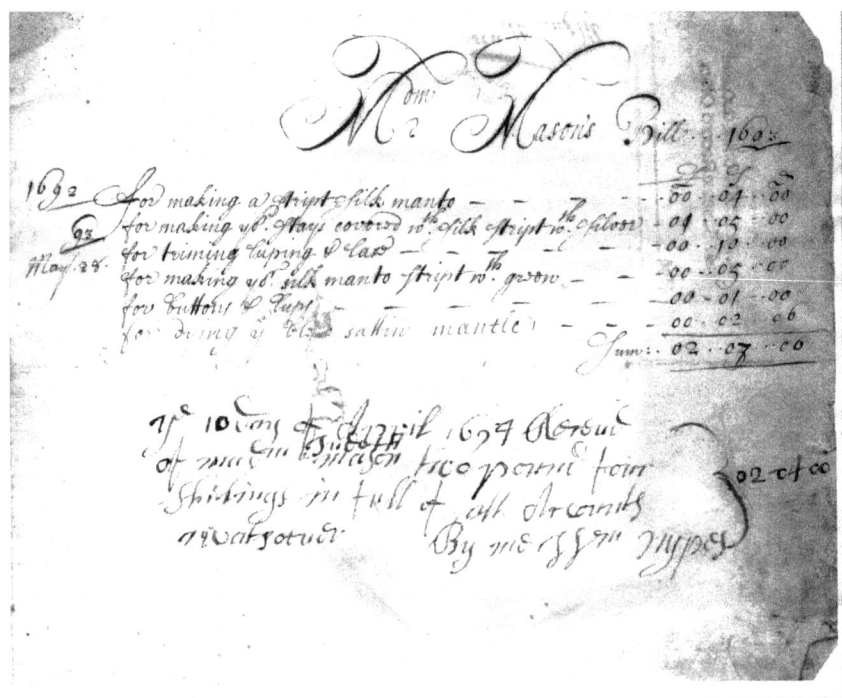

Plate 1 Madame Mason's bill, 1692–3.

with silver fringe (2s.6d) and a corset covered in black satin trimmed with silver (£1.17s.0d). A year later she had another similar outfit made.

Up to the mid-1670s, those women's garments that were not made at home had been made by tailors in the case of dresses, skirts, jackets and other 'top' garments, and by seamstresses in the case of shifts and underwear. Seamstresses worked in linen or cotton and they made men's shirts, baby linen and women's aprons as well as underclothes. The defining feature of seamstress-made garments was that they were composed of simple shapes, mostly squares and

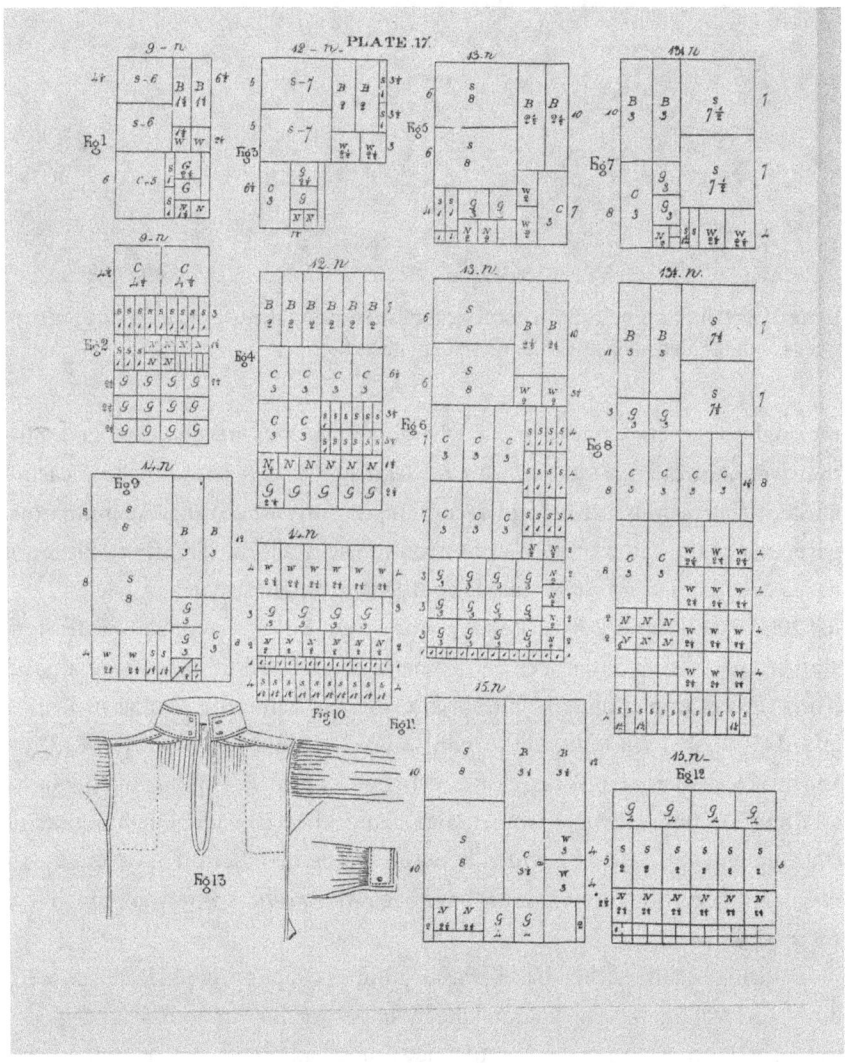

Plate 2 Page from *The Workwoman's Guide* of 1838, showing how to cut out a number of shirts at the same time to avoid wasting fabric.

Plate 3 Detail of a nineteenth-century chemise showing the use of an oblong for the sleeve and a folded square for the underarm gusset.

rectangles, gathered into a band where shaping was needed, but crucially, they were not fitted. *The Workwoman's Guide* gives details of how to measure and cut the various pieces and recommends ways of cutting out numerous garments at the same time to optimize the use of fabric. The first edition of the *Guide* dates from 1838, but it codified techniques that had been in use for 200 years. [Plates 2 & 3] Being a seamstress was a recognized profession, seamstresses took apprentices and some of them seem to have made a good living. For example, in 1638 Elizabeth Collier of Minterne Magna in Dorset left £145.00, in 1648 Margareta Dennison of Deptford (London) left £132.00 and in 1650 Margaret Wilcox of Colyton in Devon left monetary bequests totalling £67.00.[7] All three women also bequeathed considerable amounts of clothing and goods to be divided between family members. They were by no means unique, though there must have been many others who were much less successful.

Tailoring, on the other hand, was a guild occupation; guild officials were powerful local figures who guarded the monopoly of their trade and its privileges jealously. By the seventeenth century few guilds admitted female apprentices, and the merchant tailors seem to have been particularly misogynistic.[8] In 1679, for example, the Newcastle guild decreed that no woman could be taken on as an apprentice 'by bond or indenture'.[9] The employment of women was clearly a recurring problem in Oxford. In 1704 Michael Mercer was prosecuted for taking on Hannah Smith as an apprentice; on 11 May 1709 John White was fined 10s.0d for 'setting Jane Hearne, spinster on work on his board contrary to the good ordinances and Byelaws of the company'; in January 1710 Andrew Bignell was fined for employing his maidservant 'to work on his board'; a year later Richard Sherwood was in trouble for employing a journeywoman and in 1714 there were no fewer than three prosecutions of Oxford tailors who employed women.[10]

True, some tailors did involve their wives and daughters, and a tailor's widow carrying on her late husband's business could join the local guild, though seldom as a full member. However, few men were as bold about acknowledging the skills of their womenfolk as was John Porteous of Hawick in the Scottish Borders, whose widowed daughter worked as his journeyman and had learnt to cut out. In 1738 he set her to demonstrate her prowess before a representative of the local guild – and, despite the fact that he was a one-time deacon of that guild, the magistrates supported the guildsmen and he was sent to prison for it.[11] Of course, not all tailors were guild members; those who set up in business in the country, or on the outskirts of towns where the guild's writ did not run, were not subject to guild control, but nonetheless they too were almost always men who had served an apprenticeship during which they had been taught to cut and fit – skills which the seamstresses did not learn.

However, by the 1680s the supposedly traditional relationship between client and tailor was changing. More and more tailors were sub-contracting and selling goods ready-made, or keeping stocks of partially made garments that could be finished quickly to the customers' requirements. By the late seventeenth century the London Merchant Taylors' Company recognized 'cutting tailors' (who made garments from scratch) as a separate group.[12] It became less and less easy for the guilds to oversee the trade and keep track of the various sub-contractors, and in many towns the power and authority of all the guilds were already beginning to decline.

Mantua-makers

The arrival of a new, easy-to-make fashion in the 1670s enabled enterprising women, like Isobel Wood's daughter, to set themselves up as 'mantua-makers'. We know some of their names but we do not know their backgrounds or how they had acquired their skills. It may be, as Norah Waugh surmised, that some seamstresses decided to expand their repertoires.[13] Indeed, Randle Holme listed 'A ROMAN DRESS, the mantua cut square behind and round before' amongst the items made by 'seamsters'. However, as Janet Arnold pointed out, the quality of stitching on early-eighteenth-century dresses is far inferior to that on most surviving examples of linen garments.[14] It may also be that the wives and daughters of tailors decided to use skills they had learnt 'helping out' in the tailor's workshop – in the 1690s, for example, Mause Robertson, wife of Robert Lindsey, an Edinburgh tailor, worked as a mantua-maker on her own account.[15] Anne Buck also noted that many tailors' wives in eighteenth-century Bedfordshire became mantua-makers.[16]

Unsurprisingly, tailors became concerned at the prospect of losing half their trade to female entrepreneurs. In France, a guild of seamstresses called the 'Maîtresses Couturières' was established in 1675, and they were permitted by law to make all women's clothes except court dress and corsets.[17] However, French tailors were unwilling to believe they no longer controlled the garment trade and they regularly visited couturières' shops illegally and confiscated goods. As late as 1764 they seized a dress and petticoat that Madame Lahaye was delivering to a client; it resulted in a definitive court ruling that the tailors should allow the women 'to exercise their trade in peace'.[18] Merry Weisner has described how in Germany, restrictions on women working in the tailoring trades increased in the sixteenth and seventeenth centuries.[19] The records of various English tailors' guilds point to the resentment caused by the development of mantua-making as a separate trade. In 1685, for example, Priscilla Trattles was 'presented' to the magistrates in York, accused by the guildsmen of making women's garments. In 1694, also in York, Widow Lodge was 'discharged for exercising the Trade of a Draper or Taylor as she will answer the same by Law and for her neglect or refusal then she to be prosecuted against as the Law directs'. A case against Mary Yeomans ran from 1697 to 1699 and cost the York guild over £40.00 – including bribes to jurors and involving at least three indictments against Ms Yeomans.[20]

The guilds

One might have supposed that the London Merchant Taylors' Company would have been at the forefront of opposition to the women making mantuas; after all, there were more mantua-makers in the capital than anywhere else and they were doing good business. However, by the end of the 1680s the Company was chiefly concerned with managing its property and its charities, particularly the schools and almshouses, and, if the minute books are to be believed, took little interest in the day-to-day affairs of its members.[21] It was left to the provincial guilds to provide what opposition they could.

At the end of 1697 in Bristol, Mary Brobon was fined a pound for making mantuas. Whether the one prosecution was enough to deter others or whether the Bristol tailors decided it had been more trouble than it was worth is not apparent, but they did not record any other prosecutions. Similarly, the Salisbury tailors prosecuted Elizabeth Howlet in January 1699 for 'unlawful working' and fined her 40s.0d, but seem to have decided against pursuing cases against any other women.[22]

The Chester tailors had no such inhibitions. Between 1698 and 1725 they instituted at least forty-three investigations into women making women's clothes, many of which came before the mayor. It was not a cheap exercise. Firstly the guild paid informers, next searchers had to be paid to investigate, then the constable had to have a fee for apprehending the woman concerned and bringing her before the mayor, transport costs had to be covered and often there was a further reimbursement for the constable and/or the searchers for 'expenses' incurred (usually in the local pub) while waiting to apprehend the woman. The cost varied between fourpence to despatch two 'searchers' to make enquiries, and the, admittedly exceptional, two pounds it cost to prosecute Mrs Williams in 1709. Some women were prosecuted several times – Susannah Young and 'Oulton's wife' were regular offenders and they probably saw the occasional fine as a necessary business expense. However, what must have been particularly galling for the tailors was the number of offenders who, like Mrs Warmingham, another frequent offender, were the wives or relatives of members of the Chester guild.[23]

Enough was enough, and in October 1702 work began on a series of petitions to be sent to parliament – though it is not known whether the litigious Chester tailors were signatories to any of them. That month the York guildsmen instructed the Master and Wardens to 'goe to Councell about suppressing Women Mantua-makers and other garments and to know their advice therein what can be done for restraining them'. The Norwich guildsmen seem to have been of the same mind and wrote to support their brother tradesmen in York. As a result the York guild sent letters to other guilds 'to acquaint them we was going to peticon the parliamt' – they contacted tailors in Pontefract, Ripon, Wakefield, Hull (all in Yorkshire), Newcastle, and Newark in Nottinghamshire, and a Mr Jackson in London was paid £5.7s.6d 'for sillisiting the Parliamt'.[24] They were not alone.

That same month the Oxford tailors also recorded that 'the Master is desir'd to expend what shall [be] thought necessary to obtain (with other Towns) an Act of Parliament to suppress the Manto makers'.[25] Their brethren in Salisbury also decided to send a petition of their own 'to suppress Women and Others' and spent over £40.00 sending members to London and having Mr Bourgoin draw up the document.[26]

The fact that all three petitions were begun in the same month of the same year suggests that there was collaboration between the guilds. None of the petitions survive, but the *House of Commons Journal* does mention one (with no subject) which was submitted by the 'Freemen of the Merchant Tailors Company'; it seems it was sent to Parliament but never debated.[27] It may well be that MPs saw the development of a new trade, albeit one prosecuted by women, as likely to benefit the national economy, and that consideration overcame any sympathy they might have felt for the tailors.

Eventually most guildsmen bowed to the inevitable and decided that if women really wanted to make mantuas they would have to pay for the privilege. In York in 1699 they finally admitted the troublesome Mary Yeomans as a guild member on payment of £10.00. In 1704 the guild charged a Mr Johnson another £10.00 for granting permission for his wife to work 'no wages further than the making of Mantees and Peteycoates' and in 1711 they charged Mrs Elizabeth Yeomans six guineas for permission to do the same.[28] Between 1701 and 1714 four women became members of the York tailors' guild, and by 1741 out of 258 guild members, 67 were women.[29] In 1702, notwithstanding their petition to parliament, the guild began to oversee the apprenticeship of girls to the tailoring and mantua-making trades. Mary Middlebrook and Elizabeth Agar were apprenticed to their tailor fathers, and Sarah Robinson was apprenticed to Mary Yeomans, who had been such a thorn in the guildsmen's flesh just five years earlier. Bernard Johnson's 1949 survey implies that the tailors in York were particularly hostile to the mantua-makers, but in fact, while York was one of the first guilds to prosecute women, it was also almost the only one to reach a pragmatic solution in overseeing apprenticeships and allowing women to join. As a result, girls came to York from Leeds and Hull, Northumberland, Westmoreland, Leicestershire and Lincolnshire, and by the 1720s the number of girl apprentices in the city exceeded the number of boys. Indeed, it was the number of female members which enabled the York guild to survive as long as it did [Table 1].

Problems arose in different places at different times. In August 1701 the merchant tailors of Exeter prosecuted Elizabeth Bristow and fined her 3s.3d for 'intruding' on the tailoring trade. It was not enough to deter her and in October

Table 1 Relative numbers of girls and boys apprenticed by the tailors' guild in York[30] 1702–10 and 1720–28.

	1702	1703	1704	1705	1706	1707	1708	1709	1710
Girls	3	1	3	1	4	3	-	1	2
Boys	6	13	8	10	11	19	-	16	9
	1720	1721	1722	1723	1724	1725	1726	1727	1728
Girls	8	12	4	12	9	9	12	13	6
Boys	9	9	1	11	9	7	4	6	11

she was fined 6s.6d for committing a second offence. However, the complaint was not that she was a woman but that she was not a freeman of the company. Given that as a female she would have had no opportunity to gain that freedom by serving a tailoring apprenticeship, this seems a nice distinction, but it was also the basis of the company's complaints against Mary Thompson in 1704 and Hannah Stiggford in 1712, and of their prosecutions of Mary Turber in 1715, Margery Eastborough in 1719 and Susannah Savory in 1719 and 1725. A bye-law passed in 1716 spelt out the issue:

> That every person not having served an Apprenticeship of Seven Years or upwards to the Trade or Mystery of a Taylor or not being free of the said Company who shall in his or her Shop or Stall or in or about any of the Streets or places within the City of Exon or Liberties or Suburbs thereof Cutt and Sell … or make Cutt finish and expose to Sale any Garment or Garments usually made by Taylors, he or she so offending therein shall forfeit and pay for every such Offence unto the said Master, Wardens, Assistants and Comonalty the sum of Twenty Shillings.

In fact the fine was usually 6s.8d, only rising to a pound in 1725, and the 'he or she' is significant. The fines for men and women were exactly the same. Mary Eveleigh was fined 20s.0d in 1725 but refused to pay. She seems to have got away with it as hers was the last prosecution of a woman for tailoring in Exeter.[31]

In 1705, three years after parliament had ignored the petitions from York, Norwich, Salisbury and Oxford, the company of Drapers and Tailors of the city of Durham listed the following 'grievances to be redressed':

> To put off the Manty-makers.
> To put off the Skinners from making leather britches.
> To put off Broakers from selling old cloaths (except they be freemen or freemen's widows).

Competition of any sort was a threat, and along with the breeches-makers and old clothes salesmen, the tailors prosecuted three women for mantua-making. One of them was Elizabeth Browne, mentioned at the beginning of this chapter, indicted for making 'mantos and pettyeoates and taking money for the same' and for employing journeywomen (plural) – so presumably Elizabeth was running quite a substantial business. Elizabeth Lee, Mrs Ann Midleton and Mrs Elizabeth Baker, her customers, gave evidence in her favour, and Mary Mitford and Margaret Hall claimed that 'women taylors are greater artists at women's work than men taylors'.[32] There is no record of the outcome.

A year later, fourteen miles away in Newcastle, the stewards of the Newcastle guild were ordered to take the recorder's opinion about what could be done about the town's mantua-makers, and later that same year they were given permission to take such means to suppress the women as 'appeared to them most convenient' – though what they actually did went unrecorded.[33]

Not all the guilds were openly hostile to women workers, however. As early as 1683 it seems that the Bristol tailors accepted that women would be employed in their trade. That year they issued a decree against employing 'any male or female' without the prior consent of the Master of the Tailors' Guild. The Worcester guild was the 'tailors and skinners' and in 1698 and 1700 two young women were apprenticed to their fathers through the guild, though it is not clear whether those fathers made clothes or dressed hides. Mary Phillips, who had served a seven-year apprenticeship with her father and was admitted to the guild in June 1701, had certainly trained as a skinner and 'tanyer' – but the simple fact that some guildsmen's daughters could become members must have opened the Worcester men's eyes to the idea that girls were employable.[34] In Ludlow, the Company of Stitchmen never seems to have had any concerns about admitting women. The Stitchmen included representatives from a wide range of textile-related trades – tailors, drapers, skinners, felt-makers, cappers, hatters, glovers and so on – and they admitted their first 'manty maker', Ann Arundel, in 1707.[35]

Scotland

Things were rather different in Scotland and opposition went on much longer. There it was the town officials who licensed women to trade, though in

Edinburgh the Merchant Company, established in 1681, controlled all retailing of wearing apparel and the cloth used in making it. The city council could also issue licences to trade, and this caused some friction between the two bodies. In the Edinburgh town council minutes for 1692 it is recorded that a Jean Montgomerie had asked the town council for a licence to make what she called 'the new dresses' – almost certainly mantuas.[36] This seems to be the first reference to a mantua-maker in that city. There was less opposition to mantua-makers in Edinburgh than there was in smaller places in Scotland; Elizabeth Sanderson suggests that this may be because there was plenty of work and the tailors did not feel threatened. However, as late as 1752 the suggestion was made that the Edinburgh tailors' guild create a list of mantua-making women as the guild had been 'much encroached upon by the mantiemakers'. The 1752 list (the only one that was made) contained eighteen names.[37]

There were mantua-makers in other burghs too, in Aberdeen, Stirling, Dundee, and notably in Perth, who came into conflict with the Tailors' Incorporations very early in the eighteenth century when they applied for licences to trade. For example, in 1700 Beatrix Stewart in Perth had to give security that she would neither bind herself to work for another person nor work for herself, on penalty of £20.00 Scots (£1.00 Scots was worth approximately 1s.8d in the eighteenth century). Also in Perth in 1717, Isobel Moncrieff was fined for encroaching on the Tailors' Incorporation, and it was stated that she would not be fined for past offences, but was to pay £2.00 Scots from the point at which she had been found out, which rather suggests she had been making mantuas for some time before she fell foul of the guild. She also had to give £40.00 Scots security not to do so again. Other women found ways to avoid paying their fines; for example, when Martha Ross was challenged by the Perth tailors in 1725, she simply moved outside the burgh boundary. However, by 1740 Perth women could make mantuas if they paid for the privilege. That year Cecilia Foot paid 200 merks (approximately £10.00 sterling) for this 'freedom' and another £3.00 for that of her apprentice.[38]

In Aberdeen, the tailors initially prosecuted women for making mantuas, but eventually they compromised by granting them 'tollerations' – for a fee. In 1717 such a toleration was given to Rachel Baxter, on condition she only employed women, that the trade oversaw her granting of apprenticeships, and that she did not make or sell stays. In 1728 Janet Pirie was granted similar rights for an annual payment of 15s.0d sterling and on pain of a fine of £1.00 sterling. However, as the number of such grants increased the guildsmen grew worried, and in November 1728 they increased the fees.

> The Trade, taking to their consideration that the number of women mantua-makers in this burgh is very much increasing, and that the same is a great hurt and prejudice to this Trade, do therefore statute and ordain that every woman who for the future shall be tolerate to work at mantua-making by the Trade, shall pay yearly to the boxmaster of this Trade for such tolerance the sum of twenty-four shillings yearly.

The fee was raised to £30.00 Scots in April 1734.[39]

Three years later in 1737, on the banks of the River Don, the town council, on behalf of the tailors of Old Aberdeen (until 1891 a separate place from 'New' Aberdeen), published an act that was to be put up in public places:

> Several Women within the Burgh pretending to be and exercising the Trade and Employment of Mantua Making have of late years wrought at all manner of Women's Cloaths, without their being entitled to any part of the ffreedom of the Taylor Trade, which is not only a great loss and damage to each Member of the Trade, but also a notorious Incroachment upon the priveliges of the Corporation, and a considerable loss to the Publick Good.[40]

From 1 November they decreed the women were to pay an initial £24.00 Scots and 2s.0d a year subsequently. As late as 1758 complaints were still being made that 'unfree persons … particularly in the Mantua-making way' were trading without paying their dues, and on 8 November that year the boxmaster reported that he still had not received any money from any of them.

In 1738 in Dundee, Mary Whyte, a baker's wife, was fined £12.00 Scots for 'making women's clothes without being free of the trade' and was forbidden ever to do any more 'Taylor work' in the burgh.[41] In 1750, the Stirling tailors got the magistrates to insist that Isabella Bird pay a regular sum to support the poor of the craft in return for permission to work.[42] Eventually, a ruling in the Scottish Court of Sessions in 1763 established the fact that mantua-making was *not* a branch of tailoring and that tailors' guilds therefore had no jurisdiction over women making women's clothes, and this at last put paid to attempts to extract dues from Scottish mantua-makers.[43]

Conclusion

The picture is far from complete, however. Of the fifty or so tailors' guilds in Britain in the eighteenth century, only fifteen sets of records survive for the relevant period.[44] Other companies of tailors may have been as litigious as their Chester counterparts or as indifferent as their Worcester brethren. Tailors who were members of religious guilds or guilds merchant[45] in their respective towns may have been as hostile to mantua-making women as were their counterparts in the craft guilds but have had less support for expressing their concerns. All we can say is that opposition was widespread, but in most places, relatively short-lived. [Plate 4]

Plate 4 A French tailor measuring a lady customer, *Gallerie des Modes*, 1778.
Despite the rise of the mantua-maker, many tailors continued to do work for women throughout the eighteenth century.

It may at first sight appear that women had triumphed – they had successfully infiltrated a trade that had been a masculine preserve for well over a century, and over the next hundred years they would secure for themselves a near-monopoly in the making of women's clothes. At the beginning of the eighteenth century the future must have looked quite promising – as we shall see in Chapter 2.

2

'The art and mystery of mantua-making'

Britain in the eighteenth century was a prosperous nation and that prosperity was built on trade. In the 1720s Daniel Defoe boasted she was 'not only a trading country, but the greatest trading country in the world'.[1] Much of Britain's trade was with her colonies, and dressmakers benefited from the arrival of new fabrics – muslins, chintzes and silks from India; raw cotton from America; and furs from Canada. At the same time, technological developments at home ushered in the Industrial Revolution, producing, among other things, cheap printed cottons. Protectionist legislation placed heavy duties on the import of foreign fabrics, and in 1766 the importation of foreign silks was banned completely in an attempt to protect the weavers in Spitalfields. In May 1772, Mr Phillip, a Spitalfields attorney, even offered a ten guinea reward ('to be paid within twenty-four hours') to 'any Journeyman Taylor or Upholder, or any Journeywoman Mantua-maker or Milliner', or anyone else who knew of illegally imported silks being used.[2] Mantua-makers and their clients saw no shame in evading the law – in 1768, for example, Lady Mary Coke visited Deal in Kent and went to 'three of the houses that smuggle Indian goods' – she describes it as if it were a regular sightseeing trip.[3] French goods were a particular target of legislation but many dressmakers still regularly visited Paris to see the fashions and bring home samples, and French goods retained their appeal for customers.

As the century progressed, foreign visitors wondered at London's wealth and admired the fine shops and well-dressed inhabitants. Things were rather different away from the centres of population and would remain so into the nineteenth century. Travelling north from London in the early 1800s, Susan Sibbald remarked: 'What a marked difference we saw, even before we reached Newcastle, between the lower class of people as to their dress ... particularly in the females; without shoes and stockings, no caps, short petticoats and bedgowns with short sleeves.'[4] But while much of the population still lived in poverty, a new middle class was emerging, the wives and daughters of merchants, manufacturers and prosperous tradesmen, who were eager for new goods, new foodstuffs and new fashions. As Lorna Weatherill has shown from a study of probate inventories, consumption of luxury goods increased noticeably between 1660 and 1760, particularly in the towns. It is reasonable to assume that families purchasing mirrors and clocks, tea-wares and curtains also spent more on dress than had their forbears, but because garments are often not itemized in inventories, she could not prove this conclusively.[5]

Against this background it did not take long for mantua-making to become an established trade, despite the opposition of the tailors, and in the early 1700s the future still looked hopeful. Setting up in business required very little outlay. Scissors, a thimble, thread, needles, pins and a cutting-out table were all the equipment needed, though the *Description of All Trades* of 1747 suggested 'a good set of Acquaintances' would also be useful. Some money helped too – but Ann Okely set up a successful millinery business with just £50.00 worth of stock.[6] Others spent much more. In 1728 in Westminster the three Moody sisters went into partnership with Joanna Grice 'to make hoop petticoats, quilts, mantuas and all pertaining thereto' and had a lengthy legal document drawn up. They were to share the profits of the business equally and to be equally responsible for any losses. They had jointly raised start-up capital of £268.00.[7] We do not know how they fared but a large initial outlay was no guarantee of success. Hannah Glasse (1708–70) is best known as the author of *The Art of Cookery Made Plain and Easy* which was published in 1747. She was widowed in 1748, and she and her daughter set up as court milliners in London's Park Lane. Her half-brother, Lancelot Allgood, was by this time MP for Northumberland, and no doubt he urged some of his contacts' wives to patronize her. He recorded how a stream of carriages was always to be seen outside Hannah's establishment and deduced that she must be doing well. He was wrong. In 1754, Hannah Glasse's millinery business went bankrupt – to the tune of £10,000 – and she returned to writing cookery books.[8]

Fashion

Mantua-makers had to know what was in fashion; their customers depended on them for advice. John Styles has described how by the late seventeenth century the fashion, at least for decorative fabrics, had become seasonal, with new designs coming into vogue every year or two. As early as 1681 the East India Company informed its factors in Bengal:

> That in all flowred Silkes, you Change the fashion and flower as much as you can every yeare, for English Ladies and they say the French and other Europeans will give twice as much for a new thing ... than they will give for a better Silk of the same fashion worn the former yeare.[9]

It was the mantua-maker who would explain to the more fashion-conscious of her country clients that pastel colours, beiges and creams were among the 'in' colours in the 1770s; that after 1780 white fabrics or ones patterned with tiny sprigs were replacing large bold designs, and she would describe which particular configurations of stripes and flowers were in vogue that season; she would suggest what design a lady might choose for her polonaise[10] and demonstrate how the shapes of neck handkerchiefs, caps and sleeve ruffles were changing.

Paris and the French court had long been acknowledged as the centre of the fashionable world and as early as July 1748 the *London Evening Post* reported:

> By a Gentleman just arriv'd from Dover we learn, that that Road is cover'd with Coaches full of Mercers, Milliners and Mantua-makers, Taylors, &c. who are all hurrying away to Paris, in order to oblige the Town the ensuing Winter with the newest Fashions of that polite Court.

Given the dangers and difficulties of travel in the eighteenth century it is amazing that so many women braved such a journey, but it is clear that they did. Of course, visiting English mantua-makers could only have learnt about court fashions at second-hand; they would have watched fashionable ladies promenading or alighting from their carriages on the way to balls and assemblies, they would have viewed trimmings and fabrics in the shops and returned home with sketches and samples.

In France the court set the fashion, but in England Queen Charlotte was seen as dowdy and matronly, and London fashion, at least in the last quarter of the eighteenth century, was dictated by a group of elite noblewomen, of whom Georgiana, Duchess of Devonshire, was probably the most influential. Georgiana was a personal friend of Marie Antoinette and visited Paris often; when she wasn't there herself, her family and friends sent her detailed letters, complete with drawings, of what she should wear. In 1775, for example, Georgiana's mother wrote, 'You can wear no colour that is not either Dos de Puce or Ventre du Puce' (flea back or flea stomach). This was a purplish brown, deeply unflattering to pale English complexions, but it became enormously popular. In 1784 Georgiana appeared at a soiree in the latest French fashion – a robe à la Turque – which soon became all the rage; she embraced and popularized the latest fashions for

Plate 5 French fashion plate of the 1880s showing a cap decorated with enormous feathers.

elaborate hairstyles, enormous hats and huge ostrich feathers – in March 1775 she wore – 'two plumes sixteen inches long, besides three small ones: this has so far outdone all other plumes that Mrs Damer, Lady Harriet Stanhope, &c., looked nothing.' A further attempt that year to wear plumes longer than anyone else's backfired – the queen banned the wearing of feathers to her drawing-rooms.[11] [Plate 5]

Up to the Revolution, Paris retained its stranglehold on elite fashion; it was actually deemed *impolite* to wear clothes that were not à la mode. In December 1783, Frances Anne Crewe, another very fashionable lady, newly arrived in the city, determined to rest for a few days before socializing 'for my Head turns round with all that I have heard and seen already about the Paris World, and the Etiquettes which are to be observed concerning Dress'.[12]

However, one can question the idea that fashion always spread downwards from the court. Travellers from relatively humble backgrounds also disseminated news of fashion. For example, when young Fanny Herbert, a clergyman's daughter from County Tipperary, returned to Ireland in 1791 after a few months in Paris, she was judged to be 'smoking hot with fashion and Elegance from Paris' by her envious elder sister, Dorothea, who reported that local ladies in their hometown were all copying Fanny's style as best they could.[13]

Another source of information for non-travellers was the fashion doll. Wooden dolls – 'les grands courriers de la mode' – were dispatched from Paris each month, dressed and bewigged in the latest styles, to selected dressmakers across Europe, and though they were known from the sixteenth century onwards, the fashion doll or 'jointed baby' was very much a feature of the eighteenth century.[14] The war of the Spanish Succession might have been expected to have put a damper on such frivolities, but in 1704 the Abbé Prevost reported: 'By an act of gallantry … the ministers of both courts granted a special pass to the mannequin … during the times of greatest enmity experienced on both sides.'[15] In January 1783, during another war in which England and France were on opposing sides, a notice appeared in the *Kentish Gazette*:

> The report of a courier having arrived from Paris on Saturday is not true. The fact is a *French doll* arrived on that day with the ultimatum of dress … The primary novelty, it is said, is a new article of headdress. We do not hear that the above *gentlewoman* has brought any intelligence of the peace.

Some of these dolls were said to be life-size, but only small ones, like 'Lord and Lady Clapham' in the Victoria and Albert Museum, survive. They were not cheap.

Dubois, the French Ambassador to London during the Regency, commissioned a doll from Mademoiselle Filon in Paris 'to show the ladies of London how the ladies of Paris are dressed'. Mlle Filon charged 300 francs (approximately £870 in 2019 money). England also produced her own fashion dolls or 'babies' and the *Gentleman's Magazine* of 1751 described one being sent to Empress Elizabeth of Russia, while various advertisements in the *New England Weekly* describe English dolls arriving in Boston which could be viewed or borrowed for a small(ish) payment.[16]

Fabric samples and sample books also circulated widely, and perhaps for that reason, fashion often related to fabric or trimmings rather than to the shape of the gown. The late eighteenth century saw a great increase in the availability of printed material and this, too, aided the spread of news about fashion. In France, the *Journal du Gout* appeared in 1768 and in England *The Lady's Magazine* was first published in 1770. Both contained fashion prints; soon afterwards similar prints began to appear in ladies' pocket books and almanacs and in other women's magazines like *La Belle Assemblée* and the *Gallery of Fashion,* and some provincial newspapers also carried occasional news of the latest trends. English and French fashion magazines were copied in other countries, ensuring the Europe-wide adoption of many fashions.[17] [Plate 6]

After 1770 the pace of fashion change speeded up and what was worn by the Parisian haute monde was copied in London, Budapest and St Petersburg within a very short space of time. Court dressmakers in European cities seem to have had a sophisticated network of spies and couriers, primed to keep them abreast of the latest fashions worn at the French court. Furthermore, within a matter of months, fashionable ladies as far away as Buenos Aires, New York and Calcutta would be wearing garments very similar to those worn in European capitals, and the would-be fashionable in the provinces would be wearing watered-down versions. Not everyone visited Paris, but most English dressmakers of any standing made regular trips to London. They, too, would have watched ladies of the fashionable elite and made mental notes of what they were wearing and how they were wearing it. They would have visited fashionable shops, talked to former colleagues and friends and carried news and samples back to their home towns. These in turn would have influenced other dressmakers in their home areas who were too poor or too nervous to travel to the capital. There was no excuse for not knowing what was in fashion – even if you chose not to wear it.

Plate 6 Fashion plate of 1774 showing fashionable ladies in the Assembly Rooms at Weymouth.

> FASHIONABLE MAGAZINE,
> For LADIES and GENTLEMEN.
> *This Day is Published,* (*Price Sixpence only,*)
> [Embellished with the following elegant Engravings: — 1. A Lady in the Fashionable Undress of the Month. — 2. A Gentleman the same. — 3. Four Fashionable French Ladies, from the *Cabinet des Modes*, a new Magazine of Fashions now publishing at Paris, every Fortnight, at 2s. a Number; tho' every Thing important to English Readers will be constantly translated into this Work. — 4. A most elegant new Pattern for a Petticoat. — 5. An elegant new Pattern for a Gown or Train: Both Patterns incomparably superior to every Thing of the Kind ever given in any Magazine, alone worth more than four Times the whole Purchase-money]
> NUMB. II. (To be continued Monthly) Of
> THE FASHIONABLE MAGAZINE,
> For JULY 1786.

2. *Jackson's Oxford Journal,* 5 August 1786.

And not everyone cared about clothes. In March 1775 an exasperated Lucy Gildart wrote to her brother, John Herrick, at Beaumanor Hall near Leicester about their mother's obstinacy in not observing the proper forms of mourning dress:

> I am quite Tired for she does not nor never will ware what she ought to do … she ought to have Put on Black Silk Negligees and Gowns six months ago – so I told her … pray when does she intend to ware her Black Silk, for the two years mourning will be out in Sept. Sure she can't think to ware Bombazeen till then and as to her Caps she has never a one fitt to ware but that I made her a Present of last Year, and She Shd ware her rowl every day and do her Hair over it and then it would not be Such a Trouble to her when she is use to it a Little, but if you can persuade her to be a Little Like other people I shall be very Glad for its more than I can do.

Poor Mrs Herrick died three years later and bequeathed the black silk negligée and petticoat to Ann Beardsley in Stoke Newington. Lucy inherited all her other clothes, including, presumably, all the unfashionable caps and the despised bombazine gown.[18]

Mantua-makers had to be quick learners as the simple 1670s form of the mantua did not last for long. The earliest known example in the UK is in

Shrewsbury museums' collection, and is made of a lime green damask dated to 1708–9.[19] Unusually, it has had very few alterations. The simple T-shape had already disappeared, though the main part of the garment is still made from two breadths of fabric seamed together; the sleeves are set in separately and are wide, curved at the elbow and roughly pleated at shoulder and cuff. The back is also pleated and the pleats are loosely stitched and held in place by a wide piece of ribbon at the centre back, the skirt is looped up at the sides with cords and buttons, then pinned at the back, and stitched so that part of the matt reverse side of the damask would be on show. If it is typical of its period, the tailors had some grounds for their criticisms of the mantua-makers; the garment is quite crudely made, unlined and with raw edges on the inside, though the overall effect is no doubt what the client asked for. The main seams are sewn with a fairly neat running stitch in lime green thread; however, it would appear that the thread was not strong enough for the construction as there is later overstitching in at least four other types of thread to hold the heavy pleats in place. [Colour Plates III & IV]

Over time the mantua evolved, sometimes with a 'sacque (or sack) back' of wide box pleats flowing from neck to hem at the back – an excellent way of displaying the elaborately patterned silks of the early eighteenth century – sometimes with the pleats stitched flat, sometimes with the back of the skirt looped up, sometimes with it hanging loose, sometimes with a matching petticoat, sometimes made to be worn over a contrasting one. The stitching and construction also improved over time and by the 1730s most bodices were lined. By the 1780s the stitched-down pleats had become seams and the bodice fitted closely at the back; however, the front was still often open and covered by a 'stomacher' – which could be bought ready-made from the milliner or mercer – and the fronts of the skirt were open, so the mantua-maker had a little leeway when it came to making a garment fit. Today these garments are often described as 'open robes'. On bills, eighteenth-century women's dresses were usually listed as 'gown' or 'gown and coat' (i.e. petticoat), 'negligée and coat' or 'sack' rather than 'mantua', though the women who made them were still known as 'mantua-makers'. [Colour Plate V]

While the original mantuas were relatively simple to make, we do not know how women learnt to make the later, more complicated versions. The probability is that they acquired tailor-made examples and unpicked them to create a pattern. Contemporary patterns for women's dress were virtually non-existent, though Benoit Boullay's *Le Tailleur Sincere* of 1671 did contain patterns for riding habits. Not until 1769 do we find de Garsault's descriptions and diagrams for dresses in a section of *L'Art du Tailleur* entitled 'L'Art de la Couturière', and this was in French and not intended as an instruction manual. The French Maîtresse Couturières measured their customers using strips of parchment – as tailors did – cutting notches in the strip for up to sixteen different measurements – inch measures did not come into use until the early 1800s. Claudia Kidwell described how the mantua-maker used those measures to determine the length of the pieces of fabric needed to make the gown and 'progressively sewed and cut her way to a finished garment'.[20] No doubt Englishwomen learnt to do the same, but having a ready-made gown to serve as a model would have been much easier; indeed, in 1763 Mary Peers in Chester advertised 'Ladies in the Country may be fitted with the greatest exactness by sending a Gown as a Pattern' (*Adams Weekly Courant*, 5 July). Few got as lucky when unpicking such a garment as the mantua-maker who appeared in the *Norfolk Chronicle* in March 1797: 'A mantua-maker, of Louth, last week, taking to pieces an old gown, discovered between the lining of the body, bank notes to the amount of £195.' One hopes she received a reward.

One factor relating to the creation of patterns that may not be immediately obvious is that paper was an expensive commodity in the eighteenth century and dress patterns would have required large sheets which were not readily available. The price was partly because paper was made from rags which required a good deal of processing and partly because of the heavy excise duty levied on paper of all kinds after 1712. That year the duty on newspaper was a halfpenny an issue: by 1800 it had risen to fourpence. The duties were reduced in the 1830s, and by the middle of the nineteenth century the process of manufacturing paper from wood pulp had been developed, so paper became rather cheaper. However, in the eighteenth century the cost was a significant factor.[21] A letter in Dorset Record Office refers to a lost title deed and suggests that it was cut up by the local mantua-maker to make a dress pattern.[22] However, most dressmakers cut patterns from cloth and then used them as lining for the dress – which, of course, meant they could not be re-used if the customer wanted another dress a few months later.

Apprenticeship

By the early eighteenth century mantua-makers were sufficiently established to be taking apprentices. A great many of these were poor children, paid for by their parishes – though it must be remembered that parishes were more likely to retain indentures than were private families which may give a misleading impression of the relative numbers. The parish officers were probably pleased to have found a new trade for girls and seem to have been oblivious to the fact that in some quarters the existence of the trade was still controversial. While boys apprenticed to the guild-controlled trades usually served a seven-year term, many mantua-making apprenticeships were much shorter. Out of a hundred indentures from seventeen counties dating from 1701 to 1825,[23] twenty-three were for one or two years and twenty-eight were for three to five years, while eighteen were for seven years and three were for longer. Fifteen were to last until the apprentice reached the age of twenty-one or married but did not give the apprentice's age at the time of binding, and no term was specified in the remainder. Most girls seem to have been in their early teens when they were apprenticed,[24] a few were between nine and twelve – and poor little Martha Goolden was apprenticed to Alexander and Catherine Goolden in Manchester for fourteen years in 1763 at the tender age of seven to learn to make 'burying suits, blackwork and quilting'.[25] It is to be hoped they were relatives who treated her kindly. While boys were forbidden to marry until they had served their term, it seems to have been felt that the sooner a girl became the responsibility of a husband the better and most indentures did not forbid them to wed.

Because the survival of indentures is patchy it is difficult to see any regional patterns, though poor girls were more likely to have the opportunity of learning the trade if they came from a parish where there was a charity set up specifically to pay for training poor children. There were a considerable number of these – Dame Dorothy Long in Wiltshire, Edward Lloyd and William Gough in Shropshire, William Hopkins in Oxfordshire, Lady Dorothy Capel and Mr Lee in Surrey, Mrs Elizabeth Hutchinson in Bedfordshire and Mrs Jane Brigham in Cambridgeshire all left bequests that supported the apprenticeships of girls in this survey, for example. There were many others and more were established in the nineteenth century, but the random availability of such support must have had some effect on the demographic of entrants to the trade.

Apprentice premiums were often surprisingly costly – of the hundred indentures examined, twenty-five involved a premium of £10.00 or more and twenty-four cost between £5.00 and £10.00. In addition, indentures were taxed – at the rate of sixpence in the £ if the premium was under £50.00 and a shilling in the £ if it was over.[26] Mistresses seem to have raised their prices for girls from middle-class families. Mary Ann Searancke's schoolmaster father paid £29.00 to apprentice her to Lydia Blomfield in Romford (Essex) in 1814. He had paid £25.00 to apprentice her brother Charles to a plumber, painter and glazier three years previously; however, Charles' apprenticeship was for a full seven years; Mary Ann was to serve just two.[27] In 1785 Reverend Thomas Wolfe of Howick in Northumberland solicited help from a patron, Dr Sharp, towards the cost of apprenticing his daughter to a milliner for three years. The cost was £30.00 plus her living expenses and he couldn't afford it, despite having had a £20.00 grant from the Sons of the Clergy Society.[28] Schoolmasters were not particularly well-paid or well-respected in the eighteenth century, and clergymen's stipends could be very low – nonetheless, these men's daughters were seen as a cut above the average run of apprentices and charged accordingly.

However, most apprentices came from tradesmen's families and when trained, those who married mostly stayed in the same social class. This becomes clear from examining apprenticeship indentures. Where the would-be apprentice's father was alive, his trade was recorded on the indenture; where a mantua-maker was married, her apprentice was seen as the responsibility of her husband – in line with her legal status as a 'feme couvert' – and his name and profession would be on the indenture while she would be just 'his wife, a mantua-maker'. Despite the fears of commentators like the writer in the *Oxford Journal* in November 1771, 'Unequal Matches in point of Birth and Fortune are nowhere so common as in England; our Nobility are famous for it; we have many living Instances of it … Baroness Aston (a Scotch Peeress) a Mantua Maker – her Lord's first Lady a Washer Woman's daughter' – the surviving documents tell us mantua-makers' husbands were for the most part tradesmen – carpenters and blacksmiths, farmers and stonemasons, upholsterers and tailors, cordwainers and peruke-makers.

Few working-class families could afford the sort of premiums high-class mantua-makers expected. As a result, private apprenticeships were often financed by patrons or well-wishers. In Norwich in 1749, for example, Cyrill Wyches agreed to support young Sarah Scott's two-year apprenticeship to a mantua-maker in Bury St Edmunds at a cost of sixteen guineas plus the price of her 'Necessaries', even though he knew very little about the mistress as his letter to his solicitor shows.

> Name of ye Apprentice is Sarah Scott. Name of ye Mistress is — Head, her Christian Name I really do not know nor whether Maid, Widow or Wife but apprehend Blank may be left and so filld up att Pleasure …[29]

He did, however, make the unusual stipulation that Sarah be allowed the 'Liberty of going to School for her Instruction in Reading, Writing, etc.' This seldom happened in England though it was relatively common in Scotland. Priscilla Tuke in York received a letter from her sister in Chichester in 1816 telling her that the family was apprenticing their protegée, Maria Miller, to a local dressmaker. This was to cost £25.00 for two years and the family were soliciting donations from friends to raise the money because they thought it was too good an opportunity to miss.[30] In his will, made in 1819 but proved in 1827, William Pedly of Great Barford in Bedfordshire, 'gent', left £100.00 to place 'the daughter of Elizabeth Briggs of Alconbury' apprentice to a mantua-maker. There are no further details of the apprentice or her mistress, but £100.00 was a huge sum and leads one to wonder about Pedly's relationship with Elizabeth Briggs.[31]

Charity was sometimes also needed at a later stage in a mantua-maker's career. For example, in 1798 Fortescue Turvile in Market Harborough in Leicestershire received a letter from his friend, John Greenaway in Gloucester, soliciting financial support for a protegée who had the opportunity to set up in business in the Welsh town of Abergavenny. She was 'bred a milliner and understands mantua-making, etc', but she was also a Catholic convert and this had caused her numerous problems. Her vicar had opposed her taking over the local post office which her late mother had run, and dissuaded an elderly lady from taking her as a companion 'because of recent events in Ireland'.[32] The Turviles were themselves Catholics, hence the approach.

However, training with a mantua-maker was not necessarily the route to a comfortable life. Some apprentices had good mistresses and were treated reasonably well, but eighteenth-century life was precarious, mistresses died or moved on without their apprentices and girls were left high and dry. Sixteen-year-old Anne Mason, for example, was bound apprentice by the parish of St Giles-in-the-Fields to Mrs White in Drury Lane. In December 1740 she ended up in front of the overseers of the poor of St Martins-in-the-Fields because, after four years, her mistress had turned her out and she had been living rough for four months before being taken to the workhouse.[33] In June 1766, twenty-year-old Sarah Paul told the overseers of the same parish that she had served four years of an apprenticeship with Elizabeth Clarke, mantua-maker in the Strand, and was due to stay with her until she was twenty-one, but Elizabeth had died. Sarah had then become pregnant by 'William Dove, an Apprentice to his Uncle William Dove, a Waterman' – sex was probably the price she had paid for being given a roof over her head.[34] There were many similar stories.[35]

Some mistresses were actively abusive. On 27 February 1724 Mary Fitkins, a poor widow, took the relatively unusual step of petitioning the courts to release her daughter from her apprenticeship to a mantua-maker called Ann Vaughan. Ann had taken a 5s.0d premium but had beaten and starved Mary's daughter.[36] On 12 August 1730 Mary Chapman also petitioned the court to release her from her apprenticeship to another mantua-maker, Jane Roxborough, wife of Stephen. She had been with them for three years, and that during the said time the Petr. hath at several times been beat in a very barbarous & cruel manner both by her Master & Mistress without any provocacon whatsoever, and that the Petr. hath at several times wanted both victualls & drink & other necessarys.[37]

We do not know what happened to Mary Fitkins' daughter, but Mary Chapman was released from her indenture.

Other mistresses simply treated their apprentices as cheap labour. Elizabeth Kempster used Elizabeth Daniel as an unpaid nursemaid despite having received eight guineas as a premium to teach her to make mantuas.[38] Sarah Eccleston was apprenticed to Nicholas and Mary Barber but they were very negligent about training her and used her to do 'laborious work' in the house.[39] Some unhappy apprentices simply ran away. Down in Somerset, Elizabeth Clark grew up in the workhouse in Nunney, near Frome, and when she was about ten she was apprenticed to Ann Coombs, mantua-maker in nearby Holwell. After three-and-a-half years she ran away and 'travelled the county from place to place' sometimes working as a servant, sometimes doing spinning and carding. Nine years down the line she was out of work and destitute and tried to make her way back to Nunney as the only place she felt she could claim settlement (i.e. would be entitled to poor relief). She was picked up sleeping on the streets in Frome.[40]

Employment

Assuming a girl served her apprenticeship without mishap, she might do another stint with a different mistress to learn additional skills – in the nineteenth century girls in this position were called 'improvers' but the term does not seem to have been current until the end of the eighteenth century. On 22 December 1798 A. Robinson advertised in the *Northampton Mercury*:

> WANTED immediately THREE APPRENTICES to the MANTUA-MAKING BUSINESS or young persons wishing for Improvement.

This seems to be one of the first usages of the term.

Her training complete, a girl then became a 'journeywoman' or assistant. By the end of the century mantua-makers were advertising regularly in the local press for apprentices and journeywomen. Expectations were high. For example, Mrs Gambier in Canterbury ran a substantial firm, and when she advertised for a journeywoman to oversee her workroom she stressed the applicant 'must be perfect in her business' (*Kentish Gazette*, January 1783), while the author of the advertisement below made similarly high demands:

> WANTED, for a Person in full Business, A Journey-Woman Mantua-maker or two — None need apply but such as can be well recommended, and can work exceeding well and neat. — An Apprentice is also wanted — Apply to the Printer of this paper.

3. *The Newcastle Weekly Courant*, 13 November 1779.

Unfortunately, none of the advertisements mention anything as vulgar as wages, and the shortage of business records makes it difficult to say what women would have earned. Obviously wages would have been different in different types of establishment and would probably have risen as a woman became more experienced. However, Campbell, writing in *The Book of Trades* in 1747, claimed that milliners made:

> vast profits ... yet give but poor, mean Wages to every Person they employ under them: Though a young Woman can work neatly in all manner of Needle-Work, yet she cannot earn more than Five or Six Shillings a Week, out of which she is to find herself in Board and Lodging.

Mantua-makers fared no better. The accounts of wages that occur in a handful of settlement examinations suggest that Campbell's estimates were actually overly optimistic – though women claiming settlement were seeking poor relief and may not have been among the most successful practitioners of their trade.

For example, in 1739, Sarah Seaton claimed that in 1733 she had been live-in assistant to Mrs Nobbs, a mantua-maker in St Martins-in-the-Fields, and had earned £4.10s.0d a year (less than 2s.0d a week). Jane Cann worked for another mantua-maker, Mrs Fowls, between 1744 and 1748 in the same parish for £4.00 a year plus board and lodging.[41] Sarah Paine in Pulborough (West Sussex) sought settlement there in 1759. She had trained as a mantua-maker but was working as a house servant for her mother for 30s.0d a year, eking that out by doing a bit of dressmaking in her spare time – clearly she did not expect to be able to make a living from dressmaking alone.[42] Wages did not rise much over time. In 1814 in Exeter (Devon) Mary Beal claimed to have been paid four guineas a year, though in the early 1820s Mary Vaughan in nearby Chudleigh was paid double that (roughly 3s.3d a week).[43]

But dressmakers were not uniquely under-privileged. Eighteenth-century wages were low. Women doing fieldwork earned around 8d a day in the 1720s. Live-in servants' pay in the 1770s ranged from £2.00 to £8.00 pa for maids and up to £20.00 for an experienced housekeeper or cook; by contrast, a footman could expect £8.00 to £15 per year, and a coachman anywhere between £12.00 and £26.00. Independent artisans often earned as little as £15.00 to £20.00 per year, though at least £30.00 was said to be needed to keep a family in reasonable comfort – and 'respectable' people considered £100.00 a year barely adequate.[44]

Work in the clothing trades was always poorly paid and men fared little better than women. For example, in Perth (Scotland) in June 1734 fifteen journeymen tailors petitioned for a wage rise – from 5d a day to 6d a day – or 3s.0d a week.[45] They were not live-in staff and would have had to support themselves, and possibly wives and families, on the pittance they were paid. Further south, John Ravenhill of Mathon in Worcestershire, trained as a tailor and stay-maker with his father and then, in the 1750s, aged about seventeen, went to work as journeyman for another tailor, William Webb at Colwall in Herefordshire for 2s.8d a week.[46] In the early 1800s in Basingstoke (Hampshire), Samuel Attwood, a master tailor with a wife and child, seldom made more than 15s.0d a week – though he did also rear pigs and make and sell cider.[47]

In 1811 *The Book of Trades or Library of Useful Arts* was still warning that 'The business of a mantua-maker, when conducted on a large scale and in a fashionable situation, is very profitable; but the mere work-women do not make gains at all adequate to their labour; they are frequently obliged to sit up to very late hours, and the recompense for extra-work is in general a poor remuneration for the time spent'. However, the girl who had served her apprenticeship had a number of options. She could carry on working for a mantua-maker or she could work for a draper, milliner or haberdasher – her training would have given her a knowledge of fabrics and an eye for fashion that shopkeepers valued, and in many shops customers could have the fabrics and trimmings they bought made up into caps or accessories so her skills would have come in useful.

Alternatively, a trained mantua-maker or milliner could become a lady's maid. On 12 May 1778 the *Public Advertiser* carried the following advertisement:

> A Person every Way qualified for a Lady's Woman, would be glad to engage herself in a genteel Family in that Capacity; she understands Mantua-making, Millinery, and Hair-dressing; and she would be glad to live with a Lady that travels, as she has no Objection to go Abroad; her Character will bear the strictest Enquiry from a Lady of Quality.
> Direct for X. Y. Z at No. 342, Oxford street.

4. *The Public Advertiser*, 12 May 1778.

Over in Suffolk another young woman was keeping her options open:

> WANTS a Situation, as Journeywoman to a Mantua-maker, or in some genteel family, where needlework would be her chief employ; has been a regular apprentice in the above branch, and can produce an unexceptionable character. For particulars enquire of Mr. Forster, bookseller, Ipswich, or of Mr. S. Giffing, draper, Mendlesham.

5. *The Ipswich Journal*, 23 July 1796.

while the French lady who advertised in the *Bath Chronicle* in 1780 offered an even wider range of services:

> BATH, Feb. 15th, 1780.
> A French Gentlewoman just come to town, who dresses Ladies Hair, understands Mantua-making and Millinery business in all its branches, in the most elegant taste, would be very glad to enter into a genteel family, either in quality of Tutress for the French, Housekeeper, or Lady's Waiting-Maid; to be spoke with at Mr. Butler's, No. 1, Bennet-street.
> ☞ She has a most excellent character from the noble family where she lived last.

6. *The Bath Chronicle*, 15 February 1780.

Employers were often proud of their maids' talents: writing from Florence on Christmas Eve 1792, Harriet Carr told her mother that in the course of their travels Dolly, her maid, had become a 'skilled milliner, mantua-maker and tailor'.[48] Other girls were lucky enough to be able to take over their mistress's business – a favourite apprentice might be treated almost like a daughter. In *Saunder's News Letter* for 23 December 1776, for example, Bridget Sheridan, formerly apprenticed to Mrs Leslie of Bolton Street, Dublin, advertised that she was taking over her late mistress's business.

At the bottom end of the market, a trained worker could always have found employment as an outworker for an entrepreneur supplying ready-made gowns. There was already a thriving trade in ready-made garments by the end of the seventeenth century, employing an army of garret seamstresses working for pathetically low wages. [Plate 7]

Plate 7 Trade card for Mary and Ann Hogarth's ready-made 'frock shop'.

On 9 June 1711, for example, *The Spectator* informed its readers that:

The Silk Gowns formerly sold in Exchange Alley are moved to the sign of the Hood and Scarf directly over against Mill's Coffee House in Cornhill, where any Gentleman or Lady may be finished with any Size or Price, there being all sorts of Silks from rich Brocades of 6 Guineas a Gown to Thread sattins of 37s … Note, there are upwards of 50 fresh Gowns new made up and are [*to*] be seen on Tuesday next.

Ready-made garments were available across the country, from the warehouses of Bath[49] supplying middle-class visitors with affordable garments at fixed prices to Hull market where Mary Hardy bought a gown for her niece in 1803.[50]

> OXFORD, April 14, 1798.
>
> JUST arrived from the Milliner and Fancy Dress Maker to her Royal Highness the Princess of Wales, a fashionable Assortment of MILLINERY, FANCY, and other DRESSES, at C. Lovett's, Milliner, Mantua and Fancy Dress Maker, from London, at Mr. Haynes's, Glover, High Street, Oxford.
>
> C. Lovett hopes from her Attention and Experience in Business, and her Endeavour to have almost weekly some ready-made Fashions ready for the Nobility, Gentry, and Inhabitants of Oxford, to merit their Approbation.
>
> Orders from Ladies in the Country duly attended to.— The Letters must be Post paid.
>
> N. B. Milliners, Mantua and Fancy Dress Makers, in the Country, supplied with the Fashions in both Branches, on the most reasonable Terms, as soon as they arrive from London, Carriage free.

7. *Jackson's Oxford Journal*, 14 April 1798.

It is interesting to note that, in Oxfordshire at least, suppliers would provide milliners and mantua-makers with ready-made garments to use as patterns. The ready-to-wear trade probably absorbed a large number of the women who had trained as mantua-makers, but it is outside the scope of this study.

Running a business

As we have seen, by the end of the eighteenth century advertisements in the press for dressmakers wanting jobs and employers wanting staff appear with increasing frequency. This was largely due to the increasing number of local papers, but improving literacy levels may also have played a role. Not that it was essential to be literate to run a business – of the 61/100 apprenticeship indentures examined where the mistress or her husband signed their name, sixteen (roughly 25 per cent) signed with a cross. Apprentices signed their own indentures surprising infrequently, but of the 28/100 who did, twelve signed with a mark. Of course, like Sarah Scott, some may then have received a little schooling as part of their apprenticeship.

Running a business also required the ability to do sums and few girls were taught more than simple arithmetic. Schools and writing masters advertised in the press that they would teach accounting to tradesmen's sons but there was little provision for tradesmen's daughters. A few girls may have had access to one of the many books on penmanship and book-keeping – by Snell, Hatton, Ayres, London, Webster and others that appeared from the 1690s to the 1770s[51] – through their fathers or brothers, but none of these works are particularly easy for the untutored to understand.

However, some girls simply had a knack for business. Sarah Hurst was the daughter of a tailor-cum-draper in Horsham (West Sussex) and from 1759 to 1762 she kept a diary.[52] Much of it is concerned with her social life – paying calls, going for walks, holidaying with friends, dancing, playing cards, writing poetry – and she is constantly worrying about 'my dear Harry', the naval captain she eventually married – but it is clear she also spent some time working with her father in his shop and that she did some dressmaking for customers.

> Work very hard fancying the pattern of my apron, but am often interrupted by people in the shop. Allmost [sic] wish I did not love work so well, yet it passes away many hours that I shou'd probably employ by tormenting myself about what hangs like a heavy load at my Heart, the fate of my Dear Harry (26 September 1759).

> Extreamly [sic] busy in the shop with various sorts of customers & work, business is certainly the finest thing in the world for depressed spirits (16 April 1760).

'[I]s it because I carry on all his business & he wou'd find it difficult to do without me?' she wondered later that month when her father seemed unhappy about the idea that she might marry. In fact, her father was not an easy man to work with and she often records his bad temper. She seems to have been responsible for writing out bills and copying letters for him – she wrote a neat sloping script. 'Write out a great many bills. Papa a little cross and pettish ... ' (5 January 1860) or 'Write out all the Ellis's Bills which engages me all morning' (21 March 1761) or 'Very busy all the morning posting the Shop Books, a disagreeable but a necessary piece of work' (19 August 1761). She also seems to have done the stocktaking and record-keeping: 'Began casting up the Shop by Papa's order' (23 February 1762); 'Cast up my father's Cash Book, & almost stupefy myself with Accounts' (8 March 1762). Sarah also visited London regularly and did a good deal of business on her father's account, paying bills, visiting suppliers and ordering goods for the shop; he obviously relied heavily on her business sense and gave her a great deal of responsibility. 'Put several hundred pound of my father's in my stays to buy in the Stocks, am afraid I shall find it a great weight' (4 November 1761). Nonetheless she found 'doing business for fathers is attended with very great perplexity, did I carry it on for myself shou'd then be certain what wou'd please ... ' (3 May 1760).

Sarah was obviously also a competent needlewoman and wrote of working on ruffles for Captain Smith, handkerchiefs for Miss Seawall and Mrs Turner and an elaborate embroidered apron for herself which took many months and was much praised – 't'is almost enough to make one vain to have a performance so generally admir'd'. She helped a Mrs Wicker and her Aunt Tasker with their quilting and made garments – including stays – for herself. She also seems to have done some dressmaking in the shop – 'Miss Ellis here, she bespeaks a new silk gown, & I cut her out several things, very chatty' (17 March 1760); 'Busy cutting out work in the shop' (4 October 1760). They seem to have employed a Miss Tredcroft as a needlewoman and Sarah often records helping her; they also socialized with 'Miss and Mr Tredcroft' but Sarah's comments are revealing: 'Miss Tredcroft ... is a most charming girl in person ... but how infinitely short falls the intellectual part.'

It is unlikely that Sarah was unique. Tradesmen's daughters who were intelligent and educated and who had been brought up in a business environment had every chance of becoming successful businesswomen in their own right, but not all women had those advantages. The fact that no mantua-makers' business records survive from the pre-1800 period is therefore not entirely surprising. However, some records do survive from the very early nineteenth century. Magdalene Dunbar in Leith ran a millinery business which was patronized by wealthy women. When she was declared bankrupt in 1816 the courts listed her business records 'viz, a Ledger, a Day Book, a Scroll or Waste Book, a Cash Book, an Invoice Book and a Book of Payments'.[53] This is interesting because it gives a complete list and we are not left to guess her system from a few random survivals – and she certainly kept fuller records than most of the firms that will be considered in subsequent chapters. She went bankrupt because her wealthy and titled clients were tardy in paying their bills, not because she kept poor records.

Successes and failures

Against the odds, some mantua-makers were surprisingly successful. Whether many of them made the 'vast profits' Campbell attributed to them is open to question, though reports like the one that appeared in the *Stamford Mercury* on 21 July 1768 reinforced his assertion: 'A French Mantua-Maker has lately retired from London to Paris with a Fortune of £1,500 where she lives in great splendor [*sic*], on what she emphatically calls *La Follie des Dames Anglaises*.' Her success was seen as exceptional; nonetheless, an examination of mantua-makers wills shows that quite a number left considerable amounts of money and property.

In 1763, for example, Ann Sawney in Lechlade (Gloucestershire) left six messuages and tenements to various relatives, and £25.00 apiece in cash to her sisters and nieces along with a large amount of clothing and household goods. In 1772, Ann Carter of St Marylebone in Middlesex left her house and most of her estate to her foreman, John Church, 'in gratitude for his years of service', and £145.00 in bequests to tradesmen and staff with whom she had worked – it would appear she had no family. Three years later, Sarah Sutton of Streatley in Berkshire left £70.00 to be divided between her nephews and nieces. Grace Plaistow of Rickmansworth (Hertfordshire) left a similar sum to be divided between her siblings in 1790. In Nottingham in 1785 Martha Burgess left bequests totalling over £300.00 along with quantities of silver, plate and linen. Other mantua-makers had clearly lived comfortably, even if they did not leave much actual cash – in Westminster Mary Stainforth left the contents of two well-appointed parlours in 1762, and in 1793 Lucy Hitchcock, also in Westminster, had silver spoons and gold rings to bequeath to her family.[54]

Looking at how mantua-makers fared at the end of their lives is not the only way of analysing the worth of their businesses. Another is by looking at insurance records. The eighteenth-century records are not as detailed as one might like; businesses were insured for a lump sum and were only protected against fire, so though they show replacement costs for restarting a business the items to be replaced are not itemized. Most mantua-makers did not own their own premises, so the figures cover the cost of equipment and stock (lining fabrics, trimmings, bones, ribbons, etc.). Most mantua-makers made up fabric supplied by the customer so did not keep bales of expensive materials. An analysis of the sums for which mantua-makers in London insured themselves in the period 1776 to 1787, by which time the trade was well-established, is revealing. Of 232 policies, 88 were for sums between £100.00 and £200.00 and 117 were for between £200.00 and £400.00. Just twenty-seven businesses were valued at over £400.00 and of these just one – that of Elizabeth Dorothy Watson in Little Argyll Street – was insured for £1,000.00, while of the rest, two were insured for £900.00, three for £800.00 and two for £700.00.[55] However, there were many firms which were uninsured. In May 1770, for example, Mrs Catherine Bond in St Ann's parish, London, took out an advert in the *Public Advertiser* entreating her customers to provide 'benevolent Assistance' to enable her to re-establish her business after a house fire.

Old age and sickness cut short many careers. In 1776 Elizabeth Taylor and Mary Doverlie both petitioned Aberdeen Council for support from the Huison charity. Elizabeth had made a living sewing and mantua-making for sixty years but was unable to work 'through age and infirmity' – she must have started work *c*.1716. Two references attached to her application spoke of her respectable family – her grandfather had been a freeman cooper – and of her own 'unblameable' character. Mary was younger, an 'indigent gentlewoman … in a very tender and sickly state of health'.[56] Neither had found mantua-making brought 'vast profits'. Seventy-year-old Mercy Eastman in Winchelsea (Sussex) applied for settlement in 1825.[57] She had trained as a mantua-maker in Hastings and had originally been paid three pounds a year (presumably in the early 1770s). She had worked on her own account for seven years then married a hairdresser and had a son by him. Her husband had deserted her when the child was a toddler and she had worked as a mantua-maker in Winchelsea for a few years before becoming mistress of the workhouse at a salary of four pounds a year which later rose to twelve guineas. After she left that post she again worked at mantua-making but was now old and infirm. Despite her long residence in Winchelsea which should have been enough to gain her settlement, the authorities removed her to Hastings, her birthplace.

Comparatively few such records survive so we have no way of knowing how many women did well in the trade and how many fell on hard times – or, indeed, how many made an adequate living and ended their days in reasonable comfort, living on their savings or cared for by family and friends.

Conclusion

By the mid-eighteenth century the mantua-making trade was well-established though it still employed a relatively small number of women. Many of their customers were drawn from the new middle class, women who were anxious to keep abreast of fashion, not only in clothes but in household goods and furnishings. Paris remained the fashion centre of Europe and throughout the century French goods remained desirable, despite wars and prohibitions, and news of new modes of dress made its way across the UK surprisingly quickly, via London and through an increasing number of fashion publications. Many eighteenth-century mantua-makers were comparatively well-educated and many came from the middle class and the lesser gentry, though as the century wore on more and more new recruits to the trade came from the tradesman class. Some were successful and left substantial sums of money in their wills; others struggled and ended their days on poor relief or supported by charities. Records of mantua-making are few and far between, but there are sufficient similarities between those records that do survive to enable us to draw tentative conclusions about the structure of the trade and relationships between mantua-makers and their customers. In the next chapter we will look at the trade from the point of view of those customers.

3

'I bought me a gowne'

The customer experience

Like their customers, dressmaking businesses came in all shapes and sizes. The grand shops in London's Regent Street where wealthy women could while away the hours trying on bonnets and choosing fabrics and trimmings were by no means typical. [Plates 8 & 9] Even in the capital, many mantua-makers worked in their own homes and visited their customers to fit garments and discuss

Plate 8 Trade card for Martha Cole and Martha Houghton, drapers. A card with exactly the same image and legend was produced for Benjamin Cole, draper. It seems likely that the two Marthas took over his business and had the engraving reworked.

Plate 9 Draper's shop from *The Book of Trades*, 1818.

details. Alongside the women who worked in the bespoke trade there were the women sub-contracting to wholesalers and to the sellers of ready-made dresses. Between them, they clothed the nation's womenfolk, providing elaborate silk dresses for countesses and print gowns for servant girls. Different firms catered for different classes of customers – and inevitably, it is the wealthy customers who have left most information behind them [Plate 10].

London was acknowledged to be a centre of fashion, second only to Paris, and well-to-do women across the country visited town when they could or sought the help of friends and relatives who lived or travelled there. There is, for example, a list in Cheshire Record Office, dated 1755, of the items a lady called Ann Shackerley required from London:

> ## Goods from London requested by Ann Shackerley in 1855
>
> One suit of habit linen, 1 everyday round cap, 1 gause mob, gause for an apron, flower'd gause and blonde and trimmings for caps, 3 yards of a sort of different coloured ribband, a Night Gown Hoop Fan fashion, A black Capuchine and Hat of some sort, very little, 2 pr of white riding gloves, 2 pr coloured ditto, 4 prs white gloves, 2 prs lead coloured unglazed ditto, 2 prs mitts, Drawing books, Washballs, My watch mended, Pins.

There followed a list of the shops where these items were to be purchased and the instruction that 'the washballs only to be bought of Mrs Wharton at the sign of the Blue Coat Boy a Toy Shop near ye Royal Exchange in Cornhill and at Mrs Stevens milliners at the sign of ye Blue Ball near ye Middle Temple Gate in Fleet Street'. There is no record of the person to whom Ann entrusted these commissions.[1]

In 1760, Elizabeth Jervis wrote from London to her mother back home in Staffordshire:

> Sister and I think you had better have one of ye new fashion'd long short black aprons trim'd with trolly which are much more wore than white – but you might have one white if you chose it, but I think ye black would look better with that gown … shan't you want a black handkerchief they don't slope 'em as your last but just cut across ye silk and trim'd with lace or trolly … if you make new stays they should be very low before & high-behind and as thin bone as possible fear they wont be able to make' em properly in ye Country if you can stay till you come to Town next winter woud be best.[2]

She sent numerous other letters – about the high price of mourning fabrics after the death of George II, new fashions in gloves, new types of stay laces and all sorts of other information about dress that would not otherwise have reached rural Staffordshire.

Shopping for others could sometimes be a nightmare. In July 1700 Susannah Avery in London wrote to Lady Mordaunt, wife of Sir John Mordaunt MP, seventh Baronet of Massingham, in Norfolk:

> I could not get ye Gown out of ye womans hand I was often with her and she promised me from day to day and now at last she saith she cannot draw it till she washeth it she promisseth I should have it next week but I am afraid she will fail me as she hath dun offne. I have bought ye velvet and got it printed. I have bougt ye muslin and it cost four shillings and six pence and ye oringflower water it cost fifteen pence … [sic]

Susannah passed on advice from 'Mrs Rigbee', a London mantua-maker, about what Lady Mordaunt could wear as mourning for 'ye Duke'. The letter is dated 9 August so this was probably eleven-year-old Prince William, Duke of Gloucester, son of Princess (later Queen) Anne, who died on 30 July 1700. Mrs Rigbee had:

> mauve cloth gowns for ye mourning and she has one white lustring lined with black but she knoweth of no new fashion stuffs cum up yet but your Ld^{sh} being with Child she knoweth not but sumthing of whit may be proper for you. [*sic*].[3]

The tone of Susannah's letters is very respectful and it may be she was a servant to the family or a young relative.

Not surprisingly, mistakes and misunderstandings occurred. In September 1757, Christian Williamson wrote to her brother, Edmond, about a length of silk for a gown which she had acquired for her sister-in-law in Bedfordshire, and for which she had been underpaid:

> I am sorry there was such a mistake about the silks but I think I may say it wasn't mine, for nobody that ever bought a silk in their lives could have thought that pattern of my silk could be under 6s or 7s a yard of that breadth and richness ... and I am afraid there is another mistake about the other, for you desired 12 yards; now there was 13½ in that piece that I sent ... for the mercer would not cut the odd yard-and-a-half off without it was more than 7s a yard, for the yard-and-a-half would be quite lost to him. But he said if I would take it all as it was, he would give the half-yard in for nothing, and so was only to pay for 13 yards, which I thought was a good bargain for 7s.[4]

Transporting items could also be problematic. In April 1771 Elizabeth Shackleton in Lancashire received a box containing her 'good white satin petticoat' which she had sent to London to be dyed blue. It arrived 'spoiled and cut to pieces'.[5] There are numerous other examples of commissions that went wrong.

Ladies who had no contacts in the capital often relied on their dressmakers for advice. With country clients whose garments were out-of-date the dressmaker required a good deal of tact. In 1734, for example, Elizabeth Blyvers in London wrote to Mrs Buxton at Shadwell Lodge near Thetford in Norfolk:

> They now wear their Lappets so very broad that it was impossible to make the ... lappets fit to appear in any other shape which obliged me to make new ones the others will serve for mobs, tuckers or any such use. I have made the Ruffels as

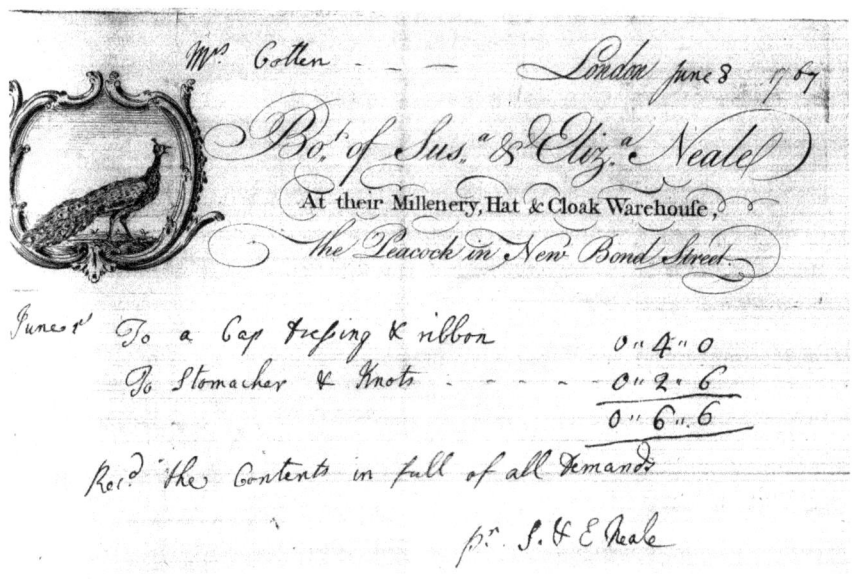

Plate 10 Bill from Susan and Elizabeth Neale, New Bond Street, 1767.

handsome as I possibly could considering the difference in the fashion at the time they were made. I hope you will like them.[6]

However, some dressmakers established remarkably amicable relationships with their out-of-town customers. A series of letters dated 1783 and 1784 survive from Mrs A. Charlton of Holles Street, Cavendish Square, London, to Lady Sabine Winn at Nostell Priory in Yorkshire.[7] They are deferential but friendly. Mrs Charlton asked after members of the Winn family, particularly the two children, and told Lady Sabine about her own indispositions. She offered plentiful advice about the latest fashions in caps and sleeves and fichus and sent bundles of samples of laces, ribbons and chintzes. [Colour Plate II] She visited Paris regularly, but selling French goods was risky: 'in regard to the gauze, it is a french one and the common width of french ones the reason we cut the selvedge of [sic] is that we may run no risk in keeping it in the house.' In another letter she described French gloves as 'too dangerous a thing to deal in'. She also sent 'bargains'.

> I recd a chemise from France a little time ago which cost me 9 guineas there –
> I have sent it to your Ladyship to see with a sash that belongs to it and if you would chuse to keep it your Ladyship shall have it for 4 guineas ... Chemise with

sashes the new coulors I have joind in a bit of paper and one is called the violet Blue all the sprind Cloaths have been of this color [sic].

In her next letter Mrs Charlton made sure Lady Winn recognized how lucky she was:

> I am happy your Ladyship keeps the chemise as I am sure it is a great bargain and I loose [sic] 5 guineas by it and could not afford it for less it is worth more than that to take to pieces and there is no one but your Ladyship should have had it at that price.

This is another indication that mantua-makers cut patterns from gowns they acquired ready-made. Interestingly too, both mantua-maker and customer were obviously well aware of the prohibition on the sale of French goods, but they seem to have seen it as a nuisance to be worked round rather than a law they were breaking. In return for her services, Lady Sabine regularly sent Mrs Charlton hampers of produce – including venison – from the Yorkshire estate.

As the century progressed more and more dressmakers advertised in the press. Given the difficulty of travelling on eighteenth-century roads, a remarkable number of them claimed that they had visited London and brought back new fashions for their customers to see, and some still visited Paris, as had Mrs Charlton.

> DERBY, May 11th, 1789.
> S. HOLMES, *MANTUA-MAKER*,
> OPPOSITE the THEATRE, *Bold-Lane*,
>
> BEGS Leave to return her moft grateful Thanks for all paft Favours, and hopes for the Continuance of the fame. Likewife takes this Opportunity to acquaint her Friends that fhe is juft returned from London, and that thofe Ladies who pleafe to favour her with their Commands may depend on them being executed in the neateft and moft fafhionable Manner, and their Favours gratefully acknowledged.

8. *The Derby Mercury*, 7 May 1789.

The custom of milliners and mantua-makers putting on displays of the latest goods to tempt customers also seems to have begun in the late eighteenth century and advertisements for fashion displays appeared regularly in the press. For example:

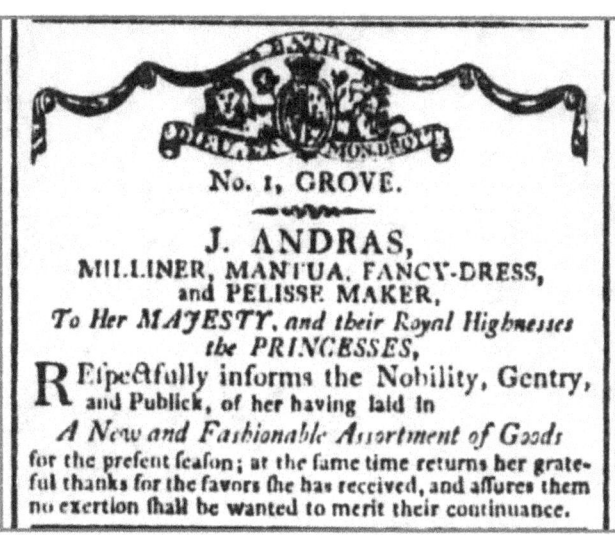

9. *The Norfolk Chronicle,* 29 May 1790.

10. *The Bath Chronicle,* 12 December 1799.

By the 1790s the custom had even reached rural Norfolk – in May 1793 Mary Hardy recorded that her daughter and younger son 'walkd up to Holt to see Miss Johnson's fasions [*sic*].'[8] A year later, a few miles away in Weston Longville, Parson Woodforde noted, 'After breakfast I walked out with Nancy to Miss Browne's to see the Fashions. Gave Nancy a very handsome Sash etc. Paid for the same 0.18.0. Nancy bought her a pretty Hat suitable to the Sash.'[9] Some women also used their premises for other forms of entertainment – on 6 April 1795, for example, Miss Newton, a Hereford milliner, advertised an entertainment by a London magician 'the powers of imagination or the senses deceived' at her premises on the Market Place.[10]

Dressmaking establishments

While there is a considerable body of evidence about dressmakers and clients, we have very little information about dressmaking establishments. There are engravings and descriptions of fashionable shops where ladies bought fabrics and trimmings, but very little about what a dressmaker's shop actually looked like or what it was like to go for a fitting. There is an illustration in Diderot's *Encyclopaedie* of a French mantua-maker's workroom, a spacious, well-lit room with one worker at a cutting-out table, two women, one being measured by the other, and a range of garments

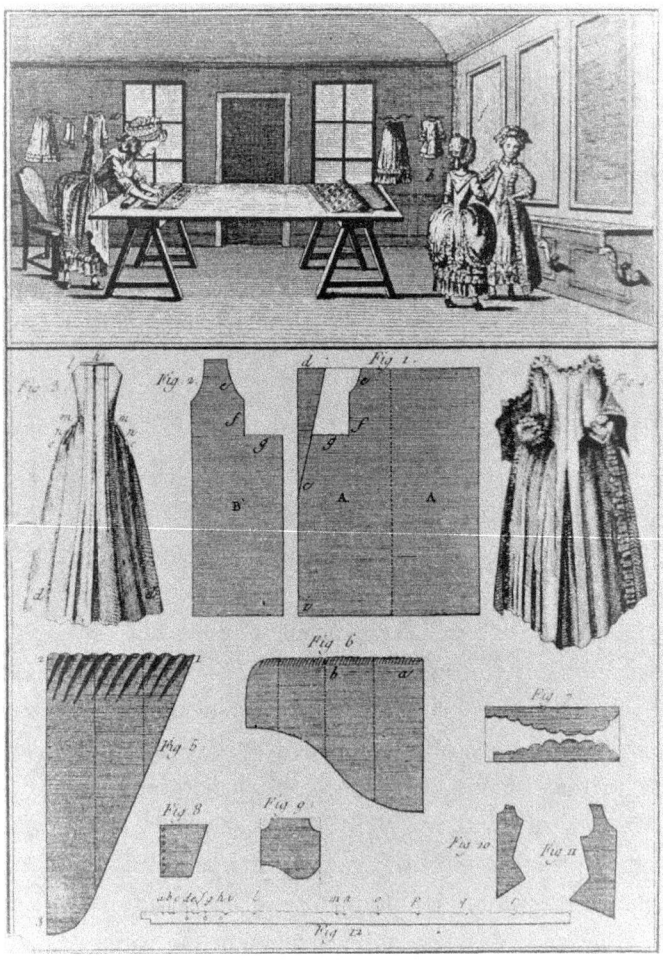

Plate 11 Mantua-maker's workshop from *Diderot's Encyclopaedia*, 1751–80.

apparently stuck to the walls but presumably hung on nails. [Plate 11] But like many Diderot illustrations it is essentially a diagram; almost certainly the appearance of space is illusory – and where are all the needle-women? Another illustration of a fitting comes in the *Book of Trades*, first published in 1811. Here the customer is trying on a dress in front of a large mirror, but there is no indication of what the rest of the shop looked like [Plate 25]. Later testimony[11] tells us that early-nineteenth-century workrooms were crowded and uncomfortable – no doubt they were in the latter part of the eighteenth century too. It would be fascinating to know more about working conditions and practices.

There are occasional clues. An inventory was made of Magdalene Dunbar's stock and possessions in Leith (near Edinburgh) in 1815.[12] She carried £235.12s.8d worth of stock, all of which was carefully listed and divided up by category – muslin, ribbons, bead clasps, feathers, fancy flowers, fancy trimmings and white laces. She had a well-furnished bedroom, parlour, kitchen and 'ware room' (linen cupboard) and silverware, china and glass valued at £127.18s.9½d. Her shop and work room contents are itemized below so we have some idea of what they must have looked like:

1 set of dining tables £5.0s.0d
1 set of tea tables £2.8s.0d
1 small square table 5s.0d
1 stove and a set of fire irons and fender £3.0s.0d
1 pair of bell handles 2s.6d
2 mirrors £8.0s.0d
1 carpet £2.5s.0d
6 rush bottomed chairs £1.10s.0d
2 poles for hanging dresses on 15s.0d
1½ dozen bonnet blocks 18s.0d
Total £42.4s.1d

Work-room
2 tables
2 work baskets
5 chairs
2 stools
1 screen
a stove, fender, shovel and tongs
Total: £3.17s.6d

This was a well-equipped, upmarket business in a fashionable part of town. It is interesting to note that far and away the most valuable pieces of equipment were the two – presumably full-length – mirrors.

Travelling in France in January 1786, Frances Anne Crewe described a visit to the famous 'marchande des modes', Rose Bertin:

> I had actually the sensation of awe on being brought into the Presence of Mademoiselle Bertin! I beg you won't laugh at this … The Duchess de Castries was waiting in one Corner of the Room for her turn to be spoken to – two Ladies had got Possession of her Ear at the moment we entered – and several Gentleman were beguiling the Time in different parts of the Room with her Apprentices or Myrmidons … I observed several large Wooden Busts and Statues dispersed about, and upon them various Parts of Dress – and, everything had on it the Stamp of Science, and, if I might judge from the sort of Ecstasy which was lavished on the Chief D'oeuvres of her Art, Mademoiselle Bertin has certainly carried it to the highest possible Pitch of Perfection.[13]

Rose Bertin was holding a sort of salon and the items on display had been made for the Duchesse de Castries to wear at Versailles. What is clear is that this was completely unlike anything Mrs Crewe had encountered at home. The reference to busts and statues is particularly interesting – it would be another hundred years before dressmakers' dummies came into use in England.

Lower down the social ladder were those women working on a smaller scale in their own homes or shops. There were many such firms in London and they seem to have been the norm in the provinces. Sometimes the dressmakers visited their clients; in isolated districts they sometimes stayed in the client's house to work. Sarah Fell records the tailor visiting Swarthmore Hall, near Ulverston, in 1677, and being paid 2s.8d for four days' work for Sarah, her mother and sisters.[14] Lynn Sorge-English has described how the stay-maker, Richard Viney, travelled to visit his various clients in the area around his home in the West Riding of Yorkshire in the 1740s.[15] In Norfolk, Mary Hardy had clothes made for herself and her daughter; sometimes they went to Holt – their nearest town, just a mile away – to the dressmaker, sometimes the dressmaker came to them. Mary also employed various seamstresses. She was the wife of a farmer-cum-brewer, and seems to have seen her dressmakers and seamstresses as her social equals – she frequently dined or took tea with them. On 14 February 1794, for example, 'Mrs Sheldrake came aftern to alter and repair my Gowns, Slept here …' Four years later Miss Braithwait was her dressmaker, and in September she visited and 'made Mary Ann [Mary's daughter] a White Muslin Gown'. Later 'Miss Braithwait drank tea here, did a job to my black Silk Gown.'[16]

It was much the same in Lancashire. Elizabeth Shackleton was a respectable gentlewoman living in a grand house, but from time to time she entertained Margaret Fielden, her mantua-maker, for tea. Letters to her from Margaret survive which are purely social – an account of her health and activities with no mention of business.[17] By 1772 one of Elizabeth's dressmakers was a Mrs Fields and on 25 September Elizabeth 'took my scarlet damask to Mrs Fields – dined with her, had my gowns tried on'.[18]

A grateful customer might even leave her mantua-maker money in her will – for example, in Hertfordshire in 1777 Ann Godfrey left £20.00 to Mrs Barnard, her mantua-maker in Bishop's Stortford, along with numerous other bequests to tradesmen and the local poor.[19]

Money worries

However they worked, the biggest problem all dressmakers faced was getting clients to pay their bills. Magdalene Dunbar in Leith provides a perfect test case. Her problems were largely due to her inability to persuade her clients to pay her and in 1816 her debts totalled an astronomical £2,549.2s.6¾d. There were two lists of debts. She was owed £281.17s.1d by seventy-eight clients and a further £91.8s.3d was classed as 'bad or doubtful' debts from twenty-nine clients who presumably had owed them for a long time or could not be traced. Some were quite large sums. Mrs McKenzie of Renton Hall owed £13.18s.3d; Mrs B. Home of York Place, £12.1s.11d; Mrs Kerr of Leith, £27.11s.11d; Mrs Graham of Annfield, £22.12s.3d; Miss Stewart of Jamaica Place, £30.10s.0d. Some of her creditors were titled ladies – like Lady Jane Stewart Greenhill, Lady Helen Hall and Lady Cathcart.[20]

Miss Dunbar in turn owed money to her suppliers, to her assistant Mary Livingstone (£20.00 of unpaid salary) and even to her baker. The trustees took steps to gather her debts and kept her and her staff at work completing orders – 'and, so far as she has gone, a much greater sum has been earned by her and her young people than has been expended in housekeeping', reported W.H. Brown smugly at the first meeting after his appointment as sequestrator. He paid off what debts he could and reduced the number of her creditors to forty-four – though some of them were owed large sums – £98.10s.11d to Mary Knox, milliner, £45.00 to the Edinburgh haberdasher, Alexander Campbell, £65.8s.9d to Solomon Davis, a London merchant, for example, as well as several hundred pounds to members of the Dunbar family who had bailed Magdalene out. In the end her creditors were paid at 2s.8d in the pound and proceedings were concluded in April 1818.

Magdalene Dunbar's clients were wealthy women and she was trading in a fashionable location. Small town dressmakers were more likely to be able to insist on immediate payment, but they, too, had rogue customers. A letter survives from 1731 to Mrs Mary Smith, a milliner in Hull. She had obviously requested the service of a bailiff, John Howden, to try to get Mr Swain in Scarborough to pay his wife's bill. Despite the presence of Mr Howden and his sidekick, Thomas Pratt, Mr Swain still refused to pay and was ordered to appear 'at the Bell in Beaverley on fryday [sic] the fifth of November'. History does not record the outcome.[21]

Prices

The cost of making clothes varied widely – from 1s.6d for a cotton frock in 1724 to eighteen guineas for a court robe for Lady Bruce, wife of the Marquis of Aylesbury, from M. Sowerby in London in 1800. This seems to have been a splendid affair of straw-coloured silk and green crepe ornamented with gold and bronze beads; worn over a hoop (hoops had long been out of fashion for normal wear but were still de rigeur at court); and accessorized with a green, bronze and gold bandeau with bronze feathers. The whole outfit cost an enormous twenty-seven guineas. Lady Bruce was always a big spender. In 1797, for example, she spent £32.6s.0d with Le Brun Boileau on hats and £13.7s.6d with Sarah Perry on gloves and trimmings, while in 1805 she spent an enormous £42.2s.2d with Hardings on fabrics, ribbons and shoes.[22]

Unfortunately, the lack of proper business records makes it very difficult to assess the profitability of mantua-making. Of the three main variables in making such an assessment – prices charged, volume of trade and outgoings (including rent and wages) – we only have information about the first. The following table lists prices for various types of garment and client, culled from a range of sources. It does not include all the garments bought or made by each of the individuals named but is intended to give a representative sample.

Table 2 Table of eighteenth-century garment prices.

Source	Date	Print/other dresses	Silk dresses	Petticoats	Court robes	Cloaks	Bonnets	Caps	Hoops	Stays
For Mrs Knyvett, Norwich	1647		5s.6d 'taffety gowne' and petticoat							
To Margaret Caton for Sarah Fell, Lancs.	1673			5s.5d						
To Mme Mason, Chichester	1692–4		4s to 5s 'mantos'							
For Lady Trumbull, Reading	1691–5		6s 'black manto'	2s-6d fringed 3s 'stuff' with ribbon						£1.17s covered in black satin and trimmed with silver fringe
John Scott paid his wife's bill with Jane Park, Shropshire	1713	2s.6d wadded calico gown	5s.6d satin dress and petticoat							

Continued

Source	Date	Print/other dresses	Silk dresses	Petticoats	Court robes	Cloaks	Bonnets	Caps	Hoops	Stays
For Lady Trumbull, Reading	1714–1716		19s.6d	13s crepe					£1.8s	£2.5s
Tailors' Guild of Orkney, register of prices	1720	10s	12s to £2							£3.16s
For Mrs Kenyon, Lancs – these were probably second-hand purchases	1724	1s to 1s.6d	1s.6d	4d						
For the Duchess of Richmond	1725–7	18s.6d blue flowered linen robe and apron	£1.0s.6d grey watered tabby 18s.1d 'fine work'd robe' 12s scarlet mantua and petticoat							
For Mrs Frances Shackerley, Cheshire	1740	£1.0s.2d poplin gown (ready made)								

Source	Date	Print/other dresses	Silk dresses	Petticoats	Court robes	Cloaks	Bonnets	Caps	Hoops	Stays
Boughton a/c Warwicks.	1741	5s 'bedgown' 3s.5d white cotton gown	£1.2s.1d white negligee £1.8s.6d polonaise	9s-6d						£1.2s.6d
Bought by the Latham family, Lancs.	1755–1767	4s.10d 'gown for outside'	15s.6d silk camlet	4s.6d			5s.1d	1s.2d		4s.3d
Gough family of Perry Hall, Birmingham to various suppliers	1745–1768	2s poplin 2s to 3s cotton dresses 3s grey Irish 'stuff'	5s.4d pink tabby 2s.4d and 8s (girls' dresses) 12s green silk, 3s crepe, 6s black silk	£1-4s quilted calamanco 1s red flannel			2s	5s.6d	9s to £1.3s	
For Elizabeth Shackleton, Lancs.	1749–1777		2 gns black satin negligee £1.0s.2d mulberry coloured nightgown and petticoat				15s	10s		18s
For Ann Hancock, Oxford	1769–1782	2s to 3s.6d	4s. 6d to 6s.6d							

Continued

Source	Date	Print/other dresses	Silk dresses	Petticoats	Court robes	Cloaks	Bonnets	Caps	Hoops	Stays
For Mary Heath, Norfolk	1771–3	5s.7d				16s 'for Bath'				
For Arabella Calley, Swindon	1777–1787		2 gns (ready made)	11s.8d quilting 'white stuff' petticoat			17s.9d	5s.6d gauze	9s.6d	£1.12s.6d 2gns
For Mrs Williamson, London										
To M & E Bennall	1781–2	11s. to 16s.4d printed linen dresses	12s gauze 16s blue lustring £1.4s 'persian' £1.19s crepe trimmed							
To S Ramsey	1791		16s to £2.15s.5d		10 gns			2 gns blonde lace		
To Miss M Daniels	1792	13s.4d long sleeved muslin	7s. gauze polonaise							
For Mary Hardy, Norfolk	1782	£1.14s. chintz gown (ready made)								

Source	Date	Print/other dresses	Silk dresses	Petticoats	Court robes	Cloaks	Bonnets	Caps	Hoops	Stays
Mrs Charlton in London for Lady Winn in Yorks.	1783		4 gns 'chemise' which allegedly cost 9 gns in Paris							
For Penelope Mead, Reading	1784–95	3s		14s		£3-14s-6d		2 gns muslin turbans		
For Miss Woodhouse, York	1787	£1.8s 'Canterbury muslin' (ready made) 1gn 'common gown' (ready made) 4s.4d chintz	£1.4s.11d pink striped, ribbon trimmed	5s.11d white silk and ribbon						£1.10s
For Miss Whittaker E. Yorks.	1792						Black satin £2.8s	Worked muslin and ribbon £1.14s		

Continued

Source	Date	Print/other dresses	Silk dresses	Petticoats	Court robes	Cloaks	Bonnets	Caps	Hoops	Stays
For Lady Lifford, Warwicks.	1793–4	13s.6d cotton gown								£1.11s.6d brown Holland corsets
For J Freeth, charity school, Stratford-on-Avon	1809	1s apiece for girls' dresses								
For Lady Bruce, Bucks, from various suppliers including M Sowerby, court dressmaker	1800–1820	15s.6d black spotted gown 12s short checked ditto Ditto black calico 6s plain muslin	17s.6d blue silk 12s white satin 5gns white crepe	5s plain muslin	18gns + 8 gns for head dress				£3.16s	18s
For Eliza Stone, Leics.	1813	10s.4d to 11s.11d 'batella' dresses	9s 'leno' frock 17s red silk							

Source	Date	Print/other dresses	Silk dresses	Petticoats	Court robes	Cloaks	Bonnets	Caps	Hoops	Stays
For Lady Grey of Dunham Massey, Cheshire, to Elizabeth Sarel	1814				16 gns					
For Lady Louisa Grey (ditto) to Barber and Co, court dressmakers	1820				£20.4s.3d					

Costs

Janea Whittaker, who manages the millinery and mantua-making store at Colonial Williamsburg, estimates that a simple mantua can be made by one person in a ten-hour day.[23] Working on the basis that a typical small town mantua-maker would have employed a journeywoman and an apprentice (records show that this was a fairly usual arrangement in the early nineteenth century), and that the average price for a dress was 4s.0d, and assuming that the mistress and journeywoman spent ten woman-days a week between them actually sewing (allowing two days a week for liaising with customers and doing fittings), supported by the apprentice who threaded needles, ran errands, made tea and stitched some of the long seams and hems, the three women between them could have produced ten dresses a week, making £2.00. If the journeywoman was paid the 5s.0d a week Campbell estimated and the apprentice was unpaid, the mistress would have had £1.15s.0d a week out of which to pay her rent, heat and light her premises and feed herself and her staff. Even if they only produced five dresses a week she would have had a higher income than that on which many working men ran a home and supported a family. Of course, this is the most simplistic of calculations and ignores many factors – simple cotton dresses usually cost less than 4s.0d; repairs and alterations were an important part of the mantua-maker's work and were time-consuming but paid less than making; many women worked more than ten hours a day; there may have been a small profit of a few pence per garment on the linings, bones and sundries the mantua-maker supplied; an experienced apprentice might have earned a little pocket money per week – and so on – but inadequate as it is, this analysis does suggest that a woman with a reasonably full order book (though she probably kept no such document) could have managed quite comfortably. It is much more difficult to produce similar estimates for larger businesses, but it seems certain that they had more staff who were probably rather better-paid, and we know they charged their customers considerably more.

The cost of making up a garment was, however, the least part of the price of a dress in the eighteenth century. Fabrics were expensive. In 1741, Mary Woollett, a milliner in Rye (Sussex), died. She left cash, clothing and household goods valued at £165.13s.8d and a shop full of fabric; various types of Holland, dowlas, dimity, huckaback, alamode silks, sarsnet, printed cotton, painted linen, calico, Scotch cloth and various types of muslin; a whole range of ribbons, tapes, braids, trimmings, buttons and buckles, silks, fringes, laces, silver and gold thread; and made-up goods like gloves, stomachers, cloaks, caps and hoods; together with

(*For ready Money Only.*)

THOMAS LOMAS,
LINEN-DRAPER, MERCER, and HABERDASHER.

At his Shop in the Market-Place, LEICESTER.

1784

Sells the following Articles Wholesale and Retail, upon the most reasonable Terms.

IRISH linens and sheetings of every breadth and sort
The greatest variety of printed linens, cottons, callicoes, & chints
Muslins, plain, flower'd & strip'd
Ditto handkerchiefs and neckcloths
Long and clear lawns
Winchelsea and Scotch cambricks
Flaxen linen
Russia diaper and huckabacks
Hempen and flaxen Russias
Russia drabs and ravenducks
Diaper and damask table cloths of all sorts
Linen and cotton checks of all breadths
Furniture checks and trimmings for beds
Strip'd cottons and linens
Nankeens and brown silesias
Printed linen and cotton handkerchiefs all sorts
Check ditto
Silk and soosee ditto
English and Scotch stitching and colour'd thread
Scotch ounce and Lisle threads
Leather and jean gloves and mits
Green netting silk for purses
Flourishing, tambour and knotting cottons
Manchester incle, tapes and filletings
Holland and diaper ditto
Broad and narrow worsted quality
Galloons and ferrets
Cotton, ferret and silk laces
Pins and needles
Skeleton and skain wires

Shirt buttons
Sewing silk of all sorts
Barbers and netting ditto
Stay trimmings all sorts
Velvet collars
Gauzes and gauze handkerchiefs, a great variety
Tiffanies of all sorts
Modes, persians and sarsnets
Plain and figur'd silks and sattins
Dutch lace
Plain figur'd and love ribbons
Mode and sattin hats and cloaks
Leghorn, covering, and fine chip hats
Scarlet and beaver cardinals
Green oil cloth
Marseilles quilting
Counterpanes
Burton, Wildbore, and all kinds of tammies
Black shalloons and camblets
A great variety of lutstrings and fancy silks for gowns
Stuff and silk petticoats
Manchester gowns
Silky stuffs, all sorts
Furr trimmings and gimps
Black crapes and bombazeens
Black lutstrings and armozeens for gowns
A large assortment of black and white lace
Blond lace
Purle twist in plain colours & shades
Scotch gauze with or without the threads drawn
Plain and spotted lenau
Lenau handkerchiefs

With every other Article in the Linen Drapery, Mercery, and Haberdashery Business.

Plate 12 Flier for Thomas Lomas, draper of Leicester.

> **At WILLIAM WOOD's WAREHOUSE,**
> **No. 9, HANWAY-YARD,**
>
> SELLING remarkably Cheap, a large Quantity of coloured Persians, Sarsenets, Lutestrings, Ducapes, Tobines, and Sattin Stripes; black Lutestrings, Armozeens, Alamodes, Bombazeens, Stuff, &c. Irish Linens, Sheetings, Dimities, printed Callicoes, Muslins, Cambricks, and French Lawns, a large assortment of Hosiery, Haberdashery, Woollen Drapery, and Mens' Mercery; all sorts of Child-bed Linen, ready-made Shifts and Shirts, of all sizes and qua'ities, Household Linen, Ladies and Gentlemens Powdering Gowns, Ladies Fancy Dresses and Caps, very good India Muslins, Morning Caps with double borders, 33s. per doz. or 3s. each; amongst the above articles is several thousand pieces of Fancy Ribbons, remarkably good, selling at very little more than half price.
>
> N. B. If agreeable to the Ladies, Goods bought at the above Warehouse made in the most fashionable manner, at reduced prices, compleat Mantua-makers and Milliners kept for that purpose.
>
> *** WOOD's Warehouse is in the middle of Hanway-Yard.

11. *The Times,* 20 September 1780.

parcels of Spanish and Scotch snuff, fans, pincushions, bird cages, snuff boxes and twenty-six looking glasses – total value, including debts owing, £894.18s.6d.[24] James Longridge, draper and milliner of Eye in Norfolk, died in 1753 and his inventory is equally informative though he was working for a poorer clientele. He sold dowlas at 7d and 8d a yard, printed cotton at 1s.8d, handkerchiefs at 4d to 10d, stays at £1.5s.0d, and, like Ms Woollett, he also sold snuff. His shop goods were valued at £282.5s.4½d.[25] Drapers' advertisements list a bewildering array of fabrics with names that mean nothing to us today. [Plate 12]

What is interesting about William Wood's advertisement is that, though he was a wholesaler, he was also happy to sell to private individuals and had found it worthwhile to employ his own milliners and mantua-makers to service them.

Bills show that customers in different places paid different rates for fabrics that sound the same, but there is no way of knowing whether that is accounted for by location, supplier or quality. And some buyers were thrifty. Mary Hardy in Norfolk was a case in point – she gleefully recorded bargains she had bought from auctions or businesses that were closing down. For example, in October

Table 3 Table of eighteenth-century fabric prices per yard.

Fabric type	1690–1700	1700–20	1720–40	1740–60	1760–80	1780–1800	1800–20
Muslins							
muslin	4s.6d		6s.10s		12s.8d		1s.6d
book muslin					13s		
'worked' muslin						18s	
Silks							
plain or figured silk	6s.3d			5s.9d to 7s.6d	3s.9d to 5s.6d		4s.6d to 7s
lustring		6s	5s.11d	5s.6d	6s.-3d to 8s.6d		3s.9d
tabby		5s.2d	11s		4s.6d to 12s	11s.3d	
'changeable shagreen'	4s.6d						
armozine					8s	6s.3d	
damask			10s.6d	11s			
satin						2s.6d to 7s	
sarsnet						5s.6d	4s to 7s.6d
Cottons and linens							
cotton				1s.2d	2s.4½d to 3s.6d	1s.10d	10d to 1s
printed cotton				1s.8d to 2s.6d	2s.8d to 5s.6d		

Continued

Fabric type	1690–1700	1700–20	1720–40	1740–60	1760–80	1780–1800	1800–20
calico					4d	2s.6d to 5s.9d	1s to 1s.6d
cambric			5s to 14s.6d		7s		
poplin			2s.6d				
dimity					3s.6d		
linen or 'holland'		1s.10d	2s.4d to 3s		1s.10d to 11s.6d	1s.6d	
chambray						5s.6d	
fustian		2s.9d to 5s.6d					
Laces and ribbons							
Mechlin lace					9s		
blonde lace					2s.8d		6s.6d
lace						£2.8s	

Fabric type	1690–1700	1700–20	1720–40	1740–60	1760–80	1780–1800	1800–20
ribbon			2d to 1s			6d to 1s	
Woollens							
broad cloth				9s.4d			
shalloon	2s to 2s.4d			2s			
calamanco		2s.8d			2s.8d		
flannel					1s.8d		1s.1d
kersey				4s.6d			
camlet				1s.2½d			
serge					5s.6d		
Mourning							
bombazine							4s.3d
crepe		2s					3s.9d

Continued

Fabric type	1690–1700	1700–20	1720–40	1740–60	1760–80	1780–1800	1800–20
Linings and interlinings							
buckram		1s			1s		
dowlas				7d to 8d			

Glossary

Armozine – a heavy, plain silk, often used for clerical robes.
Bombazine – a heavy mix of twilled silk and worsted, usually black. It is a matt fabric, hence its use for mourning wear.
Calamanco – a glossy woollen fabric with a check or brocade weave so the pattern shows on one side only.
Calico – a plain weave, unbleached, unfinished cotton.
Cambric – a fine plain linen, originally made in the area around Cambrai in France.
Camlet or camblet – originally a mix of silk and camel hair, later a mix of silk and wool or silk and cotton.
Chambray – a solid, plain weave cotton, about the same weight as denim.
'Changeable shagreen' – a shot silk, sometimes called 'watered silk' or 'moiré'.
Dimity – a light weight sheer cotton, usually woven with a pattern of checks or stripes.
Dowlas – a coarse linen used as a lining fabric.
Fustian – a strong, heavy cotton fabric with a slight nap.
Holland – fine linen.
Kersey or kerseymere – a fine wool with a fancy twill weave.
Lustring – a thin, glossy silk, a bit like taffeta.
Muslin – a light weight, open weave cotton.
Sarsnet – a fine, soft twill, usually of silk.
Shalloon – a light weight, twilled, worsted woollen fabric often used for linings.
Tabby – a simple, over-one-under-one weave. The name is usually applied to plain silks but any fibre can be tabby woven.

1779: 'I and Mr Hardy at Boornes Auction, bout some Ribbin and 6 yds of purple and White Linnen at 11s-6d and 8 pairs stockings'. She went back two days later and bought some printed cotton at 2s.4½d a yard. In June 1794 she and her husband bought tickets for a raffle at Whissonsett – she won a square of muslin; her husband won a 'piece for a Gown'. In March 1798 she bought some muslin 'off a travelling woman at Holt'; on 16 January 1799 she 'went in the evening to an Auction at the Kings Head of Drapery goods by Mr Levi, the Jew' and on 17 April 1804 she went to 'Miss Leake's sale'.[26]

Table 3 gives some idea of fabric prices per yard, taken from various bills and account books, and it is important to remember that fabrics came in quite narrow widths – usually about twenty-one inches. Fancy silks could be as narrow as thirteen inches, and even cottons were often less than thirty-six inches wide, so the yardages required for a gown were considerable – between ten and twenty-two yards, depending on the width of the fabric and the style of the garment.

Theft[27]

Garments were therefore valuable and the theft of clothes and fabrics was a serious problem. The Old Bailey and provincial Quarter Sessions records are full of histories of people who stole clothes, and servants stealing from their mistresses appear often, probably because wealthy women with large wardrobes could be extremely careless about what they owned. For example, when Mary Warndell came before the courts in September 1777 charged with stealing twenty yards of silk, 'value 50s, a sattin sack, value £2, a sattin petticoat, value 20s, a silk petticoat, value 20s, a cotton sack and apron, value 20s and a crape petticoat, value 5s', her mistress, Elizabeth Edwards, acknowledged that she had missed the items, but as they moved frequently between their country and town houses, Warndell always claimed the items were in the other house when she asked for them. Mary Warndell's defence was simply that 'if I had not acknowledged [the theft] my mistress would not have known anything of it'. She was sentenced to transportation.

Mantua-makers were especially vulnerable to theft. They might be robbed by their own staff – for example, in August 1730, Anne Barnes (alias le Grange) who worked for Jane Aliff in Westminster was transported for stealing a 'Suit of Head-Clothes, value 35s' earlier that month along with one of Jane's husband's shirts. If they kept a shop, dressmakers were even more at risk of being burgled. Shop windows were often unglazed and goods displayed there were particularly easy to steal, especially as shops stayed open late. At about nine in the evening on 18 August 1743, for example, Jacob Chapman helped himself to a part-finished cotton gown, value 12s.0d, from Susannah Buck's shop-window in London's Gray's Inn Lane. Susannah was a mantua-maker and haberdasher and the dress was for a customer.

Carrying goods through the streets to deliver them to clients was also hazardous. Edward Paild was indicted for 'feloniously assaulting Anne Wright, spinster, on the king's highway, on the 6th day of May, 1787 and putting her in corporal fear and danger of her life'. Anne was apprenticed to a mantua-maker called Elizabeth Probyn in Bishopsgate, and late that Saturday evening she was on her way to deliver a bundle of four cotton gowns to Mrs Robinson in Phils Buildings on Houndsditch when she was attacked and robbed. Phils Buildings was part of the notorious Spitalfields rag market in London, so Mrs Probyn was probably a 'translator' rather than a proper mantua-maker – someone who mended and renovated second-hand clothes – so the stolen items were probably of no great value. Nonetheless, Edward Paild was sentenced to hang.

Such thefts must have had a serious impact on their victims. As well as being shocked and possibly injured, the mantua-maker would lose any profit she could have made on the stolen garments, and if her customer was less than sympathetic she might also find she was expected to reimburse the cost of the fabric they had supplied. For women working to a small profit margin, and unable to insure themselves against any risks other than fire, such a theft could be disastrous.

Sometimes the court cases illuminate the humble circumstances in which some mantua-makers lived. Many who reported thefts were living in one or two rooms, and goods awaiting delivery to customers were hanging on doors or lying in bundles in the women's living quarters. In May 1765, for example, Sarah Shelfe brought a case against Victoire Donvilla, a Frenchwoman who had taken lodgings with her in Castle Street, Leicester Fields. Victoire had 'lain in the parlour' where there was a bundle of five linen gowns waiting to be delivered to a Mrs Rickaby. After her first night with the Shelfes, Victoire disappeared – taking the gowns with her. On finding them missing, Mrs Shelfe and her husband toured the local pawnbrokers and discovered the gowns with George Brown in Long Acre – he had given £1.11s.0d for them. Victoire claimed it was all a misunderstanding and called a fellow countrywoman, Frances Bolioe, a milliner in Dean-street, and her husband, John L'Esperance, to give her a character reference. It did her no good – she was sentenced to transportation.

But being robbed was not the only hazard dressmakers faced – there was also the risk of being seen as the thief's accomplice. Stolen fabric could often be disguised by being remade. In September 1731, for example, Margaret Thomas was indicted for stealing a large piece of crimson damask worth 39s.0d from an upholsterer. She took ten yards of it to a mantua-maker to be made into a gown and pawned the rest. Numerous court cases record mantua-makers being questioned about whether or not they had made a particular garment. It paid to be careful. Katherine Williams, a mantua-maker, gave evidence in January 1731. She had been given a letter suggesting she go to 'a certain place to fetch some materials for apparel that had to be made in haste ... but she, not knowing the person, did not go'.

The same applied to pawnbrokers. The easiest and quickest way to dispose of stolen goods was by pawning them, even though the pawnbroker seldom paid anything like their full value. The records of George Fettes, a pawnbroker who worked out of Lady Peckitt's Yard in York, survive in York Archives and give some idea of how little a thief could expect to get. Mr Fettes dealt almost exclusively with clothing and the odd watch or silver spoon. He gave out between £1.00 and £10.00 a day in small amounts ranging from a few pence to a little over a pound. On one fairly busy day – Monday 13 October 1777 – he expended £9.9s.0d on forty-two separate transactions, in sums ranging from 6d to James Atkinson of Bishophill for 'an old cravat' to £1.5s.0d to James Rother of Skeldergate for a parcel containing a coat, waistcoat, a 'fine shirt' and some hats.[28] Many of Mr Fettes' customers were regulars, but no doubt he, too, had to be careful when dealing with customers he didn't know.

Numbers

Mantua-makers had a limited number of customers. Some seem only to have worked part-time or as an adjunct to another business, for example:

> BENJ. MONTAGUE, Perfumer and Stationer, opposite the Pump-Room, Bath, informs his friends and the public, that he has taken the Stock of Mr. Lloyd, Tobacconist, late of Stall-street, and intends selling every article in the Snuff and Tobacco business. He respectfully sollicits the favours of his friends, with those of Mr. Lloyd's, in the above business, as they may depend on the strictest attention.
> All sorts of Perfumery and Stationary as usual.
> Mantuas, Sacques, Robes, &c. made in the neatest and most fashionable manner, and on reasonable terms, by CLARISSA MONTAGUE.——☞ HABERDASHERY in general.

12. *The Bath Chronicle*, 7 December 1780.

Clarissa was probably Benjamin's wife, daughter or sister, and her business was apparently a side-line to his perfumery, tobacco and stationery shop.

Some women did spend huge sums on dress – for example, Mrs Williamson (wife of General Adam Williamson who became Governor of Jamaica in 1790) had an active social life and regularly appeared at court. Between 1781 and 1792 she had at least twenty gowns made, many by the Bennall sisters in London.[29]

On the other hand, there were many women who bought very few garments. Nany Latham was the wife of a Lancashire smallholder and their family income averaged around £30.00 a year. Nany had just three new gowns in the forty-two years covered by the account book her husband kept (1724–67), and none at all between 1723, when she married, and 1742, by which time she had given birth to eight children. The family bought fabric from time to time and Nany may have used some of this to make shifts and petticoats for herself as well as clothes for her children, but for the most part she seems to have continued to wear – and wear out – her pre-marriage clothes. Regular small payments for 'taylors work' suggest the local tailor was charged with keeping these in repair, and in 1735 Nany acquired a new checked Holland (linen) apron (for three shillings), perhaps to disguise her increasingly shabby petticoats. In 1742, when all her children were earning, Nany finally had a new gown – made from nine-and-a-half yards of worsted 'camblet' (a silk and wool fabric) at 1s.2½d a yard. A further 1s.3½d was spent on thread and trimmings but there is no sum allowed for making up so Nany probably made the gown herself. She had two more new gowns in 1755 – a black and blue one 'for outside' at 4s.10d and a 'silk camlet' one for 15s.6d which both seem to have been bought ready-made – so at no point in her married life did Nany patronize a mantua-maker. Indeed, the only 'luxury' item she seems to have had in the whole of that time was a silk handkerchief, bought for 3s.8d in 1752.[30]

The Lathams were poor but they were respectable – they ate well, bought 'physik' when they were ill, sent their children to school and ensured they were adequately shod – Richard Latham bought 'clog nails' in batches of a thousand so presumably he repaired the family's everyday footwear himself.

Lower down the social scale there were women who had little more than the clothes they stood up in. Francis Place described the dress of townswomen, the 'wives and daughters of journeymen, tradesmen and shopkeepers' – who

> ... either wore leather stays or what were called full-boned stays ... They were never washed, altho' worn day by day for years ... [*they had*] petticoats of

camblet lined with dyed linen, stuffed with wool or horsehair and quilted, these also were worn day by day until they were rotten.[31]

The meagre wardrobes of many countrywomen are shown in the 'pauper inventories' created by Poor Law officials – lists of the belongings of individuals who were on long-term poor relief. When the person died the goods listed, such as they were, would be taken by the parish and sold or distributed to other paupers in a feeble attempt to defray the overall cost of poor relief. If the overseers decided a pauper household had goods they did not actually need, those items were sold before their owner died. It was a deeply unpopular system but in parts of Essex it continued into the nineteenth century. In the 1690s in Braintree, for example, Widow Doogood was allowed to keep a spare shift, two old pairs of shoes, a riding hood and a grey gown, but the overseers sold her other gown and petticoat, together with a cupboard, for 12s.0d towards her keep.[32] In Wakes Colne in the 1740s Widow Griggs had just a shift and a flannel petticoat other than the clothes she stood up in,[33] while in Finchingfield in 1734 Henry Cawell's wife's spare clothing consisted of three shifts, two gowns, two petticoats, a bonnet and a cloak.[34]

As late as 1797 Sir Frederick Eden in his *State of the Poor* claimed that labourers' wives in the midlands and the south 'seldom make up any article of dress, except making and mending cloaths for their children. In the North, on the contrary, almost every article of dress ... is manufactured at home.' Like many of Eden's statement it is a generalization. Regardless of where they lived, poor women could not afford to patronize mantua-makers, nor could they afford much fabric to make up into garments for themselves.

However, there were also well-to-do women who spent very little on clothes. We have already encountered Mrs Herrick in Leicestershire whose inappropriate mourning clothes so incensed her married daughter. She was far from unique. Over in Norfolk in the early 1800s, for example, Augusta Lady Walsingham, second wife of the second Lord Walsingham, kept accounts of her personal expenditure. She was forty-one in 1800, wealthy and well-connected, and she seems to have had a fairly active social life – playing (and losing) at cards, going to the theatre and travelling around on visits. But she records scarcely any expenditure on clothes other than on thick stockings and 'everlasting' shoes – which clearly did not live up to their name as she replaced them every few months. Lady Augusta's passion was buying and breeding caged birds – canaries (5s.6d for a hen and 6s.0d for a cock) and java sparrows (a guinea a pair) – and she spent her money acquiring bird cages (19s.0d apiece) and their accoutrements and having cages repaired.³⁵ She seems to have been the stereotypical eccentric aristocrat, stomping round her estate in the eighteenth-century equivalent of battered tweeds and green wellies.

If their accounts are to be believed, older gentlewomen like Arabella Calley in Wiltshire (see Chapter 10) and Elizabeth Shackleton, a Lancashire gentlewoman, actually spent more money on accessories like fichus, sleeve ruffles, caps and aprons – bought from the milliner rather than from the mantua-maker – than they did on dresses; in 1769 Elizabeth Shackleton owned *fifty* caps of various types. Her son married that year so she had to leave her old home, Alkincoats (near Colne), and she made an inventory of her clothes. She was forty-three. As well as the caps she had fifteen shifts, five under petticoats, five quilted petticoats, three bedgowns, ten gowns of various types and ages, thirteen neck handkerchiefs or fichus, several sets of sleeves and ruffles, a 'sute of linnen' that she had worked herself consisting of an apron, double ruffles and fichu all of the same pattern and another of 'best new Minonet Linnen', and at least fourteen aprons of various fabrics.³⁶

Many well-to-do women extended the life of their garments by having them dyed, altered or remade, sometimes several times over, priding themselves on being thrifty, and most women also did some of their own sewing. Carolyn Dowdell has analysed how Gertrude Savile altered and reused a green damask dress with gold trimming, the fabric for which cost her an exorbitant £24.00 in 1745. It was remade and retrimmed multiple times in a decade and some of the leftover fabric was even made into a pair of shoes.³⁷ Mrs Papandiek, a London courtier and Keeper of the Queen's Wardrobe from 1794, recorded acquiring a puce satin dress as a teenager in 1782 and having it 'done up' at least four times as fashions changed until in 1791 she recorded that it was 'at its last gasp'. At that date, as she explained in her journal (written in the 1830s):

> A silk gown would go on for years, a little furbished up with new trimmings – and a young woman was rather complimented than otherwise when she exhibited care of her possessions, and might, with no discredit to herself, appear time after time in the same attire.³⁸

Even Anne Lister of Shibden Hall in West Yorkshire, known locally as 'Gentleman Jack', a lesbian who prided herself on her masculine good sense, was not above doing some of her own mending. For example, on 4 May 1820 she recorded 'Sewing leather on to my clean stays' and complained that she was late starting on a letter to her beloved 'M' 'having been obliged to finish mending my bombazine petticoat'.³⁹

Throughout the century tailors continued to make clothes for women [Plate 13]. The Gough family of Perry Hall in Birmingham were hoarders and kept all the bills they received, neatly folded and tied up in brown paper bundles. In amongst the bills for shoeing horses, mending window frames, weeding the garden, buying nails and paying for the children's schooling are a number of bills for clothing for Mrs Gough and her two stepdaughters, Mary and Anne. They patronized both men and women indiscriminately (Mr Goodall, Ann Lambert, Goolden, Lawton and Co, Samuel Harper, H. Harding, William Godwin, Sarah James, Miss Jefferies, Robert Blayney and A. Harwood) between 1745 and 1770 for gowns and stays, negligées and petticoats, bonnets, caps and aprons and mourning clothes when the girls' brother was killed in a fall from his horse in 1769.[40]

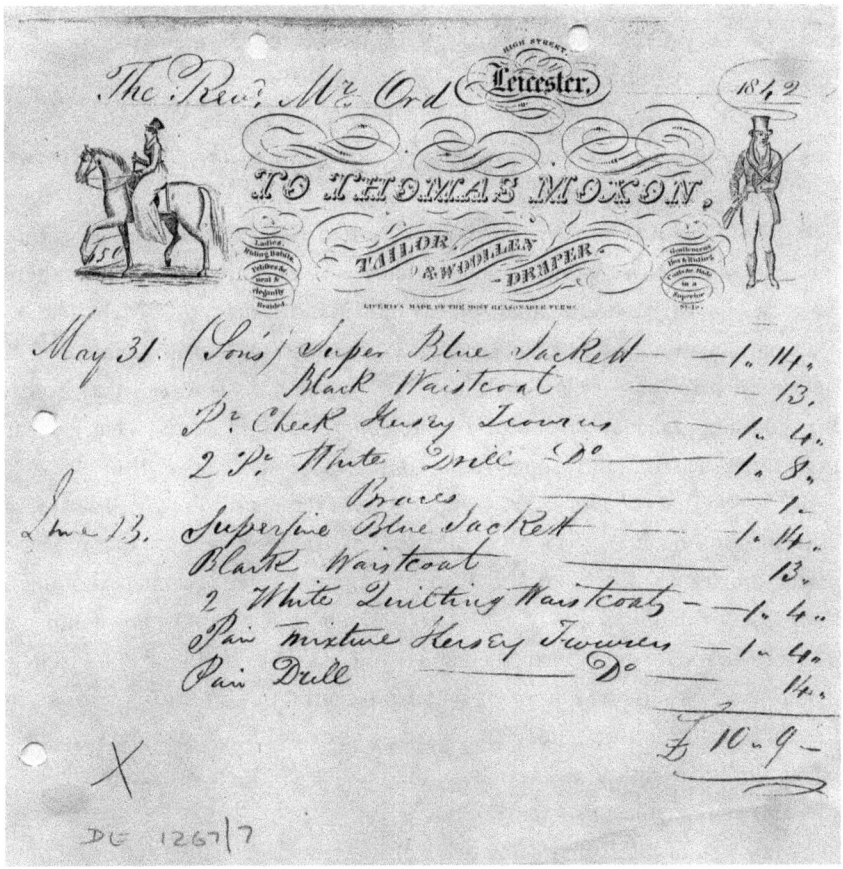

Plate 13 Thomas Moxon had premises on Leicester High Street between the late 1820s and the early 1860s. He made tailored garments for both men and women.

All of these factors meant that mantua-makers had a relatively limited client base on which to draw, particularly in the provinces, and it is hard to say just how many of them there were in the UK by 1800. One guide is the *Universal British Directory* of 1791 to 1795, but despite the claim in its prospectus to be 'an ample guide' for 'persons or families unconnected with business whose pursuit is pleasure in travelling', it is unlikely that it would have been a great deal of use if any of those travelling persons had needed a dress repairing or a new one making. In many places where we have concrete evidence that ladies patronized mantua-makers – Colne in Lancashire, Swindon in Wiltshire, Holt in Norfolk, even York and Birmingham – none are listed, despite the *Directory's* claim to record 'every extensive line of business or manufacture'.

Most bizarrely of all, *no* mantua-makers are listed in London, though we know many women went to London specifically to have their dresses made, and insurance records alone catalogue several hundred mantua-makers in the capital. Furthermore, we know nothing of the situation in Scotland and Ireland for 'Universal British' actually meant 'England and Wales'. There was apparently just one mantua-maker in Cardiff in the 1790s, with two milliner-cum-haberdashers. In Oxford in 1791 only Mary Popple described herself as a mantua-maker and there were two milliners, but in Richmond in Surrey there were five mantua-makers, while in Manchester there were twenty-three. Some small places had mantua-makers – Mansfield in Nottinghamshire had four, Evesham in Worcestershire had two, Hambledon in Hampshire had one – while large population centres like Leeds, Birmingham and Newcastle-upon-Tyne apparently had none. What is clear is that everywhere, tailors outnumbered mantua-makers many times over.

It may be that the *Directory's* compilers were reluctant to recognize women in business, though they do list women in other trades. It may be that in some places the term 'mantua-maker' was still unfamiliar and women described themselves as milliners; it may be that women who were already making a perfectly adequate living from clients they knew did not bother to submit their details; whatever the reasons, it is obvious we cannot rely on the information in the *Directory*. However, inadequate as it is, it is one of the few sources we have and it does give us some clues about the relative numbers of tradespeople in various places. Table 4 lists some of them.

A few places published directories of their own prior to 1800 and some of these tend to be rather more informative. The Norwich directory for

Table 4 Mantua-makers in the *Universal British Directory* 1791–5.

	Mantua-makers	Milliners	Stay-makers	Tailors
Bath	6	15	2	24
Bristol	2	10	7	40
Birmingham	0	2	7	28
Cardiff	1	4	1	5
Carlisle	1	5	2	7
Chester	11	11	8	26
Durham	3	6	7	16
Derby	2	3	4	9
Exeter	4	16	8	28
Hull	2	4	3	26
Lincoln	2	5	5	23
Liverpool	2	2	18	78
Manchester	23	30	14	105
Nottingham	0	6	5	18
Norwich	0	3	6	20
Oxford	1	2	2	33
Richmond	5	1	5	9
Southampton	3	2	1	14
Warwick	2	4	3	17
Worcester	1	4	1	16
Winchester	2	3	0	150
York	0	5	1	11

1783, for example, lists Elizabeth Bell, Mrs Booth, Tabitha Carver, Ann Love and E. Willem as mantua-makers.[41] In Winchester in 1784 Mrs Lavender and Ann Wayble both described themselves as mantua-makers, as did Elizabeth Rackett in Basingstoke, Elizabeth Towers in Gosport and six ladies in Southampton. There were ten mantua-makers in Manchester in 1788; four in Bristol in 1793; and twenty-three in Liverpool in 1796, despite the *Universal Directory* only listing two.[42] Leeds apparently still only had one mantua-maker in 1798, Mrs Nichols, though there were numerous milliners who may also have made dresses. This may in part explain the following advertisement:

> **William Albrecht, at London,**
> STAY, MANTUA, and HABIT - MAKER,
> BEGS Leave to acquaint the Ladies at Leeds and its Environs, That he has removed from his House in Villier-ſtreet, to No. 20, Henrietta-Street, Covent-Garden,
>
> Takes likewiſe the Opportunity of informing the Ladies, That he intends being in Yorkſhire the latter End of May, or Beginning of June.——Ladies who wiſh to be waited on, are requeſted to favour him with a few Lines directed for him at Mr Owen's, Boar-Lane, Leeds, may depend upon having their Orders executed with that uſual Taſte and Punctuality.

13. *The Leeds Intelligencer*, 23 April 1782.

William Albrecht advertised his services to the ladies of Leeds and Hull between 1780 and 1785; however, it is probable that they were actually a good deal better provided with women to make their clothes than the directories would suggest. In fact, where detailed evidence survives, we find that even very small places had local women who made mantuas. In rural Westmorland, for example, the Constables' Census of 1787 shows us that there were mantua-makers in several villages and townships – Dufton, Stainmore, Brampton, Sandford, Sockbridge and Askham, where Elizabeth Swainson made mantuas and employed Barb Winder as an apprentice. However, there were no mantua-makers in the county's biggest town, Kendal, perhaps because the tailors there made it difficult for women to trade.[43] Similarly, in Bedfordshire there were mantua-makers in the villages of Cople, Ickwell, Eaton Socon, Biddenham and Cardington.[44]

Conclusion

Clearly, across the country there were more women making mantuas than the directories show. All we can really conclude is that in the eighteenth century few women who wished to dress fashionably were unable to find someone to make their clothes, and those clothes, and the fabrics from which they were made, were expensive to acquire and became valuable assets that could be traded. We know that as the century progressed more and more women set up in business, and while there is still some debate about whether or not the numbers of women in business declined in the nineteenth century, there is no doubt at all that there was a huge increase in the number of women in what we must now call the dressmaking trade, as we shall see in the next chapters.

4

'Undeviating endeavours to please'

The nineteenth century saw the development of a thriving bourgeoisie. This class was larger than the old aristocracy and at least as important. It provided employers and senior employees, created standards of morality and behaviour and defined rules of etiquette. It was Christian and bigoted, charitable and thrifty, complacent and curious, well-read and ignorant. What is most important here, however, is that its womenfolk were much concerned with dress, outward appearances and 'correct' behaviour. Etiquette required them to have more clothes than ever before and caused a whole industry to spring up to cater for just one ritual – that of mourning the dead. There was an ever-growing market for dressmakers' services.

Fashion changed decade by decade and, in the second half of the century, almost year by year. In the 1800s women wore flowing dresses in soft fabrics like cotton and muslin, in faint imitation of what they believed had been worn by the wives and daughters of Athenian citizens. In the 1820s and '30s skirts became fuller and dresses had huge sleeves and low necklines, a romantic interpretation of sixteenth- and seventeenth-century dress inspired in part by the novels of Walter Scott. By the 1840s, bodices and sleeves were tighter and more demure, but skirts, for the next two decades, became fuller and fuller, spreading out over increasing layers of voluminous cotton underwear and crinolines of various shapes. In response to the arrival of the sewing machine in the 1850s, garments became more and more elaborately trimmed, especially about the skirt; in the 1870s and '80s first the crinolette and then the bustle replaced the crinoline. Shapes veered from full to voluminously draped to flared to narrow and columnar. A woman who started out as an apprentice dressmaker in the 1820s and carried on working into her sixties would have seen at least five major fashion changes which would have necessitated learning new ways of cutting out patterns. It is not the purpose of this book to catalogue those changes in detail, but the fashion plates on the following pages will give some idea of them. [Plates 14 A–L] [Colour Plates VI & VII] At its best, dressmaking was a highly skilled craft.

A. 1800–5 B. 1809 C. 1822

D. 1836 E. 1843 F. 1856

G. 1860 H. 1874 I. 1886

J. 1895   K. 1900   L. 1913

Plate 14 A–L Fashion plates showing the development of fashion in the nineteenth century.

While information about the dressmaking trade is hard to come by for the eighteenth century, much more survives for the nineteenth century – mostly from government reports, social reformers and the memoirs of women who trained as dressmakers.

The Children's Employment Commission[1]

Probably the most useful account of the trade comes in the two reports of the Royal Commission on the Employment of Children and Young Persons in Trade and Manufacturing (generally known as the Children's Employment Commissions), the first of which appeared in 1843. Nineteenth-century society was increasingly concerned about women's and children's working conditions. An Act of 1833 instituted factory inspection and limited working hours for women and children, and in 1847 the 'Ten Hours' bill further limited the working day for women and children under sixteen. In 1840 came the first attempt to protect sweeps' climbing boys, and in 1842 legislation banned women from working underground. These reforms were inspired by humanitarian motives, but there were other imperatives, and chief amongst them was concern about women in the workplace. Respectable Victorian men had very ambivalent views about women, and their wives and daughters led restricted, over-protected lives. Many believed working women were in moral danger from contact with men in their places of work – but women of the lower classes, who had always worked, did not always appreciate their well-meaning attempts at protection.

The Children's Employment Commission came out of this masculine mindset, and as it was already known that dressmakers often worked incredibly long hours – a letter to *The Times* on 26 June 1828 had described London milliners working eighteen to twenty hours a day and had sparked correspondence on the subject – apprentices in the dressmaking and millinery trades were among the first categories of workers to be assessed. The commissioners were middle-class male authority figures – not the sort of people with whom young working women would feel at ease, and by modern standards their methods of enquiry were seriously flawed. They had an agenda, which was to discover abuses within the trade, and though their report does include the caveat 'happily there are numerous exceptions' they did not record them, so the picture they present is unrelievedly bleak. Nicola Phillips has rightly pointed out that the report and subsequent discourse demonized mistresses, no doubt unjustly in some cases, but the sheer volume of evidence must lead us to conclude that a great many young milliners and dressmakers were indeed cruelly exploited.

Nowhere do we learn what proportion of firms the commissioners were able to visit in the towns they studied, nor do we know how they selected their interviewees or the places they chose to visit. We do not know whether they published all the interviews they were given or whether they made a selection, nor do we know whether the published interviews are a complete record of their respondents' statements. We can only deduce what questions were asked and clearly not all interviewees were questioned in the same way. Different commissioners dealt with different towns and their methods were not uniform – some reported names, some only gave initials, some used reported speech, some wrote synopses. Even when they tried to be unbiased their findings were woolly. When reporting the views of Bristol employers who supported the idea of legislation to limit hours of work, for example, they were careful to note that there were other dressmakers in the town who thought such legislation would be 'inexpedient and impracticable' but they did not name them or give the numbers for and against. Nonetheless, by allowing their informants to speak for themselves they produced a compelling and shocking record.

Typical was Miss Bryan of Birmingham (interviewee 604), who claimed considerable experience of the trade in several places:

> In Birmingham the regular hours of work are from 8AM to 8PM, but in the busy season they begin earlier, or work later, or both, generally commencing at 6am and working till 10 or 11 pm sometimes they go on later – last night they left off at 2 in the morning. Was formerly at Sheffield as an assistant, where the hours were much longer. The Young Person whose place she took had left for

her health, but she died on the day month on which she left; her health had been previously impaired by working at Leamington. During the whole time she never left off earlier than 12 … very regularly they worked until 2 in the morning, and three times all night. The two principals used frequently to work on a Sunday; she herself would never do this … In some watering places during the season [she] believes the young people often have not more than three hours sleep …

Conditions varied from place to place, but everywhere workers complained of the long hours and 'continuous sitting'. Nonetheless, conditions in the provinces were better than in London, as Bath interviewees 249 and 250 pointed out. Interviewee 250 had worked through the night three times a week in London, but considered that 'in the country the hours have always been much more moderate'. Interviewee 251 recalled that dressmakers had worked shorter hours in Cork where she had been apprenticed, and 263 had worked shorter hours as an apprentice 'in the country'; 257 had worked as a dressmaker's assistant for twenty-six years and believed that hours of work had become 'very much shorter' in her lifetime, implying that conditions at the beginning of the century must have been truly appalling. Interviewee 265, at Clifton, near Bristol, agreed with her, though, as an employer, she said she liked her young ladies to start work at 4.00 am in summer and work until 8.00 or 9.00 pm at night. She must have thought that a sixteen-hour day that finished before midnight sounded better than one that finished at 2.00 am!

Things were better in Norwich – only interviewee 273 admitted to having occasionally worked as late as midnight on Saturdays. But in Nottingham, Mary Scott (interviewee 602) reported how, as an apprentice in the town, she had often worked until 2.00 and 3.00 am; 'her health was so seriously injured that for several years it was not restored'. Nonetheless, Ms Scott had gone on to set up her own business. We do not know how she treated her staff, but Ann Abbott in Leicester (interviewee 608) normally worked her staff from 8.00 am to 8.00 or 9.00 pm, only occasionally keeping them until 11.00 pm:

> This excess very rarely occurs, because when any particular order requires it she obtains extra assistance … [She] is convinced, from a long acquaintance with the business, that these long hours are not at all beneficial to the principals, they lead to negligence and waste.

Clearly some dressmakers worked under dreadful conditions. The commissioners did their best to uncover these but they were totally dependent on the co-operation of employers. It was impossible for them to check the accuracy of everything they were told and few apprentices had the courage to criticize their employers – for example, did the Bristol fourteen-year-old (interviewee 241) really 'like the work very much', especially as she was going to have to continue with it, unpaid, for the next seven years? Forewomen and assistants were more forthcoming in their criticisms, though some of them disguised their evidence as being the experience of 'friends' elsewhere. Even so, Commissioner Grainger commented, 'I repeatedly noticed a great disinclination on the part of the young persons to state what they knew, and this owing to a feeling of intimidation which was very prevalent.' What is interesting, however, is that some of the older women interviewed must have been working in the 1820s and '30s and give us an insight into the trade as it was then.

The immediate result of the Commissioners' report was the formation, in March 1843, of the Association for the Aid and Benefit of Dressmakers and Milliners. The Association was the brainchild of a group of philanthropic ladies, and it existed as a registry for employers and employees. It offered certain safeguards in that employers were vetted before being placed on the Association's register, so employees were assured that the firms they were sent to would conform to minimum standards. The Association was also committed to the reform of conditions within the trade and offered financial and medical help in time of need. It was a worthy initiative. The Association was most active in London and did have some effect on conditions, though it was never wealthy enough to fulfil all its aims. It was joined by a number of equally impotent but well-meaning organizations,[2] but for most dressmakers, conditions changed little, if at all.

In 1864 the Children's Employment Commissioners again reported on the dressmaking trade. Mr Pitter of the Early Closing Association was cautiously optimistic: 'It is generally admitted that the efforts made some years ago succeeded in abolishing Sunday work, excepting so far as it might be voluntarily undertaken in a few instances by other than English females.' But this was the only improvement. London houses still regularly worked sixteen- to eighteen-hour days in the season and most provincial firms worked twelve-hour days. Some older dressmakers resented the change. Mrs Gregory of Cambray Villas in Cheltenham (interviewee 89), who had been in the trade for forty years, grumbled that when she was young 'in emergency' she had gone a week without going to bed, but 'now the girls complain if they have to work through one night. I think they are either much less strong than they used to be or much more idle'! Miss Holmes in Cherry Street in Birmingham (interviewee 63) assured the commissioners that it was a mistake to think that workers needed any protection from employers: 'No-one has any idea of the extent to which employers are dependent upon the caprices and intrigues of their assistants.' Dissatisfied staff, she said, could leave at a month's notice (though presumably without references) and she herself blamed the 'Milliners' Institute' in London for setting assistants against their mistresses. With employers holding attitudes like these it is not surprising that conditions in the trade had improved so very slowly.

Miss Reeves of Russell Terrace in Leamington (interviewee 102) believed that working hours were shorter in 1864 than they had been fifteen years before, but thought they were still bad and cited the case of a 'friend' in Birmingham who had worked until 4.00 or 5.00 am every night for three weeks in the run up to Christmas, and had finished at 5 am on Christmas morning. In Exeter, Mrs Treadwin's forewoman (interviewee 130), who as an apprentice in Ipswich, had regularly worked until 1 and 2 am, reported grimly that 'I call nothing late until after midnight'. But increasingly, these were the exceptions. At Edgar Buildings in the still-fashionable city of Bath, the owner's sister (interviewee 110) recalled how for several days before a fancy dress ball held the previous Easter Monday the staff had all worked sixteen-hour shifts 'which she was sure they would never forget'. She considered anything over twelve hours excessive, while in the same city, Mrs Dunning (interviewee 111) thought a ten-hour day should be the norm.

Some women who were employers in 1864 had been over-worked apprentices in 1843, and tried to spare their own staff. Miss Turner of Bertie Road in Leamington (interviewee 104) was typical: 'My own health has suffered too much from long hours to let me have anybody work late for me.' Mrs Jones, (interviewee 122) forewoman for Mrs Matthews in Clifton, said she did all-night mourning orders very occasionally, perhaps twice a year, but when she did she gave her girls a half-day break the next day.

Small businesses and greedy, ill-organized mistresses created the worst conditions. Mrs Faulder in St Ann's Square, Manchester insisted it was necessary for the hands to work long hours to give any profit. She ran a large establishment with ten live-in employees and around twenty outdoor staff, and her first hand, Miss Pringle (interviewee 3), confirmed that for their five-month season they worked a regular sixteen-hour day and added 'I can safely say that during quite two months of that time we made 17 or 18 hours a day'. Mrs Faulder was clearly a disastrous employer. Miss Pringle accused her of 'want of calculation' and described the dreadful treatment one sixteen-year-old apprentice had received. The girl was given a skirt to make:

... which was more than she could really do in the time, however hard she worked, and she did work hard all day; but the principal coming up and finding her behind-hand said that it was the girl's own fault and that she must take half-an-hour from her dinner time.

The poor girl did not finish it until 11.00 pm, even though Miss Pringle helped her for the last hour.

Many of the criticisms of the commissioners' methodology in the 1843 enquiry also apply to the 1864 one; however, there was more consistency in the questioning of interviewees. The commissioners concentrated on three aspects of working conditions – long hours and whether these had improved since 1843, wages and conditions in workrooms. The 1843 report had revealed that workrooms were often stuffy and ill-ventilated, and many of them were basement rooms where the heat and smell from gas lighting were a problem. So anxious were the commissioners to deal with this situation that the 1864 report included three pages of recommendations, effectively advertisements, complete with diagrams, for four named ventilation systems.

Apprenticeship

Apprenticeship was well-established by the end of the eighteenth century and continued into the nineteenth century, though many girls do not seem to have served a formal term and by the 1790s some mistresses were so desperate for apprentices that they advertised 'No premium required'. The 1843 report highlighted the discrepancies between apprenticeship customs in different parts of the country. For example, interviewee number 237 in Bristol was six years into a seven-year apprenticeship for which no premium had been charged. Number 257 said that the usual length for an apprenticeship in Bath was five years, while in Norwich one- or two-year apprenticeships were said to be the norm. The premiums charged also varied widely. Mayhew estimated in 1849 that London apprenticeship premiums varied between £10.00 and £50.00, and cited the case of 'a third rate house in the suburbs' where the proprietress actually rented premises and set up in business on the proceeds of the premiums she received – £110.00 from four apprentices at £20.00 each and three improvers at £10.00 each.[3]

Some private apprenticeships could still be very expensive. In July 1845 James Kent, 'gentleman' paid £40.00 to apprentice his seventeen-year-old ward, Sarah Strong Talbot, to Emma Elgar of Dorchester (Dorset) for three years.[4] Drawing up the indenture cost him £2.0s.6d and he remained responsible for paying for Sarah's keep. However, he no longer had to look after her and could persuade himself he had secured her future by providing her with the means to earn a living. By contrast, parish apprenticeships had become cheaper; many cost just £3.00 to £4.00.

Because they brought in an income and cost their employers very little, many firms had a number of apprentices. In September 1836 Miss Osborne moved her business to Hotel Street in Leicester. She advertised that she was employing an 'experienced assistant' and wanted two indoor apprentices; in December she advertised that she also needed 'several' outdoor apprentices.[5] 'Several' must mean at least two – so Miss Osborne and her assistant were running a business and trying to train four or more girls. Under such circumstances training was often minimal and the girls were simply unpaid labour. A girl who replied to an advert like this in the *Leicester Post* in 1875[6] was taking a calculated risk:

> WANTED. A respectable girl, about 14 years of age, to be APPRENTICED to the MILLINERY business, in a village, a few miles from Leicester. She will be treated with kindness and as one of the family.

By 1864 the Children's Employment Commission found that most apprenticeships were shorter and cheaper than they had been in 1843 but that conditions varied widely. In Bath, interviewee 113 reported that two-year apprenticeships were now usual and that premiums were small or non-existent – though Mrs Crowden of the Blue Coat School (interviewee 116) still paid £3.00 for three-year apprenticeships for her girls but stipulated they should be paid 1s a week for the first year, rising to 3s.0d in their third year. In Exeter, Mrs Brothers (interviewee 125) charged £3.00 to £5.00 for a three-year apprenticeship, though Mrs Brown (interviewee 132) claimed that high-class apprentices still paid £25.00 to £30.00. In Plymouth, Mrs Radford charged a £5.00 premium to her out-apprentices for a three-year term. However, in Ryde, Miss L. (interviewee 141) charged a £30.00 premium for three years, and in 1864 she had six live-in apprentices and three or four outdoor ones, so she was making good money from training girls. In the 1880s and '90s Hobson's Charity in Cambridge paid a standard £12.00 premium for girl apprentices and £15.00 for boys, regardless of the length of their apprenticeships, and usually expected the children's parents to pay for their keep and the children to receive a small wage. Frances Hicks claimed that a £20.00 premium was still the norm for an apprenticeship in the 1890s at one of the 'Madame' shops she described to Margaret Stewart and Leslie Hunter.[7] Apprentices in such businesses usually worked for six to twelve months unpaid, then for another twelve months for a nominal 2s.0d or 2s.6d a week, before becoming 'season hands' in the West End.

Women who were apprenticed in the latter years of the nineteenth century have left descriptions of what they did. Picking up pins and filling pin cushions feature largely, as do threading needles, stitching on brush-braid, making strap-holders for evening dresses and running endless errands. Apprentices were often kept at one task to maintain secrecy and prevent the girls learning too much. Alice Maud Chase of Portsmouth was apprenticed in 1895 and remained in the trade for eight years, hating almost all of it:

> To girls like myself who were shut up in one room from 8.30 am to 8 pm, the world was just one dreary round of tacking, stitching, pressing, over-sewing, boning and trimming, over and over again, being bullied and harried and insulted by over-bearing and ill-tempered task mistresses, that we all grew pale, round-shouldered, dull-eyed and depressed.[8]

At least she had a range of things to do. Ellen Gill, born in Woodhouse, Leeds, started work as an apprentice at the age of twelve in 1900, and most of her job consisted of sewing on buttons at threepence a hundred, for which she had to provide her own cotton at 4½d for 1,000 yards.[9] By contrast, Minnie Frisby was exceptionally lucky. She lived with her sister who kept a hotel and had bought Minnie a piano and paid for music and dancing lessons. After a spell in domestic service, Minnie was apprenticed in the mid-1890s, aged seventeen, to Mrs Rawlings, who

> … was supposed to be the most First Class Dressmaker in Bromsgrove … there were about a dozen of us girls in the workroom … I can assure you us girls knew what to wear, and my sister would usually pay for my clothes and provide me with pocket money.

Minnie gave the lie to the idea that all young dressmakers were downtrodden. She and her fellow workers would roll back the carpet in their employer's living room and play the piano and dance whenever 'Mrs R' went to the wholesalers. They spent some of their employer's time working on dresses for themselves and vied with each other to be 'belle of the (local) ball' – clearly these were not young women who were too exhausted by hours of toil to have any time to enjoy themselves.[10]

Many girls found their jobs through personal contacts. Rose Hackett of Chichester was apprenticed in 1897 at the age of fourteen to a Mrs Downer, her mother's friend – a typically informal arrangement and one that worked well. She was well-treated and eventually married Mrs Downer's son. She went into business on her own account in 1901 and was very successful.[11] Mrs Stent of Westbourne was also apprenticed in Chichester at about the same time – to a Mrs Dowson in West Street. Dressmaking was perhaps not the best choice of career for a girl who admitted she had been caned in school for the number of needles she broke in Domestic Economy lessons, and Mrs Stent clearly hated her job and left it as soon as she could.[12]

Some employers acted almost as foster mothers to their apprentices. Mrs Allinson in Whitehaven, Cumberland, in the 1880s, agreed to take Elizabeth Ann Hunter on as a 'trainee' at 8s.0d a week (£20.00 pa) including her board and lodging. She was to have a half-day every Saturday and Mrs Allinson had offered a fortnight's annual holiday; Anna Maria Mardon, a friend of the girl's late mother, over in Barrow-in-Furness, bargained on her behalf:

> Now would you allow her a month at a fortnight each time during the year – to come home – as she is very young and we would like her to come a little oftener than once a twelvemonth. I am quite sure you will have every satisfaction with her – but would like her kept under control and carefully taken care of as one of your own.[13]

As late as 1908, Meyer and Black found a 'Mrs P' whose only employees were three or four little girls who came to her straight from school, were paid a shilling a week, taught the trade and then, a year later, were placed by her with West End houses as 'improvers'. She reported that they 'always look in and tell me how they are getting on'.[14] She, too, was acting as a sort of mother figure.

However, it was always possible to enter the trade with much less formal training. Hannah Mitchell's mother regarded dressmaking as 'ladylike' and despatched Hannah's elder sister, Lizzie, to be apprenticed to a high-class dressmaker in Glossop (Derbyshire); she hoped that Lizzie would then come home and teach her sisters. Hannah herself was then apprenticed to 'an elderly, crippled lady who ran a small private business with two apprentices and a niece about my own age' but was summoned home again when Lizzie chose to work in town rather than return to the farm. Despite this minimal training Hannah was able to find work as a dressmaker in numerous establishments after she ran away from her neurotic mother and cheerless home, aged fourteen, in 1885.[15] She was not unique. 'Taking in sewing' is mentioned again and again in memoirs and interviews as a way working-class women eked out the family income. Some of them had trained before marriage, but a number simply capitalized on a flair for sewing.

Employment

The process by which girls served a second apprenticeship to improve their skills became formalized in the nineteenth century. 'Improvers', as they were called, were not always paid, and some girls paid a premium to be taken on in that capacity. According to Mayhew in 1849, girls usually paid a premium of between £10.00 and £50.00 and were taken on for about two years. A girl who had served her apprenticeship in the provinces and hoped to set up in business for herself saw 'that it would be hopeless to attain the patronage of the neighbourhood ladies unless she have the prestige of having been trained to the perfect exercise of London taste and skill', so she was likely to spend a term in London as an improver.[16] In 1864, the Children's Employment Commission suggested that the normal term for an improver with a London fashion house was just six months. Time in town provided the improver with contacts for when she returned to London on her own to 'see the fashions' on her clients' behalf – advertisements attest to the fact that most provincial dressmakers of any standing did regularly visit London.

Her training complete, the young dressmaker then sought paid employment. Mayhew described the structure of employment in London fashion houses in the 1840s and '50s and it was little different in good provincial firms. There were first, second and third hands and assistants – though the numbers in each category depended on the size of the firm. First hands waited on the customers, took orders, measured the clients, supervised fittings and did the cutting out. Second hands were employed to work along with the staff and supervise them, and in larger establishments, there were third hands doing the same thing. Assistants were hired at busy times and might live in or out. They were variously known as 'day workers', 'out workers', 'out assistants' or 'weekly hands' and hired by the week, month or season.[17] In London, skirt-making, a simple but time-consuming job, was sometimes 'put out' – Mayhew described the progress of a Genoese velvet skirt from 'first rate house' to squalid attic in the arms of the outworker's small son.[18]

The number of staff varied with the size of the firm for which they worked. For example, in Glossop, in the firm where Hannah Mitchell was an improver, the staff consisted of a 'workshop head', two assistants and Mona the apprentice.[19] However, in the 1860s 'Madame Elise' on Regent Street employed around seventy live-in staff and twenty-five day-workers, making it one of the largest firms in the country.[20] It was owned by Mr and Mrs Isaacson and they became notorious when, on 17 June 1863, one of their workers sent an anonymous letter to *The Times* describing the death of a colleague. The writer ended her letter: 'we do not complain of our house, which is better conducted than many, [*but*] we should be so glad if some plan could be discovered by which we could get a little less work and a little more air.' The girl who died was twenty-year-old Mary Anne Walkley and at her inquest Mr Keys, the physician, gave his opinion that the 'apoplexy' that had killed her was the result of 'long hours of work in a crowded apartment, and sleeping in a close, badly-ventilated room'. Nonetheless, difficult though it is to believe, there is evidence to suggest that, comparatively speaking, the Isaacsons were quite considerate employers.[21]

In London houses most hands lived in and their board and lodging was part of their wage, making them heavily dependent on their employer for their living conditions as well as their livelihoods. Unscrupulous employers might stint their staff; Mayhew interviewed one girl who told him how her employer's family had 'secret' meals at which they ate properly, and then other meals which the workers attended. The family, already sated, ate very little at these sessions and thus shamed the work-girls into also eating tiny portions.[22] Living conditions often left a lot to be desired – the lady who established her business by taking on apprentices and improvers had her four apprentices, three improvers, six daughters and first hand share the same bedroom! Writing in 1909, Meyer and Black noted that firms were often judged by the quality of the food they provided.

> The quality of tea given in some work-rooms is a point about which workers feel deeply. One very nice woman still recalls with satisfaction the super-excellence of the bread and butter provided by a firm for which she worked a short time many years ago.[23]

Courteous employers were also much appreciated. In Glossop, Hannah Mitchell's last post before she married was with a firm which:

> Had a good middle class clientele, and paid quite decent wages judged by the low standard of the times ... Moreover, our employer was a courteous man who treated us all with respect. If he was in the shop as we passed through, he would open the door for us, bowing to us just as he did to his best customers. I don't suppose he ever realised how much this little attention was appreciated, or the return it brought him in willing service.[24]

The long hours dressmakers worked took their toll. George Shaw MD of the Leicester Royal Infirmary wrote to the Children's Employment Commissioners in 1843 (interviewee 627):

> It is a general practice for these young persons to work long hours, to be subjected to close confinement, and to have frequently poor diet ... The young persons who are employed by the principal dressmaking establishments, are more subject to long hours of work than others. The common results are dyspepsia, derangement of the uterine action, headache and pain in the side: there are also frequently swelling about the ankles, and a general languor, accompanied with great pallor.

Many women blamed dressmaking for the problems they had when they married and had children. As late as 1914 one of Margaret Llewellyn Davies' correspondents attributed the difficulties she had had in childbirth to her work:

> My confinements (five) were however, hard, bad times ... This I have always put down to the fact that at the age of thirteen I began to learn dressmaking, which entailed sitting long hours at a stretch, at a time when the bones are in rather a soft state.[25]

Sewing was also blamed for damaging women's eyesight. It was reported to a meeting of subscribers to the North London Opthalmic Institution in 1844 that: 'Out of 669 patients during the previous year no less than 81 were poor needlewomen whose eyes had been materially injured by the incessant application at fine work to earn a precarious subsistence.'[26] Working at mourning – sewing matt black fabrics with black thread – was seen as terribly bad for the eyes, as were some other textile tasks like lace-making and white-work embroidery on muslin. One of the 1864 commissioners (Interviewee 95) interviewed three dressmakers who were in Cheltenham General Hospital. One of them, a girl of sixteen, was in hospital for the second time with eye problems which she attributed to having worked for two consecutive nights on a mourning order. She was not expected to recover.

Current medical opinion is that such work was unlikely to do permanent damage.[27] What tends to happen is that the eye finds it difficult to adjust to distance viewing after a long period working in close focus; most people's sight would recover from this naturally after a period of rest. However, the common practice of sponging the eyes with whisky or gin to sharpen the sight may well have introduced infection, which in exhausted, malnourished women would have been difficult to cure without the benefit of antibiotics and could have led to blindness. Nonetheless, census evidence shows that a significant number of dressmakers worked on well into their seventies.

Another of the disadvantages of working in a dressmaker's shop was the need to look respectable. The 1864 report described dress as a 'serious item' and showed how, even if she made her own outfits, a girl who came into regular contact with customers needed to spend at least £20.00 a year on black silk dresses. This was probably something of an over-estimate, and fortunately it was only the first hands who were likely to have to incur this expense.

Some women remained paid hands all their lives, but some used their experience to set up in business on their own account.

Setting up a business

The Book of Trades of 1811 suggested that girls should not train as dressmakers if they had no money with which to establish a business. But money did not guarantee success any more than it had done in the eighteenth century. In 1858 John Thompson of Manchester, about to sail to New Zealand, set his wife Elizabeth up in partnership with Mary Elizabeth Tasker as 'Tasker and Thompson, milliners and dressmakers'. He intended thus to provide her and their three children with an income in his absence, and a livelihood if he did not return. He took premises for them, provided £1,250.00 for furnishing and start-up costs and appointed two local businessmen as trustees to look after the women's interests.[28] Fortunately for his family he did return, for the business failed and within two years only £600.00 of the capital remained.

Mrs Agnes Dow in Leith (near Edinburgh) ran a haberdashery and millinery business and was declared bankrupt on 12 August 1834. She had employed a milliner, two shop boys and a maid, and lived in furnished rooms next door to her business at 45, Tolbooth Wynd. The sederunt books include an inventory of her stock (cottons and prints, 'Tuscan' and 'Dunstable' bonnets, caps, collars, etc.) valued at £144.12s.0d. Her equipment was worth a mere £14.5s.4d, and consisted of six rush-seated chairs, counters, shelves, a writing stool, a mahogany desk, a large hat block, one small screen, two pairs of steps, four cap blocks, a gas 'metre' and pipes, a small glass case, a grate and fire irons, a carpet, brushes and a looking-glass.[29] It was possible to run a dressmaking or millinery business with very little in the way of fixtures and fittings.

It depended how ambitious you were. Sometime in 1854 Elizabeth Taylor wrote to her sister-in-law, Louisa, in Brighton. Elizabeth worked for a Mrs Goulding, but she was planning to leave to set up on her own. She explained her plan and what she would need:

> Madame Schodeher who lived with us a year was always asking me to join her I made up my mind to try this winter to see if it will answer, if not I can always take another situation in the spring. She is very clever and I have not the slightest doubt we should do very well if we can only get up the first year – the worst is the furniture to buy, for we must have a decent showroom. I wish I had a friend to lend me £20 … The ladies are all so fond of me in Edinburgh and there are few good dressmakers there.[30]

Presumably the £20.00 was Elizabeth's contribution to the cost of setting up the new business and Madame Schodeher was to provide the remainder.

Plate 15 Chaffards' former shop on the corner of Castle Street and Princes Street, Edinburgh.

That venture was not a success, but Elizabeth and her sister eventually went into business together on the corner of Castle Street and Princes Street in Edinburgh as 'Chaffard et Cie' – Chaffard was Elizabeth's married name. [Plate 15] Theirs was a luxuriously appointed establishment. The walls were lined with seven 'large and elegant Mantlepiece and Pier Mirrors' and the room was lit with flickering gas lights adorned with lustres. There were rosewood cabinets, chairs upholstered in Utrecht velvet and a damask couch for customers to recline on if the whole business of choosing a dress was too fatiguing. Curiously, there was also an 'Elizabethan bed', though it is not clear whether this was for decoration or use.[31]

The 'first-rate establishment in the West-end' described to Mayhew by a lady correspondent was even more luxurious.

> [A] very large house, more like a mansion for a nobleman than a milliner's establishment ... A lady goes to order perhaps her wedding *trousseau,* or a train for the Queen's Drawing Room ... She alights from her carriage. The hall-door is opened by the footman of the establishment, who bows her into what is called the "premier magazin", or "first show-room". Then comes a French lady, dressed in a silk dress, with short sleeves and a very small lace cap, with long streamers

of ribbon that fall over her shoulders down to her feet. She walks before the lady to a counter and places a chair for her. These French ladies are styled "magazinières" ... There are generally five or six ... in a first-rate establishment. The first show-room is about 130 feet long and 60 feet wide. In every other panel there is a looking glass from floor to ceiling, set in a handsome carved gilt frame. The floor is covered with a very expensive carpet ... The window curtains are of a rich dark green velvet ... there are counters of polished ebony, elegantly ornamented with gilding ... After a considerable deliberation, she selects [*the fabric for*] one or two dresses.

Later:

... as soon as is convenient to the lady, the first hand goes to take her measure. For this purpose, a one-horse Brougham, with a servant in livery, is brought to the door, and the first hand goes in to measure the lady for her dress. When she returns she gives it out to another first hand, who takes it up into the work-room and cuts it out.[32]

This was service at its most obsequious. Few provincial dressmakers could aspire to such a standard which is why so many wealthy women chose to have their dresses made in London.

Up in Lancashire, Elizabeth Sarah Simpson was a typical small town dressmaker. She had been apprenticed in 1877–8. In September 1884 she married Samuel Smith Pattinson, a railway clerk and the couple set up house next door to Elizabeth's parents at 8, Upper Brook Street, Ulverston in the Furness district of Lancashire, and rented number one, on the corner, for Elizabeth's millinery, dressmaking and haberdashery business. [Plate 16] Numerous receipts survive from 1884 relating to the furnishing of her new house and business. Most of Mrs Pattinson's initial stock was bought from Ulverston drapers and suppliers and she even acquired a sewing machine from J.B. Kay, the local dealer. Her shop had a plate-glass window which she insured for 4s.0d, and Edward Dickinson charged her 6s.9d for 'writing the frieze and door'. Her only out-of-town supplier was J.H. Barrow, linen and woollen draper, a few miles away in Barrow-in-Furness. She had trouble finding a suitable supplier of paper goods and tried various firms. Weeks and Fletcher of Ulverston supplied a thousand millinery bags and a hundred billheads for 15s.3d in November 1886 and five hundred 'flower bags' for 4s.0d. Her bundle of receipts also contains invoices from plumbers, gas fitters and ironmongers but it is not clear which are for her home and which are for the shop.[33]

Frances Hicks, one-time secretary to the London Tailoress's Union, described the sort of business in which she had served her own dressmaking apprenticeship in the 1890s:

> In every suburb and working class district there are to be found a number of women, who having worked for a few years in some fashionable dressmaking establishment, have set up for themselves in business and give West End style to neighbouring tradespeople, upper-class servants, and perhaps a few wealthier patrons.

Miss Hicks, her mistress and an assistant worked in the family kitchen from 8.00 am to 8.00 pm, at a table in the window. They took their meals at the same table without stopping work, but had to clear their sewing away when the dressmaker's 'lazy husband' and two schoolboy sons came home for their tea. Most customers provided their own fabric, the dressmaker hired a sewing machine for 1s.6d a week and beyond that 'the chief requirement [*was*] a tidy room with fashion plates and magazines, a mirror and long white curtain which admits a good light yet screens the customer while garments are being tried on'.[34]

Doing the job

Comparatively few records survive that give any sort of detail about working practices, so it is worth examining those few in some depth.

Mayhew described the workroom in the 'first-rate establishment in the West-end' whose show-room was mentioned earlier.

> The work-room is nearly as large as the first showroom, with a fireplace at each end. Three large deal tables run down the middle, with a gas pipe over them, and there are as many chairs as the room will hold, all filled with young ladies working at the tables. These young ladies are generally short. If there is a tall one amongst them she is usually an "improver", and has grown up before she learned her business … [*the other women*] are so thin and pale-looking that their appearance is not very prepossessing. The first hand comes in with the dress, and throws it down on the first table she comes to … At last one ventures to ask "Who is it for?" "Oh," the first hand answers, it's for Lady or Mrs So-and-so, and she wants it tomorrow morning." "Tomorrow morning," cry half-a-dozen voices, "how is it possible when we have so many other dresses to do? Why, she has kept us up three nights this week already."[35]

In a large firm like that, workroom tasks were carefully structured. Apprentices spent their first months picking up pins and watching what went on. Cutting and fitting were the preserve of the owner or first hand and these skills were jealously guarded. Apprentices were cheap, and firms tended to take on too many at the expense of trained staff. Mrs Treadwin's first hand in Exeter explained that at Ipswich where she had been apprenticed: 'The fault was in having just one first hand, and all the rest apprentices, so that the first hand, instead of only superintending and cutting out, spent half her time in working herself or unpicking the bad work of the apprentices.'[36]

Mayhew's 'first class' firm would probably have styled itself a 'court dressmaker', but he identified other types of business too – 'second-class' firms that catered for the middle class and made everyday wear for the gentry, 'third-class' firms that were cheaper and catered to an aspiring working-class clientele or middle-class customers who were having to watch the pennies and 'fourth-class' firms that did repairs and made cheap cotton dresses. The differences were probably more marked in London and the large cities, but most places of any size had businesses to serve a range of clienteles.

In many firms girls were not taught a full range of skills but were encouraged to become expert in just one or two processes. This made them useful to their employer but unable to progress. In 1849 Eliza Ann Cory explained,

> It is well known that apprentices are seldom taught how to take a pattern from the figure: the only way in which they acquire the knowledge, is by being allowed to hand the pins to the Operator, who is always the Mistress, or First Hand.[37]

Many dressmakers therefore emerged from their apprenticeships with very little knowledge of cutting and fitting, and as a result, no prospect of being able to run their own businesses.

Elizabeth Taylor's 1854 letter to her sister-in-law has already been quoted. It sounds as if Elizabeth was an assistant or second hand. She had served her apprenticeship in Edinburgh, and it was to Edinburgh she would return to set up on her own. Her letter to Louisa continued:

> Mrs Goulding is just returned from London, she has engaged a French dressmaker. I could not put up with her temper any longer, its an old saying and a fine one with them "work a willing horse to death" in my part I told her from ½ past 7 till 11 and sometimes 12 was quite hours enough for any old work horse … I could not swallow the last tiff she and I had without cause. She thought it would all blow over again but when she found I was determined she said I should not have to take another situation she would rather give me £35 per annum and then she offered 40 the next day but I had gone to[o] far with Madam to retreat or they would have persuad'd me to stop another year, she said if she had known it she would have had a person working under me all the summer. You see they cannot get anyone to do the stays and dresses and we make nearly as many stays as dresses.

In many ways, this letter is an important document as far as long hours are concerned, because it was not written with any political agenda – Elizabeth was simply explaining to her sister-in-law why she was changing her job. It is also interesting that Mrs Goulding made her clients' stays as well as their dresses. Staymaking has usually been seen as a separate trade, sometimes allied with straw bonnet making. Both involved heavy stitching through stiff materials – much more arduous work than dressmaking.

In London on 17 September 1856, after a brief and unsuccessful spell working in Edinburgh with Mme Schodeher, Elizabeth Taylor married Leonard Ferdinand Chaffard of Limoges. On the same day her sister Mary, also a dressmaker, married John Carmichael of Edinburgh. Little is known of either of the men, but it would seem that Monsieur Chaffard was some sort of commercial traveller in hats. The two husbands spent some time looking for premises for their wives to use as a business before taking a shop in Edinburgh, at 2, Castle Street, which had a frontage on Princes Street.

Ten years later the Chaffards moved back to Brighton with their only child, Lizzie. Both were unwell and Ferdinand died shortly afterwards. [Plate 16] Mary Carmichael continued to run the Edinburgh business – she was widowed young – and wrote regular letters to Elizabeth about what she was doing. These, together with other family letters, are pasted into a large scrapbook.[38] Most of them are undated but they provide a fascinating insight into the running of an up-market dressmaking and millinery business in the 1860s:

> Yesterday I had a visit from Mrs Lawson for mourning – one of the Oliphants of Coullie is going to be married and I had to arrange for her as they are to be in tomorrow in prospect of the trousseau of which I think there will be at least five silks all in stock …

> I am fairly worn out tonight, have had such a heavy day with the Oliphants, I was from 12 till 4 without ceasing speaking and advising and arranging as all was proposed to them first and then the intended had to go over all again … I think at present there will be about twenty-one dresses without jackets, crinolines, bonnets, etc and all has to be done by the first week in October without other orders and Miss Taylor away for her holiday … I did not feel very strong after they left but I am better tonight.

> Miss Hawkins is going to be married – they've been staying in London since they got those white glacé dresses. Mrs Hawkins came in – she gave me a compliment when she said she had been to four places before to me – Semprose, Hackwood, Cameron's, Vogue – for a tulle bonnet – but she could not fix so I fixed her.

Plate 16 Elizabeth Chaffard, 1865–6.

The bonnets in question were probably made or trimmed on the premises and kept as stock items, though the firm also seems to have sold ready-made goods. Sometimes Mary waxed eloquent about her stock: 'got such a pretty grey straw hat, so light, the bateau shape, sold three already trimmed velvet the same shade and veil the same colour'.

Mary Carmichael had problems with her staff – she seems to have been a hard task mistress and was scathing about workers' complaints: 'What a case with the Hairdressers [*they had been on strike*] – our lot will be next I shouldn't wonder ... I should never be surprised at our lot wanting their hours shortened it seems such a pity to work till 9.'

'Wages are higher as you know by Miss Stark who has of where at first she had half the sum and workers are not to be had.' Miss Stark was in fact a very good worker and had taken charge of the workroom when the forewoman, Miss Taylor, was away. Even the pernickety Mary described her work as 'first-class'. No doubt in such a firm the workwomen were well-educated – a letter survives from Miss Taylor to Elizabeth, dated October 1866, by which time the Chaffards were in Brighton, and it is beautifully written and spelt:

> Thank you for your description of the fashions. We are making two dresses for a Mrs Baird staying at the "Alma Hotel" a black figured silk out of the show room, the trimming I have copied from your letter … We are still continuing busy. Mrs Dobell and her sister have sent in material for two dresses, when outfitting [*sic*] them on they made kind enquiries after your health and Mrs Dobell desired me to give you kind compliments. A Box from Paris has arrived today which they are unpacking but I have not seen the contents yet. We are still getting on very nicely but I shall be very glad to see Mrs Carmichael home again.

The personal lives of staff could not get in the way of business. 'There is no word of Miss Stark going to be married but indeed I could not spare her for any such thing', wrote Mary. Even her reporting of a tragedy was dispassionate: 'Miss Sharp, the tall apprentice is now dead, went home ill, she bled at the nose and ears, she was 14½.' Miss Muir, another member of staff, left to go to another firm, Remingtons; 'I suppose Miss Nicoll has persuaded her, they were great friends – fortunately I have one in the work room who can take her place', wrote Mary crossly, before admitting that the girl was also to be paid more for shorter hours in her new place. She was overworked herself and overworked her staff: 'I am overwhelmed with work here – 10 dresses to turn out … I could not sleep last night with the worry.'

Mary Carmichael's letters provide one of the fullest accounts available of practice in dressmaking establishments. Her customers were wealthy society ladies. At the other end of the UK, and also at the other end of the social spectrum, were the dressmaker clients of B. Thomas of Helston in Cornwall. He or she kept a haberdashery business and also made garments. Most of the work was repairs and the firm did more tailoring than either millinery or dressmaking. What is interesting, however, is that they were supplying several local dressmakers. Cornwall was not a wealthy county and Thomas's dressmaker clients seem to have been working on a very small scale indeed, probably for poor rural customers. They bought in tiny quantities for one job at a time. On 18 December 1847, for example, Mary J. Borrows, 'tailoress', bought five yards of print at 4d a yard; on the 24th Mary Julian, 'dressmaker', was unable to pay for the goods she bought and left 9s.5½d owing, but three days later she was back for 2½d-worth of tape, a pennyworth of needles and fifteen yards of binding at 1s.6½d.[39]

We have already seen how Elizabeth Pattinson established her business in Ulverston. We know comparatively little about the goods she made and nothing at all about the prices she charged or the staff she employed. But many bundles of invoices survive relating to her business and these shed light on what she bought and on her relationships with suppliers. As we have seen, young Mrs Pattinson bought most of her initial stock from local suppliers in Ulverston itself – it is surprising today that the small town could support so many drapers – the population of Ulverston in 1881 was 10,001 and Slater's 1890 *Directory* lists eight tailor/drapers and five dressmaker/drapers – but the town would also have served a large, if sparsely populated, rural hinterland. Elizabeth Pattinson bought stock from Manchester, London, Nottingham and Ripon. Most items were ordered by post and sent by rail, and odd little notes survive from the suppliers, for example: 'Sorry we cannot do the mob cap and Jack Tar cap' (1 March 1891); 'Sorry we are sold out of the brown hat, have sent the nearest' (9 November 1895); 'Sorry this is the nearest we have in all white, can have at any time made exactly to pattern, say ¼ doz of any kind' (23 April 1895). But even a quarter-dozen was a large order for Mrs Pattinson – few of her orders were for more than two or three pounds. Many were for less – on one occasion she ordered a single widow's cap for 1s.3d plus postage, all the way from Manchester. To modern eyes it is amazing that large firms were prepared to supply a small provincial milliner with such tiny quantities of goods. [Plate 17]

She bought the basic shapes for her hats – chip, straw and mob caps – roughly once a month, for about two pounds a time, from 'Rayner and Lee, wholesale dealers in straw bonnets, ribbons, flowers, feathers, millinery, etc' of North Bridge, Ripon (North Yorkshire). Batho, Taylor and Ogden, suppliers of millinery goods, and Peel, Watson and Co, manufacturers of baby linen, underwear, sun bonnets, aprons, etc., both in Church Street, Manchester, were also suppliers she used regularly. In the period October 1886 to December 1887 records survive for her expenditure with the firms which by then were her three main suppliers. She spent £141.8s.1½d with Batho, Taylor and Ogden; she placed thirty-nine separate orders – three a month – totalling £107.11s.6½d with Peel, Watson and Co; and with S.J. Watts and Co of Manchester, suppliers of ready-made clothing, laces and trimmings, aprons, etc., she spent £9.12s.6d. Her expenditure remained roughly the same with these firms until she ceased trading in 1902. Her stock

Plate 17 Mrs Pattinson's shop on the corner of High Street and Upper Brook Street, Ulverston.

books also survive, showing much of her trade was in ready-made goods – in 1891 she had stock worth £248.12.6d; by 1900 it had risen to £349.4s.8d.[40]

Most firms were prepared to provide a high level of service, whatever the cost to their workers. Indeed, it was a selling point. In Dalton in Lancashire, the Misses Dixon provided a typical example, advertising that they would make mourning 'in the neatest manner and on the shortest possible notice' (*Soulsby's Ulverston Advertiser*, 21 December 1849). The result was that dressmakers were expected to work extraordinarily long hours. Most of the dressmakers who wrote their memoirs for Professor Burnett in the 1950s and '60s remembered working an eleven- or twelve-hour day. For Hannah Mitchell in Glossop in the 1880s the 8.00 pm end of the day often became 10.00 pm, sometimes midnight, and in summer, 1.00 or 2.00 am; 'We envied the cotton workers who streamed out of the mill as soon as the "buzzer" went at ½ past 5. At least they knew when their working day would end. We never did.'[41]

Dressmaking was not an easy trade in which to make a profit and some dressmakers offered additional services. Many sold ready-made goods or tea or groceries. Mrs Smith, straw-bonnet manufacturer in Leicester's Haymarket, made a little extra money in 1840 by renting space to 'Mr S Lee, Ear and Eye Specialist' for a few days. Anne Elsworth had a shop in Leicester High Street next door to Daniel, the bookseller. She sold caps, flowers, cuffs, collars, ruches and children's lace, as well as making garments for her clients, and she also acted as agent for a mysterious drink called 'Evans Piqua Plant' which was marketed as a 'highly refreshing substitute for tea and coffee'.[42]

Relations with clients

The relationship between dressmaker and client could be an intimate one. Indeed, writing of dressmakers and milliners in nineteenth-century Edinburgh, Stana Nenadic claimed that customers expected their relationship with their dressmaker to be a personal one rather than a business one: 'This is one of the primary reasons why the sector evolved as it did, and why individual women entrepreneurs within the sector behaved in a manner that often appeared "unbusinesslike."'[43] It may also explain why some customers were so dilatory in paying their bills.

The dressmakers' shop was an all-female environment, and though it is unlikely that real dressmakers acted as matchmakers like their fictional counterparts, it is probable that many clients confided in them. The first dressmakers' trade journal – the *Drapers' and Milliners' Gazette of Fashion* – appeared in 1871. Some of the advertisements it carried are revealing. Advertisements for beauty products featured largely, including the wonderful 'Alsatian herb wash for hair' allegedly discovered by an Alsatian peasant woman, once nearly bald but 'now [*in 1877*] with hair over seven feet long!' But there were also advertisements for much more intimate products, like Land's rosebud liniment for sore nipples, Cardson's Binder Belts 'especially useful after accouchement', Southall's sanitary towels and booklets with titles like *Advice to the Married* which gave contraceptive advice. There were patent medicines, like Mother Siegel's constipation remedy and Nurse Lilley's Royal Female Pills. 'Female pills' was often shorthand for abortifacients. It is possible that dressmakers had long been providing such services for their clients; they, after all, would be among the first people to know when a woman got pregnant – her dresses and stays would need to be let out. In an all-female environment, during lengthy fittings, confidences could be exchanged and advice offered. Could the prejudice about dressmakers' immorality have some of its roots in this aspect of their activities? We can only speculate.

Of course, not all clients got on with their dressmakers. Young Mrs Smith, newly married to the Reverend Reginald Smith, visited a new dressmaker in Dorchester on 3 May 1836: 'Went to the Dress Maker. Quite a Musician of Wind – arrived at 1 o'clock and stayed till late in the afternoon', she recorded in her diary.[44] It is unlikely that many confidences were exchanged there. And not all dressmakers were conscientious. A difficult commission might be more trouble than it was worth. In 1823 Mrs C. Butlin of Rugby asked her friend, Frances Woutherington, who was on a visit to London, to try to find out what had happened to an order she had placed with a dressmaker there. Frances wrote to her:

> I went on Friday morning to Miss Forbes, No 1 York Street to make the enquiry you wished me to do respecting your pelisse and found it in the same state as it was when you returned it. Miss F told me it was a very difficult black to match and that she was fearful she should not be able to make the alterations you require, she was going into the city on business, I therefore begged she would take a piece of the silk with her and try to match it which she promised to do and let me have the result in the evening … I have not seen or heard anything of her since.[45]

The Carmichael/Chaffard correspondence throws a good deal of light on how the sisters saw their customers.[46] Clients could be amazingly selfish. Mary Carmichael described one to Elizabeth:

> Had a visit on Saturday afternoon from Miss Bateman, had a cup of tea, just in the midst –walked in Lady Braithwaite – wanted a Bonnet, this was half-past-6 and wanted me to unlock and turn out everything. I told her I knew there was nothing she would really like but could shew her some Tuesday.

Then there was:

> Mrs D Mackenzie Clark Marman – Elizabeth Maclaine that was, has removed to this address Tighnabruaich near Greenock. I have two dresses for her I think I told you in a former letter – and [*she*] has the coolness to say "pay carriage of Box."

Tighnabruaich is on the western side of the Kyles of Bute, several hours by sea up the Firth of Clyde from Glasgow. In the mid-nineteenth century it was probably at least two days' journey from Edinburgh and the cost of delivering the 'box' would have been considerable.

It was difficult to persuade some clients to pay at all. 'The Kempes have just come in and paid – there with a deduction of course.' This was probably for paying in ready money. Miss Kempe had owed £38.19s.0d and Major Kempe £1.4s.0d. Clients could simply be capricious. Mrs Hay Gordon called to get Mrs Carmichael to change a bonnet she herself had chosen 'because nobody liked her in it'. We can deduce that Mrs Nollneye's sister was also an unpopular client – Mary simply described her as 'the one who played the <u>harp</u>'. But others could be kind and congratulatory – Mary frequently passed on to Elizabeth the good wishes of their customers and one, C. Vinck of Glasgow, wrote to Elizabeth herself, enquiring about her health, wanting to visit her in Brighton and sending a present for little Lizzie.

A lengthy correspondence, mostly undated, survives between Mrs Fenton in the country and Mrs Pattinson in Ulverston.[47] Mrs Pattinson's husband collected rents for Mr Fenton, and at some point Mrs Fenton decided to patronize the rent collector's wife's dressmaking business. It was convenient – Samuel Pattinson visited regularly to hand over the rents and could deliver items for fitting. There was rather more than a business relationship between the families and at first Mrs Pattinson did occasional errands in town for Mrs Fenton. From Mrs Pattinson's point of view it must have been a less than happy arrangement for Mrs Fenton was hardly the ideal client. She had a cavalier attitude to punctuation, her pen tended to run away with her and she had difficulty making up her mind:

> My bonnet arrived safely and is very pretty but rather small, I think. I think if I had strings. of a rather wide lace it might be better and will [*you*] put them a little forwarder so as to make the sides of the face a little more – and please make me a bow to fix on for it and tie the lace – it soon looks shabby. If you have not any wider lace please send me half a yard the same as the strings – the bow as well.

> My hat fits very comfortably but after the soft silk that would bend any way it feels rather stiff – I like it very much but I am returning it to have more trimming on – some loops from the crimson round to the other side to fill it up and I think if they were made of the plain velvet they would look well – just – little fancy bows on loops and I would like a bow at the back where the gauze is tied on to fill up a bit – Mr F thinks it a beautiful hat – but I think it a little juvenile – but the members will make it all right – the velvet both plain and ribbed is very pretty. Some thought a bit of feather trimming would look nice – but leave it to you – I don't like great spreading bows – the crimson one is very nice – the canvas is very nice but I still prefer thick Turkey red cotton …

what a trouble I give you.

It sounds as if Mrs Pattinson was being urged to turn a stylish hat into an over-decorated monstrosity. The letters continued:

> [T]he cape is too short – it just cuts off in the worst place for me and shows all the worst parts of me – fortunately it just fits a friend of mine who has a good stylish figure …

> I like two frills and quilting on other people but not on myself, it makes me too round and plain …

> I thought a little cape without any lining just to reach below the waist would be nice – would you give me your advice please. I can't afford anything expensive. I have had a great deal of wear out of the crape clothes and if I live it will do well for winter … I do so dislike being fitted on … it need not be made quite the same just a change somehow and a little crape – there is a kind of embroidered crape … I am giving you a deal of trouble.

Indeed she was, and it was to get worse. The crepe dresses were mourning wear for Mr Fenton who died in 1896. Mrs Fenton had to take over responsibility for his properties, she was lonely and the strain was just too much. Her letter continued: 'When you send my bonnet would you send a bottle of whisky from Mackareth's 3/2 proof Scotch – Dr Mason said I had to have some.' Thereafter, week after week Mrs Pattinson sent her bottles of whisky hidden in corset boxes or wrapped in garments to hide them from the prying eyes of the local carrier.

Other firms had troublesome clients too. Cockshutt and Preston in Kendal in Westmorland kept a draper's shop and did millinery and dressmaking;[48] they served a large district and seem to have operated an informal mail-order service. A number of clients' letters survive and it would seem they were extremely demanding:

> The dress piece I have chosen is to [sic] dark for the occasion it is required for. Will you dispose of it if you can and let me have another much lighter. I will be in the Town soon and will call as I do not like this one now when I see it again I mean it is much to [sic] dark wrote S. Hayhurst from Milnthorpe.

Mrs Wood of Bowness had particular difficulty with her spelling:

> I right to ask if you will be so kind as to send 7 Do of buttons this sizes the morn I sent 2 Yards of paton velvet not so Dark as the Dress. Mrs Ward will be at Kendal Saturday Next Pleas to send By Moor Carryer Wensday [sic].

A lady in Stricklandgate had similar problems:

> Would Mr Cockshot send M Williamson another Peeitcote to look at with only one dress Flounce she will return them at 1 o'clock and the price on them in plain figers PS Send them by the Little girl [*sic*].

Cockshutt's were not always the most efficient of firms; they were serving a large district and were dependent on the vagaries of the local carriers, but the notes they received when things went wrong were peremptory in the extreme: 'will Mr Preston please inquire upstairs what time Mrs Thompson's dress is coming she wants it without fail by 3 o'clock' ran one pencilled missive. Jane Fleming of Ambleside became quite sarcastic:

> I think I am not to have an Ulster Coat from Kendall, I have never received one yet, although I have got a postcard saying you had forwarded it per Bennets – I would really like to know where it asgot [*sic*] to.

Even a Liverpool dressmaker, interviewed in the *Liverpool Review* in September 1887, most of whose work was making dresses for servant girls, complained about the demands of her clients. 'Some people are never satisfied but come back again and again for alterations, until you are sick of the very sight of the thing, and would like to burn it if you dared'!

Conclusion

The nineteenth century saw women establish a near monopoly of the dressmaking trade, and there were dressmakers to cater for all strata of society. However, by the middle of the century if not before, the trade had become oversubscribed. In 1841, for example, there were 89,079 milliners and dressmakers and 17,946 seamstresses in England and Wales according to the census. To compete, dressmakers offered unreasonably low prices and speedy completion of orders, which led customers to expect an almost impossible level of service. This in turn led to dressmakers' employees being grossly overworked. Not until the Children's Employment Commissions of 1843 and 1864 did the true scale of the problem become apparent and even then it would take many years before conditions improved.

And as if troublesome clients, demanding employers and long hours were not enough to put up with, dressmakers were for the most part poorly paid – as we shall see in the next chapter.

5

'At short notice ... and at most economic charges'

The development of the dressmaking trade mirrored the shifts and turns of the national economy. The period c.1780 to c.1816 was a time of unrest and rising prices. There were a series of bad harvests; Britain saw a social upheaval caused by rapid industrialization and urbanization; there was a revolution in France and wars throughout Europe. But nonetheless the economy was vibrant, the population was growing and the pace of fashion change was speeding up, so the developing dressmaking trade was buoyant.

By 1816, prices in Britain had reached an all-time high; they then fell until 1820 when inflation stabilized, and for the next seventy-five years prices for goods other than food remained remarkably static. Food production, however, was affected by the weather, and when the price of bread rose after a bad harvest, the poor were the first to suffer. Consequently, the early nineteenth century was a period of intermittent uprisings among the working poor. Demobbed soldiers returning from the Napoleonic wars swelled the ranks of the unemployed and Luddite workers damaged machines in protest at the low wages and overproduction they were thought to have caused. There was much unrest, and the government, remembering the revolution that had so recently taken place in France, feared that a protesting crowd could easily turn into a rioting mob, and legislated to ban demonstrations.

In the 1850s and 1860s, dressmakers, along with the rest of the workforce, began to see some improvement in their lot. For many people, the middle years of the nineteenth century were a golden age of prosperity and Britain's industries were the most productive in the world. In 1870 her foreign trade was worth four times that of the United States and more than the trades of France, Germany and Italy combined, she grew three-quarters of the food she needed and most of her imports of foodstuffs and raw materials came from her empire. Assisted emigration (and, up to 1867, enforced transportation) meant the empire was also a safety-valve for the problems caused by unrest and unemployment at home. Real wages and prices rose steadily from 1850 to 1870 and most working-class families experienced a 10 per cent increase in their spending power over that period; there was more demand for goods and services and more opportunity for profit.

But it was too good to last. From 1870 to 1873 wages and prices rose sharply, only to slump disastrously in 1873–4. Firstly, there was an agricultural depression, and secondly, by the mid-1870s Britain found herself in competition with Germany and the United States. Real wages and prices fell; meanwhile, the working class was becoming increasingly literate, organized and assertive. The Trades Union Act of 1871 had given trades unions legal status and the boom of the early seventies had encouraged workers to combine to press for improvements in pay and conditions; after 1875 their activities were directed to fighting wage cuts and unemployment. While unionized workers had a little bargaining power, workers like dressmakers who had no such organization were seriously disadvantaged; for many, conditions deteriorated markedly after 1874. In addition, their clients had less money to spend on clothes, production of ready-made garments increased and home dressmaking became popular, helped by the development of paper patterns. Conditions remained bad in the 1880s and unemployment was high, and though there was a temporary improvement in 1893–4 and again around the turn of the century, the depression lasted until 1914.[1]

Wages *c.*1800–1914

Throughout the nineteenth century various bodies and individuals instigated enquiries into the lifestyles of the poorest sections of society and produced horrifying findings. It emerged that market forces had created a large class of people, who, through no fault of their own, had to work desperately hard in dreadful conditions for grossly inadequate rates of pay. Many of them worked in the garment trades and some of them were bespoke dressmakers. But though there was a clearer understanding of the causes of poverty than there had been at the beginning of the century, there was disagreement about how it could best be alleviated; consequently, legislation to create Wage Boards to establish and enforce minimum wages did not reach the statute books until 1909.

Though the perception of dressmaking was that it was an impoverished profession, dressmakers were not uniquely underprivileged. Nineteenth-century wages were low in many trades. Throughout the century, a pound a week was reckoned to be the decent minimum on which a respectable working man could maintain a family, but many men earned considerably less – Charles Booth discovered that, in the 1880s, the earnings of some 178,000 East Enders fell below what he defined as the poverty line of '18s to 21s per week for a moderate family'.[2]

Women fared even worse. The wages of female servants usually included their board and lodging, as was also the case in parts of the dressmaking trade. In 1861 Mrs Beeton listed servants' wages ranging from £5.00 to £9.00 pa for a scullery maid through to £14.00 to £30.00 pa for a cook. In the towns, factories provided jobs for large numbers of women, especially in the textile trades. However, as late as 1906–7 in the cotton industry 40 per cent of women earned under 16s.0d a week, while in the woollen industry 70 per cent earned less than 14s.0d.[3] Many firms paid piecework rates which they adjusted to prevent workers earning too much – Ada Jackson, making caps for Thomas Webster and Co of Leicester, recorded delightedly in her diary in December 1883, 'I have got more money this week than I have ever got in my life, 13s.8d only fancy, I must not get too much or I will have my work docked.'[4] In fact the average female weekly wage in 1888 was found to be just 12s.8d for women and 7s.0d for girls.[5] Dressmakers, therefore, were not exceptionally badly paid.

There were several reasons why women's wages remained low. Comparatively few women were sole breadwinners – though those who were were heavily disadvantaged. Women's wages were seen as supplementary to the family income or as pocket money; men were believed to be physically stronger and thus more useful workers; a high proportion of the female labour force consisted of girls and young women who commanded little respect and had little bargaining power, whereas in the male sector their cohort was balanced by a much higher percentage of experienced older men. Much women's work was unskilled and had come about as production processes became more and more fragmented; women were channelled into unskilled work because their employment was seen as essentially temporary, something that would cease on marriage. This coloured expectations.

According to the Children's Employment Commission of 1864 the usual wage for 'assistants' in the dressmaking trade (by which they seem to have meant second and third hands) ranged from £8.00–16.00 a year to £30.00–70.00 a year in the 'best houses'. Day-workers' ordinary wages varied between 8s.0d and 12s.0d a week in the West End though some specialist day-workers were paid as much as 18s.0d or a pound. In the provinces they were paid less – 5s.6d to 6s.0d a week for ordinary workers and 11s.0d to 12s.0d for specialists. By 1864 there was also a new class of worker – sewing machinists. They tended to be well-paid, usually earning something between 14s.0d and a pound a week. First hands or forewomen were the elite of the profession and few in number; they could earn £60.00 to £120.00 a year. The commissioners interviewed several hundred women to arrive at these averages and they tally with the few surviving records.

For example, when Agnes Dow in Leith went bankrupt in August 1834 her debts included £16.1s.11d to Miss Bell, her milliner, for the period March to October. Miss Bell had lodged with her mistress, and the cost of this was assessed at £23.6s.8d for the same period, and this seems to have formed part of her wages – so Miss Bell's salary worked out at around £60.00 a year of which her lodging took well over half – the bottom end of the pay scale for first hands identified in 1864.[6] In the 1880s, Hannah Mitchell started work as a part-trained apprentice in Derbyshire at 8s.0d a week. She considered her final job to be quite well paid at 12s.0d to 15s.0d a week (£30.00 to £39.00 pa) – again, within the range of the 1864 scale.[7] Many others fared much worse, especially towards the end of the century.

Meyer and Black did a survey of wages in the London garment trade in 1908 and found that they varied wildly. Designers in first-class houses earned up to £200.00 pa, but in one smart house the 'trotter' (or errand girl) earned just 4s.6d a week (£11.14s.0d pa); in a year she wore out three pairs of boots – cost, probably about 30s.

Wages in East End firms in 1908 could vary from 5s.0d to 30s.0d a week if the workers were doing piecework, but 12s.0d or 15s.0d was the norm in a good week (£31.4s.0d to £39.00 pa). For outworkers, payments of one or two shillings for making a whole costume were not uncommon. The interviewers were told that the average dressmaking wage had fallen from 18s.0d in 1906 to 16s.0d in 1908, though they found instances of women paid between 18s.0d and 22s.0d and one cutter/fitter in a 'very good private dressmaking house' who earned an astonishing £4.00 a week. But on average, wages were actually lower than they had been fifty years earlier.[8]

Hobson's Charity in Cambridge listed the wages their dressmaking apprentices were to receive in the 1880s and '90s – they normally worked the first year for nothing, received something between 2s.6d and 5s.0d a week for the second year, thereafter their wage rose incrementally 'if merited' until the end of their term.[9]

Dressmakers may have considered themselves badly paid, but rates for seamstresses were unbelievably low. They were paid 2s.0d a dozen for corset making; 4d each for dressing gowns; 2s.0d a dozen for chemises, combinations and nightdresses; 1s.1d a dozen for blouses; and 4s.6d a dozen for skirts. Weekly earnings averaged 6s.0d to 10s.0d for which women were working up to fourteen hours a day and paying for their own needles and thread.[10] There is no shortage of evidence about the hardships caused by sweating in the clothing trade.

Selling

Any commodity has to be advertised, and as more and more dressmaking firms were established, customers had to be wooed. Sometimes it was price, or location, that determined which dressmaker a particular client would patronize, but in most areas there were many firms to choose from. Ladies were fickle, and unless they found a real 'treasure' they would take their custom elsewhere on a chance recommendation or if the price was right. Individuals would patronize different people for different jobs. Mrs Susanna Ingleby in Staffordshire (see Chapter 10), for example, used the services of at least fourteen dressmakers over a twenty-year period. Dressmakers, therefore, had actively to seek custom. Many advertised in the press, sometimes on a regular basis, more usually in April–May and October–November when new fashions came out. Most such advertisements specify particular dates and times. On 6 May 1829, for example, the Misses Fowkes advertised in the *Leicester Herald and General Advertiser* that they had:

> ... the honour to announce that they have opened a showroom opposite Miss Linwood's on Belgrave Gate ... [*showing*] an assortment of elegant Millinery and Dresses of the present fashion of the Beau Monde – to open on the 11th May.

In 1836 'Madame Ange' advertised in the *Cheltenham Looker-On* of 14 May that she:

> ... has the honour to inform the Ladies of Cheltenham and its vicinity that she has just received from Paris THE NEW FASHIONS FOR THIS SEASON for which she respectfully solicits an early inspection at her Showroom 376 High Street.

Across the country, there were hundreds of similar advertisements for what were in effect private views. Few gave any clear idea of what the ladies could expect to see. In that respect, the advertisement on 26 March 1836, by Mr C. Beales of Nottingham, acting as agent for 'fashions by Louis Stumpke' is unusual. He advertised a display of '15 elegant drawn figures richly coloured and displayed in two distinct rows ... with a report'.

Advertising was relatively cheap. Thomas Smith's *Successful Advertising* was first published in 1878 and gave some information about prices. *The Times* and other national dailies charged approximately 4s.0d for four lines of text, while most women's weekly and monthly magazines charged 3d to 6d. Amongst the books kept by Shepherd and Manning in Northampton is a scrapbook of printed matter and advertisements created by the firm between 1862 and 1909, together with notes of the printing costs. In 1862 a two-column advert for mourning in the local paper cost 2s.6d for thirteen insertions, and a slightly longer one for 'Spring novelties' cost 3s.6d. A single insertion of a similar advertisement for bridal wear cost 3s.0d, or £1.12s.6d for a quarter, £2.12s.0d for a half-year or £4.10s.0d for a full year[11] – which goes some way to explaining the repetitive nature of much newspaper advertising at this date.

But by no means all firms advertised in the press. In May 1840 eleven Leicester dressmakers advertised their fashion displays in the papers but we know that at that date there were at least fifty-four dressmaking firms in the town; it seems likely that many of the forty-three others held similar viewings but did not advertise them in the press. It would appear that quite often fliers were sent, or delivered by hand, to regular clients – for example, Mrs Walker stated in the *Leicester Journal* on 31 May 1844 that there would be 'no circulars sent' – implying that this was unusual.

Record-keeping in the dressmaking trade

Our knowledge of wages, prices and profits is hampered by the quality of firms' record-keeping. This varied enormously. At the end of the century, George Henry Richardson produced a book, *Drapers', Dressmakers' and Milliners' Accounts* (the third edition came out in 1904). His advice was aimed mainly at large firms and department stores, and he recommended a bewildering array of books and forms to deal with all eventualities, including packing, shipping and returned goods. Chapter 5 dealt with 'Dressmakers' Milliners' and Workroom Accounts', but few firms, even the department stores discussed in the next chapter, kept anything like the complex system of records he recommended.

In February 1873 the *Milliners' Dressmakers' and Warehousemans' Gazette* carried an article on 'drapery frauds' and urged its readers to keep proper client books because 'reference to a file of bills is too tedious in the pressure of daily business'. One of Scissors' many criticisms in *Why Dressmaking Does Not Pay* (1895) was that 'many dressmakers keep no book'. She pointed out that it was an offence under the Bankruptcy Act not to keep proper records and advised that at the very least, small firms should keep daybooks as a record of what had been agreed, thus avoiding disputes with customers. This implies that as late as 1895 there were firms that kept no records at all, though where records do survive, they usually are daybooks.

Efficient record-keeping was not always the key to success, however. The McCleod sisters in Edinburgh kept immaculately neat daybooks, but the entries are not all in sequence and are interspersed with notes about what clients owed and what they had spent on straw-plait, bits are cut out and pages are missing.[12] Luck and Sons in Darlington (Durham) kept the most haphazard of records – all sorts of different accounts, out of order, in books with misleading titles – but nonetheless ran a perfectly successful business.[13] D. Mitchell, drapers and milliners in Dysart, with another branch in Pathhead (Fife, Scotland), flourished but kept execrable records.[14] Like many firms they had daybooks, separate ones for the drapery and millinery parts of their business. A heavy pencil cross through an entry denoted payment had been made, but the books are hopelessly untidy, the assistants' handwriting uniformly illegible, and entries were interspersed with pencil lists of prices.

Accounts were kept in all sorts of odd books – paper was still quite expensive in the nineteenth century and books were often re-used. For example, a draper's daybook in Leicestershire Record Office is to be found amongst the papers of Thomas Deacon, clockmaker of Lutterworth. The book was originally a customer's account book, covering the period 1833–48, probably for William Hackett, tailor, grocer and draper of Barlestone near Market Bosworth – the Hacketts and Deacons were related by marriage. Later, the clockmaker used the back of it to record cleaning and repairing clocks.[15] A dressmaker's daybook (1859 to 1861) from Braintree in Essex was kept in a book recording sales of slate.[16] Elizabeth Edwards, a Welshpool (Montgomery, Wales) milliner, kept her 1859 daybook in a book that had been used for several other purposes[17] – part of it contains legal cases written in a beautiful ornate hand in 1771, by, or for, Thomas Griffiths of Clifford's Inn. Miss Clarke, dressmaker in Guildford, Surrey, kept her 1873–83 accounts in the back of a school exercise book full of mathematical problems, written out in the most beautiful copperplate script, and almost all of them refer to business activities.[18] Mrs Pattinson of Ulverston kept a monthly profit and loss account in pencil, on the back of the calendars she received from local stationers.[19]

Fabric prices

Fabric prices were lower than they had been in the eighteenth century but they were still a significant part of the price of a dress. There was little change in the cost of material between 1800 and 1900 so Table 5 is not subdivided by date:

Table 5 Nineteenth-century fabric prices.

Fabric type	Price per yard
calico (coarse cotton)	3d–1s.2d
flannel	1s.4d–2s.4d
flannelette	3¾d
muslin	4½d–6d
black muslin	1s.6d
worked muslin	7s.6d
velvet	4s.6d
merino (fine wool)	1s.9d–3s.0d
linsey (thick linen or wool-and-linen)	6d–7½d
holland (linen)	2½d–1s.3d
waterproof	4s.11d–6s.11d
satin	8s-6d–10s-6d
woollen cloth	2s.6d–10s.0d
tartan plaid	1s.2d–1s.6d
tweed	5s-6d–11s.0d
silk	2s-6d–11s
'surah' silk	2s.0d
moiré (watered silk)	2s.0d
velveteen	2s.8d
lawn	3½d–6d
Norwich crepe	10½d–2s.9d
crepe	3s.9d
paramatta (lightweight wool or wool-and-silk mix)	2s.0d+
cotton print	7d
alpaca	1s.6d

As curators of dress collections know, many nineteenth-century fabrics were of very high quality and so dresses withstood numerous alterations and re-makes. However, by the end of the century this was beginning to change. In *The Art of Dress* (1879) Mrs Haweis observed: 'Modern black silk is chiefly shoddy loaded with dye; so is much of the calico on the market weighted with china clay.'[20] By the 1890s silks were being treated with oxide of tin to make them stiffer and ensure they rustled attractively. Today, such silks that survive are as brittle as burnt paper.

Prices and profits – some case studies

Dressmaking was a precarious trade. By the mid-nineteenth century, if not before, it was oversubscribed; to stay in business dressmakers had to cut their prices to the bone. A woman working on a large enough scale to employ staff needed a good business head to work out what she could charge, when and whether to let staff go in slack times, when and if she dared turn work away when her staff were at full stretch. Sisters or friends in partnership tended to do better than women on their own. They could manage with fewer staff and when times were hard both partners could take a pay cut. Firms that had additional income streams – like haberdashery, drapery or the sale of ready-made garments or accessories – had the best chance of staying afloat. However, an examination of directories shows just how few dressmaking businesses lasted for more than a year or two. Of the eighty-three firms listed in *Slater's Leicester Directory* for 1847, for example, only twenty-five were still in business in 1850. It was a pattern repeated across the country.

The surviving daybooks are most useful as a record of what different types of firms charged their customers. Sometimes it is also possible to estimate the overall level of profit firms were making, though it is nearly always an estimate as the figures for firms' outgoings are seldom complete. The following case studies are sub-divided by type, but unfortunately there are comparatively few surviving records and none for any of the large court dressmaking businesses. The picture the case studies present is reasonably consistent, but with so few extant records any conclusions have to be treated with caution.

A. Firms catering for wealthy clients

The McCleod sisters in Edinburgh[21] ran a millinery business. Their daybooks survive for the period January 1803 to September 1805. They made and altered caps and bonnets for a wealthy clientele in Edinburgh and they also sent work to out-of-town clients as far afield as London and Fort William. They record up to five sales a day, though many days no sales at all are listed. Most of their clients seem to have been known by name – only a handful of sales related to passing trade – and there seem to have been about seventy-four regular customers. By far their most frequent customer was a Miss Macquhae, another milliner, with whom they had several transactions a month. In January 1805 she owed them £36.9s.3d. Some of their other customers bought in bulk – probably also for re-sale. For example, on 4 April 1805, Mrs Allan Cameron at Fort William bought six straw hats at 18s.0d, six white chip hats and four brown chip hats at 10s, three buff willow hats at 6s and three white willow hats at 5s.0d – a total of £12.4s.6d.

The McCleods' made-up hats were expensive. On 31 May 1803 they sold a hat to Lady Glascow for £1.8s.0d, for instance, and on 5 June 1805 Miss Simpson bought a hat for £1.14s.0d and paid a further 2s to have it lined. Even their alterations were dear – on 28 May 1803 Lady Balcarra paid 7s.0d to have a hat altered, and on 17 November 1804 they altered a 'Blue Chip' for Miss Buchanan for 5s.6d – more than some small town milliners charged for making an entire hat.

Table 6 analyzes their trade as shown in the daybooks with the figures rounded to the nearest 10s.0d.

Table 6 Transactions 1803–4, the McCleod sisters.

1803	Turnover	Number of transactions	Alterations	Made-up	Sold
Jan	£3.10s	9	5	0	4
Feb	£19.00	24	13	5	6
March	£27.00	39	22	8	9
April	£38.10s	37	41	7	9
May	£24.00	68	32	11	4
June	£31.00	70	32	18	5
July	£20.00	44	21	0	0
Aug	£24.00	31	13	3	6
Sept	£8.00	21	12	3	4
Oct	£35.10s	31	13	11	3
Nov	£23.10s	32	14	3	11
Dec	£15.10s	32	14	4	5
TOTALS	£249.10s	429	231	73	66
1804					
Jan	£13.00	24	14	5	2
Feb	£29.00	46	21	5	12
March	£25.00	56	25	13	7
April	£84.00*	121	57	22	6

May	£57.00	110	43	23	24
June	£39.00	88	34	29	10
July	£29.00	65	25	19	8
Aug	£12.00	42	16	12	8
Sept	£22.00	72	19	21	18
Oct	£18.00	31	16	1	13
Nov	£21.00	36	19	6	6
Dec	£19.00	37	10	9	9
TOTALS	£368.00	728	299	165	123

* Included £29.9s.0d-worth of straw plait.

It is impossible to tell what profit the Misses McCleod actually made as they do not itemize their bills with a sum for making. There were three sisters, and their workload implies that they would not have had to employ staff – though they may have had an unpaid apprentice or two. However, they were operating in a fashionable part of the city and may well have paid a high rental for their premises. With only the daybook as evidence, it looks as if they should have done well, but the McCleod daybook is to be found amongst the Edinburgh bankruptcy records.

Milliner in Evesham (Worcestershire).[22] This lady is unnamed but seems to have served a well-to-do clientele. The daybook starts in April 1883 and covers the whole of 1884 and January–November 1885. Most of this analysis relates to 1883 and 1884. Most of her hats cost 8s.0d or more, though turbans were usually 1s.6d and alterations often cost less than a shilling. Ten shillings seems to have been the average price per transaction, so she was charging rather less than the McCleods. She made mostly hats, caps and bonnets and there are very occasional references to making other items like collars and muffs but these made up less than 0.5 per cent of her total workload.

Our milliner's profit for the nine months of 1883 was £42.16s.0d, for 1884 it was £30.11s.6d but for the eleven months of 1885 it went down to £20.00, which suggests that this was a business in decline. The profit seems to have been approximately 10 per cent of her annual turnover – which was £340.00 for the nine months of 1883 and £290.00 for 1884. On top of this she presumably made some profit on materials but there is no way of estimating what this might have been. The firm had a client base of about forty-five. A good deal of work seems to have been making hats for 'stock' – presumably to sell as ready-made. The

Table 7 Transactions arranged by month.

	Jan	Feb	March	April	May	June	July	Aug	Sept	Oct	Nov	Dec
1883				145	144	99	70	32	50	113	25	8
1884	27	9	38	52	80	90	33	0	80	93	42	37

daybook costs these as if they were sold, and the figures given here reflect that assumption. In 1883 she made 686 hats of which 390 were for stock, 15 were what she describes as 'orders' (probably for other firms) and the remainder were for named clients. In 1884 the figures were 581 hats made, of which 284 were for stock and 53 were 'orders'.

The workload for most of 1883 and for the heavier months of 1884 would imply that our milliner employed several staff, so her profits would have been further depleted by paying wages [Table 7].

On 28 January 1884 the Countess of Yarmouth summoned her to Park Hall to order mourning bonnets. The fifth Marquis had died on the 24th. Lady Yarmouth's own three crepe trimmed hats cost £1.6s.9d, and she bought hats for 'Mademoiselle', the housekeeper, the two kitchen-maids, the head housemaid, the second housemaid, the laundry maid and her assistant, the nurse and the two nursery maids and Lady Margaret, the youngest of her six daughters. The whole order came to £6.3s.5½d. It was the only time in the period covered by the books that the countess patronized our milliner, and no doubt she did so in 1884 only because of the need to get her household into decent mourning as quickly as possible at a time of year when travelling further afield would have been difficult. Nonetheless, the fact that she chose this milliner rather than one of the five other drapery and/or millinery firms that served Evesham in the early 1880s suggests that it was the best firm in town.

B. Firms catering for the middle class

In 1894, Jeanette Davis wrote her *Elements of Modern Dressmaking* for students, apprentices and professional dressmakers. The prices she recommended apply to this section of the market and had changed little in a hundred years. She suggested that servants' print gowns could cost between 2s.6d and 7s.0d, but 3s.6d to 5s.0d was the average; fashionably made washing dresses cost 7s.6d to 15s.0d, but averaged out at 9s.6d; between 10s.6d and 17s.6d was usual for woollen dresses; washing silks fell within a similar range and evening dresses cost 15s.0d to 30s.0d. These figures were for labour costs only and seem very optimistic. There follow three sets of records for firms which provided middle-of-the-range goods for a middle-class clientele – wives and daughters of tradesmen, farmers, clergy and some country gentry.

Miss Clarke of Guildford (1873–83)[23] was the only one of the three to work in a fashionable town and the only one to leave details of her prices. The transactions are not recorded by month, but it is possible to analyse her workload year by year. She was not working on a large scale; indeed, her dressmaking seems to have been very much a part-time occupation. In 1873 she seems to have had sixteen clients, eleven in 1874, eighteen in 1875; in 1876 she did a little work for a Miss Young but nobody else. It may be that she was ill, travelling or occupied elsewhere as there are no records for 1877 and 1878, but by 1879 she was back in business with seventeen customers, none of whom, with the possible exception of a Mrs Smith, overlapped with her previous clientele. By 1880 she had twenty-two customers, nineteen in 1881, twenty-two again in 1882 and a mere thirteen in 1883. Each year saw new clients replace some of the old ones.

She made dresses, bodices, blouses, skirts, jackets, capes, cloaks, costumes and accessories and did a good deal of altering, re-making and trimming. She also washed and cleaned certain items. Tables 8 shows her yearly income from her work and the numbers of transactions for making and repairing or cleaning.

Table 8 Transactions 1873–83, Miss Clarke of Guildford.

Year	Annual income	Garments made	Garments repaired/cleaned
1873	£13.5s.3d	65	23
1874	£6.3s.11d	67	33
1875	£13.9s.10d	79	38
1876	£1.8s.0d	3	1
1879 (May–Dec)	£8.10s.9d	36	8
1880	£9.6s.4d	37	5
1881	£5.4s.3d	23	7
1882	£9.6s.10½d	31	6
1883	£5.17s.9d	23	8

We have no way of knowing what her overheads were. She did not supply fabric though she usually charged for sundries. It seems unlikely that Miss Clarke was able to manage all of this work on her own, at least not during the 1873–5 phase of her business, so she may well have employed an apprentice or shared the tasks with someone else in her household – she certainly did not earn enough from her dressmaking to employ a full-time assistant. Her charges were low. Making a dress usually cost between 3s.0d and 6s.6d, though the cotton dress she made for Miss Blanthorne on 20 March 1874 cost a mere 2s.5d. Top of her price range was the ulster she made for Mrs Ranger in November 1881 which cost 8s.0d. 'Trimming a dress' usually cost 3s.0d, while repairs seldom cost more than 1s.6d and for 'Mounting skirt into band' for Mrs Watson in July 1875 she charged just 6d. Miss Clarke could not have lived on the proceeds of her dressmaking alone. Perhaps she did something else as well, or perhaps she was partly supported by a brother or father.

Mrs Allinson[24] established a business supplying ladies and children's underclothing, baby linen and fancy goods in Whitehaven (Cumbria), sometime in the 1870s. Suppliers' invoices show she was buying from a wide range of firms in Manchester, Nottingham and London. She was buying ready-made goods, some created specifically for her, as a memorandum from Humphreys, McChlery and Shoolbred shows. She also made items from scratch, employed a 'trainee' and was an agent for Marie Bayard's paper patterns. She was able to pay her trainee 8s.0d per week (£20.00 a year) the same rate that a second hand would have been paid. Only one (undated) invoice for her work survives – for a bonnet costing £1.5s.6d. If this was typical, she was operating at the upper end of the market.

Her husband, Thomas Allinson, owned property at Cleaton Moor and in 1881 paid £3.9s.0d in income tax and inhabited house duty, implying that the household enjoyed quite a high standard of living. Odd household bills survive that reinforce this impression; for example, their monthly butcher's bill was around £2.4s.8d and their son's school fees (at Mrs Matche's academy) for the Easter term of 1880 were £13.10s.0d. However, there is insufficient evidence to tell us how great a contribution Hannah's business made to the family's prosperity.

Elizabeth Pattinson[25] of Ulverston's dressmaking accounts survive for 1895 and 1897. The 1897 account is reproduced here [Table 9]. It is taken from the pencilled accounts she kept on the back of her calendar and it is impossible to analyse it in any way, though it seems she made a loss in January and October. We have no way of knowing how many transactions the figures represent, or how much of her profit came from the ready-made goods we know she sold. She

Table 9 Mrs Pattinson's accounts for 1897.

Jan	−£5.13s.0¾d	July	£2.8s.2½d
Feb	£10.8s.9½d	Aug	£11.0s.2½d
March	£9.1s.1½d	Sept	£15.10s.10d
April	£3.2s.6½d	Oct	−£5.7s.3d
May	£13.2s.6½d	Nov	£13.4s.1d
June	£15.15s.10d	Dec	£14.16s.7½d

conducted her business in a separate property so she must have paid rent and fuel bills. Mrs Fenton's letters make no mention of employees, but it is possible that Mrs Pattinson did have an apprentice or an assistant as most months there were payments labelled 'N' and 'F', and towards the end of the 1890s her niece/adopted daughter, Maggie, probably helped her. If the account includes all her expenses, she was actually doing quite well – her total profit for 1897 seems to have been £99.3s.0d.

C. Cheap firms

Firms existed to cater for all social strata. Cheap firms did not only supply goods to the poor, they also sold everyday garments to respectable families.[26] This section deals with the records of five such firms. These businesses were working to a very low profit margin, for customers who could not always pay their bills, and, not surprisingly, three of this sample went bankrupt. Such bankruptcies were common in the nineteenth century; Stana Nenadic calculated that between 1861 and 1891, 55 per cent of male-owned businesses and 59 per cent of female-owned ones in Victorian Edinburgh went into receivership within three years.[27] What is interesting here is that in all three cases it is possible to see *why* the firm went bankrupt.

William Barwick[28] ran a millinery business in York. His daybook for 1823–5 survives in York Archives; it has very few entries, is disordered and quite difficult to read. His charges covered a wide range – from 3s.0d (for a new black bonnet for Mrs Sarah Benson on 1 October 1823) through 9s.11d (for a black bonnet with trimming for Mrs Sowerby, three days later) to £1.11s.0d (for a 'New Leghorn Bonnet' for Mrs Smith on 8 November). He sold frills (at 1s.6d and 2s.6d) and stays (usually 10s.6d a pair), cleaned and altered bonnets and cleaned feathers (2s.0d or 2s.6d). The year 1824 is the only year for which full figures are available and his turnover for that year seems to have been £30.8s.2d from about seventy transactions. This figure makes no allowance for the cost of materials as these are not listed separately, nor for any other overheads. In fact his profit in 1824 is unlikely to have exceeded £15.00. Such a workload could have been handled by one competent milliner – perhaps Mr Barwick's wife or daughter. He could not afford to live on his profit, and William Barwick was committed to the Debtor's Prison in York in 1826. [Plate 18]

Binningtons of York[29] made both dresses and headgear. A daybook survives for 18 May 1827 to September 1828, but though it is inscribed 'James Binnington' the only Binnington to appear in the York directory of 1823 (the nearest in date to this daybook) is Mrs C. Binnington, milliner and dressmaker of Bootham Row. It may well be that she was James' wife, but as a 'feme couvert' she could not go bankrupt so it was her husband and partner who was jailed. The Binnington prices were very similar to Barwick's, but the records are even poorer – faded and illegible with much crossing out. The firm also sold fabrics and accessories and did cleaning and repair work but they were working on a much larger scale than Barwicks, with almost ten times the workload. This record has been analysed on a monthly basis by numbers of transactions alone because the book is so difficult to read that it cannot be analysed by type of transaction [Table 10].

Working on an average profit of 5s.0d per transaction this implies an annual profit of around £160.00. It should have been possible for them to have paid their staff – the workload would suggest that they needed at least a first hand, a second hand, an improver and an apprentice or two. Assuming they were paying

Table 10 Transactions 1827–8, Binningtons of York.

1827		1828	
May	37	Jan	43
June	80	Feb	29
July	82	March	78
Aug	57	April	63
Sept	47	May	131
Oct	46	June	98
Nov	47	July	86
Dec	33	Aug	55
		Sept	4

low wages, their first hand would have cost them approximately £50.00 pa and the second hand approximately £20.00 pa. The improver and the apprentices would probably have been unpaid. If Mrs Binnington worked herself, they might even have managed with fewer staff. With a total wage bill of approximately £70.00 a year, the firm should have run at a profit. It is likely the firm failed because Binningtons seldom supplied the fabric for the garments they made thus reducing their profits. James Binnington therefore found himself in the Debtor's Prison in York. [Plate 18]

George Nicholson's[30] bankruptcy came before the Debtor's Court in York in February 1847. His account books were surrendered and one of them, labelled 'Mary Kemp Book', survives. Mary Kemp was a dressmaker who, presumably, worked for Mr Nicholson. The book is arranged by client rather than in date order and covers the period 1844–6; 117 names are listed for 1844 of which about 20 appear to be duplicates, giving a client base of about ninety-seven. Lady French is mentioned, as is 'Mrs Labron's servant', and some out-of-town addresses appear – Ellerstone, Buythorpe, Sutton – but for the most part it is impossible to trace who patronized George Nicholson's shop. There are some changes over the three years as new clients replaced old ones, but the number remained about 100 [Table 11].

Nicholson's was a very cheap firm. Dresses cost 3s.0d to 5s.0d, spencers 2s.0d, bonnets usually 3s.6d, cloaks 5s.0d and caps one to four shillings. The firm did washing (1s.6d for a dress), embroidery ('Scalop-work' cost 1s.3d for an unspecified length), made bustles, sleeves, berthas, habit-shirts and collars,

Plate 18 The Debtors' Prison in York.

Table 11 Transactions 1844–5, George Nicholson of York.

Dressmaking	Alterations	Caps/cloaks	Other repairs, etc.	Bonnets	Profit
1844					
118	27	46	42	19	£40.3s.0d
1845					
173	37	48	42	20	£52.9s.0d
1846					
150	29	42	38	30	£46.16s.0d

and did a large number of repairs and alterations. The profit totals exclude the cost of materials but include some estimates where making costs are left blank or are illegible.

It is not always clear from the bills, but it appears that, like Binnington's, Nicholson's usually made up dresses using fabric supplied by their customers. Of the 200 or so items made in 1844, for example, only 13 used materials supplied by the firm. This is almost certainly the reason the firm went bankrupt. There was little profit on the linings and sundries they did supply; the workload would suggest at least two employees – perhaps more at busy times – but the profits would barely cover their wages. Again, the firm could not survive on such a low-profit margin. However, perhaps they learnt from experience; in 1851, a George Nicholson, by then in his fifties, was running a draper's shop on Parliament Street in York employing six men.

Elizabeth Edwards[31] was a milliner in Welshpool in Wales whose 1859 daybook survives in the National Library. Her prices were extremely low – 8d for three 'shapes', 6d for altering a bonnet and supplying net for Mrs Jones, shoemaker, in October, 3s.6d for a new bonnet for Emma Davies at the Vicarage and a further 4s.10d for 'ribbond' and trimmings in November, and a shilling for dying and enlarging a hat for Miss Sarah Hughes in the same month. Her prices ranged between 2s.0d and 12s.0d. Many weeks she recorded only two or three transactions, but in April and May business looked up. On 19 May she had a record seven customers and on two other days that month she had four. Her profit from making hats was approximately £35.00 pa – it is impossible to be more accurate as parts of this book are illegible. However, she could easily have managed all the work by herself or with the aid of an apprentice, and if she kept her overheads to a minimum by working from home, she was, in fact, making a reasonable living – about 15s.0d a week.

Dressmaker in Rotherham (Yorkshire), 1890s.[32] This lady is unnamed. She charged 1s.9d for a cheap frock, 9s.6d for a top-of-the-range dress, 8s.6d for a costume, 5s.0d for a cloak, 3s.0d for a blouse and approximately 3s.0d for alterations. She is not always specific about what she actually charged for the job, and sometimes she seems to have sold the makings of a garment rather than the made-up article. It is impossible to work out how much she made per annum except by doing a rough multiplication of the numbers of items she made each year by the average price for those jobs she did cost. She executed about a hundred transactions each year and thus made an estimated profit of £27.00. There are several lots of handwriting in her daybook, and at the beginning of the book she records the arrivals of Miss Epworth, Miss Rees and Miss Clegg. Perhaps they were apprentices. Her profit margin would not seem to allow for paying trained staff.

It is possible to identify some of her clients from contemporary Rotherham directories. Mrs Tradewell was almost certainly the wife of Thomas Tradewell, 'foreman' in Effingham Street. Mrs Cresswell must have been the butcher's wife from the Shambles, and Mrs Galbraithe was married to the bookseller. Mrs Seiles' husband was a brickmaker, Mrs Cowlishaw's was a brewer and Mrs Russum's was a brushmaker; however, we cannot identify the dressmaker herself – there were twenty-eight dressmakers listed in the 1887 Rotherham Directory and three more in nearby Masbrough. They served a population of 42,050 (in 1891) in the town itself with more in the outlying villages. Over the six years the daybook covers, our dressmaker was patronized by 102 families. She made almost anything they needed from bridesmaid's dresses to a cycling skirt (3s.0d) for Miss Mabel Fox.

Madame Bailey in Chelmsford (Essex) left a daybook covering the period 1893 to 1915.[33] She charged between 2s.0d and 5s.6d for dresses and 9d to 3s.3d for blouses. She would make anything her customers required and seems to have specialized in children's clothes. On 15 May 1900, for example, she made eight pinafores, four white petticoats and three 'nickers plus buttons' for Mrs Matthews' family – total 9s.9d which included postage. She never had more than fifteen customers at a time but many of them had large families. Her turnover was small, ranging between £8.4s.0d for thirty-one transactions (in 1893) and £2.7s.0d for eight transactions (in 1896), so presumably she was able to do all the work herself. Like many married dressmakers, her work contributed to the household income but would not have enabled her to support herself.

D. Small drapers

Many small drapers did tailoring and/or dressmaking and millinery. Often garment-making formed a very small part of such firms' overall business. Sometimes, no doubt, the draper's wife or daughter made a little pin money by 'obliging' special customers; sometimes it was worth the firm's while to pay a local woman to do the work to retain the client's goodwill. Dorothy Davis in *Janes, Drapers of Egham* (1991) implies that the dressmaking department there was run by William Janes' daughters in the 1850s. Records survive for a number of such firms.

William Hackett of Barlestone (Leicestershire)[34] left accounts covering the period 1833 to 1848. He appears in contemporary directories as 'grocer, draper and tailor', and the accounts include payments for drapery, tailoring, millinery – especially cap-making – and dressmaking, with very occasional references to groceries which presumably have been entered by mistake in the drapery book. The accounts are laid out by customer name, but as each page was filled, that customer's account moved to a page further on in the book. Unfortunately, different client's pages filled at different rates, so the book becomes extremely jumbled and difficult to follow.

Prices and the volume of work seem to have remained pretty constant throughout the period so the accounts for just one year – 1834 – have been analysed. The firm's turnover that year for drapery and garment-making was approximately £40.00. Of that, £15.10s.6d was the profit from tailoring and £3.1s.4d was the profit from millinery and dressmaking, with a further 11s.0d earned from quilting two bedspreads; it is therefore clear that dressmaking accounted for a very small percentage of the firm's takings. The firm did not charge high prices. Men's coats cost around 7s.0d to make, women's gowns two to four shillings and caps one or two shillings. Country people could get almost everything they needed in the way of clothing from Hackett's. Between March 1833 and July 1837, for example, one of his customers, Sarah Bailey, bought two ready-made gowns (including quite an expensive print one for 9s.6d) and had eight others made. Hackett's also made her two caps and a bonnet and sold her an assortment of shifts, stays, stockings, pattens, shawls, ribbons and fabrics.

Cockshutt and Preston of Kendal were yet another such firm.[35] They were drapers who did millinery and dressmaking and unfortunately their records are not good enough for proper analysis. Again, the firm seems to have been working for a rural and none-too-fashionable market. In 1868 they were charging 6s.0d to 8s.0d for hats, and 3s.6d to 5s.6d for making dresses and 2s.6d for making an opera cloak. Most of their clients seem to have brought their own fabrics and Cockshutt's only provided lace, lining, trimmings, etc. We know from clients' letters that they employed a dressmaker, Miss Lister. She probably worked alone or with an apprentice and her work can only just have covered her wages.

E.J. Clarke of Bourn in Cambridgeshire kept daybooks but they seldom give prices.[36] His work was approximately half repairs and half making. Dying a skirt for Miss Roper cost 3s.0d, on 30 January 1889; repairing Miss Briscoe's jacket and 'working the holes' cost 8d, on 7 December 1889. Mr Clarke employed two young women, but whether they worked in the shop or did dressmaking or both, we cannot tell. He paid a Miss Custance 5s.6d a week and Miss Pepper 8s.0d (£14.6s.0d and £20.00 pa). For such firms, the fact that dressmaking was available on the premises probably encouraged clients to buy fabric from them, thus justifying the existence of a dressmaking workroom that barely paid its way. The fact that small drapers could charge such low prices, however, affected the prices that could be charged by individual dressmakers working for similar clienteles.

E. At the bottom of the heap

Dressmakers catered for all classes of society. In 1843 the Children's Employment Commissioners received a letter from Dr Shaw at the Leicester Infirmary:

> In this town there is a considerable number of dressmakers employed by the poorer classes. This depends on the fact of the wives of the mechanics being in general entirely ignorant of all domestic knowledge, and who consequently are unable to make their own dresses, etc.

The commissioners also reported complaints from working men in Birmingham about their wives' inability to sew. Sam Page (interviewee 360) was specific: 'It would be a great advantage to the family if the wife knew how to cut out, make and repair the linen.' Sixteen-year-old Caroline Ormer (interviewee 449), who worked for a London coffin-maker, confirmed that neither she nor her mother could sew. Her interviewer reported that she

> ... cannot cut out and make any part of her things; is obliged to put them out and pay for them; it would have been an advantage if she had been taught such things; her mother cannot make things for her.

In the 1850s, Matthew Arnold, in his role as inspector of elementary schools, reported on a family in a Lincolnshire village who were receiving poor relief but were nonetheless found to be in debt to the local dressmaker.[37] The many women who had started work as children and had little or no schooling had had no opportunity to learn to sew.

An interview with a 'cheap dressmaker' was reported in the *Liverpool Review* on 17 September 1887. She was probably working for just this sort of clientele. The un-named interviewee described what she was paid for different types of dresses:

> That depends on the style of it. If it were a plain servant's dress, I would get three shillings. If there was much drapery about it, seven shillings and if it was a very stylish sort of dress ten shillings.

This dressmaker was working from her bedroom – a rented upstairs room – and she employed an apprentice and rented a sewing machine for 2s.6d a week. She admitted that most of her work was servants' dresses and that each one took about two days to make. She reckoned that, on average, she took 10s.0d a week, so presumably she was actually living on about 5s.0d after she had paid her rent, machine-hire, and fed her apprentice.

Some such dressmakers took on outworkers to help with large commissions or at busy times. Mary Ann Jackson at 9, Pares Street, Leicester seems to have been one such employee.[38] She was the wife of John Jackson, a foreman, and the couple had one adult daughter, Ada, who, in 1883, wrote a diary. They were a prosperous working-class family – John Jackson owned two houses in Chestnut Street which he rented out and the family had a piano – a great symbol of working-class success. Mary Ann had no need to work, but it would seem she did occasional jobs for Mrs Dora Twigger of Havelock Street. We do not know what Mrs Jackson was paid, and fortunately she was only earning pin-money, for Mrs Twigger was a poor payer. 'Mrs Twigger sent the money for that cape last night, it has been done about twelve months – "Better late than never" I should think that is her motto', wrote Ada on 26 April.

Some cheap dressmakers did not work from home but moved from household to household making and mending. Eliza Spurrett in Leicester employed a Miss Goddard and a Miss Clayton in that capacity in the 1830s and paid them two or three shillings and their keep for a few days' work several times a year.[39] The practice was most common in country districts. For example, over in Derbyshire, Barbara Hill, a travelling dressmaker, was employed to make Emma Jane Longsdon a dress to wear on New Year's Day 1841. She arrived on

28 December and the dress was ready the following day, probably because she worked through the night.[40] Emma Jane kept a diary and from it we know that her grandfather was careful of his money and it seems that he was determined to get his money's worth out of Barbara. No dressmaker was going to sit gossiping with the servants on his watch!

A writer in the *Girls' Own Paper* on 24 January 1885 actually thought going out to work in private houses was 'one of the best openings for many girls who are not clever enough … to be clerks or book-keepers. They are well-paid and can earn from two and sixpence to three shillings a day, and are fed as well. ' However, at the same period in Hanley (Staffordshire) the Hammersley family employed a Mrs Turnock on that basis. She came twice a year. Each time she made a new dress apiece for Mrs Hammersley and her two daughters. She also refurbished old dresses for them and mended garments and bed-linen. In return she got her 'meat', some cast-off clothing, and a shilling or two[41] – it is unlikely that she would have agreed with the writer in the *Girls' Own Paper*.

Conclusion

Wages, prices and profits varied widely between different categories of firms. Conditions for dressmakers like Mrs Turnock and women working for small bespoke dressmaking firms remained grim well into the twentieth century; however, things were changing and by the third quarter of the nineteenth century some dressmakers were beginning to see positive improvements as we shall see in the next chapter.

6

The watershed of the 1870s

While the new developments in the dressmaking trade did not all take place in the 1870s and different regions experienced them at different times, that was the decade when most dressmakers, in most parts of the country, would have been aware that change was afoot. It seems appropriate, therefore, to define the decade as a watershed for the trade and to examine some of its various facets.

Machines

The first major development to affect dressmakers had come about in the mid-1850s when W.F. Thomas began to advertise and sell sewing machines in the UK. [Plate 19] They had been available rather earlier in the United States. Much has been written about the development of the sewing machine and it would be tedious to repeat it here, but by the 1860s there were a number of makes available and most dressmakers were using them. The earliest machines made a chain-stitch of interlocking loops using a single spindle, but the great disadvantage was that seams had to be finished off by hand, otherwise a tug on the loose end of the thread would cause the whole seam to unravel. In the 1840s Elias Howe developed a lock-stitch machine, using two interlocking threads, which was taken up by Singer, and these machines soon replaced the chain-stitch models. [Plate 20] The Singer firm quickly became the market leader, and by 1856 they were offering a 'family machine', and agreeing to take old machines in part exchange. Sales of Singer and Wheeler and Wilson machines in the United States totalled 1,609 in 1853, rising to 38,105 in 1860.[1] Technical improvements in the 1870s and '80s made machines increasingly reliable and affordable – by 1871 a standard Singer retailed at £6.10s.0d in the UK according to an advertisement in *The Brighton Courier of Fashion*. Their sales in Britain rose from something under 5,000 a year in 1860 (when Thomas's patent was still in force and he was

Plate 19 Advertisement for Thomas' sewing machines, 1850s.

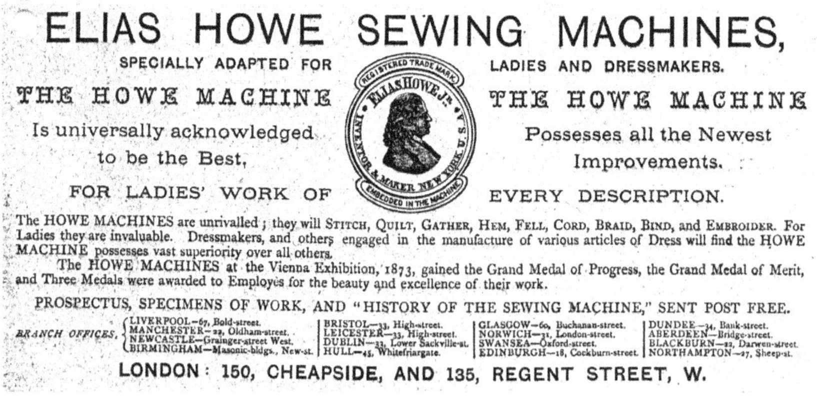

Plate 20 Advertisement for Elias Howe's sewing machine, 1871.

threatening competitors with legal action) to 88,000 a year in 1865, to 142,700 in 1884, and they remained around that level for the rest of the century. Andrew Godley believes he has proved, by reference to Singer's sales figures in relation to areas of clothing production, that the bulk of these sales were to the clothing industry.[2]

As early as 1864 the Children's Employment Commissioners reported that dressmakers were using machines and employing young teenage girls to thread the bobbins. Mrs H. Gilling of Promenade Villas, Cheltenham (interviewee 88), believed that using machines had improved her worker's health. Mrs Brothers in Exeter (interviewee 125) was sure 'The introduction of the sewing machine has done away with the need of working as long hours as formerly', while Mrs Smith at Brunswick House in Cheltenham (interviewee 98) claimed that one of her staff, a slow worker who normally took a whole day to stitch a 'body', could complete one in a quarter-of-an-hour using a machine! But opinions were mixed. Some sewing machinists complained that the machines were tiring to work and left them 'all of a tremble' and with backache and pains in their sides. Nonetheless, within a decade, almost all dressmakers were using them.

In December 1867 *The Englishwoman's Domestic Magazine* listed the available makes of machine and their prices: they ranged from £6.00 to £15.00, while 'hand' machines cost three to four guineas. Many dressmakers bought their machines on hire purchase but they were then under enormous pressure to keep up payments; if they defaulted, the supplier simply repossessed the machine, regardless of how much they had already paid on it. Some women reported that they had nearly paid for, but lost, several machines.[3] Hiring a machine by the week (for around 1s.6d to 2s.6d) was more expensive but often a safer option.

Machines tended to be temperamental and firms advertised for staff who were familiar with specific makes. For example, in 1875, John Cooper of Grantham wanted someone to work a Wheeler and Wilson machine, while Adderlys of Leicester wanted a hand to work a Howe machine.[4] Different machines functioned in different ways. The author of *Practical Dressmaking* explained how 'with some machines it is best to put a gored side of a skirt on the teeth, while with others it is best to put the straight edge downwards and ease in the gored one with the fingers on top'.[5] She therefore described all processes as they would be done by hand and left sewing machine owners to adapt her instructions to their own machines as best they could.

A survey made by the author in the 1990s of the dresses in what was then Leicestershire Museums' dress collection[6] provided some interesting insights into the use of machines. Of the twenty-seven 1850s dresses, eight were made wholly or partly by machine; however, a closer examination of these showed that dressmakers did not fully trust the new technology. All of the machine-made dresses had bodices that were lined with strong cotton fabric as was usual at the period; the technique was to tack the lining and dress fabric together and then to treat them as a single piece, the coarse lining making fine muslin or silk acceptable to the machine. Long skirt seams, which would seem to be the most obvious part of the garment for machine sewing, were only machine-stitched in garments made of robust fabrics or where the skirt was fully lined. Where skirts were unlined or made of light materials the seams were hand-stitched because the machine might have puckered or torn flimsy fabric. In only two cases were sleeves put in by machine, even when the rest of the bodice was machine-stitched. Setting sleeves is a tricky process and most Victorian dresses had very little spare fabric at the sleeve head; dressmakers do not seem to have found their machines to be manoeuvrable or reliable enough to deal with awkward seams.

By the 1860s, twenty-five out of the thirty-three dresses in the collection were machine-made, and the machines were being used much more for skirt and armhole seams. By the 1870s, twenty-four out of twenty-nine dresses were machine-made and machinists were becoming much more confident; garments were usually completely machine-made and some even had decorative top-stitching. Of all the dresses examined, only one, a black-and-white woollen dress of *c.*1860, was made using a chain-stitch machine, while two others were partly chain-stitched.

Between 1860 and the 1880s a series of inventors developed attachments that would enable sewing machines to make buttonholes[7] but few dressmakers seem to have acquired them – an apprentice with a needle was a much cheaper option and – usually – produced a better result.

Dresses of the 1870s and '80s often had bands of pleated decoration and in the late 1870s advertisements appeared for permanent pleating using the 'Wanzer' kilting (or pleating) machine. [Plates 21 & 22] Wanzer was a sewing machine company. The prices were not high – a machine that would pleat a six-inch wide strip cost 35s, one that would do a ten-inch width cost three pounds. None of the machines could cope with anything wider than twelve inches, so kilting was used at hem, cuffs, neck and for applied decoration – as yet there was no such thing as a machine-pleated skirt. Soon, other firms like Fricker and Singer developed similar machines. The workroom at White's of Ipswich had a kilting machine valued at two guineas at the time their inventory was made in 1878, but many firms patronized 'kilting establishments'. For example, throughout the 1880s advertisements appeared in the Leicester papers: 'Take all your kilting to Spencer's Kilting Establishment, 18 Regent Street … 200 varieties of plaiting.'[8]

The Watershed of the 1870s

Plate 21 Wanzer plaiting (or kilting) machine. The embossed name is on the lid of a compartment into which a heated block was placed. The strip of fabric to be pleated threaded underneath the compartment and went over a sharp blade. Each time the handle was raised and lowered, a pleat was formed.

Plate 22 Fashion plate from *Le Moniteur de la Mode* of September 1880. All the garments have kilted trimmings.

Lay figures and other services

Until the 1870s women's skirts did not need careful fitting; only the length and the size of the waist were important. The fullness varied from decade to decade, but skirts never hugged the figure, and though sometimes they were quite heavily decorated, the decoration was applied rather than integral. In the 1870s, however, skirts grew more complicated, and it became important to have some way of holding them so that they could be draped elegantly. [Plates 23 & 24] 'It is most difficult to arrange skirt draperies, such as trains in poufs, or scarves diagonally, etc., when the skirt is spread flat on a table', wrote Ms Monroe in 1879.[9] She was adamant that it was uneconomic to use a worker to model the skirt and recommended Alexander Watts, 24 Whitfield Street or Messrs Wells and Son of Wood Street (both in London) as suppliers of lay figures with 'French bodies' and wire skirts. 'French bodies' were cloth-covered so garments could be pinned in position and provided 'more substance than a mere wire cage'.[10]

Plate 23 Advertisement for the French Bust Company on Tottenham Court Road from *The Draper's Record*, 1895.

Plate 24 *Punch cartoon,* 18 November 1893. The caption reads "The problem of the day:- How to get last year's sleeves into this year's jacket"

Soon there were numerous firms producing life-size lay figures for dressmakers. Some were made of cane or wire; others were solid with detachable wire 'skirts'. Prices varied. *Myra's Journal of Dress and Fashion* recommended wicker stands in May 1881 at 1s.11d for 'brushing or mending' and at 2s.11d for fitting and in December 1888 she advertised 'Grabham's folding and adjustable dress stand' at 10s.6d. Florence White gave a list of equipment needed for a teaching workroom at the beginning of her *Easy Dressmaking* (1891) and recommended the purchase of a figure from Hall's for 25s.0d 'but a cheaper wicker one would do'. Silber and Flemming's catalogue of 1883 described 'french bodies' and advertised one with 'adjustable hips'. By the 1890s, H. Jules, the French bust company at 254 Tottenham Court Road, advertised individually customized lay figures 'any figure copied from a bodice' and claimed to be patronized by eleven royal families and 'thousands' of English and foreign nobility and gentry. The firm had been in existence at least as early as 1881 when they claimed to have exhibited at 'The Dressmakers' Exhibition [at the] Marlborough Rooms' in connection with the Scientific Dress Cutting Association of Regent's Circus.[11]

The May 1881 issue of *Myra's Journal of Dress and Fashion* advertised the Dressmakers' Supplies Stores which offered 'Economy – Certainty – Promptitude – Price,' and the area around Wood Street, off London's Cheapside had come to specialize in dressmakers' supplies. For the provincial dressmaker visiting London, an increasing variety of goods and services were available, including purpose-printed books and stationery and petersham waistbands ('beltings') woven with the dressmaker's name and address. It paid to be wary, however. Miss Payne in Sherborne (Dorset) ordered a selection of buttons from a London supplier in 1886 and was horrified to discover she had ordered several gross of buttons when she thought she had ordered in dozens. She also ordered some beltings which were unusable when they arrived because the address was misspelt.[12] The resulting negotiations and recriminations dragged on for months.

Paper patterns

According to *The Book of Trades* of 1811, dressmakers took 'the pattern off from a lady by means of a piece of paper or cloth. The pattern, if taken in cloth becomes afterwards the lining of the dress.' [Plate 25] The eighteenth-century system of taking a pattern by unpicking an existing dress that fitted the client was an easier solution and the author recommended it to amateurs. Inch tape-measures did not appear on the scene until the 1820s;[13] it took some time for them to be accepted and even towards the end of the century sets of graded paper tapes – the markings relating to particular customers' sizes – were in use.

In 1843 *The Ladies Handbook of Millinery, Dressmaking and Tatting* defined what was probably normal practice:

> Take the proper measures for the front and back of the body by fastening a paper pattern to the shape of the person for whom the dress is intended. The paper should be thin, and you commence by folding down the corner the length of the front, and pinning it to the middle of the stay bone. Then let the paper be spread as smoothly as possible along the bosom to the shoulder, and fold it in a plait so as to fit the shape exactly.

It was not a simple process.

Plate 25 Dressmaker's workroom from *The Book of Trades*, 1818 edition. The dressmaker is creating a pattern on the customer by draping and pinning a piece of fabric.

Experienced dressmakers had probably always developed their own pattern-drafting systems, based on observation and experience, but by the 1830s there were firms which provided patterns. In October 1836 *The World of Fashion* advertised:

> Every new style of dress, exquisitely formed in the exact models and colours in which they are worn, consisting of full length and small size French paper. Millinery and dresses of every description, sleeves, trimmings, etc., sold at 10s per set (comprising four articles) packed for any part of the Kingdom at 3s extra. To Ladies in Business requiring their own materials made up during their stay in London, Madame and Mrs F[ollet]'s establishment offers a combination of first-rate ability, with most moderate charges.

The Follets advertised that they had businesses at 53, New Bond Street, London and Rue Richelieu, Paris. In November 1849 the same magazine carried an advertisement for:

Mrs Dewsbury, Paper Pattern and Bonnet Shape Establishment, 3, Rathbone Place, Oxford Street, Established 1834. Mrs Dewsbury respectfully announces to her numerous customers that her showrooms are now open with a large selection of the Newest Designs in full sized Paper Patterns ... Patterns forwarded to all parts of the Kingdom.

Full-size fold-out patterns were published in the French magazine *Le Journal des Demoiselles* in 1841; the German *Bekleidungskunst für Damen Allgemeine Muster-Zeitung* produced paper patterns in the late 1840s; [Plate 26] while in America, *Godey's Magazine* pioneered the use of pattern diagrams in the 1850s. The *Englishwoman's Domestic Magazine* was giving away 'full-size' tissue paper patterns by 1860. These were single-size (small), and it still needed a good deal of skill to scale them up to fit a normal figure. Within a few years many magazines contained such patterns and manufacturers were beginning to offer a range of services; for a fee, patterns could be adjusted to fit the wearer's measurements and for a further fee, firms would cut out a toile, or even the maker's own fabric.

Pattern-designing and making soon became an industry and it was in the 1870s that it really took off. Ebenezer Butterick in America, a former tailor, began by producing graded patterns, initially for men's and boys' shirts, in the

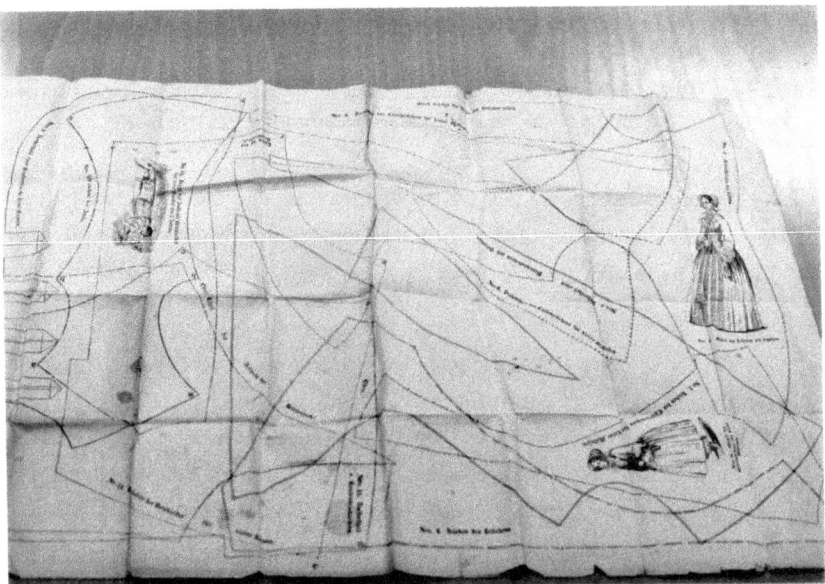

Plate 26 Give-away tissue paper pattern from the *Allgemeine Muster-Zeitung* for 1852. It measures just 50 × 81 cm and is printed on both sides with the outlines of overlapping pattern pieces for five different garments. They are distinguished by different types of line, but nonetheless, patterns like this must have been confusing to use.

1860s. He mass-produced his patterns and advertised them widely; by 1871 he was employing a staff of 140 and selling 23,000 patterns a year, retailing at ten cents a pack. Butterick had a stand at the 1876 Philadelphia Exhibition, as did one of his rivals, Mme Demorest (née Ellen Louise Curtis), who had started out as a milliner's apprentice in up-state New York in the 1850s. She married William Jennings Demorest and they established a fashionable store in New York, sent patterns by mail order to out-of-town dressmakers, sold all sorts of dressmaking supplies and ran no fewer than five fashion magazines. By the mid-1870s both firms expanded overseas, Mme Demorest to Paris and Ebenezer Butterick to premises in London. The firm flourished, and further depots were set up in Berlin, Frankfurt, Vienna, Amsterdam and St Petersburg.[14]

James McCall founded the McCall Paper Pattern Company in New York in 1870. He was a Scottish tailor who was in New York to promote his 'Royal Chart' measuring system and working as a sewing machine agent. In London, Christopher Edward Weldon established *Weldon's Ladies' Journal of Dress, Fashion, Needlework, Literature and Art* in 1879 and issued free paper patterns. These firms were all still in existence in the mid-twentieth century.[15]

Training schools

In November 1875 the Ladies' Dressmaking Association in Somerset Street opened a training school and hoped to 'induce parents to place their daughters [t]here to gain their own living'. They claimed to teach 'all the parts of the business' in 'a comfortable and well-ordered workroom with ladylike companions', and as a further incentive they offered board and lodging at 'moderate rates', stressing that 'the time ... is approaching when a lady's social position will depend not so much on the character of her calling as upon her bearing in it'[16] – in other words, dressmaking was now to be seen as a perfectly proper job for respectable young women. It was a small initiative and they could never have hoped to cater for large numbers, but it was a start.

The government schools of design established in the 1840s initially had little to offer the would-be dressmaker; their emphasis was on technical drawing and copying works of art. However, as the century progressed the schools came under a new department of the Board of Trade called the 'Department of Practical Art' and opened new technical schools specifically to teach trade skills. By the 1880s most towns of any size had a technical school, and they taught, among other things, tailoring and dressmaking and held classes in cutting and fitting. The schools were not free – in 1900 dressmaking lessons usually cost

5s.0d a week – but they attracted large numbers of pupils. Some simply hoped to learn to make their own clothes but others saw it as a prelude to working for a dressmaker.[17] However, in *Dressmaking, a Technical Manual for Teachers* (1892) Mrs Grenfell warned her readers: 'It should be borne in mind that many of the pupils, especially in the elementary classes, will never have seen a well-cut or well-made body, or can have much idea at first what they are expected to do.' She taught in Liverpool and this gives some indication of the type of students who attended her classes.

The Tailor and Cutter Academy in London taught ladies' tailoring as well as men's, and offered residential places and postal tuition, but their courses were expensive. They advertised that a course of ten evening classes cost two guineas and a single lecture cost two shillings, while full-time courses cost either five or ten guineas depending on length. By the 1890s it was also possible to sit the London City and Guilds examination in dressmaking. For more able students, it had at last become possible to enter the trade without the drudgery of an apprenticeship.

The Workshop Regulation Act of 1867

In April 1870 an anonymous letter arrived on the desk of Edward Brydges', clerk to Cheltenham Borough Council.[18] It began:

> If you have anything to do with inspecting the workrooms in Cheltenham you will be doing a great kindness on the part of the dressmakers by inspecting Miss Thomas, 13 Promenade after 5 of a Saturday evening, there the young people are kept in an underground place till 8 or ½ past or loose[*sic*] their place when every other business is closed.

Miss Rebecca Thomas had run a fashionable dressmaking business on the Promenade in Cheltenham for the best part of a decade and was successful and well-respected. Then as now, a complaint had to be investigated, so rather reluctantly – he had no desire to alienate a prominent member of the local business community – Edward Brydges despatched Mr Morgan, the Inspector of Nuisances, to number thirteen on the evening of Saturday 14 May. Sure enough, nine of Rebecca's ten employees were still at work. [Plate 27]

The Workshop Regulation Act, which had come into force on 1 January 1868, limited the working hours of women in workshops to twelve a day, banned Sunday working and working after 2.00 pm on Saturdays, as well as offering additional protection to working children. Clearly, Rebecca was breaking the

Plate 27 Rebecca Thomas's shop on The Promenade, Cheltenham from Rowe's *Guide to Cheltenham* of 1845. Rebecca Thomas took the shop over from Shipton c.1860.

law. The girls confirmed that they nearly always worked late into the evening on Saturdays and, rather foolishly, Rebecca sacked two of them 'for the Candour of their replies'. Edward Brydges was reluctant to take action, but urged on by Mr Earnshaw, the local Factory Inspector, who insisted that 'One good case is worth a thousand precepts. I would exhaust the case and prosecute it rigorously', he contacted Whitehall for advice. Did the act *really* apply to dressmakers' workshops? On 11 June he received a letter assuring him that it did.

Rebecca Thomas pleaded ignorance of the law she was accused of breaking but three days later she appeared in court. She was indicted on just three counts. The local paper reported that:

> ... this being the first prosecution under the act [*in Cheltenham*], and on account of the expense to which it would put the defendant, [*the magistrates*] thought it would be straining the law a little too tight to issue ten summonses.

Clearly neither the Council nor the magistrates wanted to upset Miss Thomas and have her take her business elsewhere. She was fined a derisory £3.00 plus costs. Rebecca promptly sacked Julia Jeens, her recently appointed first hand who she suspected of writing the anonymous letter; within a year all the other girls named in the case had left her employ – and her business seems not to have suffered in the slightest.

Rebecca Thomas was not the only dressmaker prosecuted under the act but she was one of very few. However, the mere fact that the act existed was important, and over time dressmakers' hours of work did reduce – though whether the threat of prosecution played much part is difficult to determine. Arguably, a more important factor was the rise of department store workrooms which offered shorter hours and better working conditions.

The rise of the department store workroom

Department stores have been much written about as a phenomenon of the late nineteenth century, though as Claire Walsh has shown, large stores with many of the features of department stores existed in the eighteenth century, and two of the largest and best-known – Bainbridges of Newcastle and Kendal Milne in Manchester – opened in the 1830s.[19]

Middle-class Victorian women were responsible for the display of their families' wealth both in their homes and in their clothes, and many prided themselves on their skill as thrifty and discerning shoppers. Most department stores had started out as drapers, and even in their expanded form, most concentrated on the sales of clothing, shoes, millinery, fabrics, household textiles and furnishings. As department stores were catering for a predominantly female clientele, store owners learnt, by experience and by example, that providing an environment in which respectable ladies felt safe and comfortable was good for business. To this end many provided rest rooms and restaurants, reading rooms, exhibitions and even concerts, and regular customers received mailings about sales and seasonal offers. For the less confident shopper, a familiar department store offered other advantages. It was possible to visit the shop just to look at what was on sale, the environment was unthreatening and the shopper did not risk mixing with undesirable company in the open streets. The establishment of workrooms for tailoring, dressmaking, millinery, upholstery and so on was thus a logical extension of stores' services.

Millinery and dressmaking have so far received little or no attention from department store historians. This is understandable as, paradoxically, most of the stores that have left sufficient records to enable us to analyse their dressmaking and millinery businesses in any depth were situated in small, unfashionable places. The larger and better-known firms advertised their dressmaking and millinery departments but left no detailed records of them. This does not negate the value of this section, and it certainly does not imply that department store workrooms were of no importance, but it does mean that the available data is somewhat inadequate to prove the point.

Plate 28 Caley's of Windsor letterhead, 1846.

Firms established their workrooms at different dates. At Caley's of Windsor, for example, there was a 'gown workshop' as early as 1851. This firm is unusual in that the store developed out of a dressmaking business run by Miss Caley and her sister, Mrs Noble, who moved to High Street in 1824, where they were in partnership with John William Caley (probably a relative) as haberdashers, silk merchants and lacemen. They were 'Milliners to Her Majesty and to TRH the Princesses and Duchess of Gloucester' by 1820, and in 1857 they supplied the dress the Princess Royal wore at her wedding banquet.[20] This was a firm catering for the highest strata of society. Other dressmakers sold ready-made goods and haberdashery, but there do not seem to be records of any other dressmaking business that burgeoned into a department store. [Plate 28]

Even quite small firms did dressmaking. In April 1874, an advertisement in *The Drapers' and Milliners' Gazette of Fashion* for Madame Schild's courses of dressmaking lessons stated, 'Costume making is an important part in almost all drapery establishments ... as the making of dresses leads to the benefit of many other departments.' A few stores established proper dressmaking workrooms in the 1850s and in October 1855 *The Sempstress* reported that:

> The system of large general shops combining, under one roof and one head, the business of mercer, upholsterer, milliner, etc., is, I suppose, a remunerative one, as it is daily becoming more common ... but it has this disadvantage, it tends to remove the working class still further from the public eye.

However, by the 1870s perceptions had changed and many more shops established workrooms between 1870 and 1900. As well as supplying a service to customers, these provided employees with a formal training that was thought to be superior to an apprenticeship with a private dressmaker, and for which no premium was usually charged. In addition, the large stores often kept boarding houses for their work people, though these were not cheap – Lucks in Darlington charged their boarders £26.5s.0d a year (1844 to 1871), for example.[21] However, this provision enabled staff to gain experience in places far from their homes, and as travel had become much easier with the establishment of the railway network, drapery, dressmaking and millinery assistants were remarkably mobile. It was common practice for firms to advertise in other towns – for example, the *Leicester Daily Post* of 1873 contained advertisements for dressmaking staff from firms in Newark, Horncastle, Swansea, Oakham, Oundle, Peterborough and Newcastle. No doubt informal networks also sprang up through which staff notified former friends and colleagues about promising vacancies.

Workroom staff worked much the same hours as the salespeople and though shops were open long hours, women in a department store workroom still worked shorter hours than they would have done for a bespoke dressmaker and, most importantly, knew when their working day would end. The establishing of rules for opening hours was in the hands of committees of local businessmen and there was no standardization across the country, but a ten- to twelve-hour day was usual.

In America the influence of the department store was much less benign. The stores sold ready-made goods which encouraged the rise of clothing factories and store workrooms existed only to adapt these to customers' requirements. In Philadelphia in 1860, for example, there were 308 milliners and dressmakers employing 1,138 workers. By 1870, almost 80 per cent of these had disappeared and over 80 per cent of the workers were unemployed, and by 1880 dressmaking (together with millinery) was too insignificant a trade to be a category in the manufacturing census. In the same twenty-year period the number of factories making women's clothing rose from 30 to 276, and the numbers they employed rose from 538 to 3,132. There was a slight revival after 1880, but the trade never really recovered.[22] British department stores also sold ready-to-wear clothing, but in the short term at least, they did not have an adverse effect on the market for bespoke garments.

In Britain there was also a cachet attached to working in a department store. Department store dressmakers prided themselves on their 'respectability'. As Mr Hilton, manager of the mantle department at S.H. Hannington's in Brighton, explained to the Children's Employment Commissioners in 1864 (interviewee 144):

> We try, and I think succeed tolerably well, to have none but well-conducted, respectable girls in our employ. Perhaps our greatest safeguard is the girls themselves, for if any improper character were to get into the workroom, they would be sure to take means to let the foreman know and get her out again.

In Margaret Penn's autobiographical novel, *Manchester 14 Miles*, set in the 1890s, Hilda Winstanley is immensely proud of her job at 'Hankinson & Sankey', the elite department store in St Ann's Square, Manchester: 'For Miss Jackson, Miss Robinson and Violet [*her colleagues*] she was prepared to lay down her life' and during her three months there she becomes progressively more confident and sophisticated. She describes how a department store workroom functioned:

> First of all Mrs Honeywell [*a customer*] came to the shop downstairs and selected the material. Then she spent days, even weeks, in choosing a pattern. Then she came to be measured. Then the material was given to the cutter; after this it was tacked up. Then she had to be fitted by Miss Robinson before the dress was actually made up. Several girls ... worked on different parts of it. There was, for instance, one girl who did nothing all day long except press, keeping two flat irons going for this purpose. Every seam was pressed flat as soon as it was finished.

The novel also highlights the difference between working for a small dressmaker and working for a store. Hilda had started work, aged thirteen, with Mrs Ormston where:

> She spent all her mornings doing housework, sewing only for a few hours in the afternoon. She did a fair amount of plain hemming and joining up seams ... But for the rest she had not even been shown how to lay a pattern and cut out. When customers came to be fitted, she stood by and handed pins to Mrs Ormston and threaded needles for her with tacking cotton.

Department stores generated a great deal of paperwork and only a tiny percentage survives. Even when we know a good deal about the structure of a firm, and we know that it made garments, we do not necessarily know very much about its dressmaking workrooms. Where records survive, however, they are a particularly useful source of information about wages and as an indicator of what employers regarded as desirable qualities in their staff.

Luck and Sons in Darlington is a case in point.[23] [Plate 29] It was established in the 1820s and became Luck and Sons in 1878. There is plenty of miscellaneous information about the progress of the firm and its finances, though they were not distinguished by the quality of their record-keeping – for example, the 'Staff Ledger' for 1841–58 contains details of bank loans, rents and suppliers. Nonetheless, they prospered and had a large client base – the 1839–43 account book suggests that they had about 608 regular customers from Darlington itself and the surrounding villages.

We do not know exactly when they started dressmaking or how profitable it was. The firm undertook extensive modernization of its premises in 1870; it may well be that that was when they set space aside for workrooms but we cannot be sure. The first mention of workrooms at Lucks came in 1887 when Miss Jackson changed jobs and 'went into the work room' – though presumably Miss Rees, who was employed by Lucks in 1886 for £50.00 pa and who later set up in business on her own account in tailoring, had worked there as a tailoress or dressmaker. A forewoman in the dressmaking workrooms, Miss Page, earning an exceptional £120.00 pa, left in June 1890. 'We gave her notice to quit on the 7th,' ran the note against her name in the appointments' book, 'on the 14th we found she had falsified the worker's pay bill – 30s. A very stout

Plate 29 Lucks of Darlington shop front after the renovation work of 1870.

woman with a blinking left eye, good dressmaker, not a good manager, getting her work out very slowly, given to drink'. One wonders what falsified reference had persuaded Lucks to take her on at such an exorbitant salary in the first place.

In fact few of Lucks' employees stayed a full year. Elizabeth Jane Stephenson remained at Lucks for nearly five years in which time her salary rose from £20.00 to £32.00, then to £10.4s.0d for her final quarter. Next to her name is a comment on the exceptional length of her service. Staff arrived in Darlington from London, Driffield, Leicester, Leeds, Saffron Walden, Barnard Castle, Newcastle, Tadcaster and Northallerton, and left for Pickering, Ripon, Bedford, Hull, Wolverhampton, Sheffield, Bradford, Rhyl, Hexham and Lincoln – a good example of just how mobile employees were. This is a pattern repeated elsewhere so it does not necessarily imply that Lucks were bad employers. Nonetheless, the sheer number of ordinary working women – and men – who had no qualms about travelling the length of the country to work for an employer they had never met, in a town in which they were strangers, overturns some of our preconceptions about the Victorian workforce.

Appointment books also exist for two East Anglian firms and they confirm this impression.

William Turner of Stowmarket in Suffolk[24] opened millinery and dressmaking departments in the 1880s and his appointment books survive. Turner's first appointment of a dressmaker came on 5 April 1886. She was Isabel Osborne, second dressmaker (there is no mention of appointing a first hand) who was paid £20.00 pa, and she came from Chelmsford where she had worked for twelve years 'leaving only to better herself ... personal appearance and manners quite suited to business'. Other dressmaking staff – all with salaries of £20.00 to £25.00 pa – came from Lewisham, Kingstone and Burgate. Miss Thirkettle epitomized what an employee should be 'obliging, industrious, thoroughly honest, truthful, trustworthy, often left in charge of workroom ... neat and correct, enjoys good health'. A first hand dressmaker was appointed in 1887 at £80.00 pa. She came from Dudley in the West Midlands and before that from St Ives in Huntingdonshire and went a year later to a firm in Ipswich.

On the whole, Turner was lucky in his employees – the worst he said about any of his millinery or dressmaking staff was that they were 'too inexperienced' or 'not very rapid'. It is also clear that a pleasant appearance, nice manners and good health were almost as important as skill.

W.E. White of Ipswich also kept appointment books.[25] White's began dressmaking in the mid-1870s; they paid rather better than Turner's but made much less satisfactory appointments. Miss Young, with them as milliner from November 1874 to October 1875 at £10.00 pa, was 'a very poor milliner – no talent, no taste', while Miss Reynolds who took her place at £35.00 a year from February 1875 to February 1876 was 'a pretty conceited little fool and not over fond of work'. Miss Proudman of Tamworth who worked for White's from February 1874 to November 1875 was described in doggerel:

> A rustic beauty with a skin as fair
> As lilies show in balmy morning air,
> Her teeth were pearls, her eyes soft radiance shed,
> But I must tell the truth – her hair was red.

Pre-Raphaelite looks obviously had no place in an Ipswich draper's shop.

Miss Gibson, his milliner from February 1882 to March 1883, had 'mediocre talent ... rather vulgar in manner'; Miss Dyson who got £40.00 pa in 1898 was 'No good, short, not very pleasant in manner' and Miss Simmonds, to whom he paid £36.00 pa in 1883, had 'No great ability, rather slow ... had been accustomed to a quiet trade' while her successor, Miss Eagle from Brighton, was paid £40 a year for being 'slow, no style, peculiar looking'.

His dressmakers were no better. Miss Priddell who was with him for three months in 1885 was 'dismissed summarily for refusing to execute an order for a customer. Short, short-tempered, rather bumptious and self-assertive, moderate ability'. Miss Harper was 'a fairly good dressmaker, conceited, could do well if she liked'. Miss Holdraw was 'rather antient [sic], slow, no style, dowdy looking, industrious and steady', while Miss Mitchell, as first hand in 1896, was paid £70.00 but was 'very deaf, short, overbearing to hands in workroom and not a first rate dressmaker'. Miss Vaughan was one of his worst appointments – a 'good dressmaker, bad tempered, disagreeable, bad health, vindictive and generally speaking a damned nuisance to everybody'!

Mr White had scoured the country to find these unsatisfactory individuals – they came to him from places as far away as London, Birmingham, Worthing, Nottingham, Ventnor, Folkestone and Reigate. Of course, not all his references were so derogatory, but one is left with the feeling that a spell at White's in Ipswich was the death knell to many a career. Milliners and dressmakers working in small firms were used to overbearing, unreasonable mistresses, but the personal nature of so many of Mr White's written comments, and the sheer misogyny they imply, must have made working for him extremely uncomfortable.

Dodds and Co, drapers of Alnwick,[26] left a particularly useful and detailed set of records relating to their dressmaking business and it is worth examining them in some detail. These were found in a shop in Bondgate – now 'Hansel

Plate 30 This used to be called 'Bondgate House' and was tenanted by Dodds of Alnwick from the 1880s.

House'. This was originally 'Bondgate House' from which the firm traded from the 1880s. They had had several previous addresses. [Plate 30]

Alnwick is a small country town in Northumberland. It had a population of around 6,000 for most of the nineteenth century but it also served a wide rural area. Dodds was established in the eighteenth century and the earliest surviving daybook dates from 1788–9. The firm then had around eighty-five customers and sold fabrics and haberdashery and some ready-made goods like caps and stockings, but there is no evidence that any garments were made on the premises at that point. The 1845–6 daybook shows they continued to sell ready-made garments and, though they did some making up, there are only a dozen references in the whole period covered by that daybook.

By 1864 the proprietor of the firm was Mary Dodds 'widow' and the firm traded as M. Dodds and Son until the 1930s. It was quite small, not what we think of as a department store today, but nonetheless there were many similar small town drapers' shops which operated on department store principles and which had workrooms for garment-making. Such firms knew their customers well. Molly Proctor described how in some Kent drapers' shops serving very mixed communities, tacit agreements came into play: the 'gentry' would shop in the late morning, middle-class ladies in the afternoon and working-class girls would come in the evening as they left work.[27]

Mrs Dodds was an excellent record keeper and in the late 1860s she decided to expand the dressmaking side of her firm's business. A complete series of what are called 'Journals' survives for the period 1865 to 1883. These are arranged by month and client name with all transactions listed, and were probably transcribed from daybooks; they are neat and legible, with totals and details clearly entered. It would appear that Dodds was still doing very little dressmaking and millinery between 1865 and 1867. Garment making and millinery transactions made up less than 1 per cent of the firm's transactions at this point, and the addition of some tailoring work in 1867 did not alter that balance. In fact, tailoring was never very important to the firm. Most of the work they did took the form of minor alterations for which they charged no more than a shilling or two, and quite a lot of that was done for the local military. Like many small town shopkeepers they attempted to do as their customers asked – however unusual the request – in July 1873, for example, they acted for a Mr Rennison and arranged to have three tiger skins and one leopard skin dressed for him in London.

From 1868 the dressmaking and millinery sides of the firm's activities expanded, which is somewhat surprising as Alnwick already had fourteen other drapers, twenty-five dressmaking firms and thirty-six tailors, but Dodds seems to have made a conscious effort to create a niche in the market, specializing in high-quality repairs and alterations and charging commensurately high prices. By 1873 there seems to have been a workroom – in April 'Miss Oswald, Workroom' spent 18s.6d on a jacket – and the dressmaking side of Dodds' business was clearly well-established.

The firm sold ready-made dresses and the workroom specialized in customizing them. They carried a stock of black dresses, and trimming them with mourning crepe was quite a profitable side-line. Alnwick was not a fashionable place and the canny locals seem to have been anxious to get the last ounce of wear out of their garments; rural Northumberland was not wealthy – its inhabitants were hill farmers, fishermen and miners. Dodds served a wide area, and even had the occasional customer from North Shields. Some of their clients came from local big houses – Forton Hall, Espley Hall – but for the most part they seem to have served the wives of local farmers and tradesmen.

Dodds' individual transactions varied enormously in price. Making dresses cost from 3s.6d to 18s.0d. Unpicking a dress (for Mrs Parker of Allerburn in 1876) cost 2s.6d, but unpicking and remaking a blue dress for Mrs Boland of Stamford cost 17s.6d in September 1873. Alterations ranged in price from 6d to over a pound. Dodds' prices were actually quite high – 12s.0d for re-trimming a Dolly Varden[28] dress for Mrs Sandford of Belvedere (February 1873) seems expensive when other firms were charging half that for making a complete garment, as does 11s.6d for adding crepe to a ready-made costume (which itself cost £8.12s.6d) for Mrs Dickson of Bailiffgate (January 1873) or £4.15s.6d for re-trimming a black silk dress with new silk flounces for Mrs Avery of North Shields (May 1873). However, high prices helped establish Dodds' reputation as *the* place to go for alterations, and presumably the quality of their work was equally high.

By 1876 Dodds' dressmaking department kept separate records, and their dressmaking business can be carefully analyzed from that point until 1884 [Table 12].

This averages out at about ten jobs a week. It would therefore be reasonable to assume that Dodds had a minimum of four workroom staff. A good head dressmaker at this date was normally paid about £80.00 pa and a second hand £35.00 pa, improvers earned about £10.00 pa and apprentices were unpaid. This postulates a minimum wage bill of around £125.00 pa, so the department earned around £100.00 most years. Dressmaking at Dodds was thus a relatively profitable activity, comparable to that of a reasonably successful private dressmaker. From the employees' point of view there would have been little difference between the two types of workroom; however, an apprentice training at Dodds' could have

Table 12 Transactions 1876–84, Dodds of Alnwick.

Year	Income from dressmaking	Number of transactions
1876	£162.6s.9d	566
1877	£203.18s.6d	501
1878	£204.19s.6d	526
1879	£196.15s.6d	452
1880	£156.8s.11d	494
1881	£201.11s.0d	428
1882	£238.19s.6d	495
1883	£207.16s.6d	410
1884	£136.00	415

done so without raising a premium, all the workroom staff would have worked set hours and their jobs would have been relatively secure because if the volume of dressmaking orders was down other work could have been found for them in sales or stocktaking.

Dodds' records are unique. More prestigious stores had their dressmaking workrooms but we know about them only through advertising leaflets and promotional material. It would seem that the firm managed to establish itself as the premium dressmaking business in the area, which in turn would have made it a desirable place for staff to gain experience and allowed Mrs Dodds to be selective about who she employed. We have much less information about other firms in this survey.

Lindops of Chester, for example, established a dressmaking workroom in 1884.[29] The store was originally a traditional drapers and silk mercers and William Edward Lindop was apprenticed there at the age of fifteen in 1865; in 1883 he took over the business. The year 1884 was his first full year of trading and in July that year he married Polly Tinker who had been a milliner at Owen Owen in Liverpool where he had been sent as part of his training. Perhaps because of Polly's influence, Lindops established millinery and dressmaking departments in 1884. The customer account books for 1882–99 show that the store as a whole had between 264 and 300 regular customers. It was a medium-sized concern in a fashionable, old-established town, making an annual profit of approximately £850.00. No separate accounts survive for the dressmaking section, but for a short time at least it had a prestigious employee – Miss Pinch who had trained at Redfern's, the court dressmakers in London. In her case, the arduous training had paid off and secured her a good post. An undated flier addressed simply 'Madam' announces Miss Pinch's arrival and stresses the department's selling pitch – good fit, moderate price and 'Mourning supplied at a day's notice'. [Plate 31]

Dressmaking continued at Lindops well into the twentieth century. A present-day descendant of the family remembers that when the building was renovated the floor cavity beneath the workroom was full of decades' worth of pins, threads and fabric fluff.

Bainbridges of Newcastle was typical of many large department stores.[30] It opened in 1837. By 1885, when an article about the firm appeared in the *Newcastle Daily Journal* (23 June), the shop had taken over many of the surrounding buildings and occupied 56,566 square feet over four storeys. There were twenty-one workrooms employing 200 to 300 people and amongst them were dress, costume, mantle and bonnet-making rooms [Plate 32]. The firm also did tailoring, upholstery, pit-flannel-making, French polishing and carpet beating 'by machinery', as well as

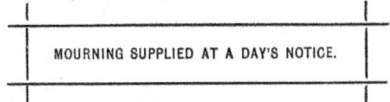

Plate 31 Flier from Lindop's of Chester announcing the arrival of Miss Pinch from Redferns.

making hosiery and running a shirt and clothing factory in Leeds, but though they advertised all these services, no records of them survive.

James Smith and Co, Clayton Street, Newcastle, did both millinery and dressmaking.[31] The wages books survive for this firm for the 1890s, and in 1891 they employed eight milliners and ten dressmakers. The head milliner was paid 21s.8d a week; the three apprentices got 3s.0d; and the others 5s.6d, 5s.4d and 10s.0d. The head dressmaker earned £2.3s.0d; her apprentices had 4s.0d; her first hand, 9s.0d; her second hand, 8s.0d; and the others 5s.0d to 6s.6d. The total annual wage bill for the two departments for 1891, therefore, was £380.11s.0d. Unfortunately we have no evidence about their turnover but they were a relatively down-market firm so it is quite surprising that they had such a large, well-paid staff.

Plate 32 Advertising calendar for Bainbridges of Newcastle, 1868.

Discipline

Even if conditions in the stores were better than they were in many dressmaking firms, they still left much to be desired. Department stores treated their employees very severely. A Draconian set of staff rules survives from Hammonds of Hull 'The Noted Shop for Cheap Drapery and Hosiery', dating from c.1889, imposing sixpenny fines for all sorts of minor misdemeanours like omitting articles from parcels, signing incorrect bills, not adding up the book properly or promising to send parcels out at given times and failing to do so.[32] Similar penalties applied in the workrooms. When wages were usually under 12s.0d a week such penalties were swingeing. At Blakes in Maidstone (Kent), the workroom rules were still on the wall in the 1970s.[33]

Blakes of Maidstone, warehouse rules

- No work to be done in workroom time without being entered
- All goods to be used carefully, and all materials to be faithfully accounted for
- Silk cuttings to be carefully saved from each table and utilised
- Punctuality to be strictly observed and absences from business not allowed except by permission of the firm
- Anyone infringing these rules will meet with dismissal

Advertising

Firms varied in the way they advertised their services. Speed of execution was important as we have seen. In Northampton, Norman and Shepherd's selling point in 1873 was typical: 'Dressmaking orders executed with care and punctuality.'[34] Walters of Chichester advertised that work would be done by 'thoroughly competent hands, and at strictly moderate charges. Satisfaction in fit, style and workmanship guaranteed'.[35] Some firms concentrated on high fashion and exclusivity. For example, Heelas of Reading had a high-class dressmaking department by the early 1900s, but no evidence survives as to when this was established. In 1907 they advertised 'The Most Expert Fitters and Cutters in the County are at your service' and described themselves as 'Maison Heelas, Court Dressmakers'. By 1929 they were holding fashion shows. A booklet illustrates the workroom in the 1920s and describes how

'The value of this Department is enormously enhanced by the close touch constantly maintained with the world's leading Fashion Designers. Exclusive models, representative of the best they have to offer, are secured each season'.[36]

Conclusion

The 'watershed of the 1870s' was made up of many strands – the arrival of machinery to speed up production and aid in the creation of ever more elaborate garments, paper patterns to simplify cutting and fitting, a whole range of goods and services offered by entrepreneurs who recognized the size of the dressmaking trade and the potential to profit from it, and legislation which – when enforced – made the length of the working day more bearable.

The development of department store workrooms provided customers with a convenient new way of getting clothes made; created a formal, organized and respectable way of obtaining training in dressmaking and millinery; and established a clearly defined career structure within those trades. Most in-house workrooms were purpose-built and designed and stores often prided themselves on the quality of the conditions they offered their work people. Terms and conditions were similar to those of other store staff, and in slack periods workroom staff were sometimes deployed as salespeople rather than being laid off.

Furthermore, experienced hands could set their own wages. In 1872 Dunn and Co of Albion House in Newcastle-upon-Tyne advertised for a mantle maker 'a superior, experienced person to take charge of the workroom, send particulars and salary required, etc'. In 1875 Hobson and Sons of Spalding requested 'Applications stating age, salary and references' for milliner/mantle makers.[37]

Dressmaking was just one of many services department stores offered. It was not necessarily an especially profitable one but it provided a way of retaining customer loyalty and of selling more fabric and trimmings. In the short term, losses in the dressmaking department could be subsidized by profits in other areas, and any calculation of the profit the department made had to take into account increased sales of fabric and sundries and impulse buys by customers who visited the store for fittings. Dressmaking departments thus worked on a completely different economic basis from that of individual dressmaking firms and this enabled them to keep their prices competitive.

However, department store workrooms did not replace bespoke dressmakers. Indeed, as late as 1914, it is estimated that department store sales of clothing and footwear (both bespoke and ready-made) accounted for only around 10 per cent of all such sales.[38] Well into the twentieth century there were still numerous dressmaking firms – ranging from one-woman businesses to large establishments employing dozens of hands – and there was a large clientele of ladies who preferred the greater degree of personal service such firms could offer. What did happen was that a marked division developed between different branches of the trade and, as always, there were winners and losers.

7

Winners and losers

There had been advances in the dressmaking trade, but as we saw in Chapter 5, the late 1870s saw one of the worst depressions in British history as Germany and the United States became industrial powers and challenged Britain's supremacy. Poor harvests drove country people to the towns and waves of Jewish immigrants arrived fleeing pogroms in Eastern Europe. The towns were already overcrowded, and under the twin pressures of an oversubscribed labour market and foreign competition, employers reduced wages.

The 1880s saw a new round of official enquiries in response to deteriorating conditions. The Women's Protective and Provident League (later the Women's Trade Union League) was set up in 1874 and reported on sweated industries in the East End. The Jewish Board of Guardians produced a survey, as did John Burnet for the Board of Trade and Factory Inspector Lakeman for the Home Office. A Royal Commission on working-class housing reported in 1885 and a House of Lords Committee on Sweating was set up in 1888. As a result, new Factory and Workshop Acts were passed in 1891 and 1895 but the legislation was patchily enforced and there were considerable discrepancies in how the law was interpreted.

Meanwhile, some members of the middle class were experiencing pangs of social conscience. Among them was Beatrice Potter; she was the cousin of Mary Macaulay (daughter of Thomas Babbington Macaulay, the historian) who married Charles Booth in 1871. Charles Booth was wealthy, a partner in a Liverpool ship-owning firm, but he had an interest in radical politics and became fascinated by the problems of urban poverty after he moved to London in 1875. He had a somewhat eccentric interest in the slums and enjoyed walking through the East End, observing the inhabitants with almost anthropological curiosity. In 1886 Booth's interest led him to attempt a proper survey of slum conditions and he recruited a group of volunteers, one of the most dedicated of whom was Beatrice Potter. She later married a fellow volunteer, Sydney Webb. The result of their enquiries was an enormous seventeen-volume series, *The Life and Labour of the People of London*, the first volume of which appeared in 1889.

Other authors produced works of a similar genre, the most successful of which was probably *The Bitter Cry of Outcast London* (1883), published by the London Congregational Union. Similar surveys were carried out in the provinces; the best known was Seebohm Rowntree's survey of the poor in York which was published in 1901 as *Poverty, a Study of Town Life* – an attempt to discover whether the conditions Booth had uncovered in the East End were replicated in the provinces. They were.

At about the same time, the particular problems of women's work came under the spotlight. Women's status was gradually beginning to change; the Matrimonial Causes Act of 1878 gave some limited protection to abused wives, the Married Women's Act of 1882 entitled deserted wives to maintenance, the Married Women's Property Act was passed in 1884 and the Guardianship of Infants Act in 1886. Some women were gaining access to university education in the 1850s and '60s; others were attending art schools and training colleges and becoming teachers and writers. New careers – like secretarial work – opened up to them. The Central Committee for Women's Suffrage was formed in 1872 after some years of agitation. Intelligent, concerned women formed pressure groups to fight for social and political rights for themselves and their less fortunate sisters. These included the National Union of Women Workers (1874), the Women's Protective and Provident League (1873–4) which became the women's Trade Union League in 1891, the Women's Co-operative Guild (1883), the Anti-Sweating League (*c.*1887), the Women's Industrial Council (1894), the Women's Labour League (1906) and the Fabian Women's Group (1908). The impetus for change thus came from groups that were largely middle class and, though well-meaning, did not always fully understand the problems they were trying to address. However, most of the groups were committed to 'special and systematic inquiry into the conditions of working women' (as Clementina Black described it to the inaugural meeting of the Women's Industrial Council in 1894) and a feature of most of these surveys is that they contain case histories. These give us some insight into the lives of some women at the lower end of the dressmaking trade in the period before the First World War.

Surveys

Lady Adele Meyer and Clementina Black published *The Makers of Our Clothes* in 1909, the result of a survey done in London in 1908, to argue for the establishment of Trade Boards in the clothing industry. They were therefore largely concerned with wages but they also reported on firms whose working practices they approved. One employer they admired operated a system of fines for late arrivals and rewards for punctuality (paid out of the fines) and found that it sorted out the girls who really needed money from the ones who were comfortably off. She also claimed to keep on in slack times those girls who most needed work and to ensure that they were the ones who were sent to work for ladies in the country. Another establishment which was 'most admirably arranged and managed' offered prizes for 'punctuality and tidy hair' and they were particularly impressed that the employer provided black ribbons for tying back the hair of the younger girls. Working hours were nominally 8.55 am to 8.00 pm but this firm usually finished at 7.30 pm; full hands earned at least 18s.0d, and the employer was a woman 'of education and culture' who inculcated 'good, quiet manners' and 'refined appearance' in her workers. They 'were impressed by the immense opportunities for good which a factory or work-room affords to an educated and enlightened woman who genuinely cares about the workers'.[1] Despite their familiarity with working-class life, Lady Meyer and Miss Black betrayed many of the prejudices of their class.

A collection of letters from Co-operative guildswomen was edited by Margaret Llewellyn Davies and published in 1930 under the title *Life as We Have Known It*. Her correspondents were asked to describe their early working lives and how guild membership had improved things for them. One lady, born in Cefyn Mawr in Wales in 1858, was one of the five children of a shoemaker father and a mother 'who went out day-sewing for a shilling a day' to supplement her husband's 12s.0d a week wage. This correspondent went into service at the age of nine, and after a series of jobs, worked in a Temperance Hotel in Oldham where her employers sent her, aged fourteen, to night school to learn to read and write. In 1880 she married a railway platelayer; 'I did a little plain sewing to help us during the week to keep out of debt. We struggled along to get a nice home together with my little sewing money.' Within a few months she was pregnant and:

> To prepare for that time, I took more sewing in, and worked night and day to save a little ... Just a week before my baby came, I made eight print, tight-fitting jackets for 1s-4d each – I had to suffer for it after. I went about with a little pillow under each arm for three months with gathered breasts.[2]

The fact that she made eight similar jackets suggests she was working for a ready-made clothing firm rather than as a dressmaker, but her story demonstrates the physical problems overwork at sewing (probably machining) could cause.

Thirteen women who worked as private dressmakers appear in Clementina Black's *Married Women's Work* (1915). They included a woman who had been a 'tea gown hand' in the West End and whose average earnings were about 12s.0d a week, while another woman and her mother earned 15s.0d to 30s.0d between them. But 'Mrs B', aged thirty-two and the mother of six children (and of five others who had died), lived in two basement rooms and let a third, had a consumptive rag-and-bone man husband and did any jobs she could as well as dressmaking – charring, washing, flower selling – for a shilling or two a week while her fourteen-year-old minded the younger children. An older woman, 'over 50', made blouses, and considered her best customer a fruiterer's wife who paid 1s.6d for fancy blouses, unlike most of her other customers who paid 6d to 9d. These were all women who were in business on their own account but whose wages were poorer than those of dressmakers' employees. Their conditions were worse, too, in that they all had families to care for, and had to pay for their own food, fuel and lighting. They were all dressmaking for their working-class neighbours and were probably typical of many girls who had some training, were not particularly talented, but found themselves married to men whose wages were inadequate to their family's needs. Their pay and conditions were very similar to those of 'slop workers' (seamstresses) described in the same report. The conclusion drawn from this limited survey was 'that a woman has not a chance of earning what she would call "good money" if she works at a trade that she has not learned properly in her early years'.[3]

It was not the whole story. *The Daily News*, bought by the Quaker, George Cadbury, in 1901, held an exhibition of work produced by sweated workers in May 1906. Visitors were attracted by lectures given by celebrities like Will Crookes MP and George Bernard Shaw. Mary Neal wrote the article on sweated dressmakers in the exhibition catalogue and felt things had improved considerably in the preceding ten years though conditions still left much to be desired. While acknowledging that the trade had different branches she concentrated on the West End. She found that a hand earned, on average, 14s.0d a week throughout the year:

> She will never earn more, because, unless a girl is exceptionally lucky in becoming a fitter or first hand, she reaches her maximum wage-earning capacity when quite young, and before a year or two is over she earns less sooner than more each time she changes her place.

She criticized the fact that girls were taught just one branch of the trade, and if they wanted to learn other skills they had to move from job to job as improvers.

She also criticized the unhealthy conditions in the trade which created 'bent backs and anaemic blood', and, in tune with her age and class, the dangers of exposing young working girls to 'display and luxury'. The exhibition attracted 30,000 visitors and 20,000 catalogues were sold – and conditions in the needle trades continued unchanged.

Charity

Dressmakers were often compelled to seek charity. The Cambridge Committee for Organizing Charitable Relief and Suppressing Mendacity,[4] for example, made various payments to individuals in the 1880s and '90s but they were very strict about who they would pay. Hannah Smith was a typical case (Case 50). In 1880 she reported: 'My dressmaking has failed the last 4 years and neither my son nor my daughter can do much for me.' She had worked for a Mr Bradwell 'opposite the station' but had been out of work for twelve months because trade was slack. Mr Bradwell acknowledged that her needlework was good, but made no comment on her character. Her neighbour and children were more forthcoming, however, and accused her of being a drunk. The committee dismissed her case – charity was only for the deserving poor. Sarah Ann Clark's case (Case 467, 1882) failed too. She was a widow with a two-year-old son and had been laid off by her employer because there was no work. She had 4s.0d a week poor relief which just covered her rent, plus a further 2s.6d from renting out a room. She had glowing character references and the doctor explained that her illness was caused by sitting up late at work and being malnourished. However, while the committee was deliberating she found a job for herself as a housekeeper. Georgina Sophia Conway (Case 714, 1893) was a dressmaker and needed a £10.00 loan to buy stock for a shop she had set up 'to help at the dressmaking which is not so efficient'. She claimed she made 12s.6d a week and her nineteen-year-old son, an apprentice, contributed a further 5s.0d. She was described as 'industrious, trustworthy and straightforward' and as someone who tried to bring her children up well. Her son's employer said he was 'very steady', and when committee members visited her home they found it 'very clean and respectable'. She got her loan but had to pay it back at 10s.0d a week – the Cambridge charity did not give away money lightly. There were many similar cases and many similar charities, but if the worst came to the worst, dressmakers who became too old or ill to work and had no one to support them still ended up in the workhouse.

Success stories

Nonetheless, by a combination of luck and talent, some nineteenth-century dressmakers were remarkably successful. For example, Madame Emily Clapham managed to establish a dressmaking firm in Yorkshire which numbered Queen Maud of Norway amongst its clients. As Emily MacVitie she had served her apprenticeship at Marshall and Snelgrove in Scarborough in the 1880s. She then had the good sense to marry a rich man, Haigh Clapham; they purchased a house in the centre of Hull in 1887 and he set her up in business. Emily Clapham had an eye for fashion but she was never really a designer. Her technique was to buy models from Paris and London fashion houses, and then copy them, mixing and matching details like sleeves and necklines, and using her own fabrics and colour schemes. From the start she aimed for an exclusive clientele and attracted the patronage of East Riding society. She did not advertise but relied on recommendations. Muriel Wilson, daughter of a shipping magnate and a renowned beauty, and Lady Ida Sitwell, Osbert Sitwell's mother, were among her early clients, but soon she was serving a clientele from beyond the East Riding, and each season she would travel to Grimsby, York, Harrogate and London, holding shows and keeping appointments with her clients at a series of hotels. She would meet Queen Maud at Sandringham.[5] Clearly Emily Clapham was a talented dressmaker and a shrewd businesswoman. [Plate 33]

Mrs Rose Downer (née Hackett) of Chichester worked as a travelling dressmaker for ladies and was also extremely successful.[6] Like Madame Clapham, most of her clients came to her by personal recommendation. She did not always give dates, but her earlier reminiscences were of the early 1900s when conditions in the trade had changed little since the late nineteenth century. Rose came from a respectable family – her father's mother, Hannah Hackett, was a gentlewoman, though admittedly one who had been disinherited for marrying the groom. Rose's own father was a coachman. Rose was apprenticed to a family friend, Mrs Catherine Downer, and this may well have eased her path, especially after she married the Downers' eldest son in 1909. As an apprentice Rose worked for General Anderson's wife who recommended her to another officer's wife whose daughter was marrying 'a famous literary critic' and needed a trousseau. Not only did Rose make the trousseau, she was also invited to the wedding as a waitress and rewarded with a gold sovereign for her pains. From there her career snowballed and she was soon invited to work for Mrs Patrick Faulkener-Wisden ('Mrs X') in Kent.

Plate 33 Madame Clapham's staff in 1908.

> I did some lovely dresses for her and we used to go to London to get materials from Liberty's, Dickins and Jones and many of the best shops ... We usually had lunch at Dickins and Jones or some other good Restaurant ... I was treated very much like a companion, and when I went out took the two King Charles Spaniels with me for a walk "Bijou" and "Mimi".

At another house, Craigwell, on the south coast she remembered:

> One of our late Kings stayed there ... Here I worked with the French maid and made some beautiful velvet coats and gowns ... I had my meals in the Servant's Hall sitting on the right hand side of the Butler, the French maid sitting on the right hand side of the housekeeper.

At Mrs X's she took breakfast in the nursery and often worked there. When she was working on one particular dress:

> I never now see such beautiful linen, it was as soft as silk. As the lace had to be let in by hand there was some close sewing and Mrs X suggested that I took it down to the beach to do. The children were going there too, and I often wonder how I managed to keep it spotless, but I did.

As she did more and more work for the family her friendship with Mrs X deepened. She was asked to use the front staircase – a mark of respect which distinguished her from the servants – and was served her meals on a tray with 'lots of very dainty food, for my supper, ice cream!'

During the war she helped Mrs X organize a hospital ball and later the family would give her theatre tickets. Mrs Downer's only son was born at about the same time as Mrs X's third child, so the two women must have been much of an age: 'After a while she wrote to ask me to go to her and if possible bring my son, which I did … The children played in the nursery while we discussed clothes!' The friendship survived a misjudgement on her part which could have proved disastrous – Mrs Downer was persuaded to copy one of the dresses she had made for Mrs Wisden for another lady and they both wore them to the same function. There were no recriminations, but Mrs Wisden never wore hers again. Mrs Downer was wise enough never to repeat her mistake, but the incident shows how fragile their relationship really was, how all-pervasive was the class system – and how important exclusivity in dress was to ladies in that social stratum.

Mrs Downer was talented, genteel and working for an upper-class clientele. She and Emily Clapham were unusual but they were not unique.

Other dressmakers had less spectacular careers but still made a good living. Elizabeth Chaffard (Chapter 4) and her sister did well, and when she became ill Elizabeth was able to spend her last years in reasonable comfort in Brighton, as a sleeping partner in the firm, living on her share of the profits.[7] However, dressmaking had taken its toll on both sisters and they died within weeks of each other in 1867, aged forty-five and thirty-five, respectively. Margaret Cameron, also in Edinburgh, trading as 'Cameron and Violard' (though in fact there was no such person as 'Violard' – Margaret's partner for much of her career was her brother, John) was in business as a milliner, dressmaker and staymaker between 1826 and 1870 and survived two near-bankruptcies – in 1839 and 1846 – by shrewd management.[8]

Stana Nenadic identified 'dovetailing', whereby women, often sisters or relatives, joined together to provide a range of related services – millinery, corset making, dressmaking, the sale of haberdashery, etc. – as a key factor in the success of a business. She cites various examples, including that of Mrs Christian Winter who founded a millinery and dressmaking business in Edinburgh in 1846, shortly before her husband's death. By the 1850s she was selling furnishings and trimmings, two of her adult daughters were dressmakers, one made straw hats, a married daughter was a laundress and a granddaughter was a furrier.[9] Individuals who provided more than one service were also more likely to succeed. For example, Elizabeth Pattinson's small haberdashery/millinery/

dressmaking business (Chapter 4) enabled her to retire in 1902 at the age of forty. She lived on in Ulverston, a lady of leisure, until her death in 1935.[10]

Despite her brush with the law, Rebecca Thomas (Chapter 6) remained in business in Cheltenham until 1887 when she retired to Weston-super-Mare and ended her days in a boarding house there within sight of the sea, living on her savings.[11] In King's Lynn (Norfolk) in 1897 Susannah Everritt died in the local almshouses, to which she had been admitted a few years earlier after a long career as a dressmaker in the town.[12] She had moved to Lynn as a young improver in 1840, having served her apprenticeship in her home town of Wells-next-the-Sea. Dying in an almshouse may not sound much like success, but in fact places in Lynn's 'Bede House' were much sought after and they were only allocated to women of good character who had had respectable jobs. Residents were given a small weekly pension (around 7s.3d in the 1890s) plus an allowance of coal, paid for from the proceeds of centuries of donations. For a single working woman of Susannah's generation it was a satisfactory and comfortable end to a life of hard work.

Some dressmakers looked beyond the business of mere sewing; dressmaking was a skilled trade and many of the women who practised it were intelligent and enterprising. Some turned to writing books of instruction; some taught, either in their own homes or in technical schools; others used their experience to develop systems of taking measurements and drafting patterns. Some went into publishing, producing magazines and fashion plates; others ran mail-order businesses producing patterns to order or cutting out fabric for ladies wishing to make their own clothes who were nervous of wielding their scissors on expensive silks and woollens. There was money to be made by acting as agents for other people's goods like dyestuffs and sewing machines, beauty products and pharmaceuticals, sanitary towels and other intimate products, novelties and everyday products like tea. Across the country, women turned these opportunities to good account. Some of them are described below.

Authors of the 1840s

Dressmaking offered various opportunities to the talented or enterprising worker. One of the earliest of these was Mrs Thomas Willimott, who published *The Young Woman's Guide* in 1841. Mrs Willimott was keen to establish a 'General Domestic Female Institution' for girls over the age of fourteen. She solicited donations from her readers and appealed for information about suitable premises in London. She planned to teach millinery, dress, straw-bonnet and stay-making, embroidery, plain work, artificial flower-making, laundry, cooking, confectionary, household work and nursery work. Mrs Willimott did not give any reason why she thought a course of instruction would be preferable to a craft apprenticeship or on-the-job training – presumably hers was purely a commercial venture. Her book was didactic, offering instructions to mothers, boarding-house keepers, women of business and various categories of female servants, and providing recipes and instructions for a range of household activities from French polishing tables to curing hams. However, the bulk of the book was given over to 'lessons' on millinery, dress and stay-making, and it contained a number of un-labelled, fold-out patterns, presented without any allowance for seams. The instructions that accompanied them were ill-written and confusing – the novice dressmaker was unlikely to come away much the wiser. Mrs Willimott charged 10s.6d for each of her lessons and also offered 'A Lady's measure taken and lined out in plans for her own use £1.1s'. As having a complete dress made usually cost under 10s.0d, it is unlikely she had many takers.

Another would-be entrepreneur was Mrs Eliza Ann Cory, who published *The Art of Dressmaking* in 1849 for the 'industrious daughters of tradesmen and … persons of limited means'. It was a tiny, pocket-sized book, only twenty-five pages long, and her instructions were rudimentary. To arrive at a pattern she advised her readers to use an old, unpicked bodice as a basis and then adapt it using a combination of measurements and pin-to-fit. Her only comment on sleeves was 'No directions can be given for sleeves as fashion alone guides the shape of them', while she considered skirt-making so simple that 'anyone who would attempt a body would know how to make them'. It is unlikely that her readers learnt a great deal. Nonetheless, Mrs Cory was convinced of her ability to teach. On Mondays, Wednesdays and Fridays she received pupils at her residence on Gray's Inn Road and on Tuesdays, Thursdays and Saturdays she taught ladies in their own homes 'if in parties of four'. A course of six lessons at Mrs Cory's cost 7s.6d.

Mrs Howell was less ambitious but more able. Her *Handbook of Dressmaking* (1845) was intended for professionals.

> No young lady that is apprenticed, or about to be apprenticed to dress-making, should be without this faithful guide, since here are displayed all the paramount features connected with the art. The information here contained will serve to educate the greatest novice in the theory of the business, allowing the practice to follow. Again, no work-room should be without a copy, since it will save the principal much time and fatigue in giving various directions.

The book is clear and reasonably easy to follow and lays great stress on accuracy and attention to detail. Unlike the previous two writers, Mrs Howell knew how to teach.

Marie Schild

There were entrepreneurs in the publishing trade whose contribution to the development of dress patterns was just as great as that of Butterick, McCall and Weldon but whose names have faded into obscurity. The most prominent of these was probably Madame Marie Schild.[13] She had showrooms at 37, Tavistock Street, Covent Garden which she claimed were the largest in England; she cut patterns to ladies' own measurements, carried large stocks of patterns which were available by mail order both at home and abroad, specialized in patterns for fancy-dress costumes and published numerous magazines for all levels of the market. Her business was established in 1852 when paper patterns were still a novelty, but Madame Schild really came to the fore in 1870 as editor of *The Brighton Courier of Fashion* and *The Drapers' and Milliners' Gazette of Fashion*.

The Brighton Courier was produced for three months of the year – November, December and January – to coincide with the Brighton season. It was published in London but was to 'be had of all booksellers in Brighton' because, as the first issue explained: 'The principal occupation of society in Brighton, during the season, is to promenade during the daylight; soirees, balls, and dinner parties at night; at all of which it is the desire of the ladies to appear the best.' The paper contained fashion plates and copious descriptions of fashionable dress, a 'Fashionable Resumé' which detailed the main events of the social calendar and who had hosted them, lists of dressmakers recommended (no doubt for a fee) for possessing 'good style with moderate charges' and numerous advertisements, many of them for Madame Schild's other publications. *The Brighton Courier* seems to have ceased publication in 1873. [Plate 34]

The Drapers' and Milliners' Gazette of Fashion was aimed at the trade rather than private individuals. It contained fashion plates, descriptions of fashions and a free tissue paper pattern for one of the dresses shown; offered a course of dressmaking 'lessons'; and contained numerous advertisements for goods and services. It was, effectively, the first trade journal for dressmakers and was printed, monthly, by Samuel Miller at 37, Tavistock Street. An annual subscription cost 14s.0d, post free. Paper patterns were available for most of the

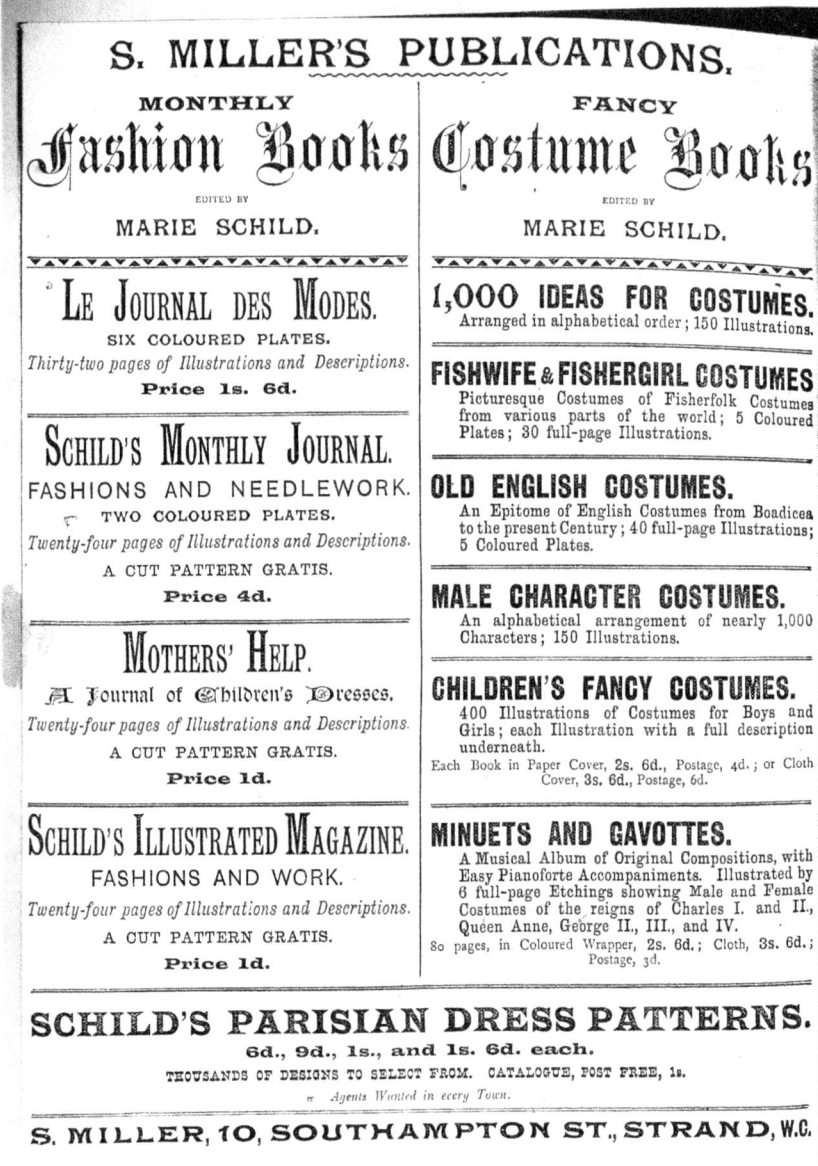

Plate 34 Advertisement for Samuel Miller's and Marie Schild's publications.

dresses illustrated or for the trickier parts of them and prices ranged from 4s.6d to 6s.6d for full patterns and 2s.0d to 2s.6d for part-patterns. These together with 'Every requisite for trade purposes' and subscriptions to the magazine were available from Samuel Miller, who was in partnership with Madame Schild –

indeed, he may well have been her husband, as 'Marie Schild' seems to have been a pseudonym. All sorts of trade goods were offered for sale. F.A. Hancock of 37-8 Wood Street, Cheapside, advertised bill heads, labels and 'Draper's Stationery'; Thomas Lomas of Manchester sold woven address labels; there were Wanzer kilting machines and hosiery machines; pentagraph tracing wheels; stocking suspenders at 3s.2d, 5s.2d and 7s.2d; dressmakers pinking irons from Paris; lead punching blocks (10s.0d) and mallets (5s.6d) for embossing fabric; hem-measuring devices, lay figures and all sorts of fabrics and trimmings.

In 1874 Mme Schild was advertising patterns based on 'a new method of cutting bodices without any seam on the shoulders. By this system the back is cut on the cross and thus a better fit ensured.' Bodices were at their most fitted at this date and a smoothly sloping shoulder line was admired. In March 1877 the magazine offered 'our usual coloured panorama of Spring and Summer [which] will be ready at the end of March'; this was 26 inches by 34 inches, showed over twenty styles and cost 3s.0d from the ubiquitous Mr Miller. In August an advertisement claimed: 'A good shaped body for trying on their ladies is a great boon to young dressmakers, first hands and ladies' maids'. These, made up in linen and tacked together, with the seam-lines marked up in ink so they could be re-used, were available at 15s.0d for a set of three.

This magazine was also short-lived. In January 1878 it was incorporated into *Le Beau Monde* – still published by Samuel Miller and edited by Marie Schild, one shilling per issue. In April 1879 it became *Madame Schild's Monthly Journal of Parisian Dress Patterns*. These publications seem to have been intended for fashion-conscious ladies rather than for the women who supplied them. On the back of her illustrated catalogue for 1877 Mme Schild advertised *Le Journal des Modes* as 'a monthly magazine by Marie Schild' at 1s.6d per issue and also *The Little Dressmaker* at 7d which consisted of patterns and illustrations of children's clothing.

By 1877 Marie Schild had come to an arrangement with Wheeler and Wilson, the sewing machine manufacturers, to act as her agents. She also had an arrangement with Judsons, the dye people, to send out one of their leaflets free with each of her patterns. By 1887 she had changed her allegiance to Singer, and she had established yet another publication, *Schild's Penny Magazine of Dress and Fashion* – twenty-three pages of cheap paper printed with black-and-white fashion plates, articles on dress and free paper patterns. Samuel Miller, her publisher, had moved to Southampton Street.

In March 1887 Mme Schild listed the hundred winners of her free prize draw for a Singer sewing machine and they came from all over the British Isles, from

Banff in the north of Scotland to Felixstowe on the Suffolk coast, and from Jersey, Dublin and County Down, demonstrating just how widely her publications were read. Her 'gratis' patterns were plain tissue-paper shapes, unmarked, and the magazine contained rudimentary instructions for making them up. For example, the *total* instructions for making up the 'Spring jacket' offered in May 1887 were as follows:

> Spring jacket illustrated on the front – No 4028. The correct pattern consists of nine pieces, viz, two fronts, half of vest and back, two side pieces, upper and under parts of sleeve, collar. Quantity of material required, two yards of cloth.

In 1893 she produced *New Skirts and How to Cut Them*, a booklet containing diagrams for cutting the new gored skirts that were becoming popular and also gave instructions for what she described as a 'stretched' bodice which relied on using a soft stretchy fabric cut on the cross to produce a close fit. As with all Marie Schild's books, it advertised her other publications, so we know that by the 1890s she and Samuel Miller were producing four monthly magazines: *Le Journal des Modes* (thirty-two pages and six coloured plates for 1s.6d), *Schild's Monthly Journal* (black-and-white fashion plates and needlework patterns, one tissue-paper pattern and one coloured plate for 4d), *Mother's Help* (illustrations of children's dress and one tissue-paper pattern for a penny) and *Schild's Magazine of Ladies Fashions* (twenty-four pages of illustrations and descriptions and a tissue pattern for a penny). By 1895 they were involved with yet another publication, *The Dressmaker's and Milliner's Butterick Quarterly*, which again concentrated on the supply of paper patterns, presumably under some agreement with the Butterick firm.

Their fancy-dress costumes are particularly interesting. Fancy-dress balls were an important feature of fashionable social life in the late nineteenth century. The 1881 catalogue contained 1,000 illustrations from 'the largest collection in the world' which belonged to none other than our old friend, her partner, Samuel Miller. She offered to 'make a paper model of any costume herein described ... and the coloured picture can be bought from Mr Miller'. Patterns could be cut to fit the buyer's own measurements. Selections could be sent to people living in the country and she even had an agent for them in Flinders Lane West, Melbourne, Australia. Judson's advertised in this catalogue, offering gold stage paint and 'the mysterious skull' – which glowed in the dark – for private theatricals.

The indefatigable Madame Schild also advertised various of her own inventions, including a patent gadget which fitted into the pocket opening and was supposed to deter pickpockets and a 'placket hole closer' which seems to have been an early form of Velcro. She did accordion pleating in various widths, priced by the yard. In June 1889 she was offering to pink ladies fabrics in various designs and Samuel Miller was advertising 'silk, plush and velvet cuttings'. She supplied 'Oxygen Water – a few applications will make the darkest hair a golden hue'. She also made sure of her future market by offering a doll for 3s.6d, which came complete with fifteen paper patterns for making up different outfits, including fancy dress, and a series of publications – *Dolly as a Baby, Dolly as a Girl* and *Dolly as a Young Lady* (undated). In the early years of the twentieth century Mme Schild diversified yet further, producing books of recipes.

Marie Schild had created a veritable empire which continued to trade into the early years of the twentieth century – yet her name is virtually unknown and nothing at all is known about her personally. She was the most prolific of the dressmaking entrepreneuses of the late nineteenth century, but she was not unique.

The Goubauds

Madame Adolphe Goubaud and her son produced a trade magazine – *The Milliners', Dressmakers' and Warehouseman's Gazette*.[14] It was founded in 1870 and in 1881 became *The Milliner, Dressmaker and Draper*. Mme Goubaud appears to have been connected with Goubaud et Cie in Paris, the firm which published *Le Moniteur de la Mode, La Modiste Parisienne* and *La Mode Artistique* (for which Gustave Janet drew the fashion plates). *The Milliners' Dressmakers' and Warehousemans' Gazette* was published in both Paris and London as an 'illustrated journal of the new modes, the coming fashions and latest novelties for wholesale and retail drapers and manufacturers in town and country'. It contained fashion plates in colour and black and white, descriptions of the outfits they showed, regular features describing the new fashions in Paris, articles by a 'Continental Correspondent' and others describing what was on sale in the Parisian wholesale warehouses, and there were short articles on general topics.

The November 1872 issue, for example, included pieces on the numbering of yarns (very detailed and technical), a report on the Committee of Patents (very critical), flowers as a source of inspiration for fabric design (very woolly), a comment on how English women dressed (well), the prospects of the American cotton crop (uncertain) and notes about Cantonese straw plait (cheaper than the English variety). The magazine appears to have received items for appraisal, and included notes that were effectively advertisements for Debenham and

Freebody's new pattern book, Allen and French's hats, Gourdet and Yates' 'Parisian Ornaments', Albert crepe, 'Little Rapid' knitting machines, Thomas Lomas's trade labels, A.R. Wells and Co's underclothes and waterproof fabrics, Judson's dyes, Messrs Wilson's bonnets, Fisher, Melles, Jones, Reid and Co's artificial flowers and a favourable review of a book by Thomas Brassey MP called *Work and Wages*.

The Goubauds were printers. Mme Goubaud advertised her own range of paper patterns which could be sent ready-made-up or adapted to fit individual requirements, and could be despatched to India and the colonies at a cost of 4d or 6d an ounce. She also published a range of handicraft books in the 1860s and '70s, giving instructions for embroidery, lace-making, crochet, tatting, knitting and netting.

Writers and teachers

Another little known entrepreneuse was Annie Tate. She was an American and in 1882:

> had succeeded in improving and perfecting a ruler (or scale measure). By the aid of this scale the veriest novice in dressmaking can, by measuring with an inch tape the exact size of the figure, draw and cut out different shaped garments … Such a system of mathematical precision has long been sought for, but had remained unfound until I brought out the "EUREKA" Dresscutter.[15]

Her system involved the use of a cardboard template with windows which could be adjusted. By 1886, she had published her system in book form and ran a dressmaking school at 61, Broad Street, Birmingham. A course of lessons cost two guineas, which included copies of her scale and her book. She also provided customized patterns for a shilling and 3s.6d and stock patterns for sixpence and a shilling. Mrs Tate was anxious to safeguard her invention, but despite her best efforts the essential features of it were soon pirated. [Plate 35]

Mrs Dobson was based in the north of England and her magazine, *The Dressmakers' Chart and Cutter,* was published in Manchester by John Heywood. Mrs Dobson developed a new system of cutting-out based on a chart of measurements 'distinguished from others by its cheapness and the ease with which it is learnt' and styled herself 'agent for the Scientific Dress Cutting Association' which was based in London's Regent Street but had branches across the country, and which, like Mrs Dobson, advocated cutting patterns based on mathematical calculations derived from a basic set of customer measurements.

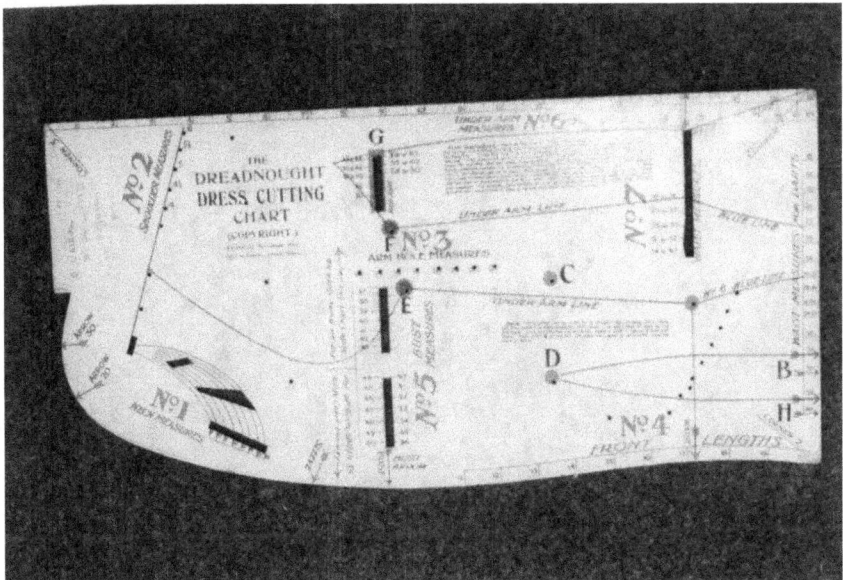

Plate 35 The 'Dreadnought' pattern-drafting template. It is very similar to Annie Tate's 'EUREKA' dress cutting system.

As dress became more and more fitted and complicated, many more measuring systems and books of instruction were produced, most of which relied on mathematical formulae to simplify pattern drafting [Plate 36]. Mrs Dobson's was one of the more successful. By 1889 she had agents across the north of England in Manchester, Southport, Seacombe, Grange-over-Sands, Barrow-in-Furness, Leek, Preston and Lancaster; her system was taught in numerous schools; and she herself was teaching domestic economy at the School of Technical Dressmaking in Preston (Lancashire).

The number of manuals and pamphlets and magazines increased rapidly after 1870. Many of their authors, like Mrs Dobson, were seduced by the idea of 'scientific' systems which created formulae by which measurements could be calculated. 'Scientific' had become a buzz word. Science was good, the high Victorians prided themselves on their modern inventions and the term was used in all sorts of inappropriate contexts – in America and France as well as in England.[16]

'Myra', editor of *Myra's Journal of Dress and Fashion* and *Myra's Journal of Dress and Needlework*, produced a series of booklets of 'Dressmaking Lessons' in 1877, and these were re-vamped and re-issued in 1887. She, too, laid great stress on measuring and supplied diagrams of exactly how this should be done. Her instructions are fairly basic, with illustrations of how to do straightforward

Plate 36 *Punch* cartoon, 26 February 1876. The caption reads '"Shall we - a - sit down?" "I should like to; but my dressmaker says I mustn't!"'

processes like gathering, sewing different types of seams and piping buttonholes. 'Myra' was associated with the Weldon pattern company – her booklets were available from them.

Mademoiselle Grandhomme's Cutting Out and Dressmaking (1879), translated from the French, advocated a confusing system of 'fixed, variable and verifying' measures, also based on 'scientific' principles. E.G. Kendall's *Instructions for the Cosmopolitan System of Dressmaking* (1892) advised making cardboard charts 'shewing the actual proportions for various measures taken' and boasted that 'the calculations being so accurately worked out by the inventor that a misfit is quite impossible'. M.A. Laughton's *Dressmaking: Guide to Freehand* (1897) showed how to plot patterns on a grid; A. Clarke's *Simple Instructions in Dresscutting by Tailors' Measures* also concentrated on pattern drawing. Mrs J. Bellhouse's *Be Your Own Dressmaker* included what she called the 'très facile' method of cutting out skirts but her instructions were garbled and the diagrams did nothing to clarify them. One wonders what Mrs Bellhouse's definition of 'très difficile' would have been.

Mrs Henry Grenfell taught at the Liverpool training school of 'Household Sewing with Home Dress Cutting'. Her best-selling work was probably *Dress Cutting-out: A Pupil's Manual for Home Study* of 1892. Mrs Grenfell claimed that it was a 'modern' idea in England that fitting and cutting-out could be taught, but in reality she was capitalizing on the fact that by the 1890s there was a shortage of fully trained dressmakers because for so long cutting-out had been the jealously guarded preserve of forewomen and principals. Sized patterns simplified cutting, but for a dress to fit really snugly, that pattern had to be adapted to the customer's measurements. Throughout the latter part of the nineteenth century numerous other books purported to offer 'new' systems of dressmaking. On examination, most of them turn out to be new ways of calculating measurements. Mrs Lowther Knight's pamphlet *How to Make a Dress from the European System of Dresscutting* (1896) gave instructions for making 'European perfect-fitting bodices' and 'Alpha skirts' (using 'Madame Knight's Alpha skirt scale'). Mrs (or Madame) Knight was the founder and principal of the Royal Counties Cutting College in Reading which opened in September 1889 and was under the patronage of HRH Princess Christian. Florence White published *Easy Dressmaking* (1892), a manual for teachers with fold-out charts and instructions for enlarging and adapting patterns. Tomlin's *Dressmakers' Guide: Cutting Made Easy* an 'entirely new and original Tailor's system' also appeared in the 1890s. Mrs Woodgate Low's *Technical and Practical Lessons in Dressmaking for Ladies Wishing to Perfect Themselves in Home Dressmaking* was published in 1893. Mrs Low recommended Butterick patterns and Singer sewing machines – presumably for a fee. She was 'an experienced teacher', and her instructions, though basic, are clear and sensible, interspersed with household hints about lining collars (with the silk from old umbrellas), cleaning black lace (sal volatile and old newspapers) and getting grease out of velvet (use salad oil). Mrs Balhatchet's *Dress Cutting and Making on Tailor's Principles*, Mme Levine's *The Rodmure System of Dress Cutting, Geometrical and Practical* and Miss Banks's *System of Self Teaching Dress Cutting* all came out in the 1890s and all attempted to show the best way of creating the smart, tailored look of the last decade of the nineteenth century.

A number of new dressmaking magazines also became available. The Tailor and Cutter's Academy published *The Ladies' Tailor*, which came out in 1884 and gave instructions and patterns for ladies' tailored wear. Weldons, the pattern firm, published monthly titles aimed at different parts of the market – *Weldon's Ladies Journal* at threepence, *Weldon's Dressmaker* at a penny, *Weldon's Bazaar* at a penny and *Weldon's Needlework* at twopence. *The Dressmaker and Milliner* had a brief run from March 1895 to November 1896.

The best of the bunch

Faraway the best and most usable of all these many manuals were R. Monroe's *Practical Dressmaking* (1879) and *The Elements of Modern Dressmaking* (1894) by Jeanette E. Davis, principal of the 'Women's Work' department at Manchester Municipal Technical School.

Monroe's instructions were very detailed even though she purported to be writing for ladies wishing to make their own clothes. She devoted a whole chapter to adapting patterns 'Fitting on and Rectifying Imperfect Fits'. It is worth quoting a short section to demonstrate her level of skill and the detail she gives. Here she is describing how best to alter a pattern that is an inch too tight at the bust. Rather than simply cutting the pattern piece a little larger at that point, she explains how:

> The alteration would be made by turning out the hem an inch wider at the waist and a quarter inch at the neck, sloping it out from one point to the other, not in a sudden slanting line, but letting it be more sudden from the neck to the chest and thence almost straight to the waist. As the waist is to remain the same size, the additional inch is used by giving one half to each of the bosom darts, which are also shifted a trifle more forward in order to preserve the same general appearance. The half-inch in each dart of course causes greater spring above them, and compensates for not having quite the full inch in the hem at the chest.[17]

It is less complicated than it sounds and works beautifully.

Dresses of the 1870s fitted smoothly, and Ms Monroe was full of tips for avoiding wrinkling. It was essential that, regardless of the shape of the bodice, the actual waistline should be cut on the straight of the fabric. Side pieces should be eased into the back rather than vice versa. Good paper patterns 'notably the American ones, have the back shoulder half-an-inch longer than the front; this is no error, and has more to do with a smooth, unwrinkled fit than many would believe'. Even the two front darts could make a bodice look bulky if the maker failed to 'draw down the piece – rather straining it, in fact, when sewing it to its adjacent side'. Skirt seams should always be stitched from top to bottom so that any unevenness was lost at the hem.

She devoted a full chapter to mourning. 'One point cannot be too strongly impressed – it is that no sewing must be visible.' Even top-stitching by machine was decorative and therefore unacceptable. Similarly 'crepe plisses' (frills of pleated crepe) were too elaborate and were 'rarely placed on the best class of mourning'. She was extremely particular: 'It looks very ill if [*the grain*] of the tucks slants from right to left, and that of the headings from left to right' and very knowledgeable about fabrics: 'Paramatta is too weak, unless lined, to stand heavy crepe trimming. Black mull muslin, about 6d a yard, is substantial enough, but should never be omitted, or the dress will split wherever a strain is given by the weight of the crepe.'[18]

Another whole chapter was devoted to different sorts of trimmings – puffings, kiltings, single box-pleats, double box-pleats, triple and quadruple pleats, feather ruches, single gathered ruches, fluted ruches, fluted flounces, single French hems, double French hems, narrow silk bindings, wide silk or velvet bindings, crossway bands, shell quilling, plain quilling, leaf trimming, upright puffs, twisted ruches, gatherings and frillings, braiding, fringing, bows and sashes, gauging, quilting and false buttonholes. Each merited a paragraph, some a page or two, of description.

Yet another chapter was devoted to the right linings for different fabrics, and again Ms Monroe was incredibly thorough. Cotton gowns should have a plain, deep hem, but longer skirts should have a facing 'laid inside with the coloured side outwards, to look like an upturned hem'. Velvet should be lined with sarsnet over Victoria lawn, and

> [L]eno is preferable to book muslin for lining between two other materials, such as to crossway bands or other flat trimmings, but bulges too much when unprotected by a backing; and though it will serve for narrow poor silk plisses, is too yielding for lining most folded trimmings, such as fluted ruches; book muslin being the better then.[19]

It is difficult to believe that Ms Monroe was really writing for amateurs. She was clearly an experienced dressmaker and the wealth of detail she provides gives an insight into best practice in an elite dressmaking establishment and shows how time-consuming such attention to detail must have been. At one shilling, her little book was a bargain.

The Elements of Modern Dressmaking by Jeanette Davis is similar. Miss Davis taught dressmaking to students sitting the London City and Guilds' examinations and intended her book to be used by professional dressmakers and their staffs. She was extremely scathing about the new systems of cutting out which supposedly did away with the need for trying on. She devoted a whole chapter to buttons and buttonholes and a large section to the merits of different types of bones; she described how to recognize and fit different figures, how to correct mistakes and how to remove wrinkles, and gave detailed instructions for methods of machining and cutting out different types of fabrics. For example:

> When cutting out good woollen stuffs, the scissors should be kept slightly outside the margins of the linings, as such stuffs draw up slightly under the scissors as they are being cut, and some small allowance should be made for this.[20]

She explained how to finish seams and considered leaving any raw edges to be 'very common work indeed'. It was, she thought, best to bind seams with ribbon, and if curves had to be cut to make them lie flat – 'Snipped curves do not look well – scallops should be used if cutting is needed.'[21] Tightly fitted sleeves presented enormous problems. Miss Davis explained that they should be stitched in two sections – down from the armhole to the elbow, and up from the wrist to the elbow, leaving a 'tiny bag. If the seam is joined down the back seam, from top to bottom, there will be no elbow, and it will not lie flat, but will twist from inside to outside in a very ugly way.'[22] She did not confine herself to descriptions of current practice but described techniques used in the past and the reasons for them. Miss Davis clearly had many years of experience under her belt and her book is still a mine of useful information.[23] [Colour Plate VII]

Experienced dressmakers like Mrs Monroe and Jeanette Davies were scathing about the idea that mathematical calculations based on a set of measurements could ever replace fitting the part-finished dress on the customer, perhaps more than once. They were right. The human body can have all sorts of bumps and hollows that would not necessarily show up however many measurements were taken. For example, in Exeter Museums' dress collection there is a dress believed to have belonged to Queen Victoria and dating from the last year or two of her life. It is of black silk trimmed with embroidered crepe and is beautifully finished.[24] The queen was just five feet tall and like many old ladies she probably shrank an inch or so in her later years, we also know from photographs that she was extremely fat – in other words, she was not easy to fit. The dress has a forty-four-inch waist, enormously wide sleeves and it is also clear that when her corset was laced up rolls of fat were pushed upwards – the back of the bodice has darts to accommodate them. Victoria in her later years was an exceptionally odd shape, but, in the days before orthopaedic surgery, there must have been many ladies who required their dressmakers to make comfortable dresses that concealed flaws or compensated for minor deformities.

Conclusion

A number of factors combined to change the dressmaking trade in the final third of the nineteenth century. The population had become larger and more bourgeois. Society decreed that respectable women should change their dress to suit different activities and different times of day – ball gowns were different from dinner gowns; afternoon dresses were different from morning dresses and different again from walking outfits; special clothes in special fabrics were deemed appropriate for seaside wear; dress for the different stages of mourning was carefully tabulated. Numerous women's magazines disseminated information about the changing forms and etiquette of fashion, and their strictures were followed even in the rural districts of Cornwall and the wilds of the Lake District. Advances in technology had created new machines and new fabrics like crepe and elastic. Publishers and printers found the market eager for as many fashion plates, patterns, magazines and manuals as they could produce. Even ordinary workers could capitalize on their talents. Meyer and Black in 1909 reported that some home workers 'make designs of their own and take them to show to firms in the hope of getting an order to make so many dozen copies'.[25] While firms did not pay well, and some pirated the designs they were shown, no doubt some women profited.

What *is* notable, however, is just how many talented female entrepreneurs the dressmaking trade produced – even if we no longer remember any of them.

Part Two

Dressmakers in fact and fiction

8

Dressmakers in fiction

Few ladies knew what really went on behind the closed doors of their dressmaker's workroom. Novelists and artists were equally ignorant but that did not stop them from painting or writing about dressmakers and seamstresses. Their work often bore little relationship to reality but nonetheless it coloured popular attitudes to women working in the trades.

As early as 1747, Robert Campbell in *The London Tradesman* warned of the low wages and long working hours in millinery and mantua-making, which suggests that by the mid-eighteenth century there must already have been underpaid, over-worked young women employed as dressmakers. However, artists and writers cheerfully ignored this reality. Eighteenth- and early-nineteenth-century cartoons and prints show dressmakers as strong, jolly and showily dressed. Milliners and dressmakers appeared frequently in plays and novels, but like maidservants they were often used as a sort of literary device to cross the social divide. Lovesick young men could be made to meet a dressmaker in the street, en route to fit a client or purchase goods (fictional dressmakers spent an improbably long time away from their workrooms), and could persuade her to pass messages to their loved ones. Dressmakers were portrayed as inveterate match-makers, and where they were given any sort of personality, they were shown as brash, vulgar, scheming and usually over-dressed, but also as clever and basically good-hearted. Robert Drury's *The Rival Milliners* of 1753 is a good example of the genre, as is *The Intriguing Milliners and Attornies' Clerks'* of 1738. This ends with a line the audience was expected to endorse: 'A clerk's a rogue, a milliner's a whore – a mighty fine discovery!' [Plate 37]

Anti-Pamela; or Feigned Innocence Detected by Eliza Haywood appeared in 1741, a year after Samuel Richardson's *Pamela*. Its 'heroine', Syrena Tricksy, was a young woman on-the-make, who saw her 'virtue' as a commodity to sell to the highest bidder. The novel was a spoof, lampooning Richardson's impossibly and irritatingly virtuous Pamela – but what is important here is that Syrena began her career as a mantua-maker's apprentice. From page one the reader knows what to

Plate 37 A dressmaker and her assistant on their way to deliver goods to a client. From the *Gallerie des Modes*, 1778. They are dressed in the height of fashion – just the sort of figures eighteenth-century playwrights had in mind.

expect. Similarly, it is no accident that Mrs Cole's brothel in John Cleland's semi-pornographic novel, *Fanny Hill* (1749), hides behind the 'outward decency' of a milliner's shop.

In John Madison Morton's *The Milliner's Holiday*, written in 1825, the Misses Potts, Dotts, Totts, Watts and Lotts are presented as a fearsome band – strong, fearless, threatening, loud and vulgar. 'Milliners out for a holiday! I'd as soon have met a drove of wild bulls!' whimpered one of the hapless young men they encountered. In fact, conditions in the trade had probably reached their nadir by 1825. We have little contemporary evidence for conditions in the 1820s, but the Children's Employment Commission report of 1843[1] gives us some clues – some of the interviewees had been working in the trade for fifteen or twenty years and described their experiences.

That report caught the imagination of novelists and artists in an unparalleled way. Subsequent investigations highlighted the plight of workers in other trades, many equally horrifying, but with much less effect. No other category of women workers – potters, calico printers, paper-makers, dyers, bleachers, straw-plaiters, lace-makers, glovers – produced the same outpouring of sentimental fiction and painting as did the poor needle-workers. Thomas Hood's *Song of the Shirt*, first published in *Punch* in December 1843 in response to the report, is still well-known:

> With fingers weary and worn,
> With eyelids heavy and red,
> A woman sat, in unwomanly rags,
> Plying her needle and thread -
> Stitch, stitch, stitch!
> In poverty hunger and dirt,
> And still with a voice of dolorous pitch
> She sang the 'Song of the Shirt'.

Its twelve lugubrious verses inspired many artists and writers. Most of the other authors whose writing is discussed here are virtually unknown, but their work has been chosen because it includes lengthy descriptions of dressmaking practice or illustrates situations that became clichés.

The young milliners

Mrs Elizabeth Stone wrote *The Young Milliners* in 1843, within months of the Royal Commission report being published, and made no secret of her agenda. She was writing:

In an attempt to awaken attention to the miseries which a great number of people ... endure in their exertions to gain their daily bread, viz., the Milliner's Apprentice, and other Needleworkers, of London, more especially.

Following a formula that was to become familiar, Mrs Stone made her heroine, Ellen Cardan, experience or witness all the abuses the trade had to offer. Ellen was apprenticed to a court dressmaker, Sally Minnow, who traded as 'Madame Sarina Mineau'. She was a relatively good employer but Ellen's job was boring. Her 'occupation was to thread needles, hand pins, find stray scissors, and so forth, till dinner time, ditto after dinner, till tea time; and ditto, repeated, after tea till supper time.' Mrs Stone gave her heroine sensitivities that would endear her to middle-class readers – Ellen was embarrassed about undressing and saying her prayers in the bedroom she shared with the other apprentices. Ellen was also, of course, beautiful, and so was expected to model bonnets for customers, showing herself off in a way no modest young Victorian woman would have been expected to enjoy: 'Your beauty will expose you to many a bold gaze and fulsome compliment. It cannot be helped, good customers must not be offended.'

Ellen worked cripplingly long hours, sometimes sitting up all night, sometimes standing at her work to keep herself awake. Early on, the forewoman told her, 'If dresses are to be made in no time, we can have no time to sleep.' One morning, having worked all night, and yawning with tiredness, she took a dress to a client 'Tired! What, at 8 o'clock in the morning exclaimed the unconscious young lady'. On another occasion Mrs Stone made her heroine work 'upwards of seventy hours consecutively' and then in a footnote referred her readers to the 'Report and Appendices of the Children's Employment Commission lately presented to Parliament, and published since these pages were written'.

Mrs Stone also introduced – rather clumsily, it must be said – a range of other characters to point up other abuses. There were the Lamberts, a family of shirt-makers, friends Ellen helped when she had time, who were struggling to survive against impossible odds. Then there was a dreadful employer called Mrs Modish who would call in on the girls toiling in her workroom, drinking a glass of gin on her way to bed, while expecting them to sit up working most of the night on her behalf. And finally there was Bessy. Bessy was a fellow dressmaker, and Ellen was made to spell out to her whose fault it was that they had to work such long hours: 'Why, the ladies themselves. You cannot imagine, Bessy, how unreasonable they are; how little thought they have for us.' Bessy soon decided there was a better way to make a living. Thereafter Ellen met her twice. The first time she was beautifully dressed, but the second, 'even Ellen, inexperienced as she was, could not doubt the vocation of the exposed wretch before her'.

The Unprotected, or Facts in Dressmaking Life

The Unprotected, or Facts in Dressmaking Life by 'A Dressmaker' was published in 1857 and relied on similar source material. The introduction is taken 'verbatim from evidence put before the House of Commons in 1855'.[2] The story follows Clara, a young apprentice working for a Mrs Morterton. Like Ellen Cardan, she is exposed to all the vices of the trade. Mrs Morterton refuses to look after girls who become ill and sends them home to their families; she stints her employees' food; she has her forewoman keep a difficult employee at 'close work' for weeks on end; she keeps a girl who has come to her without a premium as a 'runner' for five years rather than the usual three. Her girls are pestered by young men when they are out running errands after dark. Long hours are obligatory, clients must always be obliged, and Lady Emily, who takes an interest in the plight of the work-women and makes a point of ordering her dresses well in advance, is ridiculed. The proprietress urged her forewoman to ignore the girls' suffering:

> Miss Smith, however short the notice may be, never disappoint … Never see pale faces; take no notice whatever of headaches, side-aches, and finger aches, and as to fainting fits, why, girls find it convenient to faint sometimes.

Mrs Morterton had no compunction about lying to the Royal Commissioners about the hours her staff worked, and she was equally happy to deceive her customers.

> Here's a game! Lady St Aubyn innocently thinks that I am getting it [*a bonnet*] out of a case just arrived from Paris. Give me a bit of silver paper, and tuck a little into the bow, will you, because things are always most carefully packed "to cross the Channel"; and pray give the strings a light roll up, that they may look curly and as if just unrolled.

Mrs Morterton was careful to protect her own daughter, seventeen-year-old Minnie: 'I strictly forbid you entering [*the workroom*] after five in the evening; the air is too impure for a delicate girl like you.' And just in case the reader missed the point: 'If any of them are ill, and die, which they sometimes do, I can replace them; but if you were to die, what on earth should I do? No-one can replace you.' To emphasize this heartlessness the reader was reminded that the young women risking their lives in the workroom were highly respectable: 'There is Miss Wilson, she was four years at the best finishing school in Norfolk; and Adelaide Graham, she can speak French; and Clara Thompson can play, sing, draw.' Not that speaking French did Adelaide Graham much good. One day she went missing and after an anxious search she was found 'the mistress of a small establishment, but not the wife of its master; and, alas! in a fair way of becoming a mother'.

Conversation amongst the girls was frivolous and deeply distressing to a proper young woman like Clara. 'To be compelled to listen to the avowal of principles she had been taught to condemn, or the discussion of some work of fiction, the principles of which were not always of the purest kind, was abhorrent to her whole nature.' If this was not shocking enough for readers, the chapter leadenly entitled 'Stumbling Block to Religious Progress' hammered the point home. Girls were too exhausted to read their bibles, they fell asleep while in church, and some, horror of horrors, actually did their own mending on Sundays. Only the strongest would emerge from such conditions with their virtue intact.

Rather improbably, the voice of sweet reason was given to young Minnie Morterton. On page seventeen she prattled innocently to her mother:

> If I sat there [*in the workroom*] now as many hours a day as they do I dare say I should be as pale as Annie is. What a rosy cheeked girl she was when she came – and how like a ghost she has become! What is the cause of it, mamma, do you think?

By page 308, Minnie not only knew why Annie was so pale but she had a fully formulated plan to improve conditions. She would set a minimum wage of a pound a week and pay piece-rates, but make workers re-do bad work in their own time (to counter the argument that piece-rates would encourage the girls to be slapdash). She would reduce hours to a maximum of twelve a day, and less in the slack season, to keep everyone in employment, and she would bring in day workers at busy times, as well as charging live-in staff a fair rate for board and lodging. 'I would rather be thought unbusiness-like than unchristian-like at any time. I really could not let the girls work as they do,' she told her mother sanctimoniously. Mrs Morterton was predictably unimpressed.

Both these novels used the Children's Employment Commission reports as their starting points. The long hours, pitiful wages and debilitating illnesses came from evidence these contained, but the heroines' sensitivities were embellished to gain the readers' sympathies. The criticisms of uncaring clients came from evidence gathered by the Association for the Aid and Benefit of Dressmakers and Milliners, but the gin-swilling neglectful principals were their authors' own invention, as was Mrs Morterton's mockery of Lady Emily and Lady St Aubyn. The girls who resorted to prostitution harked back to the scurrilous eighteenth- and early-nineteenth-century plays discussed previously but had few real-life counterparts, while the heavy-handed moralizing and unremitting tragedy were in the tradition of many contemporary novels. Despite their professed aims, these were essentially works of fiction, and fiction is not the best medium in which to highlight real-life abuses.

May Coverley, the Young Dressmaker

May Coverley, the Young Dressmaker was published by the Religious Tract society in 1860. They hoped to persuade their readers to support good practice by describing it. May was apprenticed to an excellent employer, Mrs Browne, who employed a devout lady, Miss Davies, as forewoman. The girls were not overworked, all Mrs Browne's clients were thoughtful and ordered their dresses in plenty of time to ensure the workroom staff never had to sit up late, the girls were encouraged to go for walks in the evenings to get some fresh air but were urged to walk briskly so that they would not be accosted by young men. But all was not sweetness and light. One girl, Lucy, stole bits of fabric and trimmings. Some she sold; the rest she made into clothes for herself. She was discovered and dismissed, and was subsequently employed and dismissed by a number of other firms. The next time she was seen she was overdressed and with 'unsuitable' companions. The sensibilities of the readers of Religious Tract Society publications were too delicate to bear more information about Lucy's fate, but they were invited to weep for her *mother* who died of a broken heart!

May became friends with Miss Davies who confided in her the real problems she had encountered while working in London:

> Late hours, as I have said, formed one of the least of my troubles; for I was young and healthy, and I knew that it was only for a short time. What I felt most was the atmosphere of worldliness by which I found myself surrounded – the total absence of all religious observance; for even the Sabbath was sometimes, within the four walls of our workroom, scarcely to be distinguished from other days.

And while pious readers shuddered in horror at this revelation, they could comfort themselves with the information that long hours were not such a problem after all. Such tracts probably did as much harm as good to the workers' cause.

Paintings

Artists, too, were influenced by the Children's Employment Commission reports and produced work to tug at the viewers' heart strings. Numerous paintings added visual images to the debate. Richard Redgrave was proud of his own contribution – 'It is one of my most gratifying feelings, that many of my best efforts in art have aimed at calling attention to the trials and struggles of the poor and oppressed.'[3] As well as *The Seamstress* (1846) [Plate 38] and *Fashion's Slaves* (1847), he painted *The Poor Teacher* and *Going into Service*. Other artists were similarly inspired and many of them painted needlewomen. Examples are John Thomas Peele's *The Song of the Shirt* (1849), [Colour Plate VIII] Anna Blunden's *For Only One Short Hour* (1854), George Frederick Watts' *The Song of the Shirt* (c. 1848–50), Frank Holl's *The Slaves of the Needle* (undated), George Elgar Hicks' *Snowdrops* (1858), John Everard Millais' *Stitch! Stitch! Stitch!* (1876), Thomas Mildmay's *The Needlewoman* (1870s), and later works like *Weary* by Edward Radford (1887) or Claude Andrew Calthrop's *It's Not Your Linen You're Wearing Out, But Human Creature's Lives* (1891). Such was the power of Thomas Hood's poem that five of the above-mentioned artists used lines from it as titles for their paintings.

The sitters were often attractive young women, usually working in bleak, bare, but scrupulously clean attic rooms. But many of them were not dressmakers. Most dressmakers worked in workrooms, in groups, under the

Plate 38 *The Seamstress*, watercolour sketch by Richard Redgrave.

eye of a forewoman. Such workrooms were crowded, far from picturesque, impossible for an artist to penetrate and difficult to imagine or depict. The painters' subjects were seamstresses working as outworkers for drapers or wholesalers. Such work was even more badly paid than dressmaking, and was preferred by older women, mothers with young children or women caring for elderly or infirm relatives. Young, single, able-bodied women, particularly ones with angelic faces, could earn a much better living doing something else. Only Thomas Benjamin Kennington's *Adversity*, of 1891, showed two, recently orphaned sisters trying to earn their living as dressmakers. 'There is much quiet pathos in the drawing' ran the caption 'and the appearance of the girls but emphasises the squalor of their surroundings, and points the freshness of their loss'.[4] [Plate 39] In fact, the room is shabby but not particularly squalid; the girls, despite their mourning, look healthy; their business is quite well-equipped with a sewing machine and a lay figure; and they have plenty of work in hand. Their future might actually have been quite rosy. There was, even in the nineteenth century, considerable uncertainty about how the needle trades actually worked.

Plate 39 *Adversity* by Thomas Benjamin Kennington, 1891.

Lettice Arnold

Mrs Anne Marsh in *Lettice Arnold* (1850) exhibited just this sort of confusion. She too was trying to write propaganda in the form of a novel. Her heroines, Lettice and Myra, were the orphan daughters of a clergyman, but all the family money had been spent on medical attention for their father during his last illness and the girls were left to eke out a living by sewing. They were totally different characters. Lettice was a plain girl but impossibly good and accepted her lot cheerfully; Myra was lazy, sulky and a hypochondriac, but very beautiful. Through them, Mrs Marsh addressed herself to the problem of how poor needlewomen could make a living and decided that it was up to the ladies who ordered work, so she constructed a possible scenario. She described the commission Lettice was working on:

> It had been ordered by a considerate and benevolent lady, who instead of going to the ready-made linen warehouse for what she wanted, gave herself a good deal of trouble to get at the poor work-women themselves who supplied these houses, in order that they might receive the full price of their needlework.

Mrs Danvers, the philanthropic lady in question, was given a good deal of space to explain her cause.

Somehow, Lettice also found herself working on wedding clothes that turned out to be for an old school-friend. Such a commission would, in real life, almost certainly have been placed with a dressmaker, and if by any chance part of it had been farmed out, there is no way that the client would ever have discovered who made it up – but Mrs Marsh seldom allowed probability to get in the way of her narrative. Once the connection had been established, Catherine, the young bride, and her family effectively adopted Lettice and Myra. They arranged for Myra to be apprenticed to a Mrs Fisher, who ran a model millinery establishment – thus allowing Mrs Marsh to set out her thoughts on how millinery establishments should be run.

Mrs Fisher had married a young doctor and set up her own shop, with workrooms that were warm and well-ventilated, and where the girls were all supplied with a heated wooden pipe, wrapped in carpet, to rest their feet on 'the extreme coldness of the feet arising from want of circulation, being one of the causes to which [*Dr*] Fisher attributed many of the maladies incident to this mode of life'. She supplied 'plenty of good, wholesome, palatable food', and insisted that her workers exercise or rest for ten minutes every two hours. 'Nothing indiscreet or unseemly was ever permitted', but if the girls' parents and

Mrs Fisher approved, they could 'walk out' with young men. If the association led to marriage, the incredibly generous Mrs Fisher supplied the wedding dress, bonnet, wedding breakfast and a purse of pocket money! Myra had indeed fallen on her dainty feet, though not quite in the way she had hoped. Mrs Marsh took a swipe at popular romantic fiction in describing Myra's hopes:

> She fancied herself elegantly dressed, walking about a showroom, filled with all sorts of beautiful things ... Nay, her romantic imagination travelled still further, – gentlemen sometimes came up to showrooms with ladies ... Myra had read plenty of old rubbishy novels when she was a girl.

Mrs Marsh ensured that the reality was rather different. Myra met and married a young tailor, took advantage of Mrs Fisher's dress, bonnet, wedding breakfast and purse, but was predictably ungrateful 'married in a bonnet as if I was a tradesman's daughter, I am to be. Is it not TOO provoking?' she wrote to Lettice. But Mrs Marsh had her revenge. She turned Myra into an opium addict who died young! Lettice, on the other hand, acted as companion to Catherine's parents, charming her bad-tempered father and encouraging her sweet but inept mother. In due course she met the local curate, Mr St Leger, a schoolfriend of Catherine's husband, Edgar, who, like Lettice, Edgar and Catherine, was a paragon of saintliness. His life had been unbearably tragic; his mother had 'disgraced herself', his father had shot himself in shame, his four sisters had all died of consumption – naturally this made him an ideal companion for Lettice! Plausibility played no part in Mrs Marsh's literary universe, and unfortunately its lack (coupled with uneven writing and convoluted sentences) greatly detracted from the effectiveness of her campaigning. When her histories were so wildly romantic and improbable, few readers were likely to believe that any part of her narrative was true.

The Seamstress or the White Slave of England

The Seamstress or the White Slave of England (1853) by G.W.M. Reynolds was equally badly written and researched [Plate 40]. The heroine, Virginia Mordaunt, was a dressmaker's outworker. She was seduced, betrayed and died tragically, but it is only the circumstances of her employment that concern us here. She worked for a Mrs Johnson who sub-contracted for a court dressmaker, Madame Duplessy. Virginia was given far more responsibility than any real outworker would have had – she was given a cut-out dress of valuable velvet to make up, with just the

Plate 40 Illustration from *The Seamstress or the White Slave of England* by G.M.W. Reynolds, 1853. The dressmaker, working late into the night, is contrasted with the young women going to the ball in gowns she and her colleagues have made.

client's measurements to go on. Reynolds' source was probably Mayhew, his novel was published a year after the publication of Mayhew's *London Labour and the London Poor* which described an outworker making up a skirt in Genoese velvet.[5] Skirts required little fitting and were sometimes made by outworkers, but the bodice of an 1850s gown had to fit like a glove and would have been made in the dressmaker's workroom under the eagle eye of the first hand.

Reynolds' facts were extraordinary. Virginia was paid 3s.6d for making the dress – on which, naturally, she worked until 2.00 am. Three-and-six was a little on the low side for the making up of an evening dress, particularly when Madame Duplessy charged four guineas for the work, but given that Virginia was a sub-sub-contractor it was not an unreasonable payment for a night's work and a good deal more than most assistants earned. Anxious to reinforce his point, Reynolds invented a bill for the outfit:

18 yards velvet at 1gn a yard	£18.18s.0d
18 yards silk at 4s.0d a yard	£3.12s.0d
lace for bertha and trimmings	£15.15s.0d
making up	£4.4s.0d
Total	**£42.9s.0d**

It was an astronomical sum and though it may have been possible to buy such expensive velvet in 1853, it was certainly exceptional. Presumably the eighteen yards of silk were for lining, though lining silk cost less than 4s.0d a yard and a velvet skirt did not need to be lined. Virginia single-handedly completed the dress in a day and a night without a single fitting, another near impossibility. The bill makes no mention of the sundries all dresses needed (bones, hooks or buttons, interlinings) but suggests that the dressmaker supplied what (from the price) must have been antique lace for the bertha and trimmings. This would also have been most unusual – such laces were certainly worn but were usually heirlooms, added by the client. Reynolds' heart was in the right place but he knew too little of his subject to write about it convincingly. Unfortunately, most of his readers would have been much more familiar with prices and dressmakers' bills than he appeared to be and his inaccuracy in one area would have called into question his reliability in others.

Fanny the Little Milliner

Fanny the Little Milliner, by Charles Rowcroft, published in 1846, seemed to present a much more convincing picture. The fact that Fanny is a milliner is only incidental to the story, but the conversation she has with her friend Julia explained, without apparent artifice, the difficulties milliners faced, and clearly Rowcroft was trying to inform his readers. The girls discussed an old colleague: 'that tall pale girl who used to work extra hours' who was trying to live on 8s.0d a week (£20.00 pa):

> And obliged to dress genteelly that she might not discredit the establishment ... You can't get a furnish'd room under 3s a week. Then there's fire – say 4d a week, one week with another. She can't do without light – there's candles and soap – 6d a week, you couldn't do with less. Then there's bread – we ought to have begun with that; – what a pity it is that we can't live without eating! How much shall we put down for bread? – two quartern loaves a week? – no, that's not enough; we must say three – that's 1s – she must help herself out with potatoes say 4d a week for potatoes, We must let her have a morsel of butter with her bread and potatoes, a penny a-day for butter. Then there's tea; tea is as necessary for a poor girl almost as bread; she couldn't drink cold water always; but we can't put down much for that; suppose two ounces of tea a week, that's 6d.

It all sounds very convincing, but actually Rowcroft's figures are dubious. It was possible to rent a single room for less than three shillings a week. A quartern loaf cost 6d in 1845 (according to Mayhew) so Julia's bread would actually have cost 1s.6d but her 7d would have bought almost three-quarters of a pound of butter, though her two ounces of tea would have cost at least the 6d allowed for it. In 1900 (when prices had changed little) 4d worth of potatoes fed a family of three for a week and whole families were spending only 5d a week on soap.[6] Furthermore, if she worked for an establishment that was concerned about how she dressed, Julia was not an outworker but a daily hand. In that case, most of her working day would have been spent at her employer's, where she might also have taken her meals, so she would have paid very little for food and fuel on her own account.

Rowcroft also reflected attitudes to milliners and sex. 'Great ladies very seldom interest themselves about poor milliner girls ... They consider us as mere instruments and machines for administering to their pleasure.' And when one great lady, Lady Sarum, tries to create

> ... a benevolent association of ladies of rank and influence, desirous of alleviating the hardships, privations and temptations to which the class of young females in the employment of milliners and dressmakers is particularly exposed

she is soon led to deduce – by the gentleman Fanny has rejected – that 'these milliner girls, I have heard say, are the most artful husseys in nature'. Even her maid sees Fanny as 'a pale-faced, band-box carrying minx that is no better than she ought to be'. Here mid-nineteenth-century reformism stumbled against popular stereotype and capitulated to it. Charles Rowcroft seems to have been uncertain of his own aims.

Prostitution, immorality and dressmakers in fiction

The association of dressmaking and loose morals was never far from people's minds. In 1747, Robert Campbell had cautioned parents not to bind their daughters to milliners because:

> The vast Resort of young Beaus and Rakes to Milliners' Shops, exposes young Creatures to many Temptations ... I am far from charging all Milliners with the Crime of Connivance at the Ruin of their Apprentices; but fatal Experience must convince the Public, that nine out of ten of the young Creatures that are obliged to serve in these Shops, are ruined and undone.

And

> ... the Title of Milliner [is] a more polite Name for a Bawd, a Procuress, a Wretch who lives on the Spoils of Virtue.

As for mantua-makers:

> If a young Creature, when out of her Time, has no Friend to advise with, or be a check upon her Conduct, it is more than ten to one but she takes some idle, if not vicious Course, by the many Temptations to which her Sex and narrow Circumstances subject her ... Men pride themselves in debauching such as betray any Marks of modest Virtue.

Campbell tells us more about the views of middle-class men in the eighteenth century than about the experiences of contemporary working-class women, but he reflected and perpetuated stereotypes.

As we have seen, even well-meaning nineteenth-century novelists reinforced the idea of the dressmaker-as-prostitute, usually having some dressmakers 'go on the streets' to point up the virtue of their heroines.

Ruth

Mrs Gaskell's novel *Ruth* (1853) is probably the best-known example of a work of fiction depicting the dressmaker/prostitute. Ruth is chosen by her employer to go to a ball to do running repairs on ladies' dresses, not because she is an exceptionally good worker, but because of her beauty. At the ball she catches the eye of a well-to-do young man who seduces her and gets her pregnant.

Ruth is an orphan with no-one to support her but ultimately she is befriended by a Baptist minister and his sister who present her to their community as a young widow with a child. When this petty deception is discovered, both they and she are ostracized. Ruth only redeems herself by selfless nursing during an epidemic and by her resulting death. Mrs Gaskell was the wife of a minister, and as a child had accompanied her doctor uncle on his rounds – she had a strong social conscience and a genuine knowledge of the conditions in which people like her heroine lived. The sentiments she expressed were not necessarily her own, but only by such extreme measures could she gain her readers' sympathy for Ruth.

Novels of the 1870s and 1880s

By the 1870s novels began to present a more positive picture of the dressmaking profession. In *Nellie Graham the Young Dressmaker* (1874), C.R. Doggett's objections to the trade are still purely moral. Nellie is anxious to become a dressmaker and her parents support her, but her Aunt Rachael, crippled (and therefore made wise by suffering), opposes her plan, believing that Nellie would be better-off in service. Nonetheless, Nellie becomes a live-in apprentice to a dressmaker in a local town. She shares a bedroom with two sisters, Sophy and Esther, daughters of a local draper, who are learning the trade so that they can work for their father. They are sewing machinists – in this context the sewing machine represents modernity and the antithesis of traditional values. In case this is not clear enough, Doggett has the girls tease Nellie *because she says her prayers*. Eventually they all become friends, and Esther and Sophy persuade Nellie to make a flimsy ball gown to attend a dance their father is organizing. The gown tears the first time she wears it, and Nellie is left with a garment she is ashamed to own (presumably dancing was too frivolous an occupation for Doggett to condone) and a debt to her former friends for the fabric. She works hard to pay off the money and then returns home to marry a good and worthy man, bitterly regretting that she did not heed her aunt's advice.

> Ah' she would say to herself when at a loss in contriving a tempting dinner for her husband, "dear Aunty's words have come true! If I had gone into service, I should have known how to do everything; instead of having to learn now … There's one comfort, I can make my own, and baby's clothes; and if hard times should come, or business be dull, – I can turn to my dressmaking again. That will find food for my dear ones, though I am rather stupid at cooking it."

But Doggett's views were outdated. In *Dressmaker to the Queen* by H.J. Brooke Houston, published just five years after *Nellie Graham*, dressmaking is the salvation of two women. Jennie, a farmer's daughter, is apprenticed to Mrs Dysart. She runs a modern establishment:

> Twenty girls were at work in a large, scantily furnished room, and the whirr of sewing machines and the rustle of silken garments was the only sound to be heard … Madame was not a very severe mistress; she did not drive her apprentices cruelly, nor half-starve them, nor did she expect impossibilities.

Jennie shows considerable flair for design and is taken on as a partner: 'It was a very nice amusement to stand before a lay figure and pull a dress about until it hung prettily.' Lay figures, like sewing machines, were new in the 1870s. Jennie also found work for her widowed mother who was no longer welcome in their old home because her son had taken a wife; she became house-keeper to the establishment and transformed it.

In *Grace Myers' Sewing Machine* (1872) T.S. Arthur considered the provision of sewing machines to enable women to earn their own livings to be a positive benefit, and his male characters establish 'The Fairfield Sewing Machine Temperance Society' and save the money they would otherwise have spent on beer for this purpose.

As early as 1870 a pamphlet produced for Davis, the sewing machine manufacturer, could satirize the idea of the struggling gentlewoman-seamstress. For ten pages the heroine, Rosalie Thornton, followed a well-worn path – rejection by her social equals, separation from her aristocratic admirer and a painful struggle to earn a living. But Rosalie's problems came about only because she had chosen the wrong sort of sewing machine and 'a Spartan-like patience was required to conquer the innumerable difficulties it presented to a learner'. The booklet was entitled *Without a Penny in the World: A Story of the Period* and the 'Period' was in fact the brand of sewing-machine which solved all her problems, including re-uniting her with her lover! 'No trouble is required to learn it, it makes a beautiful lock stitch … and the worker of it is certain of constant employment'! [Plate 41]

A novel by Sarah Tytler, *Girl Neighbours*, published in 1888, presents dressmaking in a completely new light. Two girls, Pie and Harriet, from very different social backgrounds, become friends. During a smallpox epidemic,

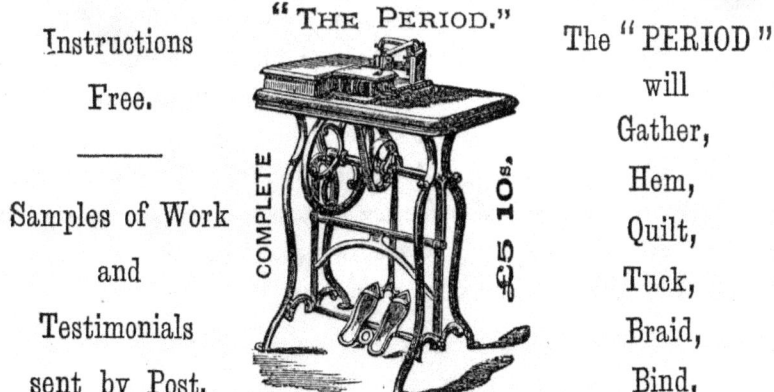

Plate 41 Advertisement for 'The Period' sewing machine, 1870.

a nurse, Emily Brandon, comes to their village to look after Harriet who has contracted the illness. Miss Brandon comes from a respectable family but both she and her two sisters earn their own livings, a fact that impresses Pie and Harriet enormously, to the extent that they persuade their parents to send them away to college, together, so that they, too, can become independent. One of Miss Brandon's sisters taught cookery; the other taught 'scientific dressmaking' and went 'about the world, teaching the trade on scientific principles to village dressmakers and their apprentices, and to sewing classes in schools'.

Finally, Margaret Penn's autobiographical novel *Manchester 14 Miles* (written in 1947 about the late nineteenth century) points up the difference between working for an old-fashioned dressmaker and working in a modern department store workroom. Hilda Winstanley is apprenticed to a village dressmaker, Mrs Ormston, learns nothing and spends most of her time doing housework. She then gets a post with 'Hankinson and Sankey', a department store in Manchester with a 'court dressmaking' department. She does well, loves the work, makes friends, enjoys being sent on errands to big stores in the city and develops sophisticated tastes. (See also Chapter 6, p.155)

Conclusion

The way dressmakers were depicted in fiction mirrored the shifts and turns of the trade's development. From being an occupation which in the eighteenth century was seen as a route into prostitution, and one which up to the 1860s was seen to exploit its employees and put their health and morals at risk, by the 1880s dressmaking was rehabilitated, at least in literature, as a modern career offering opportunities for respectable, independent young women. In fact, the late 1870s had seen one of the worst depressions in British history and wages had fallen. For dressmakers working in the new workrooms in big department stores conditions were usually tolerable, but seamstresses and many dressmakers were badly affected. Life did not always imitate art.

9

Dressmakers in fact

The women who dressed our forbears were real people, not fictional characters. Most of them were not impossibly virtuous like Clara, or Lettice Arnold, or Nellie Graham, or easily led astray like Adelaide Graham and Bessy, or opium addicts like Myra. They were ordinary women with homes and families, faults and virtues, hopes and dreams; most of them worked hard and many were highly skilled. Like most working people, they are remembered, if they are remembered at all, mainly as names or statistics, but it is possible to rescue just a few of them from obscurity.

Sadly, we have virtually no information about the enterprising women who became mantua-makers at the end of the seventeenth century, though we do know that Elizabeth Browne in Durham was the daughter of a former servant to an official of the royal court and that a number of the Chester dressmakers who fell foul of the tailors' guild were the wives and relatives of master tailors. We also know that Mary Yeomans in York – or perhaps her husband – was sufficiently well off in the 1690s to be able to pay a number of substantial fines without going bankrupt and that within a few years she was doing sufficiently well to be able to take on an apprentice.

The eighteenth century

There is not a great deal more information for the eighteenth century. Elizabeth Sanderson tells us that the women who became mantua-makers in Scotland in the eighteenth century had upper or middle-class backgrounds:

> Cicely Murray's father was the brother of William Murray of Polmaise in Stirlingshire, Christian Learmonth's mother was a daughter of Livingston of Parkhall near Falkirk, Katherine and Anne Ramsay's mother was a daughter of Kerr of Kippielaw in Roxburghshire, to mention only a few. If not gentry, then family background was probably among the professional classes. Anne

Wardrope's father was a surgeon, Carola Young's father was a minister, Janet Anderson's father was postmaster-general at Edinburgh and a writer, the equivalent of a solicitor and the most influential profession in the city. Some milliners, of course, were merchants' daughters. Fanny Mushet was the daughter of Walter Mushet, a fairly well-off merchant trading, like herself, in the Luckenbooths in the High Street.[1]

The picture in eighteenth-century England was rather different. As we have seen, Thomas Wolfe, rector of Howick in Northumberland, and Attwood Searancke, a Romford (Essex) schoolmaster, both apprenticed their daughters to mantua-makers (in 1785 and 1814), but they were unusual. Most eighteenth-century English mantua-makers came from the tradesman class. In Devon, for example, Mary Lewis's father was a mariner, Elizabeth Blackmore's was a joiner, Ann Joll's was a maltster, Ann Gliddon's was a blacksmith and Mary Hearson's was a carpenter. In Essex, Elizabeth Judd, a labourer's daughter, was apprenticed to Elizabeth Bright whose husband worked as a gardener. In Sussex, Mary Comper's husband was a flax-dresser and Mary Pattenden's father was a brickmaker. In Hampshire, Mary Wagland's husband was a carpenter and in Richmond, Lucy Smith's husband made periwigs.[2] In and around London, the Sun Fire Insurance registers list James Partridge, joiner, William Chantler, watchmaker, Reuben Robinson, mariner, Thomas Goodwin, victualler, and James Sleet and Thomas Pearson, both carpenters, among many other tradesmen, who all shared premises with their mantua-maker wives in the early 1770s.[3] The list of examples could go on and on – but they are only examples and there are insufficient of them to compile viable statistics. And confusingly, at the same period in London, the insurance registers also list a number of mantua-makers' husbands as 'gent', men like William Gough on Charlotte Street, John Edmond on Wells Street or John Bell at Charing Cross. This presumably means they did not work. No doubt some were retired men with younger wives, but it is difficult to be certain of the social position of the others.

We know that gentlewomen in the country, like Mary Hardy in Norfolk and Elizabeth Shackleton in Lancashire, socialized, to a greater or lesser extent, with their mantua-makers. Aristocrats like Lady Winn at Nostell Priory saw their dressmakers as people who would appreciate a hamper of country produce and a haunch of venison, gifts they would have been unlikely to offer their scullery-maid or labourers on their estates. Sarah Hurst in Horsham would not have described herself as a mantua-maker, but nonetheless she made gowns for her father's customers while at the same time socializing with the local gentry and eventually marrying one of them.

Of course, the mantua-makers about whom we know the most are the ones who worked for well-to-do clients. Many of these women were educated and literate, writing letters to their clients that were at least as grammatical and well expressed as the ones they received in return, and many were well travelled, regularly visiting London or Paris to buy goods and see the latest fashions. At the other end of the scale, no doubt, were the illiterate mistresses and apprentices identified in Chapter 2, working for a poorer clientele and deriving their information about fashion from the better-class firms in their nearest town; about these women we know virtually nothing.

The nineteenth century; case studies from the census

Much more information becomes available in the nineteenth century. In 1864 Miss Thomas (interviewee 90 – see Chapter 6), who ran a fashionable business on the Promenade in Cheltenham, complained to the Children's Employment Commissioners that not 'so many respectably connected girls are apprenticed ... as there used to be'. There is some evidence to suggest that this was the case, certainly if we compare the nineteenth century with the eighteenth century.

While there has been some debate about the accuracy of census data in relation to women's employment, it is nonetheless one of the best resources available if treated with caution.

A survey based on the census returns for three places – Leicester, Sidmouth and Ulverston in 1841, 1861 and 1881 – casts a good deal of light on the type of women who went into the dressmaking trade.[4] The towns were very different. Leicester is a county town in the Midlands, and by the nineteenth century it was a manufacturing centre, specializing in the making of hosiery, knitwear, elastic webbing, caps and cigars; Sidmouth was a fashionable seaside resort on the south coast of Devon, which had been catering for an elite class of summer visitors since the 1790s and which had expanded in the 1820s when a large estate was sold and a number of grand summer residences – coyly described as 'cottages' – were built; Ulverston was an isolated small town in rural Lancashire, 'capital' of the Furness district and serving a population of hill farmers, coal miners and iron workers. However, the findings for all three places are fairly similar.

The 1841 British census is the first one to list people by name, address and occupation; previous censuses had simply counted heads. By 1861 the census also detailed the relationships between people in the same household; these could only be inferred from the listings in 1841. The 1841 census rounded ages up or down to the nearest five years; subsequent censuses recorded ages as they were given to the enumerator – though clearly not all the respondents told the truth or did not know their exact ages. There are, for example, quite a number of women who apparently aged five years or less in a decade!

It was possible to assess the social status of most of the dressmakers in the survey from the occupations of their fathers, husbands or brothers, though of course, a number of dressmakers (between a third and a quarter in Leicester, fewer in the smaller towns) lived apart from their families in lodgings, with their employers or heading their own households. It was also possible to analyze the ages of dressmakers (while acknowledging that they were not always going to be entirely accurate) and thus give the lie to the idea that the work was so taxing that few women made it into old age. By comparing the numbers of women describing themselves as 'dressmaker' with the number of firms listed in contemporary directories, it was possible to determine roughly how many were employees and how many were working on their own account. Looking at the households in which dressmakers lived also gave some idea of their circumstances; it could not disprove the calumny that dressmakers moonlighted as prostitutes, but it did suggest it was unusual. While a few dressmakers did have illegitimate children, that simply showed they had had sex outside of marriage, not that they had been paid to do so. The results of the survey are given below.

Population and the numbers of dressmakers

First of all, it will be useful to compare the numbers of millinery and dressmaking firms listed in directories[5] with the numbers actually engaged in the trades in the three towns (as shown in the census) and to set this against the size of the local populations – though of course, all the towns served rural hinterlands as well as their own residents and the figures cannot accurately reflect those. These statistics are shown in Table 13.

This would suggest that by 1861 firms in both Leicester and Ulverston were employing larger numbers of staff than they had in 1841. Things were rather different in Sidmouth, probably because the town's popularity as a resort for wealthy summer residents – and thus the opportunities for dressmakers – had peaked in the 1820s and '30s. Between 1861 and 1881 the expansion of the trade slowed a little in all three places, partly as a result of the economic decline of the mid-1870s and partly because the market was saturated.

Table 13 Population, dressmakers and firms in Leicester, Ulverston and Sidmouth, 1841, 1861 and 1881.

	Leicester	Ulverston	Sidmouth
Population 1841	50,806	5,352	3,309
Dressmakers 1841	292	58	92
Firms 1841	191	17	4
Population 1861	68,052	7,414	3,354
Dressmakers 1861	1,028	122	97
Firms 1861	115	29	7
Population 1881	122,203	10,008	3,475
Dressmakers 1881	1,081	170	143
Firms 1881	191	16	9

Social status

There have been various attempts to evaluate the social status of different sorts of occupations. This study divides the jobs of husbands, fathers and other male relatives who were 'heads' of households which contained dressmakers into three main categories. It is thus a fairly simplistic analysis but it is nonetheless informative.

- Group 1 – managers, employers of labour, master craftsmen, people who described themselves as 'annuitant' or 'independent', clergymen, teachers and other individuals who appear to have had 'white collar' jobs.
- Group 2 – craftsmen, tradesmen, clerks, policemen, innkeepers, shopkeepers, commercial travellers, railway engine drivers, etc.
- Group 3 – mostly unskilled tradesmen – labourers of various kinds, miners, factory hands, warehousemen, carters, bill posters, hawkers, tradesmens' journeymen and shop assistants. It also includes members of skilled occupations which are known to have been particularly depressed in the mid-nineteenth century, like framework knitters and shoemakers.

The proportions of women from the three classes who worked as dressmakers in the three towns are shown in the pie charts below [Figure 2].

Group 3, the poorer section of the working class, predominated in all three places throughout the century. The numbers from Group 1 were larger in the

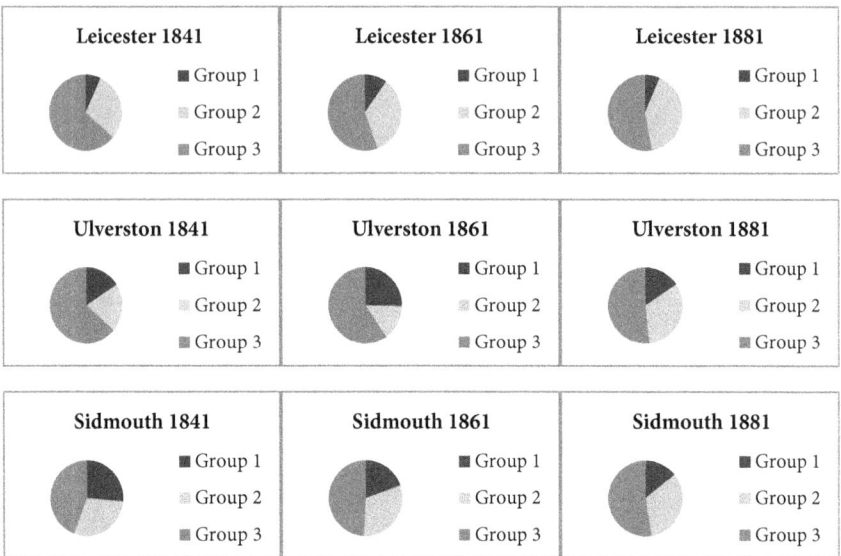

Figure 2 Social status of dressmakers in Leicester, Ulverston and Sidmouth, 1841, 1861 and 1881.

smaller places, perhaps reflecting the lack of opportunities there for girls from respectable families who needed to earn their own livings, while there was comparatively little fluctuation in the percentage of girls from the tradesman class. However, the figures suggest that Rebecca Thomas was probably right; over half of the women working as dressmakers in and after 1841 were *not* 'respectably connected'.

Age groups

Despite the fact that fictional dressmakers were always young, and the implication that few dressmakers could possibly survive into old age because of the rigours of their trade, the figures suggest that, though the majority of working dressmakers were in the twenty-to-thirty age range, a significant number were older and several were over sixty – seven in Leicester in 1841 and twenty-six in 1861, nearly all single women or widows. The majority of girls aged between fifteen and twenty were apprentices or improvers; there were just two girls under the age of fifteen in Leicester in 1841 – but that was probably due to the enumerator's practice of rounding ages up or down to the nearest five – by 1861 there were fourteen. The returns often explain why. For example in 1861, thirteen-year-old Amelia Richards, an apprentice dressmaker, was the daughter of a tailor – a notoriously underpaid profession – and out of nine children she was the eldest girl so her family desperately needed her to bring in a small wage or at least to be self-supporting. Thirteen-year-old Lizzie Hills, who was the eldest of the three children of a widowed schoolmistress, was in a similar position. Fourteen-year-old Mary A. Henson was the stepdaughter of William Appleton, a hosier, and he and her mother had five small children so Mary and her younger sister, Frances, had to work. Mary made dresses; Frances was a framework knitter. Other very young girls were working for their mothers – like Ann Williamson's two girls, fifteen-year-old Elizabeth and thirteen-year-old Lucy on Leicester's Newarke Street.

The twenty-to-thirty age group contained girls who had completed their training and were unmarried or newly married, so it is not surprising that this was far away the largest group in all three places. After the age of thirty numbers declined as family responsibilities increased or the need to contribute to the family income became less urgent. However, it may well be that there were women in that age group who did a little dressmaking on the side but did not tell the enumerators, either because it was an occasional sideline or to preserve their husband's pride in being the family breadwinner [Figure 3].

The figures were similar in Ulverston with one under-fifteen recorded in 1841 and four in 1861. However, the numbers of married dressmakers there over the age of thirty declined sharply – perhaps reflecting an old-fashioned reluctance on the part of husbands to allow their wives to admit they worked. In 1841 there were just two dressmakers in the town over the age of sixty and in 1861 there were none [Figure 4].

The age balance in Sidmouth was similar, with four under-fifteens in 1841 and seven in 1861. There were nine over-sixties there in 1841, a sixth of the total number of dressmakers in the town. Perhaps the higher percentage of older women in the trade suggests that a number had seen opportunities expand in the 1820s with the influx of wealthy new residents and had brushed up their sewing skills to take advantage of them. Alternatively, it might simply reflect the fact that Sidmouth was a healthy place to live and more working women survived into their forties, fifties and sixties. By 1860, however, though there were a significant number of Sidmouth dressmakers who were over thirty, none admitted to being over sixty [Figure 5].

The balance remained much the same in all three places in 1881, though a larger number of thirteen-and fourteen-year-olds were employed. Life expectancy within the trade, as well as outside it, had also improved considerably; in 1881 Leicester had fifty dressmakers who were over sixty; Ulverston had seven and Sidmouth nine.

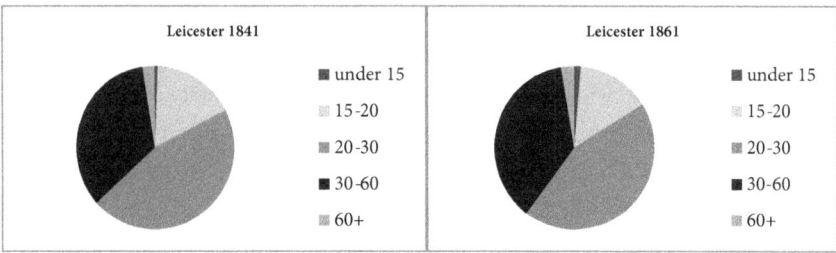

Figure 3 Ages of dressmakers in Leicester, 1841 and 1861.

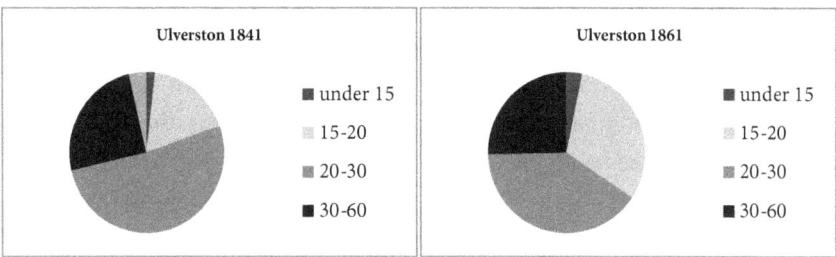

Figure 4 Ages of dressmakers in Ulverston, 1841 and 1861.

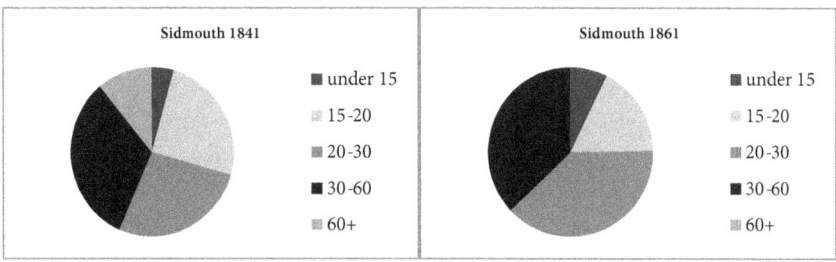

Figure 5 Ages of dressmakers in Sidmouth, 1841 and 1861.

Family lives in Leicester in 1861

Not only does the census supply statistical data, it also offers endless glimpses into the lives of individual dressmakers. It shows us, for example, that many struggled to work while looking after young families. Susannah Middleton was just twenty-three, but she was responsible for six younger siblings, three of whom who were not old enough to work. Twenty-four-year-old Ann Mason was the wife of a glover – another poorly paid occupation – and had to work despite having two babies; Mary Morris, a tanner's wife on Hill Street, had three small children; Elizabeth Almond, a sawyer's wife, had four and let space to a boarder; thirty-seven-year-old Mary Holland, wife of a turner on East Bond Street, managed to make dresses while caring for *seven* children under the age of twelve. There were dozens of other examples.

Widows who were the sole support of young families fared even worse, as did unmarried girls with children. Sarah Gill lived on Wheat Street with her two illegitimate sons – six-year-old Alfred and four-year-old Frederick. She does not seem to have had a resident partner. Neither did Jane Raby on Grafton Place who had a nine-year-old son and a baby daughter, nor Ellen Mason who lived alone on Grace Road with baby Ada.

Dressmakers from out-of-town usually lived in lodgings. Some stayed in common lodging houses; these had a very bad reputation and women living in them were often seen as little better than prostitutes. Agnes Galpin from Chard in Somerset was in a Leicester lodging house in 1861, as were two other dressmakers who were among the fifteen tenants of an umbrella maker who kept a boarding house on Britannia Street, but most dressmakers made private arrangements. Poor families often let rooms and the dressmakers who lived with them must have had a pretty uncomfortable time – for example, twenty-five-year-old Elizabeth Clayton lodged with a framework knitter, his wife and six children. Elizabeth Draycott was thirty-seven, so presumably quite an experienced dressmaker, but she boarded with the Butters family in a terraced house on Chatham Street. Thomas Butters was a druggist's clerk and he and his wife had five daughters, ranging in age from seventeen to two months, and also took in two (male) lodgers. Catherine Roberts boarded with an agricultural labourer, his rag-picker wife, their five children, the man's widowed cousin – a charwoman – and her seven-year-old son. They all crammed into rooms in a house on Lower Green Lane. For women like these, going to work must almost have been a relief.

By contrast, some of the dressmakers who lived at home came from relatively well-to-do families. Seventeen-year-old Sarah Young was the daughter of 'a manufacturer of hosiery employing 20 men'; Mary Ann Bass's father was a frameholder[6] employing thirty men; Mary and Martha Cockerill were the daughters of a grazier who had twenty-three acres of land. Emmeline and Clara Weston's father was a 'Professor of Music' while Mary Harriet Boyd's father was an artist, one of her brothers was a jeweller and another a 'photographic artist'. Emma Bland was the daughter of a builder with seventy-four men and eight boys working for him, and her family employed a nursemaid and a housemaid. Seventeen-year-old Mercy Fossett was the milliner granddaughter of Charles

Smith, a Baptist minister at the Ebenezer Chapel – the nearest approximation to a clergyman's daughter that Leicester could produce. Sarah Goodwin was the wife of a watchmaker and jeweller and the couple let a room to Mary Ward, another dressmaker, no doubt one of Sarah's colleagues, who came from Liverpool. They probably both worked for their neighbours, Mary and Sarah Leach. The Leach sisters were in their early twenties; dressmakers were apprenticed in their teens and could be running their own businesses at what, to modern eyes, appear remarkably early ages.

Some families were obviously prosperous. At 38 Gallowtreegate in Leicester town centre, Priscilla Bark, aged forty-one, the milliner wife of a hatter and with two children still at home, employed a shop assistant, two millinery assistants, a cook and a housemaid, all of whom lived in [Plate 42]. Employing a servant was a good indicator of working-class prosperity, especially when the household was small. Twenty-seven-year-old Ann Morris, the childless dressmaker wife of a gas-fitter-cum-bell-hanger on Upper Charles Street, employed a sixteen-year-old skivvy, for example.

> WHOLESALE AND RETAIL LACE AND MILLINERY, &c. WAREHOUSE,
> HIGH-STREET, AND 14, BELGRAVE-GATE.
>
> **MRS. BARK**
>
> MOST respectfully acknowledges the very liberal patronage she has received since her commencement in business, and begs to inform her Friends and the Public, that she has this week visited London, in order to select a choice assortment of FANCY GOODS, which she purposes to offer at such prices as cannot fail to give satisfaction and ensure a continuance of support, which she most respectfully solicits.
>
> A large assortment of Ladies WORKED COLLARS, Widows' Caps, White and Black Crape, and Crimped Collars, always on hand. French and English Pillow Laces, of all kinds, in great variety; Flowers, Ribbons, Blondes, Bonnet Shapes, Best French Hosiery, Gloves, &c. &c.
>
> Children's French and Scotch Cambric Caps, Robes, Frocks, &c. &c.
>
> Mrs. B. has, during the last few weeks, commenced in the above Business, in Belgrave-gate, No. 14, opposite Mr. Needham's, and has engaged an experienced person to assist in that Establishment, where she hopes to receive that share of patronage which attention to business and moderate prices have never yet failed to ensure.
>
> The Trade supplied most advantageously.
>
> High-street, 9th October, 1845.

14. *Leicester Chronicle,* 11 October 1845.

Other dressmakers were clearly impoverished. At 19 Grafton Place lived three generations of unsupported women – Mary Campbell, a forty-four-year-old widowed dressmaker, her seventy-eight-year-old mother and her eighteen-year-old pupil teacher daughter. Phoebe Selvidge lived with her woolcomber father who was still working at the age of seventy-three, while her sixty-eight-year-old mother ran a little grocer's shop. Two of her brothers worked, but at poorly paid, unsocial jobs – one was a bone sawyer, one a factory porter. Maryann Robinson's husband was a dyer's journeyman – another dirty, unsocial job – and she helped support their family of four children by millinery and dressmaking. Dressmakers

Plate 42 Mrs Priscilla Bark, milliner in Leicester, 1870s.

in poor families had to work for as long as they could. Ann Granger, wife of a coal higgler on Abbey Street, was still dressmaking at the age of seventy-two, Catherine Pettifor was still working at the age of seventy-four while living in Castle Yard with her 'bible-woman' daughter.

These are only a handful of examples out of many hundreds, but they serve to illustrate the range of circumstances and family arrangements within which dressmakers lived. Studies of the census for other dates and places would undoubtedly provide many similar insights.

Dressmakers and prostitution

As early as January 1731 a writer in the *Caledonian Mercury* announced his intention to write a *History of the Seduction of London* which he recommended to 'the serious Consideration of all Spinsters, particularly Milleners [*sic*],

Mantua-makers, Waiting women, Laundry maids, and Parsons' Daughters, whose Misfortunes must take up a great Part of this Work'. In 1792 'Cherub', the self-styled 'Guardian of Female Innocence', listed 'Corrupt Milliners' along with the stage, fortune-tellers and girl's boarding schools, as places inimical to female virtue:

> Oft has an anxious CHERUB observed the secret scenes, the nocturnal orgies of sensuality, the midnight immolations of female virtue, which are made and celebrated behind the folding shop doors of a millinery deception.[7]

The association between dressmaking and prostitution lingered on into the nineteenth century, fuelled by preachers and novelists. However, only one of the Children's Employment commissioners' interviewees (no 585) in 1843 referred to prostitution – she spoke of young colleagues who had 'gone on the town' when they were laid off from work. Henry Mayhew's articles for the *Morning Chronicle* are much quoted and in November 1849 he wrote a series on London needlewomen.[8] Twenty-five of his interviewees admitted to 'immorality', but most of them were actually common-law wives, living with men who were not their legal husbands, rather than prostitutes. One of the few who admitted to prostitution was a widow: 'For three or four years after my husband's death, I struggled on and kept true to his memory, but at last all my clothes were gone [*to the pawnshop, presumably*] and I was obliged to transgress.' She had earned 3s.0d a week as a slop trouser-maker. Another was a clergyman's daughter:

> My father was an Independent preacher, and I pledge my word, solemnly and sacredly, that it was the low price paid for my labour that drove me to prostitution. I often struggled against it, and many times have I taken my child into the streets with me to beg rather than I would bring shame upon myself and it any longer. I have made pincushions and fancy articles – such as I could manage to scrape together – and taken them to the streets to sell, so that I might get an honest living, but I couldn't … I brought home 2s.6d by my shame and stopped [*my child's*] cries for two days.[9]

This testimony may well account for the large number of fictional clergymen's daughters who resorted to prostitution. The woman herself had, at the time of the interview, been in service 'with a Christian gentleman' for some years; her wretched child was in the workhouse. However, what is significant is not that Mayhew found a handful of needlewoman-prostitutes but that he found so few.

Nonetheless, the perception of the immoral needlewoman lingered on. Thomas Hughes, principal of the London Working Men's College, was telling his hearers what they expected to hear when he quoted an interviewee in his 1852 *Lecture on the Slop System*:

> I am sure no girl can get a living at slop work without prostitution; and I say as much after thirteen years' experience of the business. I never knew one girl in the trade who was virtuous: most of them wished to be so, but were compelled to be otherwise for mere life.[10]

He re-enforced his listeners' prejudices and did the poor needlewomen no favours at all – and because few of his listeners made a distinction between slop workers, seamstresses and dressmakers and milliners, they too were often tarred with the same brush. As a result, most dressmaking houses were careful to cultivate a reputation for moral propriety to encourage customers to patronize them.

However, the stereotype persisted and it threatened more than reputations. In the 1860s, concerns about prostitution centred on the increasing incidence of venereal disease within the armed services, supposedly as a result of the men's reliance on the services of prostitutes. The infamous Contagious Diseases Acts of 1864, 1866 and 1869 gave the police the power to arrest women suspected of prostitution and force them to be examined by a doctor. These powers were much abused and unsurprisingly, they were much resented; from 1870 there was increasing middle-class opposition to the Acts from the Ladies' National Association. Judith Walkowitz[11] has examined this subject in detail, with especial reference to the ports of Plymouth and Southampton. She found evidence of two needlewomen who actually left Plymouth because of the threat of police harassment. Miss Duffett, a seamstress,

> left after her mother's death because she had seen that there was NO SAFETY FOR A WORKING WOMAN living alone in a town where a malicious whisper, or the mere suspicion of a policeman, paid in proportion to his success in bringing up unhappy women, was sufficient legal evidence to condemn to intolerable punishment, with consequent loss of character and employment.

The other recorded victim 'left Plymouth because of the system of police intimidation, [*and*] claimed that malicious neighbours contributed to this reign of terror by threatening you "with the Water Police"'. We know about these women because they were both subsequently recruited by the LNA and went back to their hometown as paid agents of the repealers. How many other needlewomen were intimidated in this way is a matter for speculation.

One factor which may also have contributed to the Victorian attitude to dressmakers' immorality was the fact that a small but significant number of them lived in lodgings. The Victorians demonized boarding houses as representing the way in which family life had broken down in industrialized society, and lodging houses were generally seen as being little better than brothels. The Common Lodging Houses Act of 1850 actually gave agents of the Metropolitan police the right to inspect London lodging houses, at any time and without notice, to check up on who was sleeping with whom.

Maude Royden's *Downward Paths* of 1916 was the first semi-scientific enquiry into the causes of prostitution. She solicited case histories from magdalen homes, clergymen, social workers and the women themselves, and using 830 of these, she constructed a thesis about the factors that drove girls to prostitute themselves. While poverty – through the loss of either work or the family breadwinner – was one cause, it was by no means the main one and she elicited many others. These included girls preferring 'tangible clothes' over 'intangible chastity' and the influence of families whose moral codes were very different from those of middle-class reformers. The recognition of such factors was an important breakthrough. From our point of view, however, the most important finding is that of her 830 prostitutes, a mere fourteen had formerly worked as dressmakers and only four as milliners. Of these, she included case notes about three. 'CE' came from a bad home and left at the age of seventeen, met a man who pimped her and abandoned her when she became too ill to work. 'MW' went into prostitution when she lost her job. She had come to London from the Midlands to work in a West End firm, but was dismissed five months later at the end of the season and became a prostitute because, as she said, 'one must live'. 'XC' came from a respectable working-class home and worked 'irregularly' for a dressmaker's shop. She was described as 'a spoilt, wilful, high-spirited, wild colt'. She went to skating rinks in the evenings and met a man who 'motored' her to a 'house of ill-fame'. He took her to a neighbouring town for the night – she told her mother she was staying with friends – then, 'the man gave her a sovereign, which they spent together on sweets and skating the next day and her career of shame began'.[12]

Certainly from the actual evidence it would seem that the link between needle-workers and prostitution was grossly exaggerated – but it dies hard. In 1993 in Terry Pratchett's *Men at Arms* featuring Ankh-Morpark in the Discworld, a seamstress is described as 'a lady of negotiable affection. One who might provide a certain intimate service for a reasonable price, and is unlikely to have any use for a needle and thread, unless that's the way the client likes it'!

Personalities

Not only is there statistical evidence about nineteenth-century dressmakers in the census; enough evidence survives elsewhere to give us an idea of some of their personalities and even to show us what some of them looked like. Rachel Thomas in Cheltenham was overbearing and a bully; Mary Carmichael in Edinburgh was demanding and had a sharp tongue, but she was respected by her staff and was a fond aunt to her niece, 'wee Lizzie'. Hannah Mitchell in Derbyshire was enterprising, hard-working and politically aware; Minnie Frisby in Bromsgrove was a sociable young girl who loved dancing; Mrs Rose Downer was genteel and able to blend into upper-class society; Mrs Pattinson in Ulverston was patient and tolerant and had high aspirations for her little niece, Maggie Simpson, who she brought up as her own. Maggie learnt to play the piano and the violin, travelled, went to children's theatre performances, and, in the few years between Mrs Pattinson's retirement and her own marriage, ran the little business on the corner of Upper Brook Street. Elizabeth Chaffard had married a Frenchman and, it seems, spoke his language, for letters survive written to her after his death, in French, by his colleagues and friends. Elizabeth and her husband were also excessively fond of their pet dogs and obviously – from his letters – spoilt them dreadfully, even letting them share their bed.

Conclusion

Most dressmakers came from across the lower reaches of the social spectrum. Some were successful and reaped the benefits of their hard work, while others struggled all their lives. There is, if we look for it, a good deal of evidence in documents, and particularly in the census, to put flesh on the bones of many of the individuals who worked in the trade. They were real people, with real lives, and many of them had enduring relationships with at least some of their customers as we shall see in the next chapter.

10

Ladies and their dressmakers

In the eighteenth and nineteenth centuries many ladies kept personal account books in which they detailed their expenditure. It was considered to be a useful discipline for girls to learn, and it was also a way husbands and fathers could keep control of the allowances they made to their womenfolk. Many of these account books survive, and they are an invaluable source of information about real expenditure on dress, particularly if taken in conjunction with other personal documents like letters and diaries. Five examples are given below, the accounts supported by some biographical information about the ladies who kept them. They may provide an indigestible amount of detail for some readers, but they do serve to demonstrate the sheer wealth of information available in such sources.

Arabella Calley (1715–92)

Arabella Calley was the daughter and heiress of Thomas and Arabella Browne of Minety in north Wiltshire. She married William Calley of Burderop House, Chiseldon (now in Swindon), in 1743 and they raised four children – Anne, known as Nancy, William, who died in 1775 at the age of twenty-eight, Thomas Browne Calley and Charles Pleydell Calley. Arabella was widowed in 1768, while her eldest son was at Oxford and her two younger boys were away at school. From 1769, as mistress of Burderop, she kept detailed accounts of her expenditure which she described as 'an account of what I spent for clothes and pocket money' though they also include some payments to her servants.[1]

Arabella was a wealthy lady. She had a personal annuity of £500.00 a year from the Burderop estate, but her account books show she never spent the full amount and many years she spent less than half. Nonetheless, she went to Bath almost every year and the visits apparently cost her between £30.00 and £70.00 a time. In 1772 she spent £65.17s.1¼d on a trip to London; in 1776 a similar trip cost £85.9s.8d. She did not stint herself, but she was also generous, paying her maidservants between five and eight guineas a year when many received considerably less. She frequently records gifts to poor people she met on her travels – usually two shillings or five shillings at a time when a penny or sixpence was reckoned to be an appropriate donation. She was equally generous to her children, paying a pound for the 'boys' expenses on road' as her two younger sons made their way home to Burderop from Marlborough where they were at school (all of twelve miles) in 1771. She covered her sons' bills at Oxford without complaint – Thomas's 1771 account totalled £60.11s.6d and included payments for repairing his gun, buying shot, keeping a dog, mending windows he had broken and for copious quantities of alcohol. Books and tuition came to less than a quarter of the total; nonetheless in 1774 she lent him £40.00 over and above his allowance. Her youngest son, Charles, went into the army, and purchasing his commission cost her over £120.00 in 1778. She also spent more on her daughter's dress than she did on her own.

Arabella was fifty-four in 1769, elderly by eighteenth-century standards; that year she must have been wearing mourning for her husband, but presumably it was purchased before she started keeping accounts as there is no reference to her buying it. In 1769 her only expenditure for herself was on flannel for petticoats and two pairs of wooden clogs, but she did make her twenty-four-year-old daughter a present of ten guineas 'to buy her a gown'. The following year she paid Miss Rumbell 5s for making a 'grey silk nightgown' and later spent £7.8s.0d on grey lustring at 8s.3d a yard – so she must have bought about eighteen yards. She seems to have liked wearing grey; perhaps she thought it a respectably sober colour for a widow who was no longer obliged to wear black. A snippet of a rich, heavy, grey figured silk with a gold stripe is attached to the account book; Arabella may not have bought many clothes but clearly she valued quality. She also paid 'Miss Smith ye milliner in full' £7.4s.6d in 1770 – perhaps for having the lustring made up. In 1771 she spent very little money on her own clothes but had a gown made for 'Jane', a servant, paid her daughter's millinery bill (£9.3s.0d) and bought twelve yards of calico at 4d a yard, perhaps for underclothes for herself or her servants. She also paid a Mrs Smith to quilt a grey silk petticoat, no doubt to go under her various grey dresses. It cost 10s.0½d.

In 1772 Arabella paid 8s.3d to the 'Swindon mantua-maker' and bought twenty-three yards of grey watered tabby silk from Carr and Co at 11s.3d a yard. That seemed to cover her for the whole of 1773, but in 1774 she visited Bath and spent 16s.0d on caps, the same on muslin handkerchiefs and three guineas on cambric, probably for sleeve frills or fichus. In 1775 she paid Mrs Crook the mantua-maker £1.6s.3d and Mrs Smith the milliner £3.7s.5d but does not tell us what they supplied. In 1777 it was time for a new pair of stays or 'jumps' and they came from 'the Wroughton staymaker' (Wroughton is near Swindon) and cost £1.12s.6d. She also bought new shoes, had an apron mended and some silk dyed black. In 1778 she had new stockings and gloves and an expensive black-and-white silk apron.

It would seem she was beginning to take more interest in what she wore, and 1779 and 1780 saw her buying numerous pairs of gloves, stockings, shoes and clogs, and muslin and dimity for caps and aprons, a hoop for 9s.6d and two lots of black-and-white striped silk to make dresses – thirteen yards for £5.10s.6d and twenty yards for £4.15s.0d. She seems to have bought the makings of two new gowns in 1781 – eighteen yards of grey 'renal' (it is not clear what this was) at 6s.8d a yard and eighteen yards of grey striped silk for six guineas. She obviously still liked herself in grey. Ann Perriman was now her mantua-maker and she received a total of £5-15s-6d that year, though it must have been for making up fabric Arabella already had in stock. Her only significant purchase of fabric in 1782 was for twelve yards of armozine (a thick plain silk) from William Prattenton, the local draper; she did, however, buy a bonnet from Miss Mayo in Bath for £1.5s.2d and spent a lot on ribbons and trimmings, shoes, stockings and gloves. Six pairs of stockings were bought in Tewkesbury while she was on her way to Bath, and they cost £1.13s.0d. She also made contact with Elizabeth Prynn the seamstress, and over the next ten years Miss Prynn did numerous small jobs for her for which she was paid a shilling or two a time [Table 14].

Between 1783 and 1787 Arabella's expenditure on clothes increased considerably. She bought several pairs of shoes a year – women's shoes were flimsy and did not last long – and the occasional bonnet and pair of stays, but for the most part her money went on trimmings and laces, handkerchiefs and caps, aprons and ruffles. Her favourite milliner still seems to have been Miss Mayo in Bath. She spent two guineas on a gown in 1785 with a Mrs Kilner – it sounds as if this was a ready-made one – and still made occasional payments to Ann Perriman, though by 1789 she was also patronizing Miss Ross locally and a Mrs Colen in Cirencester. Their payments may well have been for altering and remaking gowns she already owned as she was only buying fabric in small quantities – enough for caps or aprons. She paid to have muslin 'worked', Mrs Curtiss had 11s.8d for quilting 'my white stuff [*petti*]coat' and Sarah Thomas received 14s.6d for making new shifts in 1787. With the exception of Mrs Colen we do not know where any of these women lived. Swindon in the 1780s was a small place, its tradespeople did not warrant a mention in the 1790s *Universal British Directory,* so we can only deduce that most of them

Table 14 Arabella Calley's expenditure on dress, 1779-89.

	Total spend on dress	Additional noteworthy purchases
1779	£17.19s.4d	7s.6d for white silk handkerchief, hoop 9s.6d, seven pairs gloves 11s.8d, muslin for apron 11s.10d
1780	£5.5s.10d	18s.0d for clogs and two pairs shoes, black silk handkerchief 6s.0d, making cap 5s.4d
1781	£8.4s.7 ½d	coloured gloves and ribbon 8s.0d, gauze apron 15s.0d
1782	£23.6s.6d	8s.0d on gloves, shoes 16s.0d (one pair were of 'silk stuff'), 10s.0d for dying silk black
1783	£31.5s.10½d	£2.2s.0d 'jumps', clogs 10s.6d, green leghorn hat 8s.3d, apron and ruffles £1.0s.3d, gauze handkerchief 10s.0d
1784	£22.5s.11d	£1.0s.11d for gloves and lace, gauze apron £1.0s.0d, shoes 5s.0d, muslin apron 19s.0d
1785	£16.4s.3½ d	£4.3s.0d for muslin for shawls, etc., bonnet £1.6s.8d
1786	£23.14s.1d	7s.0d on flannel for a bathing gown, 12 yards of lace for cloak, plus ribbon and making £1.12s.6d, 'jumps' £1.16s.0d
1787	£10.12s.6d	gauze cap 5s.6d
1788	£11-1s-3d	13s.9½ d to Miss Prynn, 5s.8d to Mrs Parslie for making caps
1789	£5.2s.6½d	All on paying off bills to drapers, seamstresses, milliners and mantua-makers

worked in the villages around Burderop and Minety – Arabella seems to have gone back to Minety quite frequently.

Arabella's spending tailed off in 1788–9 and at that point either she ceased keeping accounts or the final account book has been lost. She seems to have had her last dress made in 1788 – from fourteen yards of 'sarge' and a similar quantity of 'black stuff', both at 5s.6d a yard. She was seventy-three.

Arabella Calley died in 1792 and in her will she left £50.00 and an emerald and diamond ring to her son Thomas, £50.00 and a brilliant and diamond ring to Charles, gold jewellery and all her other belongings to her daughter Anne and a gold bracelet to her granddaughter, another Arabella. She left money to the poor of two parishes and six guineas to a widow she sponsored. Most of her clothes went to her maid.[2] The Burderop estate and the income from it passed to her eldest surviving son, Thomas Browne Calley.

Ann Williamson (c. 1746-94)

Ann Jones married Major Adam Williamson at Woolwich on 10 August 1771. We know very little about her but he was a career soldier from a military family, a military engineer who had already served three terms in North America, distinguished himself at the siege of Quebec and been part of the expeditionary force to the West Indies that captured Martinique and Guadeloupe. Four years later he was promoted lieutenant colonel and sent back to North America where he took part in the Battle of Bunker's Hill. In 1776 he was back in England, and in 1782 he was promoted colonel.

As the wife of a rising military star, and living with her sister's family in Mayfair, Ann Williamson led an active social life and dressed to match. Between December 1781 and November 1782 she spent £19.9s.0d with the Bennall sisters in London on a silk 'suit of cloaths', two trimmed white satin gowns, a grey gown and petticoat, a purple gown and petticoat with pinked decoration, a brown Persian gown and petticoat, a flowered calico gown, a pink satin sack and petticoat, gowns of gauze, calico and linen and having a white satin sack altered. They also made her a blue striped gown and one of blue lustring. She must have gone into mourning at some point in 1781 because she also spent £1.19s.0d on 'a suit of cloaths trimm'd with crepe', a bombazine dress and twenty-nine yards of crepe at 2s.4d a yard (£3.7s.4d).[3]

She spent £1.10s.4d having eleven fans mended by William Wendly. In 1779 she spent £1.4s.6d with Barnaby Darley in Covent Garden on fabric, fringe, a cloak and two gowns – something of a bargain in view of her usual extravagant spending. Gilbert and Roget, milliners in Jermyn Street, supplied her with £8.6s.1d worth of caps and trimmings in 1783, and Thomas Hill, glover on Pall Mall, supplied £2.13s.0d worth of gloves. Between 1781 and 1783 she spent £6.10s.6d with W. Hayhurst, staymaker, who supplied or altered nine pairs of stays for her, while Hornby and Harris, the hoop makers in Soho, charged her £9.2s.1d between 1777 and 1778 for numerous items. Pantins and Coates provided £1.9s.5d worth of ribbons and fabrics in 1781, perhaps for the Bennall sisters to make up, but her biggest expenditure that year was on millinery goods – £11.14s.7d to Gaillard and Toussain on Golden Square.[4]

In 1790 Adam, now a general, was appointed Governor of Jamaica. Ann was invited to court and in 1791 she spent a total of £75.15s.10½d with S. Ramsay, the court dressmaker – including ten guineas on a gown and petticoat with silver stripes and tassels, six pairs of coloured gloves for 12s.0d and a 'superfine blonde dress cap with a wreath of feathers and fine beads' for two guineas. She also bought three pairs of silk slippers at 19s.6d apiece and other shoes to the value of £6.4s.0d from Daniel Godwin.[5] Ann Williamson was nothing if not a big spender.

Her husband's friends and associates seem to have been aware of her passion for clothes. A letter to her from P. Atlee in July 1779 suggests he ask a friend visiting Lyons to bring her back lace and dresses and petticoats of 'the richest and gravest silks', and in 1791, J. Wilson in China sent her a fan decorated with her 'cipher'.[6] We do not know who they were – perhaps military men who had served with her husband.

Adam Williamson went out to Jamaica in 1790 and Ann was desperate to join him. She wrote him long affectionate letters, heavy with underlinings and protestations of undying love and of her willingness to endure all the hardships the Jamaican climate could throw at her to be by his side. Her worldview was naïve though probably typical of her gender and class. Paris – in mid-revolution – was, she had been told, 'in a most unpleasant state'; Wilberforce, already campaigning against slavery, was dismissed as misguided – Adam had assured her of 'the happiness of ye Black slaves' and she made it her business to pass that information on to the Queen through her friend, Mrs Cheveley, who was a Lady of the Bedchamber. The Queen's response was that Adam was 'a good little man' – Ann repeated this patronizing remark to her husband as if it was a great compliment.

The letters are full of regimental gossip. It is clear that there was some uncertainty about how long Adam would stay in Jamaica and that there was very considerable resentment about the £4,000.00 a year he was being paid. Ann was convinced that many people were green with envy at Adam's success and anxious to bring him down – 'Mrs Cheveley kindly hinted to me, we ought to be very careful what we say to [Colonel] Marsh as Goldsworthy, [General] Tom Garth and he are all one' and the letters are full of snide comments and backbiting remarks about colleagues and acquaintances, interspersed with approving descriptions of others' 'civility' towards her.[7]

In 1789 Ann inherited Avebury Manor in Wiltshire from her uncle, but the bequest was also burdened with the need to pay out various legacies. Despite her husband's £4,000.00 a year and her own extravagant expenditure on dress, Ann professed herself unable to pay them and saw the trip to Jamaica as a way to evade her responsibilities. All in all, she does not come over as a particularly likeable lady.

Ann Williamson did eventually join her husband in Jamaica. In 1794 she died there of yellow fever and was buried in the cathedral in Spanish Town. Adam returned alone to Avebury. He died there in 1798, a few months after his return, probably of a stroke. He and Ann were childless and after his death the estate was sold.

Eliza Spurrett (1797–1885)

Leicestershire Record Office contains a collection of diaries kept between 1813 and 1885 by Mrs Eliza Spurrett.[8] She was born Eliza Stone in 1797 and her first diary dates from the year she was sixteen. That diary and subsequent ones up to 1835 contain details of her personal expenditure. In 1836 she switched to a different diary format and unfortunately the later ones contain no financial accounts.

Eliza was the daughter of a gentleman, though it is quite difficult to ascertain precisely what her social position was. Her father had the tenancy of a farm at Knighton (now a suburb of Leicester but then a rural village) that belonged to Sir Edward Hartopp and he also valued land and collected rents for various noblemen and gentlemen, including the Duke of Rutland at Belvoir and Lord Lanesborough at Swithland. Her mother was the daughter of a wealthy local businessman.

Eliza was one of nine children, and in 1804 was sent to school at Mansfield with her three elder sisters. She returned home when she was ten and continued her education with a series of French, arithmetic and drawing masters who came out from Leicester, but she and her sisters also did work that sounds quite menial:

> We used to plait straw and have it made up for our hats. It was sold in bundles ready for splitting and plaiting. It was nice work, and pillow lace I liked making, but I did not like spinning so well … My mother used to employ three or four women in the winter to spin Flax and in the Spring a Weaver from Wigston made it into linen for sheets etc.

It sounds as though the Stone girls were being brought up able to earn their livings if the need arose – though perhaps most gentleman farmers' daughters were expected to have such skills. Later, in her diaries, Eliza would record that she had money from her mother 'per lavora' by which she seems to have meant helping with housework.

She married in 1829, a year later than intended, as her father died in 1828 and the wedding was postponed: 'I was married in a Silk Dress and Bonnet to match, in a half-mourning colour.' Her husband described himself as 'a landed proprietor' in 1851. They lived in Leicester until 1842, then moved to Banbury, then to Bath and then back to Leicester. Samuel Spurrett died in 1854 but Eliza lived on to the grand old age of eighty-eight, dying in 1885.

In her memoirs she described how she had dressed as a girl:

> We girls always wore coloured prints in the morning and put on white when we dressed for the 3 o'clock dinner. Short sleeves were sometimes worn with the morning dress, but more frequently long sleeves. A "Spencer" was put on for going out. Waists were very short and skirts were short too, so as to shew the sandal which crossed the instep and was then brought round and tied in a bow. We varied our white dresses by having different coloured ribbons, sometimes sashes, sometimes braces, and in other fanciful ways.

It was dresses like these that sixteen-year-old Eliza recorded buying in 1813 in her first diary. She was then receiving a quarterly allowance of £1.15s.0d plus £2.2s.0d 'cash' and at the same time her parents usually made her a present of a few shillings, so she had roughly £16.00 a year to spend. Eliza's family were quite generous but she often overspent. Most of her money went on clothes, though a little went on church collections, charitable donations, presents and card playing.

In 1813 Eliza bought a pelisse for £4.00; 10s.3d worth of white muslin for a frock; 8s.0d worth of 'batella' for a frock (batella was a type of cotton cloth); and two – presumably ready-made – batella frocks at 10s.6d and 10s.4d; a batella gown for 11s.11d; a leno frock for 9s.0d and a red frock for 17s.0d; 1s.11½d worth of batella for a spencer; 2s.6d worth of yellow ribbon and sarsnet for a 'body'; eleven pairs of gloves of various lengths and colours; a pair of boots for 12s.0d and some coloured boots for 8s.6d; and six pairs of shoes – including pairs in white satin, black kid, sealskin and lemon kid. No payments were recorded to dressmakers, so perhaps young Eliza made her own clothes at this stage in her life. She also bought four chemises for £1.1s.0d and 9s.6d worth of calico for two night gowns, a parasol for a guinea, a pink handkerchief for 3s.0d, a green veil for 3s.3d, a white necklace for 6s.0d, a petticoat for 6s.1½d and bonnets for 10s.0d and 10s.7d. She bought a toothbrush, a tooth comb, had her hair cut each month, had her boots, shoes, stays and a brooch mended, had feathers curled, silk stockings re-footed and a petticoat glazed. The rest of her expenditure went on trimmings – ribbons, sashes, shoe-bows, flowers, collars, handkerchiefs and the like. Sometimes she mentions what the trimming was for, so we learn that she already had in her wardrobe a grey dress, a pink frock, a green frock and at least two bonnets. Her total expenditure in 1813 was £21.5s.9d (more than

Table 15 Eliza Spurrett's dress purchases, 1817–35.

	1817	1818	1819	1820	1821	1823	1824	1825	1826	1827	1828	1829	1830	1831	1832	1833	1834	1835
Dresses	4	3	3	2	1	5	4		5	5	1		1			1	2	
Hats/bonnets	1	1			1	2	1	1	3	2	1	1	1	1	1		1	1
Boots/shoes	4	5	5	3	1	1	3	1	6	3	6	4	3	3	8	2	1	2
Gloves	1	4	4	6	2	4	1	2	5	2	2			4		1		1
Stays	1	1	1		1	1		1	1				1	1				1
Nightwear/underwear	5	11	5	2	5	7	2	11		8		2	4			2		1
Scarves, etc.		2			1	3	1		1			1			1			
Cloaks/pelisses				1				1					1	1			1	
'Bodies'	4	1	1	1		1		3	2		1		1					
Skirts				1							1							

her recorded income, so perhaps she had some savings, and more than she ever spent in a year again). Young Eliza was on the brink of adulthood and was replacing the clothes of her childhood.

The next diary to survive dates from 1817, and by then Eliza was twenty and slightly less extravagant. The rest of her expenditure is recorded in tabular form for simplicity's sake. The diary for 1822 is missing [Tables 15 & 16].

She was still spending most of her money on ribbons and trimmings to revamp her existing wardrobe, and even after her marriage, all but a few shillings of her personal money went on clothes.

By 1820, Eliza was patronizing dressmakers and milliners rather than making clothes herself – Mrs Pegg (who advertised in the Leicester papers) and Jackson's were the first firms she went to. In 1821 she patronized a Mrs Hitchcock and settled on Holmes as her shoemaker. In 1823 Mrs Bracey was making her stays, and, though she was still going to Mrs Pegg, Miss Pochin also

Table 16 Eliza Spurrett's annual expenditure, 1817–35.

	Total personal expenditure	Expenditure on dress
1817	£12.4s.1½d	£11.17s.1½d
1818	£10.6s.9d	£10.1s.6d
1819	£15.15s.3½d	£14.17s.3½d
1820	£11.11.2½d	£11.4s.11½d
1821	£12.18.11½d	£12.1s.9½d
1823	£23.9s.3½d	£22.16s.6½d
1824	£18.7s.7d	£17.11s.1d
1825	£19.15s.5d	£19.2s.10d
1826	£11.11s.2d	£10.12s.2d
1827	£19.6s.8d	£18.14s.8d
1828	£9.1s.2d	£8.12s.7d
1829	£10.13s.6d	£10.6s.6d
1830	£6.4s.8d	£5.19s.2d
1831	£22.19s.5d	£22.15s.11d
1832	£12.11s.2d	£12.8s.2d
1833	£6.3s.8½d	£6.3s.8½d
1834	£7.8s.8d	£7.8s.8d
1835	£18.17.10½d	£18.17s.10½d

> MRS. PEGG, with much respect, informs the Ladies of Leicester and its vicinity, that she is now in London, selecting an assortment of MILLINERY DRESSES, LEGHORNS, CHIP, STRAW HATS and BONNETS, which will be ready for inspection on THURSDAY, the 24th instant, when a call will be esteemed a favour.
>
> South-gates, Leicester, May 18, 1827.

15 *The Leicester Chronicle*, 19 May 1827.

made some of her dresses. In 1830 she began to go to Miss Webb for bonnets and caps, and by the following year she was buying drapery and millinery from both Jackson's and Cooper's. She was married by this point and her first child was born in 1831, so her accounts began to show expenditure on baby clothes – in 1831 at least £3.5s.0d was spent on things for her baby. Sadly, the child was stillborn, but she went on to have four daughters and two sons, one of whom died in infancy.

In 1832 she was again pregnant and began to build up her stock of babywear. She also bought an India rubber apron – presumably to wear while bathing the baby – for 6s.0d. She began to patronize another dressmaker, Miss Goddard, who came to the house and who charged just 3s.0d for two day's work. Eliza now bought caps for herself – and possibly also for the child – from Mrs Thornton. In 1833 she paid her 19s.0d. She seems to have been pregnant again in 1834 for the accounts include a lot of children's wear – including a dozen size-three cotton socks and another waterproof apron. That year Miss Clayton replaced Miss Goddard as the family's home dressmaker. In 1835 she was employed for three days making mourning – probably for the little boy who died – at 3s.9d, and the same year she was paid an unspecified amount for 'making children's things at 9 different times'.

The picture of Eliza's wardrobe in later years is somewhat distorted, as she then simply paid a lump sum to Mrs Pegg or Miss Pochin without itemizing what they did. Her 1830 accounts also contain a cryptic reference against one of these entries 'See book' which may mean she kept another account book for accounts with firms that were not to be paid immediately. If so, our picture of her expenditure on dress after she was married is incomplete – certainly she spent very little in the 1830s considering she was also clothing a young family. [Plate 43]

Plate 43 Eliza Spurrett, c. 1855.

Charlotte Kenyon's trousseau, 1833 (1813–84)

My dear Mrs. Kenyon,

> I wrote to you under an impulse that was irresistible – as I would have done to my own flesh and blood and I am sorry that I did do so – you cannot follow the advice and opinions of all who may be interested in the welfare of Charlotte – and you must be the best judge of the state both of her body and mind – when I compared her with the everyday girls that one sees – and marked the intelligence of her expression, the simplicity and modesty, and affection of her manner I could not help saying to myself what a beautiful blossom Mrs Kenyon has cultivated and raised with her own hand – and what a pity it would be to see her mixed with the world and become as others – go on therefore as you have begun finish your own work in your own way and with God's blessing all will go well for your comfort and hers.[9]

The letter was written in 1829 by Mrs Hill, wife of Colonel John Hill. Charlotte was then sixteen. Two years later she was presented at court which she 'enjoyed very much' according to the extremely uninformative diary she kept that year. The Kenyons and the Hills were on friendly terms, and in December 1833 Charlotte would marry the Hills' second son, another John Hill. Both families were wealthy and well connected. Charlotte's father was the Honourable Thomas Kenyon of Pradoe in Shropshire, the youngest son of Lloyd Kenyon, first Baron Kenyon, Baron of Gredington, Chief Justice of Chester, MP and Attorney General from 1783 to 1784. Colonel John Hill's eldest brother was General Rowland Hill, first Viscount of Almaraz and Colonel Hill's eldest son, Charlotte's brother-in-law-to-be, Rowland, would inherit the title.

Like many second sons of gentry families, John Hill the younger went into the church and at the time of his marriage was curate of Weston-and-Wixhill-under-Red-Castle in Shropshire, though he had a private income and the couple never actually had to live on his stipend. Charlotte was twenty when they married, John was thirty-one, and a curious set of handwritten verses referring to 'Old Lochinvar' suggest that Charlotte may have turned down another suitor at the last minute to marry John:

> Your nephew wooed my niece, his suit was denied.
> Love swells like the Severn and ebbs like the tide.[10]

It reads like a family in-joke and may be what Mrs Kenyon meant when she referred to 'all [John] has so patiently endured for her sake' (see below).

Charlotte was an only daughter, her parents were clearly anxious to do her proud and gave her an extremely large and expensive trousseau. Mrs Kenyon kept two accounts of exactly what she had spent on it, one for local suppliers and one for what they had spent in London – the total came to £330.3s.6d.[11]

They spent £106.18s.11d in London, mostly on fine lingerie and caps from Ware and Co on Davies Street, off Berkeley Square, Robertshaws on Oxford Street and Christian and Son on Wigmore Street where they also bought some gowns – two ready-made muslin ones at £1.11s.0d and £1.15s.0d, a green one for an unspecified sum, and a sprigged muslin one they had made for 18s.0d. Redmaynes on New Bond Street provided an expensive sable boa for £6.00. Back home, they patronized firms in Shrewsbury and Oswestry – Lucas and Rogers in Oswestry supplied large quantities of long cloth and diaper and a merino cloak with a velvet cape, while Pritchard and Lloyd in Shrewsbury sold them yards of silk and merino, at least four dresses (a green printed merino, a black figured silk, one of 'chaly' (challis) and another of foulard), three dozen pairs of gloves of various colours and lengths, a Chantilly lace veil for £5.10s.0d and an ermine 'mantilla' for £5.5s.0d. Miss Nightingale in Oswestry and Mrs Ellis in Shrewsbury made up numerous dresses. Worton, the Oswestry staymaker, supplied a pair of French stays for £1.5s.0d, while Mr Jones the shoemaker sold her six pairs of walking boots and a pair of 'dressing slippers' for a total of £3.13s.6d. But the biggest local beneficiary of Charlotte's wedding was Miss Pritchard, of Pritchard and Lloyd in Shrewsbury, who received a total of £69.2s.4½d for bonnets and for making up five dresses.

Madame Devey – probably a London dressmaker – made up a figured white silk dress for £7.17s.6d and supplied a pair of stays at three guineas to go under it. This, with the Chantilly veil, was very probably Charlotte's wedding outfit. Hillhouse on Bond Street provided a muslin dressing gown for a guinea and a nightcap trimmed with Valenciennes lace for 18s.0d, possibly for the wedding night. There were numerous other suppliers and dressmakers, but it is not possible to trace them all.

Charlotte started her married life with three chemisettes, six stomachers, three dozen pairs of gloves, six pairs of white satin shoes, six of black satin and six of black 'stuff', six pairs of boots and several pairs of clogs. She had three shawls (including a green one that had cost twelve guineas), a cloak, twelve 'capes' (probably the large fancy muslin cape-collars that were in vogue in the early 1830s), an ermine tippet, a chinchilla muff and a sable boa, two white bonnets, a velvet one and a leghorn one. Her lingerie collection included thirty day chemises and twenty-four night ones, nine dressing gowns, twelve petticoats and nine nightcaps, not to mention thirty-six handkerchiefs (fancy and plain) and a selection of combs and hairbrushes. She listed eight morning dresses – a green merino, a puce merino, a dark green silk, a puce silk 'as yet unmade', a washing silk, a challis, a black silk and a muslin one lined with primrose silk – 'with a promise of four more when the Spring fashions are out'. Curiously, she had even more evening dresses than day dresses – a figured pink silk, a figured white silk, a blue challis, a yellow challis, a dark challis, a black printed muslin, a washing silk, a pink foulard trimmed with black, an embroidered muslin, a plain book muslin, the figured white satin that may have been her wedding dress, a satin 'slip' and a velvet dress. Challis was a new material, a soft mixture of silk and worsted wool, first produced in Norwich c. 1832, so Charlotte's dresses were at the cutting edge of fashion, at least as far as their fabric was concerned.[12] However, there are bills for a number of muslin dresses over and above the ones on this list and for a riding habit (nine guineas) and hat (£1.8s.0d) so she may have been even better provided for than her inventory suggests.

A few days after the wedding Mrs Kenyon wrote to Mrs Hill who apparently had not attended because of illness:

Wednesday, 18th Dec.
What shall I say to you my dear Mrs. Hill upon this occasion, but that as the hopes and wishes of our dear Children are at length realised may every

succeeding day and year prove that their choice of each other has not been lightly or inconsiderately made, and that as husband and wife they may be dearer to each other than they have ever been as lovers. The blank in this house will be long severely felt by us all, to me her loss is what I cannot trust myself to think of, she has long been my right hand, my companion, my comforter, and in resigning her to John I can only pray that she may fulfil the duties of a wife in as exemplary a manner as she has those of a daughter, may she make him happy, and reward him for all he has so patiently endured for her sake … The people here have subscribed upwards of £70 for rejoicings, and I hope the poor will benefit by it, but of course much will go in eating and drinking we hear of two great dinners in Ruyton, where they say such a wedding never was seen before. It was certainly a much gayer affair than I had anticipated and had the day been finer the Church would not have held the people, as it was Mr Evans told me he had never seen it so crowded before. We were very glad that John had the support of his Brother and Uncles and it was very kind of them to come here. I could have wished that you had been of the party and then nothing would have been wanting. The Kenyons mustered strong, 15 in number, Hills 4, Lloyds 6,[13] in all 25 in six carriages and four, and those who could see the turnout said nothing could have been better done, the day was rather stormy but no rain of any consequence and there were occasional gleams of sunshine, and Arthur observed that one bright gleam darted through the window upon them just as Mr Evans gave them the blessing![14]

It is to be hoped the marriage was indeed a happy one, but it is unlikely that Charlotte got her parents' money's worth out of the dresses they provided for her. Dresses in 1833 had huge sleeves worn over sleeve 'muffs' or frames – Charlotte bought a pair of cane sleeve frames for 3s.0d – low, almost off-the-shoulder necklines and high waists. But by 1840, styles had changed. Dresses were more demure with high necks, long fitted sleeves, low waists coming to a point at the front and very full skirts. It is unlikely that many of the trousseau dresses could have been remade to the new fashion.

Charlotte and John lived in some style – in 1851 they were living at the Citadel, Weston, with a live-in staff of ten which included a butler and a footman.[15] Charlotte died in 1884, John outlived her by seven years. The couple had four sons between 1840 and 1847, all of whom lived long, productive lives. John, the eldest and Brian Hubert, the youngest, remained in Shropshire. George William became a Vice-Admiral; Clement Lloyd had a distinguished career in the foreign office and was knighted. Their families could not have asked for more. [Plate 44]

Plate 44 Charlotte Hill (seated centre left), her husband, sons and grandchildren, early 1870s. The older man, standing in the doorway between two of Charlotte's sons, was the family butler. It is curious that he was included in the photograph when the children's mother is absent.

Susanna Ingleby (1831–91)[16]

Mrs Susanna Ingleby was a gentlewoman who kept house for her widowed brother and his young son. She was the seventh of the Reverend John Sneyd's fourteen children and had been born at Basford Hall, a large house on the family estate, at Cheddleton near Leek in north Staffordshire, which her father inherited in 1851. She grew up in a house full of servants – at the time of her birth her parents kept an indoor staff of twelve – and there was a canary-yellow carriage in the coach house which bore the family coat-of-arms on its doors. Her grandfather, who lived a mile or so away across the fields at Ashcombe, the fine house he had built when her father was a boy, lived in even greater luxury. The Sneyds were an old-established family, well known and respected in north Staffordshire, but in the 1850s they lost all their money as a result of ill-advised mining speculation. In the aftermath of that disaster, tempers had run high and John Sneyd had quarrelled with his eldest son, John William, and disinherited him; thereafter John William survived on the rents of a couple of farms and an allowance of £100.00 a year. In 1861 he married Agnes Cotton of Etwall Hall in Derbyshire, but she died just a year later, shortly after the birth of their first child, a son, grandly named Ralph De Tunstall Sneyd.

Susanna married the Reverend Charles Ingleby, curate of Ellastone, who lived at Oakamoor. It was a tragic mistake. It seems he was homosexual (Susanna's father referred to him as 'the hermaphrodite'). Susanna wrote an account of the events of her marriage for her father and his solicitor; she came from a large family, had married sisters and younger brothers and it appears she knew what to expect on her wedding night. When she 'hinted that more active measures were called for' in the bedroom, Charles was horrified – she was not the innocent bride he thought he had married and he 'exclaimed at the way [*she*] had been brought up'. Thereafter both he and his elderly mother subjected Susanna to a reign of terror and abuse. Two months to the day after her wedding, on 11 June 1860, John Sneyd arrived at Oakamoor to rescue his daughter. Divorce was virtually unheard of at that date and an annulment would have necessitated Susanna undergoing a humiliating physical examination. Instead, her father's solicitor forced through a legal separation under the terms of which she would receive an allowance of £100.00 a year from Charles Ingleby, which would rise to £150.00 when his mother died and he no longer had her to support. Mrs Ingleby in fact died in 1871, Charles Ingleby in 1873. More importantly, Susanna was also to retain her 'marriage settlement' – a lump sum of £8,000.00 plus a £50.00 annual allowance from her father. In the days when women lost all rights to their property and money on marriage, well-to-do families tried to protect their daughters by setting up marriage settlements which consisted of lump sums, sometimes supplemented by an allowance. This money was put into a trust to be administered on the wife's behalf by trustees approved by both families.

For two years after her marriage broke down, Susanna lived with a sister and cousin in one of the houses on the family estate, keeping out of society as much as possible and trying to live down her disgrace. When it was clear that Agnes was not going to survive, John William wrote to her asking her to live with him and help raise his son. 'It is', he wrote sadly, 'dear Agnes's wish as well as my own'. Despite the fact that John Sneyd was no longer on speaking terms with his son, he raised no objections to his daughter going to him as housekeeper. They were to live in the house in Armitage (mid-Staffordshire) that John William had rented as his marital home but had never lived in – it was out of visiting range of Basford Hall and no doubt John Sneyd saw it as a way of getting rid of two embarrassing children at the same time. From the time she moved to Armitage, Susanna Ingleby kept meticulous accounts in separate books for household, personal, garden, coal and travel expenditure. It is her personal accounts that concern us here.

Susanna paid her brother £50.00 a year board and lodging. Armitage Cottage cost them £30.00 a year in rent and they employed a servant and a nursemaid for the baby at a cost of £12.00 and £8.00 a year. They lived reasonably comfortably, though in circumstances much reduced from the life they had known as children at Basford Hall. For the eight years they lived in Armitage, Susanna, John William and little 'Ralphy' led an active social life. The Wilsons at the Rectory, the Birches at nearby Armitage Lodge and Josiah Spode just down the road at Hawkesyard Park were their closest companions, but they had numerous other friends and acquaintances, and their lives were a long round of dinners, concerts, picnics, croquet and archery parties, dances and other festivities.

In 1870 they moved to Abbot's Bromley, to another rented house. Though only a few minutes away by car, they were out of reach of their Armitage friends and had to establish a new social circle. They were older, Ralphy had gone away to school and their social life became more sedate. Then in 1873, their father died. There was no death bed reconciliation between father and son, John William remained disinherited of Ashcombe Park (which went to a younger brother) but inherited the old family home, Basford Hall (usually left to the second son), and in 1874 he returned there with Susanna and the then twelve-year-old Ralph. Susanna had managed her money well, but she was anxious to leave a reasonable sum to Ralph who would inherit little from his impoverished father. Over the years, particularly after their father's death, Susanna was also called upon to bail out various of her relations, and in particular, her youngest brother, Gustavus.

The Reverend Gustavus Sneyd was rector of Chastleton in Oxfordshire, but he was a profligate and dishonourable young man who cost his family much worry – and in Susanna's case – money. Her annuity of £50.00 from her father had often not been paid, and she had been forced to dip into her capital to keep the household afloat. As her capital diminished, so did her income from its interest, so neither she nor her brother could really afford to live at Basford Hall. It was a large house, and had fallen into disrepair, the roof leaked, it was cold and isolated and Susanna managed it with the aid of just two servants – a drunken cook and a maid-of-all-work – and did much of the housework herself. They could not afford to entertain and both she and John William suffered frequent bouts of illness; Susanna no longer needed a fashionable wardrobe.

We know so much about Susanna Ingleby because she kept diaries and these, together with diaries kept by her parents, grandfather and brothers, are in Keele University library. Large collections of family papers survive in the hands of various Sneyd descendants and these contain bills from dressmakers as well as Susanna's personal account books for the period 1866–91, which contains details of everything she purchased – down to the last halfpenny on lemon drops and penny to a beggar. Her diaries tell of the occasions on which she wore the dresses that her various dressmakers made for her. It is a unique collection of resources.

Susanna seems to have been a skilled needlewoman. She records making shirts for her brothers, clothes for her young nephew and garments for herself and helping out at various village schools teaching the girls to sew. On occasion she made or remade complete dresses. It is difficult to know how typical she was, but certainly many girls from well-to-do backgrounds did much of their own sewing. However, Susanna's 'best' dresses were made by dressmakers.

Susanna had a trousseau when she married in 1860, and many of her wedding presents were clothes and jewellery – she made a list of them in the back of her diary together with the names of the people who gave them:

2 work'd P-hands [*pocket handkerchiefs*]
a brown silk dress
a blue silk dress
a linsey dress & a watch chain
a bracelet
an opera cloak
a parasol
a scarf
a brooch
a shawl
a shawl, a work table, a bible, a brooch [*from her husband-to-be*]
an ornament for the neck £8.10s.0d [*from her father*]
a pair of slippers
a ring
a set of pearl and amethyst ornaments [*from her mother-in-law-to-be*]
collar and cuffs
collar and sleeves
a headdress
pins for the hair
a Honiton veil
a ring & pins for the hair
a wreath
a drab silk dress
a brooch
some pairs of cuffs

Fortunately for Susanna, fashion changed little between 1860 and 1862, so the outfits that had been provided for her married life could continue to be worn in her new role. But before long she needed to extend her wardrobe. Charles Ingleby and his mother socialized very little so the trousseau did not include much in the way of evening wear. In the spring of 1862, at Etwall Hall, staying with John William and Agnes and Agnes's family, Susanna had twice worn her wedding dress for evening parties; Victorian brides expected to reuse their wedding dresses, but Susanna had been violently abused and humiliated by her husband and her wedding dress must have brought back unhappy memories. She wore it only because she had no alternative evening outfit. On 26 August 1862, barely a month after she arrived in Armitage, she sought to remedy this omission. She went to the nearby town of Rugeley to be measured for a tulle dress by Mrs Dinsdale, possibly on the recommendation of her new friend, Mrs Birch. The dress arrived on 11 September. It contained twenty-one yards of tulle at 2s.6d a yard, forty-six yards of narrow ribbon at 4d a yard and eleven yards of wide ribbon at 1s a yard; the bodice was lined with black glacé silk and had pads (to enhance the bust – Susanna was very slim) and bones, the whole cost £4.18s.4d of which 10s.6d was the cost of making it up.

Mrs Eliza Dinsdale was rather a special dressmaker and it is not clear when – or why – she settled in Rugeley. (There were forty-seven dressmakers, seamstresses and milliners in Rugeley in 1861, serving a population of just over 4,000. In Armitage and the nearby hamlet of Handsacre, with a population of 937 there were nine.) Mrs Dinsdale was born in Farnborough, Hampshire, but was the wife of a Yorkshireman, John Dinsdale, who described himself to the census enumerator as a 'commercial traveller for a dressmaking establishment employing five assistants'. That establishment was his wife's. The 1861 census shows that one of the assistants was their niece, twenty-five-year-old Laetitia Holbrook, also Farnborough-born, and there was also a live-in apprentice, sixteen-year-old Elizabeth Mary-Anne James from Wetley Rocks in north Staffordshire. The other assistants probably lived out. It is possible that Susanna had known Elizabeth James back home. Wetley Rocks was her uncle's parish and was only a mile or so from Basford Hall. Before her marriage, both Susanna and her sister, Emily, like many philanthropic ladies of their class, taught sewing at Cheddleton and Wetley Rocks schools. Had they perhaps taught Mrs Dinsdale's apprentice?

In March 1863, Susanna received news from home of the death of her brother 'poor dear Wettie' – Richard Wettenhall, aged twenty-one. It cannot have been entirely unexpected. Wettenhall had suffered from rheumatoid arthritis since early childhood; he was crippled, weakly, and there are indications that he may have had learning difficulties. A death in the family required the surviving members to go into mourning, and it was on the women that mourning fell most heavily. Men wore black suits, ties, buttons and watch-chains, but even for a wife, a man was only expected to wear mourning for three months. A widow, on the other hand, wore mourning for at least two years, and society looked askance at her if she went back into colours as soon as the obligatory period was expired. Numerous magazines and manuals were published giving advice to the bereaved on the various grades of mourning. The consensus was that a sister should mourn a sibling for six months. For eleven days after the news of Wettenhall's death reached her, Susanna worked at altering the black dresses she already had, then, on 18 March: 'I went in Mrs Birch's carriage to Rugeley & was measured for my black dress by Mrs Dinsdale.' The black dress would have been trimmed with wide bands of black crepe, which could be narrowed after two months and removed altogether after a further four weeks. Mrs Dinsdale's bill survives:

To 15yds of black glacé at 5s.0d	£3.15s.0d
14yds of muslin for lining skirt & crape tucks at 6s.2d	7s.7d
4/4 wide patent crape at 7s.0d	£1.9s.9d
Body lining, braid, bones, buttons etc.	3s.0d
Sleeve lining	2s.9d
Wrist band & Jet clasp	3s.9d
To making Dress	7s.6d
Set of crape sleeves & collar	6s.6d

On 15 June, Susanna put fresh black crepe on the dress. Crepe was difficult stuff; it spotted, it stained, it flattened out, it turned a rusty colour and as the mourning period progressed less of it was needed and it had to be replaced. On 9 July she went to see Mrs Dinsdale about a new black dress – the crepe-less one that she was allowed to wear for the fourth and fifth months of mourning. For the final month she could, if she chose, go into half-mourning – dresses of purple, grey or white trimmed with black.

In November we find her in mourning again – this time for 'poor Barbara Scott' – a friend or distant relation for whom she was not obliged to mourn, but whose death Susanna wished to mark in some way. This time, she mended an old black silk dress which she wore for a few days. Such brief periods of mourning recur from time to time. In August 1868, for example, she put 'black in my bonnet for poor Tom Adderley' – a distant cousin who had recently died.

But being in mourning did not stop Susanna taking an interest in fashion. On 29 April 1863, less than two months after her brother's death, she wrote in her diary: 'I went with Miss Wilson in the carriage to Rugeley & saw Mrs Dinsdale's & Mrs Bown's fashions.' Mrs Bown (of Ottley and Bown, linen and woollen drapers, Lower Brook Street) later advertised in the *Staffordshire Advertiser* on 22 October 1863:

> OTTLEY and BOWN apprise the Ladies of RUGELEY and its vicinity of their return from the London Market, and that their STOCK comprises the most prevailing NOVELTIES for the present and approaching seasons.

In December 1863, with the New Year festivities looming (Christmas was celebrated by church attendance and very little else), and out of mourning, Susanna had a white silk dress made in Rugeley. It was fitted on 21 December, and again on the 29th, and as an extra, she revamped an old dress: 'December 30. I spent most of the day altering my pink barège dress. Very cold.' One hopes she wore it to events in well-heated houses, for barège is a fine muslin with a fancy woven stripe, usually overprinted with a pattern, and often used for summer dresses. It must have been worn for evening wear in winter too – in November 1864, Susanna was altering another barège dress, this time a black one.

Between 1862 and 1864 Mrs Dinsdale helped Susanna expand her wardrobe for her new and full social life. In May 1863 she provided a headdress for 10s.6d, and in July she altered a pink evening dress, adding four yards of tarlatan at 18d, one yard of pink satin at 4s.6d, 1s.4½d worth of book muslin, two yards of satin ribbon at 1s.8d, plus 'Lace taken & chemise sleeves 2s.6d'. A brown silk dress (possibly the one Susanna had been given as a wedding gift) was remade in September at a cost of 7s.6d plus 6s.6d worth of material, and a muslin evening dress with black lace cost £1.4s.6d in January 1864.

On 26 April 1864 Susanna and Miss Wilson again went to Rugeley to see Mrs Bown's and Mrs Dinsdale's fashions, and the following day they returned to Rugeley to see Mrs Wesson's fashions. She appears in the directories as a partner in Aughton and Wesson, milliners in Horse Fair. Susanna must have approved for she bought a mantle from Mrs Wesson. It was not the first time she had patronized her – she had a dress and other things from 'Wesson's' in October 1863. Wesson and Aughton were a firm of some standing employing at least one assistant. On 26 October 1863, Susanna 'walked to Rugeley to have my dress altered by Miss Cook at Mrs Wesson's' but in May 1864 she was back at Mrs Dinsdale's buying a hat, and at the end of that month there were more purchases of mourning in Rugeley for her cousin 'poor Clement' – possibly from

Mrs Dinsdale but no bills survive. Certainly the black silk jacket she ordered on 10 June came from Wesson's.

Technically, she only needed to mourn for a cousin for six weeks, and she may well have been back in colours when she went back home to Cheddleton for a holiday in September. By the time she returned to Armitage, however, there had been another death – this time her brother Freddy, a consumptive for some years, had died of what sounds like septicaemia; on 2 October Susanna records three weeks and three days spent nursing him, and then, while still at Cheddleton: 'October 3. Mrs Gwynne came. We chose our black things.' So this time Susanna's patronage went to a Leek dressmaker. Mourning for Freddy lasted until early April 1865, and later that month Susanna contacted Miss Stevens, a dressmaker in Lichfield. Over the next couple of years she patronized Miss Stevens for her 'best' clothes, bought some items in Rugeley and, while visiting Dover, tried out a Miss Knight, a dressmaker recommended by John William's sisters-in-law who lived there, and did a fair amount of making and mending herself.

Mrs Dinsdale seems to have left Rugeley but in 1867 she surfaced again. In July that year Susanna went to London for an operation (for haemorrhoids) which she had at 90, Harley Street in what was Florence Nightingale's old hospital, by then a 'Home for Gentlewomen in Time of Sickness'. Almost her first act after she had checked in was to go to 21 Wigmore Street where Mrs Dinsdale had taken premises. She left a dress to be altered – very much an act of faith considering the risks inherent in mid-nineteenth-century surgery. She also purchased and sent 'the hair' to her sister Emily. Victorian ladies kept their heads covered most of the time – caps indoors, bonnets and hats out-of-doors and nightcaps in bed. It played havoc with their hair. False chignons, fringes, ringlets and hairpieces were much in demand and dressmakers seem to have provided them together with a whole range of beauty treatments. As Susanna recovered, Mrs Dinsdale brought the newly altered dress, and other items, to 'the Home' to be tried on. Susanna did not pay the bill until July 1868:

To Hat finishing, own Feather	£1.1s.6d
To Violet & Black Bonnet	£1.6s.6d
To making up Grenadine evening dress with silk body, Grenadine under skirt & trimmed with bugles [beads]	£3.19s.6d
Lace Tucker etc Compleat [sic]	
Wreath etc.	10s.6d
	<u>£6.18s.0d</u>

With respectful thanks & Compts

Presumably, therefore, at some point between 1864/5 and 1867 Mrs Dinsdale had moved to London. By 1871 she had moved again, for on 19 April that year Susanna received a violet silk dress which she had ordered from her. The bill for it survives and is dated August 1871. The address was then 54 Wigmore Street:

To handsewn Violet Poult de Soie Morning Dress trimmed with Satin Tunic to match	£10.10s.0d
2 yds of silk at 10s.9d	£1.1s.0d
Collar & sleeves	10s.0d
Dress Preservers	1s.0d
Dress Improver	5s.0d
White Embroidered petticoat	£1.1s.0d

Dress preservers were rubberized underarm pads to prevent tight-fitting bodices becoming stained by perspiration – in her account book Susanna called them 'guards'. They were a novelty in 1871. A dress improver was a type of half-crinoline or 'crinolette'. It was succeeded by the bustle – a small pad or frame which went at the back and tied on round the waist but Susanna's account book actually describes this 'dress improver' of 1871 as a 'bustle'. Skirts in the 1860s were enormously full and worn over crinoline 'cages' of wire or whalebone. By the early 1870s the shape had changed and the fullness was largely at the back, requiring a differently shaped frame to support them. The crinolines, dress improvers or bustles were worn over layers of cotton undergarments. Susanna made nearly all her own underclothes but she bought her stays – a pair of 'Eva's stays' cost her 3s.10d in January 1869. The petticoat referred to in Mrs Dinsdale's bill would have been a decorative top petticoat. These usually had tucks or lace or embroidery round the hem as there was just a chance that the hem might be seen if the day was windy or the wearer moved carelessly.

A stiff little note from Mrs Dinsdale to Susanna survives:

> 54, Wigmore Street
> August 17th

Mrs Dinsdale begs respectfully to inform Mrs Ingleby that she does not allow discount, her charges being as close as possible, particularly to those ladies she works for in the Country. The silk dress with parasol sent to Mrs Ingleby would have been either 11 or 12 guineas to any other Lady or any Dress would have been the same taking 16 yards of silk at that price besides satin etc. The two yards sent extra not included.

This is interesting in that it suggests that Mrs Dinsdale supplied various 'ladies in the country'. It would seem that she was running a sort of mail-order business – probably using the railway parcel service. Certainly her husband's entry in the 1861 census suggests that even from Rugeley she was supplying more than a purely local clientele. Susanna clearly thought highly of Mrs Dinsdale but she remains something of an enigma and tracing her is not easy.

We do not know how often Susanna availed herself of Mrs Dinsdale's services for country ladies. Certainly by 1873 when she spent a long spell in London, she again visited her. On 14 May 1873, Susanna and John William left Armitage and went to London. John William suffered from what Susanna described as a 'quinsy throat' and went to London to consult Dr (later Sir) Morrell Mackenzie, *the* throat specialist of the day. Dr Mackenzie practised Galvanism, a sort of electric shock therapy which was fashionable at the time. It was painful, expensive, and there is no evidence to suggest it did any good. They stayed in London until the end of June, and John William had thirty-seven treatments. Between 18 August and 7 September they were back in London and he had a further seventeen. Susanna treated these visits as holidays and did a good deal of shopping in town. Her clothes-buying was again constrained because she was in mourning, this time for her father who had died in February. Mourning for a parent went on for a year, broken up into four periods – three months in deep mourning, three months in black with reduced crepe, three months in black and three months in half-mourning. Just as she moved into the second phase, reduced the amount of crepe on her dress and felt able to wear jet jewellery, she heard of the death of her estranged husband, the Reverend Charles Ingleby. She immediately paid another visit to Wigmore Street.

> 54 Wigmore Street March 1873
> Mrs Ingleby
> To E Dinsdale

Black silk dress with Tunic & Mantle high & low Bodies trimmed with Crape & lined with Silk & trimmed with fringe	£14.14s.0d
Costume of Poplin de laine with Tunic & Jacket trimmed with Crape & fringe. 5s.6d	£6.6s.0d
Two sets of Collars & Cuffs with sleeves	11d
To Bonnet & Veil	£1.1s.0d
Head Dress	10s.6d
Box	3s.6d
	£23.15s.0d

Susanna's widow's weeds cost considerably more than the five guineas that had been spent on her wedding dress back in January 1860. Her black dresses

Plate 45 Susanna Ingleby in the widow's weeds made for her by Mrs Dinsdale in 1873.

were the best quality she could afford; they were less a signifier of grief than a celebration of her freedom. As a widow she would be socially acceptable in a way she could never have been as an estranged wife, and without the impediment of a husband who was nominally responsible for her, she had full control over her own money. Furthermore, women of her age wore a lot of black; when her period of mourning was over and the crepe was removed, the dresses and jacket would last her for many years. [Plate 45]

In 1874 she, John William and twelve-year-old Ralph moved back to Basford Hall. By this date, Susanna was forty-three and John William was fifty-two. Neither of them was in the best of health. Perhaps memories of John William's quarrel with his father and of the shameful outcome of Susanna's marriage made them unwelcome in some homes in the area; for whatever reason, their social life declined sharply after their return to Basford.

In April 1876 Susanna visited London to spend a few days with an old friend. She bought a sealskin jacket from Barker's of Kensington (£7.17s.6d), a travel bag from Whiteley's (£1.1s.9d) and paid a visit to Mrs Dinsdale. The diary does not tell us what she ordered and no bill survives, but in her account book for

January 1877 Susanna records a payment of £5.13s.0d to Mrs Dinsdale for a violet and black silk dress. She had bought twenty-four yards of violet and black silk at 2s.4½d a yard from John Adams of Leek the month before she went to London – it sounds as if this was a discount price. Violet and black were half-mourning colours. The period of mourning for Charles Ingleby was up in December 1875, and for the last six months of it Susanna could have worn half-mourning; again, she was wearing her weeds for longer than was strictly necessary. This was not unusual. Many women never wore colours again after their husbands died – but given the circumstances of Susanna's marriage, her response seems a little excessive. This was to be Susanna's last trip to London, and as far as we can tell, her last contact with Mrs Dinsdale.

In the late 1870s and 1880s Susanna's social life declined even further: she was old and ill, and much poorer. John William had become deaf and increasingly bitter and reclusive. Her nephew grew up and left school; he was becoming very eccentric and devoted much time to travel and the collection of 'curiosities' – financed largely by Susanna. Her youngest brother, the Oxfordshire clergyman, was constantly in trouble – getting a young maid servant pregnant and being the subject of a Consistory Court hearing, defaulting on a mortgage, constantly in debt and finally going bankrupt in 1883. Between 1879 and 1883 he 'borrowed' thousands of pounds from Susanna and towards the end of her life she wrote in a letter to her solicitor, with some truth, 'I have to watch every penny I spend.' There was little money left over for new clothes and few occasions to wear them. Susanna Ingleby died in January 1891, six months short of her sixtieth birthday.

Her patronage of Mrs Dinsdale had lasted for fourteen years and survived three moves on Susanna's part and more on Mrs Dinsdale's. But Mrs Dinsdale only provided Susanna's 'best' clothes. We have already seen that she patronized other dressmakers. In fact, her account books and diaries combined refer to fourteen different ones. There were some whose work she only tried once. Mrs Payne, wife of Alexander Payne the Rugeley draper, made her one outfit in 1868: 'a muslin dress and slip, finding the muslin and narrow black lace £1.7.1d & a garibaldi 4s.6d, white mantle 15s, leghorn hat 5s.6d' and remade a dress for her a few weeks later for 4s.0d, but was never employed again. [Plate 46] Perhaps her work was not up to scratch, her prices were reasonable enough. Others like Miss Knight in Dover and Mrs Gwynne in Leek were used only once because Susanna was away from home when she needed them.

However, there were several dressmakers who were employed regularly, whose charges were low and who probably worked on everyday items of clothing. Bessie Conway in Handsacre (a hamlet just outside Armitage) was one such. She was the wife of an agricultural labourer and mother of three young children. Between 1869 and 1870 she did a good deal of work for Susanna, mostly altering dresses, for example: 'Sept 13th 1869, altering skirt of violet dress 1s.6d, remaking skirt of pink barège 2s … altering drab dress in the folds 6d, remaking brown dress and altering bodice again 5s.'

These are all dresses we have encountered before and two of them date back to Susanna's trousseau. As the fashionable dress shape changed in the late 1860s, again in the mid-1870s and again in the 1880s, new dresses had to be bought or old ones remade. Victorian silks were of far higher quality than contemporary fabrics; they were expensive, and their owners expected them to last and survive many alterations and remakes. In October 1869 Bessie Conway altered a tulle dress (almost certainly the one Mrs Dinsdale had made in 1862) for 1s.3d and in September 1870 she altered four dresses for 10s.0d.

Susanna made or altered many items herself. In Armitage in April 1869 she unpicked and remade a blue silk dress. In later years she did much more of her own sewing. She bought large quantities of calico to replenish her stocks

Plate 46 Susanna Ingleby with her brother and nephew. She is wearing the dress made for her by Mrs Payne in 1868.

of voluminous cotton underwear as well as to make shirts for her brother and nephew. And in September 1871, as soon as they became readily available, she bought herself a sewing machine from Willcox and Gibbs for '£5.15s.6d, box 10s.6d, case 2s'. Her friends and neighbours came to see – and borrow – it. On 3 April 1872, for example, she wrote in her diary, 'I lent my sewing machine to Harriet.' But despite all these purchases, Susanna's expenditure on clothes averaged less than £14.00 a year.

And when that is set against the other information in her personal account books an even more surprising picture is revealed. From her diaries, Susanna appears as a conventional Victorian lady, not particularly well educated, whose chief preoccupations were her home and her family and whose main recreations were sewing and gardening. She could write and spell, but her vocabulary was limited and her style tedious. But the account books show us what books she bought – religion, history, natural history, biography, philosophy, science, child-care, cookery and household management. She subscribed to the *Ladies Treasury*, a magazine which, along with language lessons, history and philosophy, published articles by women whose contribution to science is only now being recognized. Susanna Ingleby was not totally disinterested in clothes, and she was certainly not eccentric enough to defy the fashionable conventions of her age, but she preferred to spend her money on books for her library and plants for her garden rather than on finery for herself.

(A longer version of this section was originally published as 'Buttons, braids, bones and body linings; a Staffordshire lady and her London dressmaker' in *Staffordshire History* [Spring 1997])

Conclusion

The five sets of accounts were all kept by ladies who were reasonably well-off; they all had choices about what they wore and who made it. But the accounts are only snapshots. It is quite possible, for example, that Arabella Calley was much more interested in fashion when she was a young woman than she was in her fifties. It may be that Charlotte Kenyon was less extravagant in her dress once she was married. We can see that Eliza Stone's youthful enthusiasm for clothes declined once she became Mrs Spurrett and the mother of a young family. Inevitably, age and circumstances affected the women's spending patterns in ways the accounts cannot show.

What they do, however, is reinforce information we have already gleaned – that there was a hierarchy in the dressmaking trade and different dressmakers occupied different places within it: it was not so much that they worked for different clienteles but that they produced work of differing qualities. Ladies saw no harm in paying less for having their everyday clothes made or altered than for having their 'best' clothes made – despite the fact that the time and effort that went into making the two types of garments were very similar. They saw it as thriftiness, not parsimony, and thrift was a virtue. For example, Mrs Kenyon saw no shame in having the less important parts of Charlotte's trousseau made in Shropshire, despite having spent weeks shopping around the most expensive shops in London. Arabella Calley shopped in Swindon but she bought her more fashionable caps from Miss Mayo in Bath. Susanna Ingleby was happy to wear mourning made by Leek or Rugeley dressmakers when her brothers died, but her widow's weeds were important enough to be made by Mrs Dinsdale in London. Even Ann Williamson had a few everyday gowns made by a Miss Daniels who charged roughly half the price she would have paid at Bennall's.

No doubt London firms like S. Ramsay, the Bennall sisters and Lady Winn's Mrs Charlton and Rebecca Thomas in fashionable Cheltenham had higher overheads than Mrs Gwynne in Leek or Mrs Pegg in Leicester, Elizabeth Shackleton's dressmakers in Colne or Mary Hardy's in Holt – but their charges for making-up were two, three sometimes four times as high. The fact that their 'best' customers went elsewhere for special purchases affected small town dressmakers' status as well as their profits and deprived them of the experience of working on really high-quality fabrics and garments. This in turn influenced the prices they could charge and consolidated their lowly place in the hierarchy. Dressmaking was a precarious business, and it is women in this stratum of the trade whose businesses were most likely to fail.

The other thing an examination of the actual expenditure of real individuals shows is how unreliable fashion writers could be. In the latter part of the nineteenth century a series of writers – 'Sylvia' in *How to Dress Well on a Shilling a Day* (1876), Mrs Haweis in *The Art of Dress* (1879), Mrs Praga in *Appearances and How to Keep Them Up on a Limited Income* (1899) and a host of others – offered advice aimed at the new middle class about how to dress respectably without spending a fortune. 'Sylvia' was the most detailed. She listed the number of dresses a lady should own (at least ten), plus a winter hat, jacket and bonnet and another set for summer, to be replaced every couple of years, keeping to a single colour palette (she favoured brown) to ensure outfits could be mixed and matched – and she advised buying the best quality the reader could afford. She subscribed to the view that you could 'tell a lady by her gloves and her shoes' and to that end advocated spending at least £3.00 a year on footwear and another

£1.00 on gloves (eight pairs at 2s.6d each plus 1s.6d for cleaning them). 'Poverty', she stressed, must never have the appearance of poverty'. Good quality and shabby was acceptable, shoddy was not.

Mrs Haweis urged ladies to make their own clothes and not to trust dressmakers who would swindle them by asking for more fabric than was needed and then keeping a yard or two for themselves – but she didn't see fit to explain exactly how they would use all those odd yards of different fabrics.

Mrs Praga recommended following her own example:

> I was fortunate enough to discover a little woman in our vicinity who fitted really well, and whose charge for making was only half a guinea ... though I was careful to have my gowns as well made as my means would allow, I never invested in anything ultra-fashionable, for I knew that markedly fashionable soon becomes markedly unfashionable.

She did not say what ladies were supposed to do if they failed to discover a suitable 'little woman'.

Susanna Ingleby and Eliza Spurrett both had limited money to spend on clothes but both managed to dress respectably on significantly less than the pundits suggested; neither owned ten dresses at any one time and neither bought eight pairs of gloves in a year. Ann Williamson, on the other hand, owned and spent considerably more.

Five sets of accounts are simply a random sample. Nonetheless, examining them makes a significant contribution to our knowledge. They reinforce impressions gleaned from other sources. They tell us what clothes cost and give some indication of what the women who made them might have earned. They demonstrate how fickle customers could be. And above all, they give a fascinating insight into how a handful of fairly well-to-do ladies lived and dressed.

Conclusion

This study has drawn on many types of material – from bills and account books to novels and paintings. There is no single key source; it is the aggregate of pieces of information that is telling.

What makes a study of the dressmaking trade unusual is that it was a trade carried on almost entirely by women, exclusively for women. Furthermore, the women who entered the profession were often enterprising and able. Fortunately for us, the dressmakers and milliners of Britain were not completely nameless and faceless: a small but significant number left records behind them. They employed staff, despatched bills and fell foul of the law; they advertised in newspapers and sent promotional material to their clients; they wrote letters and had their photographs taken; magazines were written for them and advertisers courted them; their customers remembered them and they were described in diaries and correspondence. This study has brought a few of these women into the light. Some, like Elizabeth Browne in Durham in the 1700s, Mrs Carmichael in 1860s Edinburgh and Madame Clapham in late nineteenth-century Hull, were clearly appreciated in their own lifetimes; others are now known simply because of the chance survival of documents, and at least one – Marie Schild – has proved to be a woman of exceptional energy, productivity and importance. For whatever reason, her contribution to fashion has gone largely unrecognized, and yet for fifty years she developed an empire, providing paper patterns, fashion magazines and a whole range of goods and services. Other dressmakers used their skills in similar ways though not always with the same degree of success. The importance of these women as pioneers in the world of commerce, albeit a small corner of it, should be recognized and appreciated.

Nonetheless, dressmaking has often had a bad press. From the seventeenth-century guildsmen who saw mantua-makers as a threat to be 'suppressed' through the eighteenth-century authors of scurrilous plays and novels that depicted milliners and mantua-makers as vulgar, over-dressed and willing to lose their virtue to the first man who came along, to the poisonous 'Cherub' imagining lurid goings-on behind 'the folding doors of a millinery deception' in 1792, women making women's clothes were deeply suspect, at least in the minds of some men.

Attitudes did not improve much in the nineteenth century. Even as they tried to describe abuses within the trade, mid-Victorian novelists followed their eighteenth-century predecessors in reinforcing the idea of the dressmaker-prostitute, if only in their efforts to highlight the virtue of their heroines. As we saw in Chapter 9, the evidence suggests that dressmakers were in fact *less* likely to become prostitutes than were other categories of young female workers, but the stereotype persisted. There were various reasons. Some dressmakers lived apart from their families, unprotected by male relatives and – in the view of self-righteous men whose womenfolk did not have to work – they were therefore at imminent risk of being seduced. Women were fragile creatures, so the argument ran, so of course they would be unable to resist temptation or make wise decisions. Furthermore, young dressmakers were in constant contact with fashionable clothes. Too great an interest in dress was sinful, particularly in young working women who might, heaven forbid, choose to wear clothes that were inappropriate to their station in life. Men's unease about dressmaking establishments was probably also fuelled by suspicion of all-female environments in which ladies were in intimate contact with members of a lower class. What did they talk about? What harmful views or influences might they encounter? The advertisements in trade magazines may also offer some clues. If by the 1870s (some) dressmakers were supplying 'female pills' and booklets of 'advice to the married' to (some of) their customers – what other services might they have been providing? However groundless the fears and suspicions, they lingered in the back of people's minds.

In reality, dressmaking usually attracted girls from respectable, aspirational families who could afford to pay an apprenticeship premium or could persuade a patron to pay it for them, or whose daughters the local parish or charity officials deemed worthy of support. However, the belief in dressmaking as an occupation of impoverished gentlewomen died hard, and articles like the one in *The Sempstress* on the Distressed Needlewomen's Home (supported by the Distressed Needlewomen's Society which produced the magazine) reinforced it. [Plate 47] The inmates were not all dressmakers, but some were:

> Very many it has assisted who once enjoyed the comforts of life, and had at their command the carriage, the servant, etc: but, from causes over which they have had no control, have been reduced to penury and want. Many of the parties assisted are officers' daughters and widows, clergymen's daughters and widows, and widows and daughters of those who have been independent.[1]

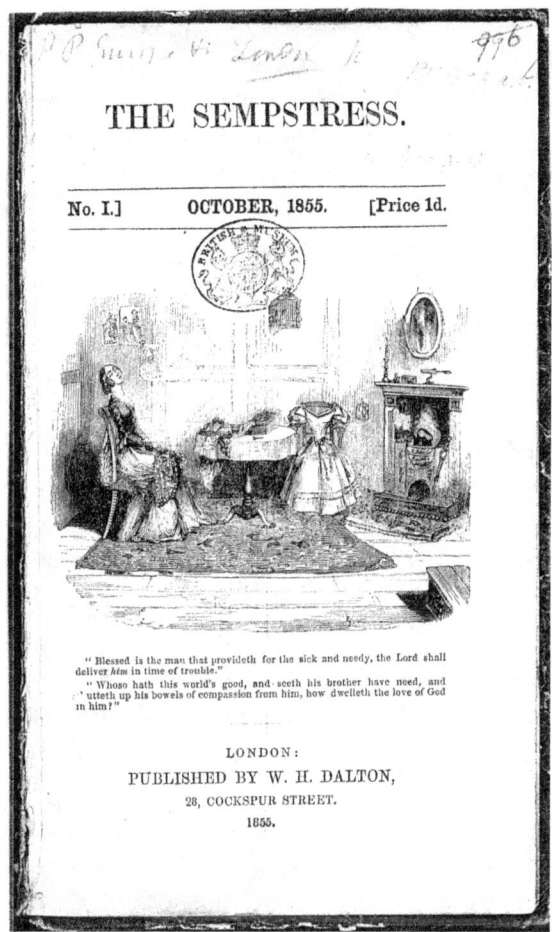

Plate 47 Cover of the first – and only – issue of *The Sempstress*, dated October 1855.

The value of the study of census data – for all its limitations – is that it enables us to say with certainty that the majority of nineteenth-century dressmakers actually came from what can loosely be described as working-class homes, as had their eighteenth-century counterparts. Many were members of the small tradesmen/craftsmen class. Many came from the class below. A handful came from semi-professional families and about a third cannot be placed in any social category because they lived apart from their families. It is possible, even probable, that some of these were the stereotypical gentlewomen-fallen-on-hard-times. However, it seems fair to deduce that such women formed a minority of the work force, though it is possible that, like middle-class families today, they were more adept at finding support services when things went wrong than were their less educated colleagues, hence the (alleged) preponderance of them in the Distressed Needlewomen's Home.

Class mattered. According to Ms Monroe, writing in 1879, some dressmakers offered formal tuition, but this, she was careful to stress, was for ladies' maids and milliners' assistants wishing to go into business on their own account, and 'naturally, such associates are objectionable to private people'. Her brief was to drum up business for the 'Ladies' Dress Making and Embroidery Association' which had workrooms open six-and-a-half days a week which ladies could attend (at one guinea a month or five guineas for six months) to 'learn the basics of the craft', but the social distinction she makes is revealing and again gives the lie to the idea of the genteel dressmaker's apprentice so popular in fiction.

Ladies sewed; they did fancy work and many of them also did plain sewing, making at least some of their own underclothes, shirts for their menfolk and garments for their children, mending tears, sewing on buttons and altering trimmings. But dressmaking was actually a very different task. Patterns were complex and dresses had to fit, while shirts and underwear were voluminous and made from basic geometric shapes that simply required diligence to put together neatly. Some ladies, and some working women, made their own everyday frocks and wrappers, but best dresses, cut from narrow breadths of expensive silk, were usually professionally made throughout our period. And as we have seen, many nineteenth-century working-class women had never learnt to sew and so had to buy any new clothes they had. Dressmakers were skilled craftswomen, providing a service that many of their clients simply could not undertake for themselves.

This brings us to a very important point. Women's paid, non-domestic work has usually been regarded as essentially temporary – a way of filling the gap between childhood and marriage and accumulating a little capital with which to start married life – and this has been used to explain the relatively lowly status accorded to it. But dressmaking required a lengthy training. The minimum period for a formal apprenticeship was a year and many women served much longer. Many of them paid for the privilege and some went on to further unpaid, or poorly paid, training as improvers. A study of dressmakers therefore leads us to question this nostrum about women's work. Few individuals would have invested so much time and money in acquiring skills that would be discarded on marriage. It is therefore reasonable to assume that women who trained as dressmakers expected to work for most of their lives, either within marriage or without it. Furthermore, by providing them with apprenticeship premiums, their families, or, in the case of charity children, their communities or sponsors, encouraged and legitimized this decision.

While middle-class writers seem to have seen domestic service as the most respectable occupation for working-class girls, the young women themselves saw things rather differently. Being in service was 'low and degrading', involving 'an almost total loss of personal liberty'. Even factory workers described themselves as being 'above that poor scum what mustn't wear a feather or a ribbon, or breathe the fresh air, without asking somebody's leave'.[2] To modern eyes, dressmakers' assistants seem to have fared little better, but perception was important; they saw themselves as employees, not servants, and that informed their view of their employment.

It is crucial to our understanding of the trade to realize that most girls did not drift into dressmaking through poverty and ill-fortune; they chose the most prestigious of the skilled trades open to young women, and, for the most part, they accepted the rigours that went with it. It was not an easy life, but then neither was working in a factory, or a shop, on a farm or in domestic service, doing laundry or knitting or making lace. Dressmaking itself was not especially arduous, but the cripplingly long hours were. For the young woman who became ill but had no time to rest and recuperate, a dressmaking apprenticeship could be a death sentence.

But some – many – girls worked out their apprenticeships and moved up the trade. They became improvers, assistants, second and first hands, and their wages improved. If Campbell is to be believed, a dressmaker's assistant in the middle years of the eighteenth century could earn around £12.00 a year, comparable to the salary of a housekeeper and not much less than that of a male labourer. Young Elizabeth Stone in Brighton, as a second hand in the middle years of the nineteenth century, was offered £40.00 a year – a very respectable wage, more than the salary of many country schoolmasters. Lucks paid one of their first hands £120.00 a year in the 1890s, an excellent wage even by men's standards – a pound a week was reckoned to be the basic living wage for a working man with a family for most of the nineteenth century and up to the First World War.

By the 1870s dressmaking also offered the opportunity for young women from modest backgrounds to travel to different parts of the country to work, a much more adventurous proposition at the end of the nineteenth century than it now seems. There were, of course, many different types of dressmaking establishment and many different types of client. Conditions, prices, wages and workrooms varied, and so did individuals' attitudes to their trade. But at every level the job required much the same skills, regardless of conditions in the workroom, the type of fabrics being sewn or the social status of the clientele.

The rewards dressmakers reaped varied widely. Anne Sawney in Lechlade, working in the middle years of the eighteenth century, amassed a substantial amount of property; Martha Burgess left over £300.00 when she died in

Nottingham in 1785. However, Hannah Glasse in London in the 1750s and Magdalene Dunbar in Leith in the 1810s were turning over several thousand pounds a year but still went bankrupt. Mrs Carmichael in Edinburgh in the 1860s and Madame Clapham in Hull in the 1890s enjoyed prestige and lived in comfort, even if they worked long hours and had undergone exhausting apprenticeships. Miss Goddard in Leicester in the 1830s or Mrs Turnock in Hanley in the 1880s, eking out their livings by moving from household to household to make and mend, and dependent for subsistence on the generosity of their employers, had a much less enviable lot – but even they led less miserable lives than did Sarah Paul and Ann Mason, abandoned apprentices in mid-eighteenth-century London, or Mrs Faulder's hapless apprentice in Manchester and Miss Reeves' 'friend' in Birmingham in the 1860s. Bessie Conway of Handsacre in altering Susanna Ingleby's four dresses for ten shillings in September 1870 was probably making a significant addition to her family's income that month, earning at least as much as her labourer husband would have brought home in a week; forty years earlier Agnes Dow in Leith, who had often charged more than that for a single hat, went bankrupt. Circumstances altered cases.

But whatever the advantages, dressmaking was not an easy profession, though the true scale of the problem did not really come to light until the 1840s. One after another, young dressmakers in different parts of the country reported to the Children's Employment Commissioners how they worked past midnight for days or weeks on end, how they were ill-fed, unable to do anything other than work and constantly at the mercy of capricious employers. Contemporaries were rightly outraged; organizations were formed, articles were printed, novels were penned and pictures painted. But none of them made any immediate difference. The *Song of the Shirt* was a classic; references to it were readily understood half-a-century after it was written, but for most people, it was fiction, as were Mrs Gaskell's novels, or Mrs Stone's, or the Religious Tract Society's. The connection between the overworked milliner's assistant in a story and the girls who worked for the reader's own dressmaker was hard to make, and lady readers had not been taught to be critical of what they read. John Thomas Peele's or Richard Redgrave's or Millais' paintings were affecting – but they did not, the viewer was vaguely aware, depict 'real' workers.

It is unlikely that many ladies *wanted* to cause young women to be overworked, and no doubt many heeded the pleas of the Association for the Aid and Benefit of Dressmakers and Milliners and its successors to order their dresses well in advance of need – at least when it did not inconvenience them too much to do so. Even *The Sempstress* admitted that 'it may occasionally happen that circumstances beyond our control will oblige us to give a hasty order, but do we never, without such necessity, defer sending a dress to be made up until the last moment?' It was an implicit, class-based assumption, even among the reformers of the Distressed Needlewomen's Society, that in extremis, a lady's 'need' for a new dress took precedence over her dressmaker's need for sleep.

Magazine articles described working conditions, but in fact Victorian society colluded in keeping supposedly sensitive ladies in ignorance of any unpleasantness that might distress or disturb them. Dressmakers kept their workroom doors firmly closed and any pale consumptive little apprentices stayed well out of sight. Even in the 1920s, Madame Clapham 'lost' apprentices in cupboards and passages when the inspectors called.[3] There is a contemporary parallel in the purchase of garments made in third-world countries. No amount of television documentaries or magazine articles on sweat-shops in the Far East has had any noticeable effect on sales of cheap clothes, or of designer-label goods made in Indonesia or Bangladesh. We are driven by many imperatives when buying our clothes but charity is not usually the chief of them.

And clothes were disproportionately important in the eighteenth and nineteenth centuries. Fashionably dressed wives and daughters, paying and receiving calls, leaving cards and drinking tea, demonstrated – to other fashionably dressed wives and daughters, similarly engaged – the social position to which their family aspired. Society was mobile and many people were anxious to move up the social hierarchy rather faster than their means would allow. 'Poverty,' wrote 'Sylvia', 'should never have the appearance of poverty'[4] – a stricture which applied equally to the genteel lady fallen on hard times and the tradesman's wife trying to move onto the next rung of the social ladder. Dress proclaimed to the world the social pretensions of its wearer. From Lucy Gildart's criticism of Mrs Herrick in 1770s Leicestershire to the March sisters in 1860s Massachusetts in *Little Women*, we see evidence of the importance of clothes in representing social status. Even working-class families saw dress as a signifier of respectability. For working-class women, a clean white apron covered a multitude of sins; patches and darns were acceptable – raggedness was not.[5]

Clothes had many meanings. Too great an interest in dress was a sign of vanity, and vanity was sinful. 'Modesty' in dress, which meant plain dresses in drab colours (greys, beiges, browns, soft blues and greens and the ubiquitous black), was much praised. Trimmings were to be muted and kept to a minimum. There was a good deal of inverted snobbery too; fabrics were to be good quality; lace and jewellery should be old and real. By the nineteenth century it was felt that bright colours and loud patterns were vulgar and suggested that their wearer was, too, but on the other hand, shabby clothes, or clothes that had been mended too often or too obviously, also branded their wearer as being unable to keep up appearances and therefore socially undesirable.

At the same time clergymen, and books of domestic economy, preached the virtues of thrift in all areas of expenditure. Household items were made to last, and even wealthy families had pans re-bottomed and broken china mended with rivets. Clothes had to survive several re-makes, and in the eighteenth century there was no shame in bequeathing your used dresses to friends and family. Even well-to-do ladies tended to have limited clothing allowances for which they often had to account to their husbands or fathers – hence the keeping of personal account books. Anything that could be regarded as unnecessary extravagance was likely to incur censure; there was thus economic, moral and social pressure to keep expenditure on dress to a minimum and this in turn affected the prices that all but the most elite of dressmakers could expect to charge. Writers like Ms Monroe[6] might accuse dressmakers of charging excessive rates, but few surviving bills substantiate this. The key to the trade's problem was that most dressmakers charged too *little*.

This study indicates the types of businesses which were most likely to succeed. Small businesses tended to be more viable than large ones. For example, two women in partnership, both working, with an unpaid apprentice or one who was paid only a few shillings a month, could manage reasonably well. Between them they could make four or five dresses a week from which they could earn at least a pound. If a family could live adequately on a pound a week, so could two women, even with a live-in apprentice and perhaps a maid-of-all-work to pay and feed. Working on such a small scale they could even afford to take on temporary help at busy times – the extra work would more than pay for itself. Married women whose husbands were in work tended to be even more successful. Like Mrs Pattinson in Ulverston, they could make a temporary loss but still continue to trade because there was a second income to tide them over. Profits from dressmaking were also often enhanced by the sale of ready-made goods and haberdashery. Even work people could live quite comfortably if conditions were right; Clementina Black quoted the case of two sisters of eighteen and twenty-one in 1908 who worked together

> … in the workroom of a well-known shop, earning 18s.0d and 7s.0d respectively, with overtime at 6d an hour. They lived together in one room paying 4s.6d for it, keep it beautifully and are very comfortable on their joint income of 25s.0d a week.[7]

The economics of a large workroom were much more difficult to manage than those of a small concern. Even the department store workrooms do not seem to have made much actual profit, but, as we have seen, they had a different raison d'être and brought profit to their owners in other ways. To judge by the records that survive, a modest workroom in the latter years of the nineteenth century containing a first hand, a second hand, four improvers/assistants and two unpaid apprentices, would have had an annual wage bill of at least £120.00 (£60.00 for the first hand, £20.00 for the second and £10.00 each for the others). The apprentices would not have done much actual making, but they would have lightened the load for the six others, by picking up pins, threading needles, tidying up, making tea and doing jobs like sewing on buttons and brush-braid. Six needlewomen, dividing the tasks between them according to skill and experience, and served by the apprentices, could comfortably make twelve ordinary dresses (or their equivalent) a week, working a ten-hour day and a five-and-a-half-day week. But if those dresses were charged for at a basic rate of five shillings each, the firm would have made £156.00 pa, giving the owner a surplus of just £36.00 a year out of which to rent premises, feed (if not house) eight staff and live themselves. It was not an economic proposition – hence the bankruptcies of the likes of James Binnington and George Nicholson in York.

Working on the same basis – an average of two dresses a week per workwoman, costed at 5s each – each hand 'earned' the establishment for which she worked £26.00 a year, assuming, of course, that demand always matched capacity. To make a profit, therefore, the average annual wage paid to staff members had to be less than £26.00, and/or the number of garments made per head per week had to increase. No amount of early ordering by clients could alter the fact that, for their labour to be economic, hands often had to produce more garments than was realistically possible – hence the extraordinarily long working hours.

Wages remained low for a number of other reasons. As we have seen, women's wages generally were lower than men's and there was no expectation that it should be otherwise. Widows and older spinsters were penalized by this but they were a minority of the workforce. Dressmaking was virtually the only craft trade open to women so there was no community of craftswomen with whom to compare pay scales, and no tradition of parity with skilled male workers. Dressmakers compared their salaries (probably quite favourably) with those of unskilled and semi-skilled women and women in service, but because there were comparatively few jobs which were open to women, those areas in which women could find reasonably good employment were likely to be oversubscribed. By the mid-nineteenth century there were more dressmaking firms than the market could support, so to compete, proprietors offered not just quality, but cheap rates and speedy service. This inevitably led to low pay and long hours, but the workwomen were unable to protest because there were plenty of unemployed hands able and willing to take their places.

In the union sense, therefore, dressmaking was never an organized trade. Workers were isolated and many worked in their own homes – the type of situation that even today defies attempts at unionization. Women in live-in posts, even in department stores, were subject to strict rules imposed by their employers and risked losing their place of residence as well as their job if they disobeyed them. In the late 1880s Hannah Mitchell's employer forbade her staff to attend a meeting about reducing hours; they defied her, only to find her sitting in the front row, pretending to support the motion.[8] They were unusual. To women who had no political power, the concept of political action was often foreign, or even morally suspect, and the exceptional length of the working day left dressmakers' assistants particularly short of time and energy with which to agitate for improved conditions.

Another reason for low wages was probably 'custom and practice'. Ladies became used to paying a certain price for their clothes and were unwilling to accept price rises, particularly in a period when inflation was not general. In an oversubscribed market this left little room for manoeuvre. From the early eighteenth century onwards there was also increasing competition from ready-to-wear clothing.

Dressmaking did not have to be an impoverished profession. In America, economic conditions were similar to those in the UK, but dressmakers' status was higher. In New England in the 1770s Rebecca Dickinson worried endlessly about money and having enough work as did her British counterparts, while in 1803–4 Polly Lathrop charged 3s.0d for a cotton gown and 4s.0d for a silk one – very similar prices to those charged in Britain.[9] But opportunities were greater. Mary Molloy in Minnesota was the daughter of Irish immigrants but she rose to be one of St Paul's most influential businesswomen and was listed in the Blue Book of the twin cities in 1907.[10] Carrie Taylor in Kentucky had a college degree but saw dressmaking as a respectable way of earning a living and was also a noted local hostess.[11] From Elizabeth Ashridge in eighteenth-century New York buying herself out of a miserable apprenticeship with wages earned doing extra sewing ('then I fell to my needle, by which I could maintain myself handsomely') to the two feisty old needlewomen in *A Mistaken Charity* who fled an old peoples' home to return to their own tumbledown cottage, Americans seem to have viewed dressmaking as synonymous with independence rather than as a route to poverty.[12] In England, dressmakers had no time to host lavish soirées, few eighteenth-century apprentices had leisure for extra sewing, and most old ladies lucky enough to find themselves in a charitable institution other than the workhouse would have been quite happy to stay put.

However, it is misleading to see dressmaking conditions as a purely female problem. The parallels with the tailoring trade were very close. Live-in journeymen tailors and male shop assistants were subject to their employers' dictates in much the same way as the women were. Tailoring unions, though they existed, were largely unsuccessful in controlling wages and working conditions. Charles Kingsley's *Alton Locke* (1850) experienced poverty, unemployment, unhealthy workrooms and excessive hours that were very similar to those described by many young dressmakers. Men were no more anxious to pay a proper price for their clothes than women were, and small town drapers made even less profit from their tailoring than they did from their dressmaking. The fact that dressmakers were women may have added an extra dimension to their problems, but it was not their cause. Nor is this a case of women being exploited by the patriarchy; the exploiters were other women – employers and customers. They were not wholly responsible for the economic climate in which dressmakers worked, but they contributed to, and colluded with it.

The combination of moral and economic pressure from customers to keep expenditure on clothing as low as possible made it unlikely that garment workers could ever be well paid. Even the establishment of Wage Boards in the early years of the twentieth century, and the great social catalyst that was the First World War, did not really improve dressmakers' conditions. Helen Bagrie in Aberdeen[13] and Madame Clapham in Hull paid their staff appallingly little even in the 1930s, and as late as the 1980s May Verita,[14] working for herself, seldom earned more than a pound an hour. Wages in the 'rag trade' are still notoriously low.

However, in a world in which they were heavily disadvantaged, dressmaking provided many women with a lifeline. It enabled them to augment the family income, to provide for their children if they were widowed or deserted, or simply to live independently. It was a trade they could take up and drop at will. They were poorly paid, but not in comparison with other women workers; for decades, women's wages would remain much lower than men's. Of the 3 million women in full-time work at the time of the 1911 census, for example, a million earned under 12s.0d a week, and a further million-and-a-half earned between 12s.0d and 15s.0d. Of the 13 million *men* in full-time work, only 4 per cent earned less than 15s.0d, while the majority – 62 per cent – earned over a pound.[15] In this context we should not judge dressmaking simply on its profits. Its exponents may have been badly paid and overworked but this does not detract from the craft skills most of them developed, the real artistry that some of them showed, the managerial ability of many workroom heads or the entrepreneurial endeavours of a significant minority. Women in high-class firms were often proud of their status even if their financial rewards were low. Working-class women who made clothes for their neighbours had a skill which defined their worth in the community, benefited their families and could be traded for reciprocal services as well as for cash. At the very worst, women with a dressmaking training behind them were the ones most likely to be offered seamstress work when times were bad.

But the key thing was that dressmaking offered the *possibility* of success. The head of a workroom was an important figure, earning good money. That was something to aspire to. A woman who could save or borrow a little capital could even set up in business on her own account, and if she was reasonably talented – and lucky – she could make a decent living. Some were successful. Many others, to judge by the rapid changeover of names in trades' directories year by year, were not. We can only guess at the personal tragedies that lie behind those statistics, but the fact remained that, for those with reasonable stamina and ability, dressmaking offered women the possibility of a good wage and the hope of independence. However unattainable it was for many, it was that hope that persuaded young women – and their parents – that the years of training, the long hours and the meagre wages might, in time, bear fruit. For girls who needed to work, despite all the disadvantages, dressmaking remained one of the more attractive options.

Notes

Introduction

1. *Norwich Directory* (1783) and *Lewis's Directory of Manchester and Salford* (1788).
2. Buck, Anne (1993), 'Mantua-Makers and Milliners: Women Making and Selling Clothes in 18th Century Bedfordshire', *Bedfordshire Historical Miscellany*, Bedfordshire Historical Society, pp. 142–155.
3. Pinchbeck, Ivy (1930), *Women Workers and the Industrial Revolution 1750–1850*. London, Virago reprint; Clark, Alice (1919), *The Working Life of Women in the 17th Century*, Frank Cass reprint, 1968. The quotation comes from Pinchbeck, p. 287.
4. Bray (1857), *The Industrial Employment of Women* (pamphlet, n.l).
5. Nenadic, Stana (1998), 'Social Shaping of Business Behaviour …', *Journal of Social History* 31(3).
6. Children's Employment Commission Report, Vol. X (1843), p. F32.
7. Phillips, Nicola (2006), *Women in Business 1700–1850*, 2006, Section 1. Woodbridge, Boydell.
8. Aston, Jennifer and Martino, Paolo (2017), 'Risk, Success and Failure', *Economic History Review* 70(3).
9. Notably by Roszika Parker (1984), *The Subversive Stitch*. London, Women's Press.
10. *Wikipedia*.

Chapter 1

1. Trueman (1858), 'The First Mantua Makers in Durham', *Aeliana Archaeologica*, 2(II). R. Hope was appointed as one of the clerks of the Spicery in 1660, but in 1671 he was demoted to 'Supernumary' as it had been decided that only two clerks were needed, not three. http://www.british-history.ac.uk/office-holders/vol11/ The whereabouts of the documents Trueman used are no longer known.
2. By Michael John Wright.
3. Lambert, Miles (1999), 'Sent from Town', *Costume* 43.
4. W. Sussex CRO, Buckle Mss 432.
5. Berks. CRO, D/ED/F19. She married Sir William Trumbull of Easthampton Park in 1706.

6   A mixture of silk and worsted.
7   PRO PROB 11_265_161; PROB 11_209_529; PROB 11_179_426.
8   There were exceptions. See Collins, Jessica (2013), 'Jane Holt, Milliner and Other Women 1606–1800', *Textile History* 44 for a reappraisal of women's role in the Clothworkers' Guild.
9   Newcastle RO, GU/TY/12.
10 Bodleian, Ms Morrell 16.
11 Maxwell, Stuart (1972), 'Two 18th Century Tailors', *Hawick Archaeological Society Transactions*, p. 6
12 Sleigh-Johnson, Nigel (2003), 'Aspects of the Tailoring Trade in the City of London', *Costume* 37.
13 Waugh, Norah (1973), *The Cut of Women's Clothes 1600–1930*. London, Faber.
14 Arnold, Janet (1973), 'The Dressmaker's Craft', *Costume* 6.
15 Sanderson, Elizabeth (2001), '"The New Dresses": A Look at How Mantua-Making Became Established in Scotland', *Costume* 35.
16 Buck, *Bedfordshire Miscellany*.
17 Crowston, C.H. (2002), 'Fabricating Women, the Seamstresses of Old Regime France 1675–1791', *Business History Review* 76(2), pp. 414–427.
18 Coffin, Judith (1996), *The Politics of Women's Work: The Paris Garment Trades 1750–1915*. Princeton University Press, pp. 33–34.
19 Wiesner, Merry E. 'Spinsters and Seamstresses' in Ferguson, Quilligan and Vickers (eds) (1986), *Rewriting the Renaissance*. Chicago University Press.
20 Johnson, Bernard (1949), *The Acts and Ordinances of the Merchant Tailors of York*. London and York, Ben Johnson and Co, pp. 81–91.
21 Davies, Matthew and Saunders, Ann (2004), *History of the Merchant Taylors' Company*. Leeds, Maney, Chapter 15.
22 Bristol RO, 4954.3; Wilts. CRO, G23/1/254.
23 Cheshire CRO, G22.1.
24 Johnson, *Merchant Tailors*, pp. 158–159.
25 Bodleian, Morell 16. Unfortunately, the 'other towns' are not specified.
26 Wilts. CRO, G23/1/254.
27 Correspondence with the Parliamentary Archivist, July 2018.
28 Johnson, *Merchant Tailors*, pp. 81–91.
29 Dobson, R.B. and Smith, D.M. (2006), *The Merchant Taylors of York,* from the table of 'Conjectural Estimates of the Membership of the Merchant Taylors' Company'. York, Borthwick Publications, p. 101.
30 Borthwick Institute, MTA series.
31 S. Devon CRO, Q4.
32 Trueman, *Mantua-makers*.
33 Newcastle RO, GU/Ty/12.

34 Worcs. CRO, 496.5BA9360/C9/Box1/2.
35 Salop CRO, LB fiche 3027.
36 Sanderson, 'The New Dresses'.
37 Ibid.
38 Ibid.
39 Bain, Ebenezer (1887), *Merchant and Craft Guilds: A History of the Aberdeen Incorporated Trades* [n.l.], pp. 258–259.
40 Aberdeen CRO, DD71/B/1.
41 Warden, Alexander (1872), *Burgh Laws of Dundee* [n.l.] and Dundee Archives, Tailors' Boxmaster's Accounts.
42 *Stirling Natural History and Archaeological Society Transactions* (1922–3), pp. 60–61.
43 NAS, Processes CS234/T1/12.
44 Hoffman, Tom (2011), *Bibliography on the Guilds*. London, Birkbeck College. Extant records exist for Aberdeen, Bristol, Chester, Dundee, Edinburgh, Exeter, London, Ludlow, Newcastle, Old Aberdeen, Oxford, Perth, Salisbury, Stirling and Worcester.
45 These included members from a range of trades and were usually to be found in towns too small to support a range of craft guilds.

Chapter 2

1 *The Complete English Tradesman* (1726), Chapter XXII. London, Rivington.
2 *The Public Advertiser*, 5 March 1772.
3 Home (ed) Letters and Journal, quoted in Ribeiro, Aileen (1984), *Dress in 18th Century Europe*. London and New York, Yale, p. 50.
4 Hett, Francis Paget (ed) (1926), *Memoirs of Susan Sibbald*. London, John Lane, p. 112.
5 Weatherill, Lorna (1996), *Consumer Behaviour and Material Culture in England 1660–1760*. London, Routledge, and (1991), 'Consumer Behaviour in the Late 17th and Early 18th Centuries', *Textile History* 22(2).
6 Buck, *Bedfordshire Miscellany*.
7 Wilts. CRO, 88/9/19.
8 Dodds, Madeleine (1938), 'The Rival Cooks: Hannah Glasse and Ann Cook', *Archaeologia Aeliana*. Society of Antiquities, Newcastle-upon-Tyne, 4(15).
9 Styles, John (2011), 'Fashion and Innovation in Early Modern Europe', in Welch, Evelyn (ed), *Fashioning the Early Modern*. Oxford, OUP, p. 42.
10 The looped up back of a skirt. This could be created in numerous ways, see Van Cleave and Welborn (2012), 'Very Much the Taste and Various Are the Makes', *Dress* 39(1).

11 Chrisman-Campbell, Kimberley (2004), 'French Connections', *Dress* 31(1).
12 Allen, Michael (ed) (2011), *An English Lady in Paris. The Diary of Frances Anne Crewe*, 1786. Oxford, Stockley. Introduction.
13 Baudis, Macushla (2014), 'Smoaking Hot with Fashion from Paris', *Costume* 48(2).
14 McKendrick, Brewer and Plumb (1982), *The Birth of a Consumer Society*. London, Europa, p. 46.
15 Fraser, Antonia (1963), *Dolls*. London, Weidenfeld and Nicholson, Chapter 3.
16 Ibid. See also Welch, Evelyn (ed) (2011), *Fashioning the Early Modern*, Oxford University Press, pp. 16–19.
17 For more information, see McNeil, Peter, 'Beauty in Search of Knowledge' in Welch (2011).
18 Leics. CRO, DG9/2529.
19 Shrewsbury Museums T1973/6/16
20 Kidwell, Claudia (1979), *Cutting a Fashionable Fit*. Washington, Smithsonian, p. 11.
21 See Dagnall, H. (1998), *The Taxation of Paper in Great Britain 1443–1861*. Edgeware, BAPH.
22 Dorset CRO, D-FRA/T/208.
23 Beds, Berks, Cambs, Devon, Essex, Glos, Hants, Norfolk, Northants, Northumbria, Notts, Oxford, Salop, Somerset, Surrey, Sussex, Wilts. It does not include the apprenticeships listed in the York Tailors' Guild books as these were all for seven year terms and apparently no premiums were paid. Similarly it does not include the numerous apprenticeships for poor children arranged by the Bedford and Barnstaple charities which paid a standard rate of two pounds up front and another two pounds at the end of the apprenticeship period.
24 This tallies with Alysa Leven's findings (2012), 'Parish Apprenticeship and the Old Poor Law in London', *Economic History Review* 63(4) that the average age for girl apprentices was 12–13 and for boys 11–12.
25 Manchester Archives, L89/9/16/60.
26 Cheshire CRO, memorandum book, DLT 4196/55/11.
27 Essex CRO, D/DTcB1/11&12.
28 Northumberland CRO, DN/S/2/1/4/6.
29 Norfolk CRO, BL/CS/1/22/1/13.
30 E. Sussex CRO, Addmss49717/11.
31 Beds. CRO, X290/356.
32 Leics. CRO, DG39/1438.
33 St Martin-in-the-Fields Pauper Examinations, www.londonlives.org
34 Workhouse admission and discharge register, www.londonlives.org
35 See www.londonlives.org for more examples.
36 Justices' working documents, Middlesex Sessions, www.londonlives.org
37 Ibid.

38 Ibid.
39 Ibid.
40 Somerset CRO, Q/SR332/1/1-48.
41 St-Martin-in-the-Fields Pauper examinations, www.londonlives.org
42 W. Sussex CRO, PAR153/32/4.
43 N. Devon CRO, 1710A/P010/16, S. Devon RO, 3009/99/16/882.
44 www.oldbaileyonline.org. For a more detailed analysis of wages, see Lane, Penelope et al. (2006), *Women, Work and Wages in England 1600–1800*. Woodbridge, Boydell.
45 Perth CRO, B59.29/66.
46 Settlement examination 1856, www.Mathon.org
47 Inder, Pam (2016), *The Rag Trade*. Stroud, Amberley, Chapter 4.
48 Northumbria CRO, ZCE/F/1/1/4/6.
49 Fawcett, Trevor (1992), 'Bath's Georgian Warehouses', *Costume* 26.
50 Bird, M. (ed) (2013), *Diary of Mary Hardy*, Vol. 4. Kingston-upon-Thames, Burnham.
51 For further details, see Edwards, J.R. (2010), 'Writing Masters and Accountants in England – A Study of Occupation, Status and Ambition in the Early Modern Period', *Journées d'Histoire de la Comptabilité et du Management* 24(6).
52 Djabri, Susan (ed) (2003), *The Diaries of Sarah Hurst 1759–62*. Stroud, Amberley.
53 Edinburgh RO CS96.3562.
54 PRO PROB11.891_143; PRO PROB11.983_365; PRO PROB11.101_66; PRO PROB11.1326_148; Notts CRO PR/NW; PRO PROB11.889_455; PRO PROB11.1227_144.
55 www.locatinglondon.org/static/LondonLives.html Phillips (2006), *Women in Business* claims that between two-thirds and three-quarters of all categories of business were insured in the lower ranges – £100–£400.
56 Aberdeen CRO, CA/8/P230/1/5&6.
57 E.Sussex CRO, AMS2277/2330/23.

Chapter 3

1 Cheshire CRO, DSS1/6/40/2.
2 Hayden, Peter (1988), 'Records of Clothing Expenditure Kept by Elizabeth Jervis of Meaford 1746–79', *Costume* 22.
3 Warwicks CRO, CR1368/Vol4/67&68.
4 Quoted in Lambert, Miles (2009), 'Sent from Town', *Costume* 43.
5 Lancs. CRO, DDX1096/1.
6 Cambridge University Library, 105/158.
7 W. Yorks (Wakefield) CRO, WYW1352/3/4/6/8.

8   *Diary of Mary Hardy,* Vol. 2.
9   Woodforde, James (1985 edition), *A Country Parson: James Woodforde's Diary 1758–1802*, London, Century.
10 Bodleian Library, John Johnson collection, handbill, ESTC number T185986.
11 See the CEC reports in Chapter 4.
12 Edinburgh RO, CS96/3562.
13 Allen (ed) (2011), *An English Lady in Paris*, p. 117.
14 Penney, Norman (1920), *The Household Account Book of Sarah Fell*. Cambridge University Press.
15 Sorge-English, Lynn (2011), *Stays and Body Image in London*. Oxford, Routledge.
16 *Diary of Mary Hardy,* Vol. 4.
17 Lancs. CRO, L207.
18 Ibid., DDX 1096/1.
19 Beds. CRO, AN/12/1.
20 Edinburgh RO, CS96/3562.
21 E.Yorks. CRO, DDBC15/404.
22 These suppliers were all in London. Salop RO, 112/23/3/17/40.
23 http://www.history.org/media/podcasts_transcripts/MillinerandMantuaMaker.cfm
24 E.Sussex CRO, PBT1/10/2869.
25 Norfolk CRO, DN/INV82A/153.
26 *Diary of Mary Hardy,* Vols 1 and 4.
27 All these examples are from www.oldbaileyonline.org
28 York RO, PAW1.
29 Wilts. CRO, 271/17. See also Chapter 10.
30 Weatherill, Lorna (1990), *Account Book of Richard Latham 1724–67*. Oxford University Press.
31 Quoted in Hitchcock, Tim (2004), *Down and Out in 18th century London*. London, Hambledon and London, p. 99.
32 Essex CRO, D/P264/18/14.
33 Ibid. D/P88/18/7.
34 Ibid. D/P14/18/11.
35 Norfolk CRO, WLS XV/3.
36 Lancs. RO DDX1096/1.
37 Dowdell, Carolyn (2017), 'Gertrude Savile's green damask …', *Clothing Culture* 4(1).
38 Delves Broughton, Mrs Vernon (1887), *Court and Private Life in the Time of Queen Charlotte: Being the Journals of Mrs Papendiek, Assistant Keeper of the Wardrobe and Reader to Her Majesty*. London: Richard Bentley & Son, Vol. 1, p. 247.
39 Whitbread, Helena (ed) (2010), *The Secret Diaries of Miss Anne Lister*. London, Virago.

40 Birmingham RO, MS3145/295/.
41 Mrs Booth was a 'mantua maker and milliner', Tabitha Carver also made stays.
42 *The 1784 Hampshire Directory, Lewis's Manchester and Salford Directory, Matthew's New History of Bristol, Gore's Liverpool Directory, General and Commercial Directory of Leeds.*
43 www.edenlinks.co.uk/RECORDS/CC/EW/CCINEAST.HTM
44 Bartlett's *List of Masters and Apprentices 1763-74*, quoted in Buck, *Bedfordshire Miscellany*, p. 147.

Chapter 4

1 Irish University Press reprints, CEC Vols X and XIV. The page numbering systems in these volumes are complicated; it is easier to find entries by the interviewees' reference numbers, hence these are the identifiers used.
2 For example, the Distressed Needlewomen's Association (1847), the Milliners' and Dressmakers' Provident Association (1849) with short-lived branches in Glasgow and Manchester, and the Dressmaking Company (1865).
3 Yeo and Thompson (1971), *The Unknown Mayhew*. Harmondsworth, Penguin, p. 530.
4 Dorset CRO, D1369:A14/1/19.
5 *Leicester Chronicle,* 24 September.
6 On 17 August.
7 See Stewart, Margaret and Hunter, Leslie (1964), *The Needle Is Threaded*. London, Heinemann, pp. 127–129.
8 Un-numbered mss in Brunel University Library, collected by Professor John Burnet in the 1960s.
9 Ibid.
10 Ibid.
11 W. Sussex CRO, Add Ms 18805. See also Chapter 7.
12 Ibid., oral history tape 1.
13 Cumbria CRO, YDB17.
14 Meyer, Lady Adele and Black, Clementina (1909), *The Makers of Our Clothes: A Case for Trade boards*. London, Duckworth, p. 87.
15 Mitchell, Hannah (1977), *The Hard Way Up*. London, Virago.
16 Yeo and Thompson, *Mayhew*, pp. 519–521.
17 Ibid.
18 Ibid., p. 522.
19 Mitchell, *Hard Way Up*.
20 Walkley, Christina (1981), *The Ghost in the Looking Glass*. London, Peter Owens, pp. 36–38.

21 Ibid., Chapter 5.
22 Yeo and Thompson, *Mayhew*, p. 531.
23 Meyer and Black, *Trade Boards*, p. 69.
24 Mitchell, *Hard Way Up*, pp. 80–81.
25 Llewellyn Davies, Margaret (1930), *Life as We Have Known It*. London, Leonard and Virginia Woolf (Virago edition, 1977), p. 61.
26 *Illustrated London News,* 27 January 1844.
27 Conversation with Dr Alun Davies of Newcastle-under-Lyme, 1999.
28 Manchester Central Reference Library, M/C1402-4.
29 Edinburgh RO, CS96.3562.
30 National Library of Scotland, MS9685.
31 *Edinburgh Evening Courant* advertisements for their closing-down sale in May 1868.
32 Yeo and Thompson, *Mayhew*, pp. 521–522.
33 Cumbria CRO, BDB/38. See also Inder, *Rag Trade,* Chapter 2.
34 Stewart and Hunter, *Needle Is Threaded*, p. 128.
35 Yeo and Thompson, *Mayhew*, p. 522.
36 CEC Vol. XIV, no. 130.
37 *The Art of Dressmaking.*
38 National Library of Scotland, MS9685.
39 University of Glasgow Business Records Centre, HF24\1.
40 Cumbria CRO, BDB/38.
41 Mitchell, *Hard Way Up,* p. 70.
42 *Leicester Chronicle,* 18 January 1840 and *Leicestershire Mercury,* 23 December 1843.
43 Nenadic, Stana (1998), 'The Social Shaping of Business Behaviour in the Nineteenth-Century Women's Garment Trades', *Journal of Social History* 31, 625–45.
44 Dorset CRO, D500/11.
45 Northants. CRO, 206p/240.
46 National Library of Scotland, MS9685.
47 Cumbria CRO, BDB/38.
48 University of Glasgow Business Records Centre, DB96/10.

Chapter 5

1 For a more sophisticated review of the economic trends, see Fischer, D.H. (1996), *The Great Wave, Price Revolutions and the Rhythm of History*. Oxford University Press, pp. 121–177.
2 Fried and Elman (1971), *Charles Booth's London*. London, Pelican, pp. 55–63.

3   *Beeton's Book of Household Management* (1861), p. 8; Morris, Jenny (1986), *Women Workers*. Aldershot, Gower, pp. 68–73.
4   Blow, M.M. (1993), *The Diary of Ada Jackson*. Leicester City Council.
5   Morris, *Women Workers*, p. 12.
6   Edinburgh RO, CS96.3562.
7   Mitchell, *Hard Way Up*, p. 80.
8   Meyer and Black, *Trade Boards*, p. 68.
9   Cambs. CRO, Hobson's charity CB/10/2/6/.
10 Cadbury and Shann (1907), *Sweating*. London, Headley Bros.
11 Northants. CRO, ZA666.8.
12 Edinburgh RO, CS96/3824-25.
13 Durham CRO, Acc134(D) RefD/Lu.
14 University of Glasgow Business Records Centre, CS245/1434/5.
15 Leics. CRO, 9DF/1/20.
16 Essex CRO, D/F95/2/1.
17 National Library of Wales, J.R.Hughes mss and papers 127.
18 Surrey CRO, Ref 1261.
19 Cumbria CRO, RDB38.
20 p. 49.
21 Edinburgh RO, CS96/3824-25.
22 Worcs. CRO, 899:251.
23 Surrey CRO, Ref 1261.
24 Cumbria CRO, YDB17.
25 Ibid., RDB38.
26 For much more information on this topic, see Richmond, Vivienne (2013), *Clothing the Poor in 19th Century England*. Cambridge, Cambridge University Press.
27 Nenadic, Stana (1993), 'The Small Family Firm in Victorian Britain', *Business History* 35(4).
28 York RO, Acc203[F] series.
29 Ibid.
30 Ibid.
31 National Library of Wales, J.R.Hughes mss and papers 127.
32 Rotherham Local Studies Library, 182/Z/13/1.
33 Essex CRO, D/DU 246/9.
34 Leics. CRO, 9D5/1/20.
35 University of Glasgow Business Records Centre, HF24/1.
36 Cambs. CRO, R82/102.
37 Dyhouse, Carol (1981), *Girls Growing Up in Late Victorian and Edwardian England*. London, Routledge, p. 81.
38 Blow, *Ada Jackson*.

39 Leics. CRO, 7D54. See also Chapter 10.
40 Derbys. CRO, D3580/FP/5.
41 Information from Barbara Fishburn, Anne Hammersley's granddaughter, 1999.

Chapter 6

1. Davidson, Joan and Jenson, Sue (eds) (1984), *A Needle, a Bobbin, a Strike: Women Needleworkers in America*. Philadelphia, Temple University Press, p. 32.
2. Godley, Andrew (1984), 'Singer in Britain', *Textile History* 27(1).
3. Schmeichen, James (1984), *Sweated Industry and Sweated Labour*. London, Croom Helm, p. 27.
4. *Leicester Daily Post,* 16 January and 1 September.
5. Monroe, R. (1879), *Practical Dressmaking,* n.l., Introduction.
6. The collection has since been divided between the Leicestershire Museums Service and Leicester Museum Service.
7. Godfrey, F. (1982), *The International History of the Sewing Machine*. London, Hale, pp. 96–97.
8. E.g. *Leicester Chronicle,* 3 April 1880.
9. Monroe, *Practical Dressmaking*.
10. Ibid., p. 54.
11. *Drapers' Record,* 1895.
12. Dorset CRO, D148/25/43.
13. Waugh, *Cut of Women's Clothes*, p. 188.
14. Walsh, Margaret (1979–80), 'The Democratization of Fashion', *Journal of American History* 66.
15. Ibid.
16. Coventry RO, PA919/34/A, proof copy of an article of 1879 by 'AW' for an unknown publication.
17. Foden, F.E. (1961), *A History of Technical Examinations in England ...* (PhD thesis, Reading).
18. Glos. CRO, CBR B1/4/8.
19. Walsh (1999), 'A View for the 18th Century', in Crossick, Geoffrey and Jourdain, Sarge (eds), *Cathedrals of Consumption 1850–1939*. Aldershot, Ashgate, p. 69.
20. John Lewis Partnership Archive, no. 179.
21. Durham CRO, Acc 134(D)/Lu.
22. Baron and Klepp (1984), 'If I Didn't Have My Sewing Machine ...: Women and Sewing Machine Technology', in Jenson and Davidson (eds), *A Needle, a Bobbin, a Strike: Women Needleworkers in America*. Temple University Press, p. 49.
23. Durham CRO, Acc134(D) RefD/Lu.

24 Suffolk CRO, HC425:1533 Box 2.
25 Ibid., Whites of Ipswich.
26 Northumbria CRO, NRO 00808.
27 Proctor, Molly (1987), *Are You Being Served?*. Kent, Rainham and Meresborough, p. 3.
28 Dolly Varden was a character in Charles Dickens' historical novel, *Barnaby Rudge*. A Dolly Varden dress was a bit like an eighteenth-century polonaise – an overdress, usually of printed cotton, looped up at the back and worn over a plain, brightly coloured petticoat, often accessorized with a straw hat.
29 Cheshire CRO, CR641.
30 John Lewis archive, no. 265.
31 Tyne and Wear archives, DT.JS.
32 Glasgow University Business Records Centre, HF20.
33 Ibid.
34 Northants. CRO, ZA666.8.
35 W. Sussex CRO, Add Mss 38303.
36 John Lewis Partnership Archive, 194/A/4.
37 *Leicester Daily Post,* 5 August 1872 and 16 January 1875.
38 Crossick, G. and Jourdain, S. (1999), *Cathedrals of Consumption 1850–1939*. Aldershot, Ashgate, pp. 1–5.

Chapter 7

1 Pp. 85–86.
2 P. 61.
3 Virago edition, pp. 86–90.
4 That is the title though they probably meant 'mendicancy'! Cambs. CRO, CCOS case files.
5 Tyler and Parsons (1999), *Madame Clapham, Hull's Celebrated Dressmaker*. Hull City Council.
6 W. Sussex CRO, Add Ms18805.
7 Inder (2017), Rag Trade, Chapter 2. Edinburgh RO, MS9685.
8 Nenadic (1998), 'The Social Shaping of Business Behaviour …'.
9 Ibid.
10 Inder, *Rag Trade,* Chapter 4. Cumbria CRO BDB/38.
11 Ibid., Chapter 3. Glos CRO CBR b1/4/8.
12 Inder, Pam and Aldis, Marion (2013), *Nine Norfolk Women*. Cromer, Poppyland, Chapter 6.
13 Nearly all the information about Marie Schild comes from advertisements in her own publications.

14 Similarly, information about the Goubaud's empire comes from advertisements in their own publications.
15 Tate, Annie (1886), *The "Eureka" Guide to Dressmaking*. London, Charles Gee.
16 For example, in 1890s America Nellie Hamilton and Harriet A. Brown both published books claiming to have invented a 'scientific system' of pattern making, while in France, Devereux advertised 'Scientific Dress and Sleeve Cutting'.
17 P. 9.
18 P. 52.
19 P. 54.
20 Pp. 6-7.
21 P. 32.
22 P. 23.
23 For examples of beautifully made garments, made by skilled nineteenth-century dressmakers, see Johnston, Lucy (2016), *19th Century Fashion in Detail*. London, Victoria and Albert Museuml.
24 Accession number 51.1969.
25 Meyer and Black, *Trade Boards*, pp. 73–74.

Chapter 8

1 See Chapter 4.
2 No such report was submitted in 1855; it seems she actually meant 1843.
3 Quoted in Vicinus (1972), *Suffer and Be Still*. Indiana University Press, p. 60.
4 Text from the catalogue of the 1891 Summer Exhibition of the Royal Institute of Painters in Oil. The whereabouts of the painting are now unknown.
5 See Chapter 4, endnotes 16 and 17.
6 Figures from (1) Yeo and Thompson, *Mayhew,* (2) Pember Reeves, Maud (1913), *Round about a Pound a Week* (Virago, 1979).

Chapter 9

1 Sanderson, Elizabeth (1986), 'Edinburgh Milliners', *Costume* 20.
2 Apprenticeship indentures in Devon, Sussex and Hampshire CROs.
3 www.londonlives.org
4 Inder, Pam, *English Provincial Dressmakers in the 19th Century* (PhD thesis, De Montfort University, 2000), see pp. 307–330 for more information.

5   The directories are: for Leicester, Slater's 1847, Drake's 1861 and Wright's 1882; for Ulverston, Slater's 1848, Mannex and Co 1866 and 1882; for Sidmouth, Pigot's 1844, Billings' 1857 and White's 1878–9.
6   Someone who rented out knitting frames. Framework knitting was a major local industry in the East Midlands, and knitters worked from home using hired machines.
7   Pamphlet. (1792), *Exposing the Arts of Boarding Schools, Lewd Fortune-tellers, Corrupt Milliners ....* London, W. Lock.
8   These appeared on 13, 14 and 23 November.
9   Ibid., 14 November.
10   Quoted in Purvis, June (1989), *Hard Lessons.* Cambridge, Polity, p. 34.
11   Walkowitz, Judith (1980), *Prostitution and Victorian Society.* Cambridge University Press, pp. 175 and 208–209.
12   For a more recent study of prostitution and the effect it could have on a town, see Pearson and Rayner (2018), *Prostitution in Victorian Colchester: Controlling the Uncontrollable.* Hatfield, Essex Publications.

Chapter 10

1   Salisbury and Wilts CRO, 1178/296.
2   Ibid., 1178/394.
3   Ibid., 271/1.
4   Ibid., 271/17.
5   Ibid.
6   Ibid., 271/16.
7   Ibid., 271/2.
8   Leics. CRO, 7D54.
9   Salop CRO, 811/50.
10   Ibid., 821/50.
11   Ibid., XHIL/838/4/67, 68, 70.
12   Johnston (2016), *19th Century Fashion in Detail.* Glossary.
13   Mrs Kenyon's family.
14   Salop CRO, 838/68.
15   1851 census returns for Weston-and-Wixhill.
16   The information in this section comes from Susanna Ingleby's diaries in Keele University Library Special Collections and from huge collections of privately owned family papers. See also Inder, Pam and Aldis, Marion (2002), *Finding Susanna.* Leek, Churnet Books.

Conclusion

1. Volume 1, October 1855. It was the only issue.
2. Herbert P. Miller (1876), *The Scarcity of Domestic Servants*, London, quoted in Richmond (2013) *Clothing the Poor*, p. 259.
3. Tyler and Parsons, *Madame Clapham*.
4. *How to Dress Well on a Shilling a Day* (1879), London, Home Help series.
5. Richmond (2013), *Clothing the Poor,* Chapter 5.
6. Monroe, *Practical Dressmaking*.
7. Black, Clementina (1915), *Married Women's Work* (Virago edition, 1983), pp. 71–72.
8. Mitchell (1977), *Hard Way Up,* pp. 75–77.
9. Miller, Marla (2003), 'Gownmaking … in 18th century New England', *Dress* 30(1).
10. Jerde, Judith (1981), 'Mary Molloy, St Paul's Extraordinary Dressmaker', *Dress* 7. The 'Blue Books' listed local people of note.
11. Clark, Sallye (1980), 'Carrie Taylor, Kentucky Dressmaker', *Dress* 6.
12. Ashridge, Eliza (1904), *Quaker Grey, Some Account of the Forepart of the Life of Eliza Ashridge*. n.l., Astolat Press. and Freeman, Mary E. Wilkins (1883), 'A Mistaken Charity', *Harper's Bazaar* XVI(21).
13. Whyte, Anne (1982), 'Helen Bagrie, Costumiere, 343, Union Street, Aberdeen; Reminiscences of a Dressmaker's Workroom', *Costume* 16.
14. Verita (1995), *Tailoring, Twopence an Hour*. London, Excalibur.
15. Fabian Society pamphlet no. 178, *The War, Women and Unemployment*.

Bibliography

Abbreviations

CEC – Children's Employment Commission. CRO – County Record Office. RO – Record Office. County names will be abbreviated in standard form in the endnotes, e.g. Wilts. for Wiltshire, Yorks. for Yorkshire, etc. The only one that may cause confusion is Salop for Shropshire.

Manuscript sources

These are fully referenced in endnotes.

Newspapers

Numerous references to mantua-makers and dressmakers appear in local and national papers and journals from 1770 on. The ones cited in the text are all fully referenced there or in endnotes. Newspaper articles are listed below:

Dressmaker, a cheap *Liverpool Review*. 17 September 1887.
E.M *Manchester Guardian*. 24 May 1858.
The Milliners, Dressmakers and Warehouseman's Gazette. November 1872, January and February 1873, August 1879.
Tweedie, Mrs Alec, 'Needlework', *Home Notes*. 18 August 1896.

Unpublished theses and dissertations

Davies, Julian Paul (2003) *Artisans and the City: A Social History of Bristol's Shoemakers and Tailors 1770–1800*, PhD thesis, Bristol University.
Foden, F.E. (1961) *A History of Technical Examinations in England, with Special Reference to the Examination Work of the City and Guilds of London Institute*, PhD thesis, University of Reading.

Inder, Pamela M. (2000) *English Provincial Dressmakers in the 19th Century*, PhD thesis, De Montfort University, Leicester.
Lemire, Beverley (1984) *The British Cotton Industry and Domestic Market, Trade and Fashion in Early Industrial Society 1750–1800*, PhD thesis, Balliol College, Oxford.
Sanderson, Elizabeth (1993) *Women's Work in 18th Century Edinburgh*, PhD thesis, Edinburgh University.
Simon, Amy (1993) *She Is So Neat and Fits So Well, Garment Construction and the Millinery Business of Eliza Olivia Dodds 1821–33*, MA dissertation, Winterthur, Delaware.
Sleigh-Johnson, N.V. (1989) *The Merchant Taylor's Company of London 1580–1645*, PhD thesis, London University.
Walker, M.J. (1986) *The Extent of Guild Control of Trades in England c. 1660–1820*, PhD thesis, Cambridge University.

Websites

www.britishnewspaperarchive.co.uk
www.edenlinks.co.uk/RECORDS/CC/EW/CCINEAST.HTM
www.londonlives.org
www.oldbaileyonline.org

Published sources pre-1900

Anon (1977) *The Book of Trades or Library of Useful Arts*. 1811 and 1818. London, Tabart. Wiltshire Family History Society reprint.
Bain, Ebenezer (1887) *Merchant and Craft Guilds; A History of the Aberdeen Incorporated Trades* [n.l., n.d.].
Brown, Davis and Halse (1857) *The ABC Guide to Haberdashery* [n.l., n.d.].
Campbell, Richard (1747) *The London Tradesman* [n.l., n.d.] David and Charles reprint 1969.
Cherub, or the Guardian of Female Innocence (1792) *Exposing the Arts of Boarding Schools, etc*. London, W. Lock.
Children's Employment Commission Reports, Vols X and XIV, 1843 and 1864. Irish University Press reprints.
Delves Broughton, Mrs Vernon (ed) (1887) *Court and Private Life in the Time of Queen Charlotte: Being the Journals of Mrs Papendiek, Assistant Keeper of the Wardrobe and Reader to Her Majesty*, 2 Vols. London, Richard Bentley and Son.
Eden, Sir Frederick (1797) *The State of the Poor* (Facsimile edition, 1966).
Faunthorpe, Rev J.P. (1881) *Household Science Readings in Necessary Knowledge for Girls and Young Women*. London, E. Stanford.

Grindrod, R.B. (1845) *The Slaves of the Needle*. London and Manchester, Brittain and Gilpin.
Hood, T. (1863) 'Living – and Dying – by the Needle', *Englishwoman's Domestic Magazine*.
Knight, Charles (1843) *The Dressmaker and Milliner*. London, [n.d.].
Place, Francis (1771–1854) *The Autobiography of Francis Place*. Cambridge University Press reprint 1972.
Smith, Thomas (1886) *Successful Advertising, Its Secrets Explained*. London, Smith's Advertising Agency.
Smith, William (1863) *Advertise How? When? Where?* London [n.d].
Spurrett, Eliza. (*c.* 1880) *Reminiscences*. Leicester, privately printed.
Trueman, Mr. (1858) 'The First Mantua Makers in Durham', *Aeliana, Archaeologica*, 2(II).
Warden, Alexander J. (1872) *The Burgh Laws of Dundee*. London, Dundee, [n.d.].

Novels and plays

Anon (1738) *The Intriguing Milliners and Attornies' Clerks*. London, [n.d.].
Arthur, T.S. (1872) *Grace Myers' Sewing Machine and Other Stories*. Glasgow, The Scottish Temperance League.
Doggett, C.B. (1874) *Nellie Graham the Young Dressmaker*. Dorking, [n.d.].
Drury, Robert (1753) *The Rival Milliners*. London, [n.d.].
Coyne, J.S. (1852) *Wanted, 1000 Spirited Young Milliners*. London, Thomas Hailes Lacy.
Gaskell, Mrs E. (1848) *Mary Barton*. (Numerous editions available).
Gaskell, Mrs E. (1851–3) *Cranford*.
Gaskell, Mrs E. (1853) *Ruth*.
Guignard, Mary A. (1852) *The Unprotected, or Facts in Dressmaking Life*. London, [n.d.].
Houston, J. Brooke (1879) *Dressmaker to the Queen! Or Jennie's ambition*. [n.l., n.d.].
Jerrold, Douglas W. (1825) *The White Milliner*. London, Duncombe.
Keats, Chatterton (1870) *Without a Penny in the World; a Story of the 'Period'*. London, [n.d.].
Marsh, Mrs (1850) *Lettice Arnold*. London, Henry Colburn.
Morton, John (1825) *The Milliners' Holiday*. London, Duncombe edition of the British theatre.
Otis, Belle (1867) *Diary of a Milliner*. New York, [n.d.].
Religious Tract Society (1860) *May Coverley, the Young Dressmaker*. London, Religious Tract Society.
Reynolds, G.W.M. (1853) *The Seamstress or the White Slave of England*. London, John Dicks.
Richardson, Samuel (1740) *Pamela* (Numerous editions available).
Rowcroft, Charles (1846) *Fanny, the Little Milliner, or the Rich and the Poor*. London, [n.d.].

Stone, Mrs Elizabeth (1843) *The Young Milliner*. London, [n.d.].
Tytler, Sarah (1888) *Girl Neighbours*. London, Blackie.

Dressmaking manuals and advice about dress

NB. These are the ones I have cited. There are numerous others.

Balhatchet, Mrs Grace (1895) *Dresscutting and Making on Tailors' Principles for County Council and Other Technical Classes*. Bristol, Pole and Son.
Banks, Miss (1899) *Miss Banks' Self-teaching System of Dresscutting*. Romford, Wilson and Whitworth.
Bellhouse, Mrs James (1893) *Be Your Own Dressmaker*. Rochdale, Ormerod Bros.
Clarke, A. (1899) *Simple Instructions for Dresscutting by Tailors' Measures*. Preston, T. Snape and Co.
Cory, Mrs Eliza Ann (1849) *The Art of Dressmaking*. London, Groombridge and Sons.
Davis, Jeanette E. (1894) *The Elements of Modern Dressmaking*. London, Cassell and Co.
Dobson, Mrs (ed) (1888–90) *Dressmakers' Chart and Cutter*. Manchester, [n.d.].
Grandhomme, Mlle E. (1879) *Cutting-out and Dressmaking ....* London, Macmillan.
Grenfell, Mrs H. (1892) *Dress Cutting-out: A Pupil's Manual for Home Study*. London, Longmans.
Grenfell, Mrs H. (1892) *Dressmaking, a Technical Manual for Teachers*. London, Macmillan.
Grenfell, Mrs H. (1894) *The Teacher of Dressmaking ne Plus Ultra*. Manchester, J. Heywood.
Grenfell, Mrs H. (1894) *Under-linen Cutting-out: A Pupil's Manual for Home Study*. London, Longmans.
Haweis, Mrs (1879) *The Art of Dress*. London, [n.d.].
Howell, Mrs (1845) *The Handbook of Dressmaking*. London, Simpkin, Marshall and Co.
Howell, Mrs (1847) *The Handbook of Millinery*. London, Simpkin, Marshall and Co.
Kendall, E.G. (1892) *Instructions for the Cosmopolitan System of Dressmaking*. London, Cosmopolitan Dresscutting Association.
Knight, M.J. Lowther (1889) *The European System of Dresscutting by Measure*. Leeds, Harrison Waide.
Lady, A. (1838) *The Workwoman's Guide* (reprinted Doncaster, Bloomfield 1975).
Laughton, M.A. (1897) *Dressmaking: A Guide to Feehand*. Bacup, Priestley.
Levine, Mme (1896) *The Rodmure System of Dresscutting*. Glasgow. n.d.
Low, Mrs E. Woodgate (1893) *Technical and Practical Lessons in Dressmaking*. Carshalton, self-published.
Monroe, R. (1879) *Practical Dressmaking*. London, 'Bazaar Office'.
'Myra' (1877) *Dressmaking Lessons*. London, Goubaud.
'Myra' (1888) *Myra's Half-yearly Budget of Paris Fashions*. London, Hendon.
'Myra' (1888) *Myra's Journal of Dress and Fashion* (1–4) continued as *Myra's Journal of Dress and Needlework*. London, Weldon and Co.

Praga, Mrs A. (1899) *Appearances and How to Keep Them Up on a Limited Income.* London, J.Long.
Schild, Mme Marie (n.d.) *Old English Costume.*
Schild, Mme Marie (1871–3) *The Brighton Courier of Fashion.*
Schild, Mme Marie (1871–6) *The Drapers' and Milliners' Gazette of Fashion.*
Schild, Mme Marie (1876–9) *Illustrated Catalogues 1–5.*
Schild, Mme Marie (1876–9) *The Little Dressmaker.*
Schild, Mme Marie (1876–9) *Madame Schild's Journal of Parisian Dress Patterns.*
Schild, Mme Marie (1876–9) *Schild's Penny Magazine of Dress and Fashion.*
Schild, Mme Marie (1879) *Dolly as a Baby.*
Schild, Mme Marie (1881) *Album of Fancy Costume.*
Schild, Mme Marie (1893) *New Skirts and How to Cut Them.*
Schild, Mme Marie (1896) *The Dressmakers' and Milliners' Butterick Quarterly.*
Schild, Mme Marie (1907) *One Hundred Creams and Jellies.*
'Scissors' (1895) *Why Dressmaking Does Not Pay and the Dressmakers' Future.* London, Marlborough.
'Sylvia' (1876) *How to Dress Well on a Shilling a Day.* London, Home Help Series.
Tate, Annie (1886) *The Eureka Guide to Dressmaking.* London, Charles Gee.
Tomlin, J. (1892) *Dressmakers' Guide, Dresscutting Made Easy.* [n.l., n.d.].
Walker, George (1834) *Walkers' Tables of Quantities ... or the Tailor's Ready Assistant.* London, [n.d.].
Walker, George (1835) *The Tailor's Masterpiece.* London, the author.
Walker, George (1836) *The Art of Cutting Ladies' Riding Habits, etc.* London, [n.d.].
White, Florence (1892) *Easy Dressmaking.* London, J.Smith.
Willimott, Mrs Thomas (1841) *The Young Woman's Guide.* London, [n.d.].

Published sources post-1900

Adams, Suzanne (2005) 'Purchasers from the Parsonage: Observations on Bath Dress and Reactive Shopping by the Penrose Family 1776–7', *Costume* 39.
Adburgham, Alison (1979) *Shopping in Style: London from the Restoration to Edwardian Elegance.* London, Thames and Hudson.
Adburgham, Alison (1989) *Shops and Shopping: Where and in What Manner the Well-dressed Englishwoman Bought Her Clothes.* London, Allen and Unwin.
Airey, Angela and John (1979) *The Bainbridges of Newcastle, a Family History.* Newcastle-upon-Tyne, privately published.
Aldrich, Winifred (2000) 'Tailors' Cutting Manuals 1770–1870', *Textile History* 31(2).
Alexander, Sally (1983) *Women's Work in 19th Century London, a Study of the Years 1820–1850.* London, Journeyman.
Allen, Michael (ed) (2011) *An English Lady in Paris. The Diary of Frances Anne Crewe 1786.* Oxford, Stockley.

Arnold, Janet (1964) *Patterns of Fashion 1660–1860*. London, Wace and Co.
Arnold, Janet (1966) *Patterns of Fashion 1860–1940*. London, Wace and Co.
Arnold, Janet (1970) 'A Mantua 1708–9 in Clive House Museum', *Costume* 4.
Arnold, Janet (1973) 'The Dressmaker's Craft', *Costume* 6.
Arnold, Janet (1972) 'A Mantua of c.1740', *Costume* 6.
Arnold, Janet (1975) 'Decorative Features, Pinking, Snipping and Slashing', *Costume* 2.
Aston, Jennifer and Di Martino, Paolo (2017) 'Risk, Success and Failure: Female Entrepreneurship in Late Victorian and Edwardian England', *Economic History Review* 70(3).
Attfield, J. and Kirkham, P. (1995) *A View from the Interior, Women and Design*. London, Women's Press.
Barker, Hannah (2006) *The Business of Women: Female Enterprise and Urban Development in Northern England*. Oxford University Press.
Batchelor, Jennie (2005) *Dress, Distress and Desire*. Basingstoke, Palgrave Macmillan.
Baudis, Macushla (2004) 'Smoking Hot with Fashion from Paris', *Costume* 48(2).
Bedfordshire Historical Record Society (1993) *A Bedfordshire Historical Miscellany, Essays in Honour of Patricia Bell*. Bedford.
Berg, Maxine and Clifford, Helen (1999) *Consumers and Luxury: Consumer Culture in Europe 1650–1850*. Manchester University Press.
Bird, M. (ed) (2013) *The Diaries of Mary Hardy*. 5 Vols. Kingston-upon-Thames, Burnham.
Black, Clementina (ed) (1915) *Married Women's Work*. London, G. Bell and Sons. (Virago edition, 1983).
Blow, M.M. (ed) (1993) *Ada Jackson's Diary*. Leicester City Council.
Blum, Dilys E. (1983) 'Englishwomen's Dress in 18th Century India: The Margaret Fowke Correspondence 1176–1786', *Costume* 17.
Bosomworth, D. (1991) *The Victorian Catalogue of Household Goods (Silber and Fleming)*. London, Studio Editions.
Brandon, Ruth (1977) *Singer and the History of the Sewing Machine: A Capitalist Romance*. London, Barrie and Jenkins.
Brewer, John and Porter, Roy (eds) (1993) *Consumption and the World of Goods*. London and New York, Routledge.
Buck, Anne (1979) *Dress in 18th Century England*. London, Batsford.
Burman, S. (1979) *Fit Work for Women*. Oxford, Croom Helm.
Burnett, John (1994) *Destiny Obscure*. London and New York, Routledge.
Burnette, Joyce (2008) *Gender, Work and Wages in Industrial Revolution Britain*. Cambridge University Press.
Bythell, Duncan (1978) *The Sweated Trades, Outwork in 19th Century Britain*. London, Batsford.
Cadbury and Shann (1907) *Sweating*. London, Headley Bros.
Cherry, Deborah (1983) 'Surveying Seamstresses', *Feminist Art News* 9.
Cherry, Deborah (1993) *Painting Women, Victorian Women Artists*. London and New York, Routledge.

Chinn, Carl (1988) *They Worked All Their Lives, Women of the Urban Poor in England 1880-1939*. Manchester University Press.

Chrisman, Kimberley (1998) 'Rose Bertin in London?' *Costume* 32.

Chrisman-Campbell, Kimberley (2004) 'French Connections: Georgiana Duchess of Devonshire and the Anglo-French Fashion Exchange', *Dress* 31(1).

Clabburn, Pamela (1971) 'Parson Woodforde's View of Fashion', *Costume* 5.

Clabburn, Pamela (1977) 'A Provincial Milliner's Shop in 1785', *Costume* 11.

Clark, Alice (1919) *The Working Life of Women in the 17th Century*. London, Routledge. (Frank Cass reprint 1968).

Clark, Sallye (1980) 'Carrie Taylor, Kentucky Dressmaker', *Dress* 6.

Coffin, Judith (1996) *The Politics of Women's Work: The Paris Garment Trades 1750-1915*. Princeton University Press.

Collins, Jessica (2013) Jane Holt, Milliner and Other Women 1606-1800', *Textile History* 44.

Cox, Nancy (2016) *The Complete Tradesman, a Study of Retailing 1550-1820*. London, Routledge.

Crossick, Geoffrey and Jourdain, Sarge (1999) *Cathedrals of Consumption 1850-1939*. Aldershot, Ashgate.

Crowston, Clare Haru (2002) 'Fabricating Women, the Seamstresses of Old Regime France 1675-1791', *Business History Review* 76(2).

Crowston, Clare Haru (2006) 'Women and Guilds in Early Modern Europe', in Lucassen Jan et al. (eds), *The Return of the Guilds*. Cambridge, Press Syndicate of the University of Cambridge.

Cunnington, Charles Willett and Phyllis (1970) *A Handbook of Women's Costume in the 19th Century*. London, Faber and Faber.

Cunnington, Charles Willett and Phyllis (1972) *A Handbook of English Costume in the 18th Century*. London, Faber and Faber.

Dagnall, H. (1998) *The Taxation of Paper in Great Britain 1643-1861*. Edgeware, BAPH.

Davidoff, Leonora (1973) *The Best Circles*. Oxford, Croom Helm.

Davidoff, Leonora and Hall, Catherine (1987) *Family Fortunes 1780-1850, Men and Women of the English Middle Class*. London, Hutchinson.

Davies, Margaret Llewellyn (1915), *Maternity Letters from Working Women*. Women's Co-operative Guild. [n.l.]. (Virago reprint 1978).

Davies, Matthew P. and Saunders, Ann (2004) *The History of the Merchant Taylors' Company*. Leeds, Maney.

Davis, Dorothy (1966) *A History of Shopping*. London, Routledge and Kegan Paul.

Davis, Dorothy (1991) *Janes, Drapers of Egham*. [n.l.], Egham and Runnymede Historical Society.

Djabri, Susan C. (ed) (2009) *The Diaries of Sarah Hurst 1759-1762*. Stroud, Amberley.

Dobson, R.B. and Smith, D.M. (2006) *The Merchant Taylors of York*. York, Borthwick publications.

Dyer, Christopher (1989) *Standards of Living in the Middle Ages: Change in England 1200-1520*. Cambridge University Press.

Dyhouse, Carol (2012) *Girls Growing Up in Late Victorian and Edwardian England*. London, Routledge.
Edwards, J.R. (1990) 'The Development of Industrial Cost and Management Accounting before 1850: A Survey of the Evidence', *Business History* 331(1).
Edwards, J.R. (2010) 'Writing Masters and Accountants in England: A Study of Occupation, Status and Ambition in the Early Modern Period', *Journées d'Histoire de la Comptabilité et du Management*, 24(6).
Ehrman, Edwina (2006) 'Dressing Well in Old Age: The Clothing Accounts of Martha Dodson 1746-65', *Costume* 40.
Emery, Joy Spanabel (1997) 'Development of the American Commercial Pattern Industry 1850-80', *Costume* 31.
Ewing, Elizabeth (1989) *Everyday Dress 1650-1900*. London, Batsford.
Fabian Society (1914) *The War, Women and Unemployment*. Pamphlet 178.
Fawcett, Trevor (1991) 'A Case of Distance Shopping in 1763', *Costume* 25.
Fawcett, Trevor (1992) 'Bath's Georgian Warehouses', *Costume* 26.
Ferguson, Margaret, Quilligan, Maureen and Vickers, Nancy (eds) (1986) *Rewriting the Renaissance, the Politics of Sexual Difference in Early Modern Europe*. Chicago University Press.
Fernandez, Nancy P. (1987) 'Pattern Diagrams and Fashion Periodicals 1840-1900', *Dress* 13.
Finnegan, Frances (1979) *Poverty and Prostitution: A Study of Victorian Prostitutes in York*. Cambridge University Press.
Fischer, D.H. (1996) *The Great Wave, Price Revolutions and the Rhythm of History*. Oxford University Press.
Fleischman, Richard K. and Parker, Lee D. (1991) 'British Entrepreneurs and Pre-Industrial Revolution Evidence of Cost Management', *Accounting Review* 60(2).
Fowler, Christina (1997) 'Robert Mansbridge, a Rural Tailor and His Customers', *Textile History* 28(1).
Fox, Francis (n.d.) *The Merchant Taylors' Guild of Bristol*. Unpublished.
Fraser, Antonia (1963) *Dolls*. London, Weidenfeld and Nicholson.
Fried, Albert and Elman, Richard (eds) (1971) *Charles Booth's London*. London, Pelican.
Gamber, Wendy (1997) *The Female Economy, the Millinery and Dressmaking Trades*. Champaign, University of Illinois.
Gazeley, Ian (1989) 'The Cost of Living for Urban Workers in Late Victorian and Edwardian Britain', *Economic History Review*. Second series XLII(2).
Ghering van Irlant, Marie J. (1983) 'Anglo-French Fashion, 1786-9', *Costume* 17.
Ginsburg, Madeleine (1972) 'The Tailoring and Dressmaking Trades', *Costume* 6.
Godfrey, Frank (1982) *The International History of the Sewing Machine*. London, Hale.
Godfrey, G.W. (1903) *My Milliner's Bill*. [n.l.] Lacy's acting edition of plays.
Godley, Andrew (1966) 'Singer in Britain, the Diffusion of Sewing Machine Technology and Its Impact on the Clothing Industry in the United Kingdom 1860-1905', *Textile History* 27(1).

Godman, Melina (1989) 'A Georgian Lady's Personal Accounts', *Costume* 23.
Goose, Nigel (ed) (2007) *Women's Work in Industrial England, Regional and Local Perspectives*. Hatfield, Local Population Studies.
Hall, Catherine (1992) *White, Male and Middle Class*. Cambridge, Polity.
Hayden, Peter (1988) 'Records of Clothing Expenditure for the Years 1746–79 Kept by Elizabeth Jervis of Meaford, Staffordshire', *Costume* 22.
Hett, Francis Paget (ed) (1926) *The Memoirs of Susan Sibbald*. London, John Lane.
Higgs, E. (2016) 'Women and Occupations and Work in the Victorian Censuses Revisited', *History Workshop Journal* 81.
Hill, Bridget (1993) *Eighteenth Century Women, an Anthology*. London and New York, Allen and Unwin.
Hoffman, Tom (2011) *Bibliography on the Guilds*. London, Birkbeck.
Holland, Vyvyan (1955) *Hand-coloured Fashion Plates 1770–1899*. London, Batsford.
Hope, Madeleine (1938) 'The Rival Cooks: Hannah Glasse and Ann Cook', *Archeologia Aeliana*, Society of Antiquaries, Newcastle-upon-Tyne, series 4, Vol. 15.
Horrell, S. and Humphries, J. (1992) 'Old Questions, New Data and Altered Perspectives, the Standard of Living in the British Industrial Revolution', *Journal of Economic History* 52(4).
Houart, Victor (1984) *Sewing Accessories: An Illustrated History*. London, Souvenir.
Hudson, Pat and Lee, W. Robert (1990) *Women's Work and the Family Economy in Historical Perspective*. Manchester University Press.
Inder, Pam (2017) *The Rag Trade: The People Who Made Our Clothes*. Stroud, Amberley.
Inder, Pam (2018) *Dresses and Dressmaking*. Stroud, Amberley.
Inder, Pamela and Aldis, Marion (1997) 'Buttons, Braids, Bones and Body Linings, a Staffordshire Lady and Her London Dressmaker', *Staffordshire History*, 25.
Inder, Pamela and Aldis, Marion (2002) *Finding Susanna*. Leek, Churnet Valley Books.
Inder, Pamela and Aldis, Marion (2013) *Nine Norfolk Women*. Cromer, Poppyland Publishing.
Innes, Isabella (1913) *Scientific Dressmaking and Millinery*. Toronto, self-published.
Jackson, R.V. (1987) 'The Structure of Pay in 19th Century Britain', *Economic History Review*, Second series XL(4).
Jarvis, Anthea (1981) *Liverpool Fashion, 1840–1940*. Liverpool, Merseyside Museums.
Jenson, Joan M. and Davidson, Sue (1984) *A Needle, a Bobbin, a Strike, Women Needleworkers in America*. Philadelphia, Temple University Press.
Jerde, Judith (1981) 'Mary Molloy, St Paul's Extraordinary Dressmaker', *Dress* 7.
John, Angela (1985) *Unequal Opportunities, Women's Employment 1800–1919*. Oxford, Blackwell.
Johnson, Barbara (1987) *A Lady of Fashion. Barbara Johnson's Album of Styles and Fabrics*. London, V&A Museum.
Johnson, Bernard (1949) *The Acts and Ordinances of the Merchant Tailors of York*. London and York, Ben Johnson and Co.
Johnston, Lucy (2016) *Nineteenth Century Fashion in Detail*. London, V&A Museum.

Kidwell, Claudia (1979) *Cutting a Fashionable Fit, Dressmakers' Drafting Systems in the US*. Washington, Smithsonian Institute.

Kimberley, Christian (1997) 'Rose Bertin in London', *Costume* 32.

Kynnersley, E. Sneyd (1908) *Some Passages in the Life of One of Her Majesty's Inspectors of Schools*. London, Macmillan.

Lambert, Miles (1999) 'Sent from Town: Commissioning Clothing in Britain during the Long 18th Century', *Costume* 33.

Lancaster, Bill (1995) *The Department Store, a Social History*. Leicester University Press.

Lane, Penelope, Raven, Neil and Snell, K.D.M. (2004) *Women, Work and Wages in England 1600–1850*. Woodbridge, Boydell.

Laver, James (1943) *Fashion and Fashion Plates*. London and New York, Penguin.

Lemire, Beverley (1991) 'Peddling Fashion: Salesmen, Pawnbrokers, Tailors, Thieves and the Second Hand Clothes Trade in England c.1700–1800', *Textile History*, 22(1).

Lemire, Beverley (1995) 'Redressing the History of the Clothing Trade in England: Ready-made Clothing, Guilds and Women Workers 1650–1800', *Dress* 21.

Lemire, Beverley (1997) *Dress, Culture and Commerce, the English Clothing Trade before the Factory 1660–1800*. Basingstoke, Macmillan.

Lemire, Beverley (1999) '"In the Hands of Workwomen": English Markets, Cheap Clothing and Female Labour 1650–1800', *Costume* 33.

Leven, Alysa (2012) 'Parish Apprenticeship and the Old Poor Law', *Economic History Review* 63(4).

Lewis, June (1994) *The Secret Diary of Sarah Thomas*. Moreton-in-the-Marsh, Windrush.

Llewellyn, Sacha (1997) 'Inventory of Her Grace's Things, 1847', *Costume* 31.

Mahood, Linda (1990) *The Magdalenes, Prostitution in the 19th Century*. London, Routledge.

Maxwell, Stuart (1972) 'Two 18th Century Tailors', *Hawick Antiquarian Society Transactions*.

McKendrick, Brewer and Plumb (1982) *The Birth of a Consumer Society, the Commercialisation of 18th Century England*. London, Europa.

Meyer, Lady Adele and Black, Clementina (1909) *The Makers of Our Clothes, a Case for Trade Boards*. London, Duckworth.

Miller, Marla (2003) 'Gownmaking as a Trade for Women in 18th Century New England', *Dress* 30(1).

Miller, Michael B. (1981) *The Bon Marché, Bourgeois Culture and the Department Store 1869–1920*. London, Allen and Unwin.

Mitchell, Hannah (1977) *The Hard Way Up*. London, Virago.

Morris, Jenny (1986) *Women Workers and the Sweated Trades*. Aldershot, Gower.

Moss, Michael and Turton, Alison (1989) *A Legend of Retailing: The House of Fraser*. London, Weidenfeld and Nicholson.

Mui, L. and Mui, H. (1989) *Shops and Shopkeeping in 18th Century England*. Montreal, McGill University Press.

Nenadic, Stana (1993) 'The Small Family Firm in Victorian Britain', *Business History* 35(4).
Nenadic, Stana (1998) 'Social Shaping of Women's Behaviour in the 19th Century Garment Trades', *Journal of Social History* 31(3).
North, Susan (2018) *Eighteenth Century Fashion in Detail*. London, V&A Museum.
Parker, Rozsika (1984) *The Subversive Stitch*. London, Woman's Press.
Parmal, Pamela A. (1997) 'Fashion and the Growing Importance of the Marchande des Modes in Mid-18th Century France', *Costume* 31.
Penn, Margaret (1947) *Manchester 14 Miles*. Sussex, Firle.
Penney, Norman (ed) (1920) *The Household Account Book of Sarah fell of Swarthmore Hall*. Cambridge University Press.
Perkin, Joan (1994) *Victorian Women*. London, John Murray.
Phillips, Nicola (2006) *Women in Business 1700–1850*. Woodbridge, Boydell.
Pinchbeck, Ivy (1981) *Women Workers and the Industrial Revolution 1750–1850*. London, Virago.
Potter, Beatrice (1926) *My Apprenticeship*. London, Longman and Co.
Proctor, Molly G. (1987) *Are You Being Served? Shopping at the Drapers in Bygone Kent*. Kent, Rainham and Meresborough.
Purvis, June (1989) *Hard Lessons, the Lives and Education of Working Class Women*. Cambridge, Polity.
Quennell, Peter (1987) *Mayhew's London*. London, Bracken Books.
Reeves, Maud Pember (1913) *Round about a Pound a Week*. London, Bell. (Virago reprint, 1979).
Ribeiro, Aileen (1983) *A Visual History of 18th Century Costume*. London, Batsford.
Ribeiro, Aileen (1984 and 2002) *Dress in 18th Century Europe*. London and New York, Yale.
Richards, Thomas (1990) *The Commodity Culture of Victorian England, Advertising and Spectacle 1851–1914*. Stanford, Verso.
Richardson, George (1904) *Drapers', Dressmakers' and Milliners' Accounts*. London, The Accountants' Library.
Richmond, Vivienne (2013) *Clothing the Poor in 19th Century England*. Cambridge University Press.
Roberts, Elizabeth (1984) *A Woman's Place, an Oral History of Working Class Women 1890–1940*. Oxford, Blackwell.
Ross, Adrian and Greenbank, Percy (1909) *Our Miss Gibbs*. London, [n.d.].
Rothstein, Natalie (ed) (1984) *Four Hundred Years of Fashion*. London, V&A Museum.
Royden, A. Maud (1916) *Downward Paths, an Inquiry into the Causes Which Contribute to the Making of the Prostitute*. London, G. Bell and Sons.
Sanderson, Elizabeth (1984) *Sweated Industry and Sweated Labour: The London Clothing Trade 1860–1914*. London, Croom Helm.
Sanderson, Elizabeth (1986) 'The Edinburgh Milliners 1720–1820', *Costume* 20.
Sanderson, Elizabeth (1996) *Women and Work in 18th Century Edinburgh*. Basingstoke, Macmillan.

Sanderson, Elizabeth (2001) '"The New Dresses" a Look at How Mantua Making Became Established in Scotland', *Costume* 35.

Schmiechen, James (1975) 'A State Reform and the Local Economy', *Economic History Review*, Second series XXVIII.

Shickle, Rev C.W. (1902) *The Guild of the Merchant Tailors of Bath*. Bath, Herald Office.

Sigsworth, E.M. and Wyke, T.J. (1972) 'Prostitution and Venereal Disease in Independent Working Women', in Vicinus, Martha (ed) *Suffer and Be Still*. Bloomington, Indiana University Press, pp.77–99.

Snell, K.D.M. (1985) *Annals of the Labouring Poor*. Cambridge University Press.

Sorge-English, Lynn (2016) *Stays and Body Image in London*. Oxford, Routledge.

Steer, Francis W. (1953) 'The Inventory of Anne, Viscount Dorchester', *Notes and Queries*, CXCVIII, March.

Stewart, Margaret and Hunter, Leslie (1964) *The Needle Is Threaded, the History of an Industry*. London, Heinemann.

Styles, John (1994) 'Clothing the North, the Supply of Non-elite Clothing to the North of England', *Textile History* 25(2).

Styles, John (2007) *The Dress of the People, Everyday Fashion in 18th Century England*. New Haven and London, Yale.

Styles, John and Vickery, Amanda (2006) *Gender, Taste and Material Culture in Britain and North America 1700–1830*. New Haven and London, Yale.

Sweated Trades (2006) Exhibition catalogue. [n.l.].

Takeda, Sharon Sadako and Spilker, Kaye Durland (eds) (2010) *Fashioning Fashion: European Dress in Detail 1700–1950*. Los Angeles Museum of Art.

Tarrant, Naomi (1994) *The Development of Fashion*. Edinburgh, London and New York, Routledge.

Thompson, F.M.L. (ed) (1990) *The Cambridge Social History of Britain 1750–1950. Vol 2, People and Their Environment*. Cambridge University Press.

Tilly, L. and Scott, J. (1978) *Women, Work and Family*. London and New York, Methuen.

Trautman, Pat (1979) 'Personal Clothiers: A Demographic Study of Dressmakers, Seamstresses and Tailors 1880–1920', *Dress* 5.

Tyler, Jayne and Parsons, Clare (1999) *Madame Clapham, Hull's Celebrated Dressmaker*. Hull, Hull City Council.

Van Cleave, Kendra and Welborn, Brooke (2012) 'Very Much the Taste and Various Are the Makes', *Dress* 39(1).

Verita, May (1995) *Tailoring, Twopence an Hour*. London, Excalibur.

Vickery, Amanda (1998) *The Gentleman's Daughter, Women's Lives in Georgian England*. New Haven and London, Yale.

Vicinus, Martha (1972) *Suffer and Be Still, Women in the Victorian Age*. Bloomington, Indiana University Press.

Walkley, Christina (1981) 'Charity and the Victorian Needlewoman', *Costume* 14.

Walkley, Christina (1981) *The Ghost in the Looking Glass*. London, Peter Owens.

Walkowitz, Judith R. (1980) *Prostitution and Victorian Society, Women, Class and the State*. Cambridge University Press.

Walsh, Margaret (1979–80) 'The Democratization of Fashion', *Journal of American History* 66.

Waugh, Norah (1973) *The Cut of Women's Clothes 1600–1930*. London, Faber.

Weatherill, Lorna (1988) *Consumer Behaviour and Material Culture in England, 1660–1760*. London, Routledge.

Weatherill, Lorna (1990) *The Account Book of Richard Latham 1724–67*. Oxford University Press for The British Academy.

Weatherill, Lorna (1991) 'Consumer Behaviour in the Late 17th and Early 18th Centuries', *Textile History*, 22(2).

Welch, Evelyn (ed) (2011) *Fashioning the Early Modern: Dress, Textiles and Innovation in Europe 1500–1800*. Pasold Studies in Textile History, Oxford University Press.

Whitbread, Helena (ed) (2010) *The Secret Diaries of Miss Anne Lister*. London, Virago.

Whyte, Anne (1982) 'Helen Bagrie, Costumiere, 343, Union Street, Aberdeen: Reminiscences of a Dressmaker's Workroom', *Costume* 16.

Yeo, Eileen and Thompson, E.P. (1973) *The Unknown Mayhew*. Harmondsworth, Penguin.

Index

Abbey Street 223
Abbot, Ann 89
Abbot's Bromley 246, 246
Aberdeen 21, 22, 47, 271, 275, 277, 286
Abergavenny 37
abortifacient 109
abuse 37–38, 40, 88–92, 171, 198–201
Academy of Armory, 1688 12
Adams, John of Leek 255
Adderlys of Leicester 141, Colour Plate VII
Adderley, 'poor Tom' 249
adulteration of fabric 122
Adversity 203, Plate 39
advertisements 3, 4, 30, 39, 41, 44, 54, 70, 92, 96, 109, 119, 142, 154, 179, 183, 262, 280
Advice to the Married 109, 262
Agar, Elizabeth 18
ages of dressmakers in Leicester, Sidmouth and Ulverston 216, 220
Albrecht, William 84
Alexander, Lady Judith 12
Aliff, Jane 75
Alkincoats 80
Allen and French 184
Allgood, Lancelot MP 26
Allinson, Mrs 95, 128
Almond, Elizabeth 221
Alnwick 158, 159, 160, 161
'Alpha skirts' 187
Alsatian hair wash 109
Alton Locke 271
America 25, 148, 154, 183, 184, 185, 188, 233, 270, 282, 284
analysis of indentures 35–36
Anderson, Janet 214
Anderson, General 174
Andras, J. 55
Ange, Madame 119
Aniston, Jennifer 5
Anti-Pamela 195

Anti-Sweating League 170
Appearances and How to Keep them up on a Limited Income 258
Appleton, William 219
apprenticeship 3, 15, 18–19, 20, 21, 34–38, 40, 44, 92–95, 96, 101, 102, 103, 150, 154, 174, 177, 262, 264, 265, 266, 270, 276
aprons 13, 44, 45, 51, 62, 75, 78, 80, 81, 107, 231, 232, 239, 267
arithmetic 2, 44, 235
Armitage 245–256
armozine 71, 74, 231
Arnold, Janet 16, 274
Arnold, Matthew 136
Art of Cookery made Plain and Easy, The 26
Art of Dress, The 122, 178, 258, 280
Art of Dressmaking, The 178, 280
Arthur, T.S. 210
Arundel, Ann 20
Ashcombe Park 246
Ashridge, Elizabeth 270
Askham 84
Association for the Aid and Benefit of Dressmakers and Milliners, The 90, 200, 266
Aston, Baroness 36
Atkinson, James 77
Atlee, P. 234
attitudes to domestic service 264–265
Attwood, Samuel 40
Aughton and Wesson 250
Avebury 234–235
Avery, Mrs 161
Avery, Susannah 51
Ayres 44

B., Mrs 59
Bagrie, Helen 271, 286
Bailey, Sarah 134
Bainbridges of Newcastle 152, 162, 164, Plate 32

Baird, Mrs 106
Baker, Mrs Elizabeth 20
Balcarra, Lady 124
Balhatchet, Mrs 187
Banff 182
Bangladesh 267
Bankruptcy Act 1880 5, 120
bankruptcy 26, 45, 46, 99, 118, 120, 125, 129–132, 176, 213, 255, 266
Banks, Miss 187
banyan 11
Baptist minister 209, 222
Barber, Nicholas and Mary 38
barège 250, 256
Bark, Priscilla, 222, 223, Plate 42
Barker's of Kensington 254
Barlestone 121, 134
Barnard, Mrs 59
Barnard Castle 157
Barnes, Anne 75
Barrow-in-Furness 95, 101, 185
Barrow, J.H. 101
Barwick, William 129–130
Basford Hall 244, 245, 246, 248, 254
Basingstoke 40, 84
Bass, Mary Ann 221
Bateman, Miss 110
Bath 43, 64, 83, 89, 91, 92, 93, 229, 230, 231, 236, 258, 277
Bath Chronicle 41, 55, 77
Batho, Taylor and Ogden 107
Baxter, Rachel 21
Bayard, Marie 128
Beau Monde, Le 181
Be Your Own Dressmaker 186
Beal, Mary 39
Beales, C. 119
Beardsley, Ann 32
Bede House 177
Bedford/Bedfordshire 2, 8, 16, 35, 37, 52, 84, 157, 273, 274, 275, 276, 279
Beeton, Mrs 117
Bekleidungskunst für Damen Allgemeine Muster-Zeitung 148, Plate 26
Bell, Elizabeth 81
Bell, John 214
Bell, Miss 118
Belle Assemblée, La 30
Bellhouse, Mrs J. 186

Bennall sisters 64, 78, 233, 258
Benson, Mrs Sarah 129
Berkshire 8, 12, 46
Bertin, Rose 58
'Bessy' 198, 213
'bible-woman' 223
Biddenham 84
Bignell, Andrew 15
Binningtons 130, 131
Birch family 246, 248, 249
Birmingham 1, 8, 63, 81, 82, 83, 88, 90, 91, 135, 158, 184, 266, 279
Bishops Stortford 59
Bishopsgate 76
Bitter Cry of Outcast London, The 170
Black, Clementina 170, 172, 268, 279, 286
Blackmore, Elizabeth 214
Black's Law Dictionary 5
Blakes of Maidstone 165, 165
Bland, Emma 221
Blanthorne, Miss 128
Blayney, Robert 81
blocks and mallets 181
Blomfield, Lydia 35
Blue Coat School 93
Blunden, Anna 202
Blyvers, Elizabeth 52
Boland, Mrs 161
Bolioe, Frances 76
Bondgate House 159, Plate 30
Book of Trades, The 39, 40, 50, 57, 99, 146, 147, 288, Plates 9 and 25
Boornes Auction 75
Booth, Charles 117, 169, 280
Booth, Mrs 83, 279
Borrows, Mary J. 106
Boston 30
Boullay, Benoit 33
Bourgoin, Mr 18
Boyd, Mary Harriet 221
Bracey, Mrs 238
Bradford 157
Bradwell, Mr 173
Braintree 79, 121
Braithwait, Miss 58, 59
Braithwaite, Lady 110
Brampton 84
Brandon, Miss 212
Brassey, Thomas, MP 184

Bray, Charles 3
Briggs, Elizabeth of Alconbury 37
Brigham, Mrs Jane 35
Bright, Elizabeth 214
Brighton 8, 99, 104, 106, 111, 139, 155, 158, 176, 179, 265
Brighton Courier of Fashion, The 139, 179
Briscoe, Miss 135
Bristol 8, 17, 20, 83, 84, 88, 89, 90, 92, 274, 275, 279
Bristow, Elizabeth 18
Britannia Street 221
Brobon, Mary 17
Bromsgrove 94, 227
Brothers, Mrs 93, 141
Brown, George 76
Brown, Mrs 93, 201
Brown, W.H. 59
Browne, Elizabeth 11, 20, 213, 261
Browne, Miss 55
Browne, Mrs 201
Bruce, Lady 60
Brun Boileau 60
Bryan, Miss 88
Brydges, Edward 150–151
Buchanan, Miss 124
Buck, Anne 16, 273
Buck, Susannah 76
Budapest 30
Buenos Aires 30
Burderop House 229
Burgate 157
Burgess, Martha 46, 265
Burnet, John 169, 279
Burnet, Professor John 108
Butlin, Mrs C. 110
Butterick, Ebenezer 148, 149
Butters family 221
Buxton, Mrs 52
Buythorpe 131

caged birds 79
Cadbury, George 172
Calcutta 30
Caledonian Mercury, The 223
Caley's of Windsor 153, Plate 28
Calley, Arabella 80, 229–232, 257, 258
Calley family 229, 230, 231
Calthrop, Claude Andrew 202

Cambridge 8, 35, 93, 118, 135, 173, 277, 278, 281, 285
Cambridge Committee for Organizing Charitable Relief and Suppressing Mendacity, The 173
Cameron's 104
Cameron and Violard 176
Cameron, Mrs Allan 124
camlet/camblet 74, 78
Campbell, Alexander 60
Campbell, Mary 222
Campbell, Robert 195, 208
Cann, Jane 39
Canterbury 38, 65
Cantonese straw plait 183
Capel, Lady Dorothy 35
capuchine 51
Cardan, Ellen 198, 199
Cardiff 82, 83
Cardington 84
Cardson's binder belts 109
Carlisle 83
Carmichael, Mary 104, 105, 106, 110, 227
Carr and Co 230
Carr, Harriet 42
carriers 113
Carter, Ann 46
Carver, Tabitha 83, 279
Castle Yard 223
Castries, Duchesse de 58
Cathcart, Lady 59
'Catherine' 204–205
Catholicism 37
Cawell, Henry's wife 79
'CE' 226
Cefyn Mawr 171
census 3, 84, 98, 113, 154, 215, 216, 220, 223, 227, 248, 253, 263, 271, 285
Chaffard et Cie 100, Plate 15
Chaffard, Elizabeth, Leonard Ferdinand and 'Wee Lizzie' 105, 176, 227, Plate 16
challis 241, 242
Chantler, William 214
Chapman, Jacob 76
Chapman, Mary 37, 38
Chard in Somerset 221
Charles II 11
Charlton, Mrs A. 53

Chase, Alice Maud 94
Chastleton 246
Chatham Street 221
Cheddleton 244, 248, 251
Chelmsford 8, 133, 157
Cheltenham 90, 98, 119, 141, 150, 151, 177, 215, 227, 258
Cheltenham Looker On, The 119
'Cherub' 224, 261
Cheshire Record Office 50
Chester vii, Figure 1, 17, 34, 83, 162–163, 213, 241
Cheveley, Mrs 234
Chichester 12, 36, 61, 94, 165, 174
Children's Employment Commission 1843 Children's Employment Commission 1864, 87–92, 93, 96, 117, 135, 141, 155, 197, 198, 200, 201, 215, 266
Chiseldon 229
Christian and Son 241
Chudleigh 40
Church, John 46
Circulars 120
Cirencester 231
Citadel, The 243
Clapham, Emily (née MacVitie) and Haigh 174–175,176, 261, Plate 33
'Clapham, Lord and Lady' 29
'Clara' 199–200
Clark, Alice 3, 273
Clark, Ann 173
Clark, Elizabeth 37, 38
Clark, Miss 121, 127, 128
Clark, Sarah Ann 173
Clarke, A. 186
Clarke, E. J. of Bourne 135
Clarke, Elizabeth 37
class, social of dressmakers 36, 217–218
Clayton, Elizabeth 221
Clayton, Miss 136, 239
Cleaton Moor 128
Clegg, Miss 133
Cleland, John 197
Clifton 89, 91
climbing boys 87
clothes brokers 19, 20
coal higgler 223
Cockerill, Mary and Martha 221

Cockshutt and Preston 112, 134
Coke, Lady Mary 25
Cole Martha and Houghton, Martha 49, Plate 8
Colen, Mrs 231
Cole's brothel 197
Collier, Elizabeth 14
Colne 79, 80, 82, 258
Colonial Williamsburg 68
Colwall 40
Commissioner Grainger 90
Committee of Patents 183
Committee for Women's Suffrage 170
Comper, Mary 214
Constables' Census of Westmoreland 1787, 84
Contagious Diseases Acts of 1864, 1866 and 1869, 225
Conway, Bessie 255, 256, 266
Conway, Georgina Sophia 173
Cook, Miss 250
Coombs, Ann 38
Cooper, John of Grantham 141
Cooper's 239
Cople 84
Cork 89
corsets (see also stays) 12, 16, 66
Cory, Eliza Ann 103, 178
costings for running a dressmaking business 68, 268–269
Cotton, Agnes of Etwall 245
Court of Sessions 22
Craigwell 175
crepe 60, 62, 63, 64, 66, 73, 112, 122, 126, 160, 161, 184, 188, 189, 190, 191, 233, 249, 253, 254
Cresswell, Mrs 133
Crewe, Frances Anne 29, 58, 276
Crookes, Will MP 172
Cropton, M. 55
Crowden, Mrs 93
Curtiss 231
Custance, Miss 135
'cutting tailors' 15

Daily News, The 172
Dalton 108
Damer, Mrs 29
Daniel, Elizabeth 38

Daniels, Miss 258
Danvers, Mrs 204
Darley, Barnaby in Covent Garden 233
Davies, Emma 132
Davies, Margaret Llewellyn 98, 171
Davies, Miss 201
Davis, Dorothy 134
Davis, Jeanette E. 188
Davis, sewing machine manufacturer 211
Davis, Solomon 60
de Garsault 33
Deacon, Thomas 121
Deal in Kent 25
Debenham and Freebody 183–184
Debtors' Prison 131, Plate 18
debts 59, 70, 118
Defoe, Daniel 25
Demorest, Madame 149
Dennison, Margareta 14
Department of Practical Art 149
department stores 120, 152–166, 212, 270
Derby 54, 83
Derby Mercury, The 54
Description of All Trades 1747 26
Devey, Madame 242
Dewsbury, Mrs 148
di Martino, Paolo 5
Dickins and Jones 175
Dickinson, Edward 101
Dickinson, Rebecca 270
Dickson, Mrs 161
Diderot's Encyclopaedie 56, Plate 11
Dinsdale, Mrs 248, 249, 250–258
discipline 165, 229
displays of new fashions 54–55, 119–120, 250
Distressed Needlewomen's Home, The 262, 263
Distressed Needlewomen's Society, The 262, 267
divorce 245
Dixon, Misses 108
Dobell, Mrs 106
Dobson, Mrs 184–185
Dodds and Co 158, Plate 30
Doggett, C.R. 209
Dolly as a Baby 183
Dolly as a Girl 183

Dolly as a Young Lady 183
Dolly Varden 161, 283
Donvilla, Victoire 76
Doogood, Widow 79
Dorchester 92, 110
Dorset Record Office 34
Dove, William 37
Dover 27, 251, 255
Doverlie, Mary 47
'dovetailing' 176
Dow, Agnes 99, 118, 266
Dowdell, Carolyn 80, 278
Downer, Mrs Rose (née Hackett) 94, 174–176, 227
Downward Paths 226
Dowson, Mrs 94
Drapers', Dressmakers' and Milliners' Accounts 120
Drapers' and Milliners' Gazette of Fashion 153, 179
Draper's Record 144, Plate 23
Draycott, Elizabeth 221
'Dreadnought' pattern drafting system 185, Plate 35
Dress, Culture, Commerce 3
Dress Cutting-Out, a Pupil's Manual for Home Study 186
'dress improver' 252
dress of the poor 25, 78–79, 135–137, 267
Dressmaker to the Queen 210
Dressmaker's and Milliner's Butterick Quarterly, The 182
Dressmakers' Chart and Cutter, The 184
Dressmakers' Guide Cutting made Easy, The 187
Dressmaking: Guide to Freehand, The 186
Dressmaking; a technical manual for teachers 150
The Ladies' Handbook of Millinery, Dressmaking and Tatting 146
Driffield 157
Drury, Robert 195
Dubois, the French ambassador to London 30
Dudley 157
Duffett, Miss 225
Dufton 84

Dunbar, Magdalene 45, 57, 59, 60, 266
Dundee 21, 22, 275
Dunn and Co of Newcastle 166
Dunning, Mrs 91
Duplessy, Madame 205–206
Dysart 121, 210
Dysart, Mrs 210
Dyson, Miss 158

Eagle, Miss 158
Earnshaw, Mr, Inspector of Factories 151
East India Company 26
Eastborough, Margery 19
Eastman, Mercy 47
Easy dressmaking 145, 187
Eaton Socon 84
Eccleston, Sarah 38
Eden, Sir Frederick 79
'Edgar' 91, 205
Edgar Buildings 91
Edinburgh 8, 16, 21, 57, 60, 99, 100, 103, 104, 109, 111, 121, 123, 125, 129, 176, 214, 227, 261, 266, 275, 277, 278, 280, 281, 283, 284
Edmond, John 214
Edwards, Elizabeth 75, 121, 132
Elements of Modern dressmaking 126, 188, 189
Elgar, Emma 92
Elgar, George 202
Ellis, Mrs in Shrewsbury 241
Ellerstone 131
Ellis family 45
Ellis, Mrs, Shrewsbury 241
Elsworth, Anne 109
Emily, Lady 199, 200
Empress Elizabeth of Russia 30
Englishwoman's Domestic Magazine, The 141, 148
Epworth, Miss 133
Espley Hall 160
'Esther' 210
Etwall Hall 245, 248
"Eureka" system 184–185, 284
Evans piqua plant 109
Eveleigh, Mary 19
Everritt, Susannah 177
Evesham milliner 125–126
Exchange Alley 43

Exeter 1, 8, 18, 19, 39, 83, 91, 93, 102, 141, 190, 275
Eye in Norfolk 70
eye problems 98

Fabian Women's Group 170
fabric names 12, 68–75, 122, 226
fabric prices 71, 75, 121, 122
fabric samples 30, Colour Plate II
fabric widths 75
Factory and Workshop Acts 1891 and 1895 170
Factory Inspection Act 1833 87
family life – dressmakers' in Leicester 220–223
fancy dress 43, 91, 183
Fanny Hill 197
Fanny the Little Milliner 207
Farnborough 248
fashion, changes 7, 11, 26–34, 51, 52, 53, 60, 80, 85, 86–87, 119, 191, 243
Fashionable Magazine, The 32
fashion doll 29, 30
Fashion's Slaves 202
Faulder, Mrs 91, 266
Faulkener-Wisden, Mrs Patrick 174
Felixstowe 182
Fell, Sarah 58, 61, 278
'feme couvert' 5, 36, 130
'feme sole' 5
feminist history 3
Fenton, Mrs 111, 112, 129
Fettes, George 77
Fielden, Margaret 59
Fields, Mrs 59
Filon, Mlle 30
Finchingfield 79
fines 19, 21, 165, 171, 213
Fisher, Dr and Mrs 204–205
Fisher, Melles, Jones, Reid and Co 184
Fitkins, Mary 37, 38
fitting 56, 57, 68, 96, 99, 102, 103, 110, 111, 144, 145, 149, 166, 187, 188, 190, 206, 207
flawed enquiry methods 88
Fleming, Jane of Ambleside 113
Folkestone 158
Follets, the 147
Foot, Cecilia 21

For Only One Short Hour 202
Forbes, Miss 110
Forton Hall 160
Fort William 123, 124
Fosset, Mercy 221
Fowkes, Misses 119
Fowls, Mrs 39
Fox, Miss Mabel 133
France 27, 30, 53, 74, 115, 185, 274, 284
French bodies 144, 145
French Bust Company, Tottenham Court Road, Plate 23
French goods 25, 48, 53, 54
French, Lady 131
French mantua-maker 41, 46, 56
French Revolution 234
Fricker 142
Frisby, Minnie 94, 227
Frome 38

Galbraithe, Mrs 133
Gaillard and Toussain on Golden Square 233
Gallerie des Modes 23, 196, Plates 4 and 37
Gallery of Fashion 30
Galpin, Agnes 221
Galvanism 253
Gambier, Mrs 38
Garth, General Tom 234
Gaskell, Mrs 209, 266
General Domestic Female Institution 177
Genoese velvet 96, 206
Gentleman's Magazine 30
Georgiana, Duchess of Devonshire 27
Germany 16, 115, 116, 169
Gibson, Miss 158
Gilbert and Roget 233
Gildart, Lucy 32, 267
Gill, Ellen 94
Gill, Sarah 221
Gilling, Mrs H. 141
Girl Neighbours 211
Girls' Own Paper, The 137
Glascow, Lady 124
Glasgow 110, 111, 279, 280, 281, 283
Glasse, Hannah 26, 266, 275
Gliddon, Ann 214
Glossop 95–97, 108
Gloucester/Gloucestershire 8, 37, 46, 52, 153

Goddard, Miss 136, 239, 266
Godey's Magazine 148
Godfrey, Ann 59
Godley, Andrew 141, 282
Godwin, Daniel, shoemaker 234
Godwin, William 81
Going into Service 202
Goldsworthy 234
Goodall, Mr 81
Goodwin, Sarah 222
Goodwin, Thomas 214
Goolden 81
Goolden, Alexander, Catherine and Martha 35
Gordon, Mrs Hay 111
Gosport 84
Goubauds 183, 184
Gough family of Perry Hall 81
Gough, William 35, 214
Goulding, Mrs 99, 103–104
Gourdet and Yates 184
government schools of design 149
Grabham's folding dress stand 145
Grace Myers' Sewing Machine 210
Graham, Adelaide 199, 213
Graham, Mrs 59
Grainger, Commissioner 90
Granger, Ann 223
Gray's Inn Lane 76
Gray's Inn Road 178
Greenaway, John 37
Gregory, Mrs 90
Grenfell, Mrs Henry 186
Grice, Joanna 26
Griffiths, Thomas of Clifford's Inn 121
Griggs, Widow 79
Guadeloupe 233
Guardianship of Infants Act 1886, 170
Guildford 121, 127
guilds 2, 3, 14, 15, 16–24, 261, 275
Gwynne, Mrs 251, 255, 258

Hackett, Hannah 174
Hackett's 134
Hackwood 104
hair, false 251
hairdressers' strike 105
Hall, Lady Helen 59
Hall, Margaret 20

Hambledon 82, 278
Hammersley family 137
Hammonds of Hull 165
Hancock, F.A. 181
Handbook of Dressmaking 178
Handsacre 248, 255, 266
Hankinson and Sankey 212
Hanley 137, 266
Hanningtons, S.H. 155
Harding, H. 81
Hardings 60
Hardy, Mary 43, 55, 58, 70, 214, 258, 277, 278
Harwood, A. 81
Harper, Miss 158
Harper, Samuel 81
Harriet 211–212
Hartopp, Sir Edward 235
Hastings 47
Hatton 44
Haweis, Mrs 122, 258, 259
Hawick 15, 274
Hawkesyard 246
Hawkins, Miss 104
Hayhurst, W., staymaker 233
Hayhurst, S. of Milnthorpe 112
Haywood, Eliza 195
Head, Mrs or Miss 36
health of dressmakers 4, 47, 89, 91, 106, 111, 141, 157, 158, 173, 203, 212, 219, 271
Hearne, Jane 15
Hearson, Mary 214
Heelas of Reading 165
Helston 106
Henson, Mary A. and Frances 219
Herbert, Fanny and Dorothea 29
Herrick, John 32
Herrick, Mrs 32, 79, 267
Hexham 157
Hicks, Frances 93, 101
Hicks, George Elgar 202
Hill, Barbara 136
Hill, Mrs 240, 242
Hill, Colonel John 240, 241Hill, Rev John and Charlotte, 241–2, 244–5, Plate 44
Hill, Rowland 241
Hill, Thomas, glover on Pall Mall 233

Hillhouse on Bond Street 242
Hills, Lizzie 219
Hilton, Mr 155
History of the Seduction of London, A 223
Hitchcock, Lucy 46
Hitchcock, Mrs 238
Hobson and Sons of Spalding 166
Hobson's Charity 93, 118, 281
Hogarth, Mary and Anne's ready-made frock shop 42, Plate 7
Holbrook, Laetitia 248
Holdraw, Miss 158
Holl, Frank 202
Holland, Mary 221
Holme, Randle 12, 16
Holmes, Miss 90
Holmes, S. 54
Holt 55, 58, 75, 82, 258
Holwell 38
Home for Gentlewomen in Time of Sickness 251
Home, Mrs B. 59
Honeywell, Mrs 155
Hood, Thomas 197, 202
hoops 60–67
Hope, R. 11, 273
Hopkins, William 35
Hornby and Harris, hoop makers in Soho 233
Horncastle 154
Horsham 44, 214
Houndsditch 76
House of Commons Journal, The 18
Houston, H.J. Brooke 210
How to Dress Well on a Shilling a Day 258, 286
How to Make a Dress from the European System of Dresscutting 187
Howden, John 60
Howe, Elias 139, 140, Plate 20
Howell, Mrs 178, 179
Howlet, Elizabeth 17
Hughes, Miss Sarah 132
Hughes, Thomas 225
Huison Charity 47
Hull 17, 18, 43, 60, 83, 84, 157, 165, 174, 261, 266, 271, 283
Humphreys, McChlery and Shoolbred 128
Hunter, Elizabeth Ann 95

Hurst, Sarah 44, 214, 277
Hutchinson, Mrs Elizabeth 35

Ickwell 84
immorality – see also prostitution 6, 261–262
improvers 38, 92, 95, 97, 161, 172, 218, 264, 265, 269
Indian goods 25
Ingleby, Reverend Charles 245, 253
Ingleby, Susanna 119, 244–257, 258, 259 285, Plates 45 and 46
instruction manuals 177–179, 182, 184–189
Instructions for the Cosmopolitan System of Dressmaking 186
insurance 46, 82, 214
Intriguing Milliners and Attorney's Clerks, The 195
Ipswich viii, 41, 91, 103, 142, 157, 158, 283
Ipswich Journal 41
Isaacson, Mr and Mrs 96
Italy 115
It's not your linen you're wearing out, but human creatures lives 202

Jackson, Ada 117, 281
Jackson, Miss 155–156
Jackson, Mr 17
Jackson's 238, 239
Jackson's Oxford Journal 32, 43
Jamaica 59, 78, 233, 234
James, Elizabeth Mary-Anne 248
James, Sarah 81
Janes, Drapers of Egham 134
Jeens, Julia 151
Jefferies, Miss 81
'Jennie' 210
Jersey 182
Jervis, Elizabeth 51, 277
Jewish Board of Guardians 169
Johnson, Bernard 18, 274
Johnson, Miss 55
Johnson, Mr 18
Joll, Ann 214
Jones, Mrs 91, 132
Jones, Mr the shoemaker 241
Journal des Demoiselles, Le 148
Journal des Modes, Le 182

Journal du Gout 30
journeywoman 15, 25, 38, 39, 41, 68
Judd, Elizabeth 214
Judsons (dyes), 181
Jules, H. 145
'Julia' 207–208
Julian, Mary 106

Kay, J.B. 101
Keele University Library 246, 285
Kempes, the 111
Kempster, Elizabeth 38
Kendal 84, 112, 113, 134
Kendal Milne of Manchester 152
Kendall, E.G. 186
Kennington, Thomas Benjamin 203, Plate 39
Kent, James 92
Kentish Gazette, The 29
Kenyon, Charlotte 62, 240–257
Kenyon family 240–244, 257, 285
Kerr, Mrs 59
Kerr of Kippielaw 213
Keys, Mr 96
Kidwell, Claudia 34, 276
Kilner, Mrs 231
Kingsley, Charles 271
King's Lynn 177
Kingstone 157
Knight, Miss 251, 255
Knight, Mrs Lowther 187
Knighton 235
Knox, Mary 60

Labron, Mrs 131
Ladies' Dressmaking Association, The 149
Ladies' Dress Making and Embroidery Association, The 264
Ladies' Handbook of Millinery, Dressmaking and Tatting, The 146
Ladies National Association, The 225
Ladies' Tailor, The 187
Ladies' Treasury, The 257
Lady Peckitt's Yard 77
Lady's Magazine, The 30
Lahaye, Madame 16
Lakeman, Factory Inspector 169
Lambert, Ann 81
Lambert family 198

Lancashire 8, 52, 59, 78, 80, 82, 101, 108, 185, 214, 215
Lanesborough, Lord of Swithland 235
L'Art de la Couturière 34
Latham, Nany and Richard 63, 78, 278
Lathrop, Polly 270
Lavender, Mrs 84
Lawson, Mrs 104
Lawton and Co 81
lay figures 144–145, 181, 210
Le Tailleur Sincere 33
Leach, Mary and Sarah 222
Leake, Miss 75
Leamington 89, 91
Learmonth, Christian 213
Lechlade 46, 265
Lee, Elizabeth 20
Lee, Mr S 109
Leeds 8, 18, 82, 84, 94, 157, 163, 274, 279
Leeds Intelligencer, The 83
Leek 185, 244, 251, 255, 258, 285
Legal position of women in business 5
Leicester/Leicestershire 1, 6, 8, 18, 32, 37, 69, 79, 81, 89, 93, 97, 109, 117, 119, 120, 121, 123, 134, 135, 136, 142, 154, 157, 215, 216, 217, 218, 219, 220, 221, 222, 223, 235, 236, 238, 239, 258, 266, 267, 279, 280, 281, 283, 285
Leicester Chronicle 222, 239, 279, 280, 282
Leicester Daily Post, The 154
Leicester Fields 76
Leicester Herald and General Advertiser 119
Leicester Journal, The 120
Leicester Post, The 93
Leicestershire museums' dress collection 141, 282
Leith 45, 57, 59, 99, 118, 266
Lemire, Beverley 3
Leslie, Mrs 42
L'Esperance, John 76
Lettice Arnold 204–206, 214
Levi, Mr 75
Levine, Madame 187
Lewis, Mary 214
Lewisham 157
Liberty's 175
Life and Labour of the People of London, The 169

Life as we have known it 171, 280
Lilley, Nurse's Royal Female Pills 109
Limoges 104
Lincoln 8, 18, 83, 136, 157
Lindops of Chester 162
Lindsey, Robert 16
Lister, Anne of Shibden Hall 80
Lister, Miss 135
literacy levels among dressmakers 3, 44
Little Dressmaker, The 181
Little Argyll Street 47
'Little Rapid' knitting machine 184
Little Women 267
Liverpool 83, 84, 150, 162, 169, 186, 222, 279
Liverpool Review, The 113, 136
Livingstone, Mary 59
Lloyd, Edward 35
Lloyd family 243
Lochinvar 241
Lodge, Widow 16
lodging houses 221, 226
Lodging House Act 226
Lomas, Thomas 69, 181, 184, Plate 12
London 5, 6, 7, 8, 11, 14, 15, 16, 17, 18, 25, 26, 27, 30, 44, 45, 46, 47, 48, 49, 50, 51, 52, 53, 54, 55, 58, 60, 64, 65, 76, 78, 80, 82, 88, 89, 90, 91, 92, 96, 97, 98, 101, 103, 104, 107, 110, 118, 123, 128, 135, 144, 146, 147, 149, 150, 157, 158, 160, 162, 169, 170, 174, 175, 178, 179, 183, 184, 198, 201, 214, 215, 224, 226, 229, 233, 241, 242, 250, 251, 252, 253, 254, 255, 257, 258, 266, 273, 274, 275, 276, 277, 278, 279, 280, 281, 282, 284, 285, 286
London City and Guilds Examinations 150
London Evening Post, The 27
London Merchant Taylors' Company 15, 16
London Tradesman, The 195
London Working Men's College 225
Long Acre 76
Longridge, James 70
Longsdon, Emma Jane 136
Long, Dame Dorothy 35
Louth 34

Love, Ann 83
Low, Mrs Woodgate 187
Lower Green Lane 221
Lucas and Rogers, Oswestry 241
Lucks of Darlington 156, Plate 29
'Lucy' 201
Ludlow 20, 275
Lutterworth 121

Macaulay, Mary 169
Macaulay, Thomas Babbington 169
Mackenzie, Dr (later Sir Morrell), 253
Macquhae, Miss 123
'Madame Elise' 96
Madame Schild's Monthly Journal of Parisian Dress Fashions 181
'Madame' shops 93
Mademoiselle Grandhomme's Cutting Out and Dressmaking 186
magazinière 101
Maîtresses Couturières 16
Makers of our Clothes, The 170, 279
Manchester 2, 8, 35, 82, 83, 84, 91, 99, 107, 128, 152, 155, 181, 184, 185, 188, 266, 273, 276, 279, 280
Manchester 14 miles 155, 212
Mancini, Hortense, Duchess of Mazarin 11
Mansfield 82, 235
mantua/mantua-maker 2, 7, 11, 12, 13, 15, 16, 17, 18, 19, 20, 21, 22, 23, 25, 26, 27, 29, 31, 32, 33, 34, 35, 36, 37, 38, 39, 40, 41, 42, 43, 45, 46, 47, 48, 49, 52, 54, 56, 59, 60, 62, 68, 70, 75, 76, 77, 78, 79, 80, 82, 83, 84, 195, 209, 213, 214, 215, 224, 230, 231, 232, 261, 273, 274, 278, 279
mantua-maker, use of term 7, 12, 15–16, 33
March sisters 267
Mardon, Anna Maria 95
Marie Antoinette 27
Market Bosworth 121
Market Harborough 37
Marman, Mrs D. Mackenzie Clark 110
marriage settlement 245
Married Women's Acts 1882, 1884 170
Married Women's Work 172, 286
Marsh, Mrs Anne 204

Marsh, Colonel 234
Marshall and Snelgrove 174
Martinique 233
Mary Kemp Book 131
Mason, Ann 220, 266
Mason, Dr 112
Mason, Ellen 221
Mason, Madame 12
Matche's Academy 128
Mathon 40, 277
Matrimonial Causes Act 1878, 170
Matthews, Mrs 91, 133
Maud, Queen of Norway 174
May Coverley, the Young Dressmaker 201
Mayhew, Henry 224
McCall, James 149
measuring systems 185
Men at Arms 226
mercer 7, 27, 33, 52, 154, 162
Mercer, Michael 15
Merchant Company, Edinburgh 21
Meyer, Lady Adele 170, 279
Middlebrook, Mary 18
Middleton, Susannah 220
Midleton, Mrs Ann 20
Mildmay, Thomas 202
Millais, John Everett 202
Miller, Maria 36
Miller, Samuel 179, 180, 181, 182, 183, Plate 34
milliner/millinery 2, 3, 4, 5, 7, 25, 26, 27, 33, 36, 37, 39, 40, 42, 43, 45, 51, 54, 55, 60, 68, 70, 76, 80, 82, 83, 84, 88, 90, 91, 93, 99, 100, 101, 104, 106, 107, 112, 113, 118, 119, 121, 123, 124, 125, 126, 129, 130, 132, 134, 147, 149, 152, 154, 157, 158, 160, 162, 163, 166, 176, 178, 195, 197, 198, 200, 204, 207, 208, 214, 216, 221, 222, 223, 224, 225, 226, 230, 231, 232, 233, 238, 239, 248, 250, 261, 262, 264, 266, 273, 274, 278, 279, 284, 285
Milliner, Dressmaker and Draper, The 183
Milliners' Dressmakers' and Warehouseman's Gazette, The 183
Milliner's Holiday, The 197
Minety 229, 232

Minnow, Sally/Mineau, Madame Sarina 198
mirrors 26, 57, 58, 100
Mistaken Charity, A 270, 286
Mitchell, D. 121
Mitchell, Hannah 95, 96, 97, 108, 118, 227, 270, 279
Mitchell, Miss 158
Mitford, Mary 20
Mode Artistique, La 183
modesty in dress 267
Molloy, Mary 270, 286
'Mona, the apprentice' 19, 96
Moncrieff, Isobel 21
Moniteur de la Mode, Le 143, 183, Plate 22
Monroe, R. 188, 190, 282
Montague, Benjamin and Clarissa 78
Montgomerie, Jean 21
Moody sisters, the 26
Mordaunt, Sir John and Lady 51
Mordaunt, Virginia 205
Morgan, Mr, Inspector of Nuisances 150
Morning Chronicle, The 224
Morris, Ann 222
Morris, Mary 220
Morterton, Mrs and Minnie 199–200
Morton, John Madison 197
mourning 32, 51, 52, 73, 74, 79, 81, 85, 91, 98, 104, 108, 112, 120, 126, 160, 162, 188, 191, 203, 230, 233, 235, 239, 249, 250, 251, 253, 254, 255, 258
Moxon, Thomas of Leicester 81, Plate 13
Muir, Miss 106
Murray, Cicely 213
museum 1, 29, 33, 141, 190, 276, 282, 284
Mushet, Fanny and Walter 213
'MW' 226
'Myra' 185, 186
Myra's Journal of Dress and Fashion 145, 146, 185
Myra's Journal of Dress and Needlework 185

National Register of Archives, the 2
National Union of Women Workers, the 170
Neal, Mary 172
Neale, Susan and Elizabeth, New Bond Street 53, Plate 10
needle trades 5, 173, 203
Needlewoman, The 202
Nellie Graham the Young Dressmaker 209–210
Nenadic, Stana 109, 129, 176, 272
New England Weekly, The 30
New York 30, 149, 270, 275
New Skirts and How to Cut Them 182
Newarke 154, 219
Newcastle Daily Journal, The 162
Newcastle Weekly Courant, The 39
Newcastle-upon-Tyne 8, 82, 166, 275
Nichols, Mrs 84
Nicholson, George 131, 132, 269
Nicoll, Miss 106
Nightingale, Miss 241
Nobbs, Mrs 39
Noble, Mrs 153
Nollneye, Mrs 111
Norfolk Chronicle, The 34, 55
Norman and Shepherd 165
North London Opthalmic Institution 98
North Shields 160–161
Northallerton 157
Northampton 8, 38, 119, 165
Northampton Mercury, The 38
Northumberland 6, 8, 18, 26, 36, 159, 160, 214, 276
Norwich 2, 8, 17, 19, 36, 61, 82, 83, 89, 92, 122, 242, 273
Norwich Directory, The 1783, 83, 273
Nostell Priory 53, 214
Nottingham 8, 17, 46, 82, 83, 89, 107, 119, 128, 158, 266
numbers of dressmakers per head of population 78–84, 216–7
Nunney 38

Oakamoor 245
Oakham 154
Okely, Ann and Francis 2, 26
Old Aberdeen 22, 275
Old Bailey 75
Oldham 171
Oliphants, the 104
opening hours 154
Ormer, Caroline 135

Ormston, Mrs 155, 212
Osborne, Isabel 157
Osborne, Miss 93
Oswald, Miss 160
Ottley and Bown 250
'Oulton's wife' 17
Oundle 154, 262
outworkers 118, 136, 203, 206
Owen Owen 162
Oxford 8, 15, 18, 19, 35, 63, 82, 83, 229, 230, 246, 255, 275, 276, 278, 280
Oxford Journal, The 36
Oxford Street 148, 241
Oxygen Water 183

P., Mrs 95
Page, Miss 156
Page, Sam 135
Paild, Edward 76
Paine, Sarah 39
Pamela, 196
Pantins and Coates 233
Papandiek, Mrs 80
paper, cost of 34
paper patterns 1, 2, 116, 128, 146–149, 166, 179, 181, 182, 183, 184, 188, 261
Paris 25, 27, 29, 30, 46, 48, 50, 53, 54, 65, 106, 119, 147, 149, 174, 181, 183, 184, 199, 215, 234, 274, 278
Parker, Mrs of Allerburn 161
Parslie, Mrs 232
Partridge, James 214
Pathhead 121
Pattenden, Mary 214
Pattinson Elizabeth Sarah (née Simpson) 101, 107–108, 111–112, 128–129, 176, Plate 17
Paul, Sarah 37, 266
pauper inventories 79
pawnbrokers 76, 77
Payne, Miss 146
Payne, Mrs 255, 256
Pearson, Thomas 214
Pedly, William 37
Peel, Watson and Co 107
Peele, John Thomas 202, 266, Colour Plate VIII
Peers, Mary 34

Pegg, Mrs 238, 239, 258
Penn, Margaret 155, 212
Pepper, Miss 135
The Period, a Story of 211, Plate 41
Perriman, Ann 231
Perry, Sarah 60
personal account books 3, 229, 247, 257, 268
Perth 21, 40, 275, 277
Perth journeymen tailors 40
Peterborough 154
petitions 17, 18, 19
Pettifor, Catherine 223
Philadelphia 149, 154, 282
Phillips, Mary 20
Phillips, Nicola 5, 88, 273
Phils Buildings 76
Pickering 157
'Pie' 211–212
Pinch, Miss from Redferns 162, 163, Plate 31
Pinchbeck, Ivy 3, 273
pinking irons 181
Pirie, Janet 21
Pitter, Mr 90
Place, Francis 78
Plaistow, Grace 46
plumes 29
Plymouth 8, 93, 225
Pochin, Miss 238, 239
politics, dressmakers and 227, 270
Pontefract 17
Poor Teacher, The 202
Popple, Mary 82
Porteous, John 15
Portsmouth 94
post office 37
Potter, Beatrice 169
Potts, Dotts, Totts, Watts and Lotts, the Misses 197
Poverty, a study of town life 170
Practical dressmaking 141, 188, 282, 286
Praga, Mrs 258, 259
Pratchett, Terry 226
Pratt, Thomas 60
Pratenton, William 231
premiums 35, 36, 92, 93, 264, 276
Preston 112, 134, 185
Preston, Mr 113

Prevost, Abbé 29
Priddell, Miss 158
prices 6, 35, 43, 60, 61, 62, 71, 75, 91, 107, 113, 115, 116, 119, 120, 121, 122, 123, 126, 127, 130, 132, 134, 135, 137, 141, 142, 145, 160, 161, 166, 180, 207, 208, 255, 258, 265, 268, 270
Pringle, Miss 91, 92
Pritchard, Miss 241
Pritchard and Lloyd, Shrewsbury 241
probate inventories 26
Probyn, Elizabeth 76
Proctor, Molly 160, 283
professor of music 221
Promenade, The 150, 151, 215
prosecutions 15, 17, 19
prostitution 200, 208, 212, 223–226, 285
Proudman, Miss 158
Prynn, Miss Elizabeth 231, 232
Public Advertiser, The 40, 41, 47, 275
puce 27, 80, 242
Pulborough 39
Punch 145, 186, 197, Plates 24 and 36

Quarter Sessions 75
Quebec 233
quinsy throat 253

Raby, Jane 221
Rackett, Elizabeth 84
Radford, Edward 202
Radford, Mrs 93
raffle 75
Ramsay, Katherine and Anne 213
Ramsey, S. 64
Ranger, Mrs 128
Ravenhill, John 40
Rawlings, Mrs 94
Rayner and Lee 107
ready-made dresses 50, 160
record keeping 120–121
Redferns 163
Redgrave, Richard 201, 202, 266, Plate 38
Redmaynes, New Bond Street 241
Rees, Miss 133, 156
Reeves, Miss 91, 266
Regent Street 6, 49, 96, 142, 184
Reigate 158

Religious Tract Society 201, 266
Remingtons 106
Rennison, Mr 160
rental of property, difficulty of 5
Reynolds, G.W.M. 205
Reynolds, Miss 158
Rhyl 157
Richards, Amelia 218
Richardson, George Henry 120
Richardson, Samuel 195
Richmond 62, 82, 83, 214, 281, 286
Rickaby, Mrs 76
Rickmansworth 46
Rigbee, Mrs 52
Ripon 17, 107, 157
Rival Milliners, The 195
Roberts, Catherine 221
Robertshaws, Oxford Street 241
Robertson, Mause 16
Robinson, A. 18, 38
Robinson, Maryann 222
Robinson, Miss 155
Robinson, Reuben 214
Rodmure system of Dress Cutting, Geometric and Practical, The 187
Romford 35, 214
Roper, Miss 135
Ross, Martha 21
Ross, Miss 231
Rother, James 77
Rotherham dressmaker 133
Rowcroft, Charles 207, 208
Rowntree, Seebohm 170
Roxborough, Jane and Stephen 37
Royal Commission – see Children's Employment Commissions
Royden, Maude 226
Rugeley 248–258
Rumbell, Miss 230
Russum, Mrs 133
Ruth 209
Rutland, Duke of 235
Ruyton 243
Ryde 93
Rye 68, 112

Saffron Walden 157
Salisbury 8, 17, 18, 19, 275, 285
Sanderson, Elizabeth 21, 213, 274, 284

Sandford 84, 161
Sandford, Mrs 161
Saunder's Newsletter 42
Savile, Gertrude 80, 278
Savory, Susannah 19
Savoy, Duke of 11
Sawney, Ann 46
Schild, Marie 179–183, 261, Plate 34
Schild's Magazine of Ladies' Fashions 182
Schild's Monthly Journal 181, 182
Schodeher, Mme 104
'scientific' 185, 186
Scientific Dress Cutting Association 146, 184
'Scissors' 1, 291
Scotland 8, 20–22, 36, 40, 82, 121, 182, 213, 274, 280
Scott, Barbara 249
Scott, Mary 89
Scott, Sarah 36, 44
seamstress 5, 6, 13, 14, 15, 16, 42, 58, 113, 118, 172, 195, 202, 203, 211, 212, 225, 226, 231, 232, 248, 272, 274
Seamstress, The 202, Plate 38
Seamstress or the White Slave of England, The 205, 206, Plate 40
Searancke, Mary Ann and Charles 35
Seaton, Sarah 39
Seawall, Miss 45
sederunt books – see also bankruptcy 99
Seiles, Mrs 133
Selvidge, Phoebe 222
Semprose 104
Sempstress, The 153, 262, 263, 266, Plate 47
'separate spheres' 3
settlement examinations 3, 39
sewing machines 139, 140, 142, 177, 187, 210
Schild's Penny Magazine of Dress and Fashion 181
Shackleton, Elizabeth 52, 59, 80, 214, 258
Shackerley, Ann 50, 51
Sharp, Dr 36
Sharp, Miss 106
Shaw, George MD 97
Shaw, George Bernard 172
Sheffield 88, 157
Sheldrake, Mrs 58
Shelfe, Sarah 76

Shepherd and Manning 119
Sherborne 146
Sheridan, Bridget 42
Sherwood, Richard 15
Shrewsbury 33, 241, 242, 276
Shrewsbury mantua 32–33, Colour Plates III & IV
Sibbald, Susan 25, 275
Sidmouth 8, 215, 216, 217, 218, 219, 220, 285
Siegel, Mother's Constipation Remedy 109
Silber and Flemming 145
Simmonds, Miss 158
Simple Instructions for Dresscutting by Tailors' Measures 186
Simpson, Maggie 129, 227
Simpson, Miss 124
Singer 139, 141, 142, 181, 187, 282
Sitwell, Lady Ida 174
skinners 19, 20
slate 121
Slater's Leicester Directory 107, 123, 285
Slaves of the Needle, The 202
slavery 234
Sleet, James 214
Smith, Charles 222
Smith, Captain Harry 44–45, 214
Smith, Hannah 15, 173
Smith, James and Co of Newcastle 163
Smith, Lucy 214
Smith, Mary 1, 60
Smith, Miss 199, 230
Smith, Mrs 109, 110, 127, 129, 141, 230
Smith, Reverend Reginald 110
Smith, Thomas 119
Snell 44
Sneyd family 244, 246, 248, 249, 251
Snowdrops 202
snuff 70
social status of dressmakers in Leicester, Sidmouth and Ulverston 218
Sockbridge 84
Somerset 8, 38, 149, 221, 276, 277
Song of the Shirt 197, 202, 266, Colour Plate VIII
Sons of the Clergy Society 36
Sophy 210, 257
Sorge-English, Lynn 58, 278
Soulsby's Ulverston Advertiser 108

Southall's sanitary towels 109
Southampton 8, 83, 84, 181, 225
Sowerby, M. 60
Sowerby, Mrs 129
Spectator, The 43
Spencer's Kilting Establishment 142
spinning 38, 235
Spitalfields rag market 76
Spode, Josiah 246
Spurrett, Eliza (née Stone) 235–240, 257, Plate 42
St Aubyn, Lady 199, 200
St Giles-in-the-Fields 37
St Ives 157
St Martins-in-the-Fields 7, 37, 39
St Marylebone 46
St Petersburg 30, 149
Staffordshire 8, 51, 119, 137, 244, 245, 248, 250, 257
Stainforth, Mary 46
Stainmore 84
Stamford Mercury, The 46
Stanhope, Lady Harriet 29
Stark, Miss 105, 106
State of the Poor, The 288
stays (see also corsets) 12, 21, 45, 51, 61–68, 70, 78, 80, 81, 103, 109, 129, 134, 231, 233, 236, 237, 238, 241, 242, 252
Stent, Mrs 94, 95
Stephenson, Elizabeth Jane 157
Stevens, Miss 251
Stevens, Mrs 51
Stewart, Beatrix 21
Stewart Greenhill, Lady Jane 59
Stewart, Margaret and Hunter, Leslie 279
Stewart, Miss 59
Stewkley, Katherine 11
Stiggford, Hannah 19
Stirling 21, 22, 213, 275
Stitch! Stitch! Stitch! 202
Stitchmen, Ludlow Company of 20
Stoke Newington 32
Stone, Mrs Elizabeth 197
Story of the Period, A 211
straw plait 125, 183
Streatley 46
Stumpke, Louis 119
Successful Advertising 119

Suffolk 8, 41, 157, 182, 283
Sun Fire Insurance Co 214
Sutton 46, 131
Sutton, Sarah 46
Swain, Mr 60
Swainson, Elizabeth 84
sweating system 118, 169, 170, 281
Sweated Labour exhibition 172
Swindon 64, 82, 229, 230, 231, 258
Swindon mantua-maker, the 230
'Sylvia' 258, 267
System of Self Teaching Dress Cutting 187

Tadcaster 157
Tailor and Cutter Academy 150
tailors 2, 3, 11, 13, 14, 15, 16, 17, 18, 19, 20, 21, 22, 23, 26, 33, 34, 36, 40, 62, 81, 82, 83, 84, 160, 213, 271, 274, 275, 276
tailors employing women 15
tailors' hostility to mantua makers 3, 11, 14–24
Talbot, Sarah Strong 92
Tamworth 158
Tasker and Thompson 99
Tasker, Aunt 45
Tate, Annie 184, 185, 284
Taylor, Carrie 270, 286, 293
Taylor, Elizabeth 99–100, 103–104, Plate 16
Taylor, Miss 104, 106
Technical and Practical Lessons in Dressmaking 187
technical schools 149, 177
'Ten Hours Bill' 1847, 87
Tewkesbury 231
theft 75–76
Thetford 52
Thirkettle, Miss 157
Thomas, B. 106, 184, 203
Thomas, Margaret 76
Thomas, Rebecca 150–151, 177, 218, 258, Plate 27
Thomas, W.F. 139–140, Plate 19
Thompson, John 99
Thompson, Mary 19
Thornton, Mrs 239
Thornton, Rosalie 211
Tighnabruaich 110

Times, The viii, 4, 70, 88, 96, 119
Tinker, Polly 162
Tipperary 29
'tollerations' 21
Tomlin 187
Towers, Elizabeth 84
Trades Union Act 1871, 116
Tradewell, Mrs 133
transportation 75, 76, 115
Treadwin, Mrs 91, 102
Tredcroft, Miss 45
Tricksy, Syrena 195
trimmings 7, 27, 30, 40, 47, 49, 51, 56, 57, 60, 68, 78, 80, 107, 132, 135, 143, 147, 166, 176, 181, 189, 201, 206, 207, 231, 233, 236, 238, 264, 267
trotter 118
trousseau 100, 104, 174, 240, 241, 243, 247, 248, 256, 258
Tuke, Priscilla 36
Turber, Mary 19
Turner, Miss 91
Turner, Mrs 45
Turner, William of Stowmarket 157
Turnock, Mrs 137, 266
Turvile, Fortescue 37
Twigger, Mrs Dora 136
Tytler, Sarah 211

Ulverston 8, 58, 101, 107, 108, 111, 121, 128, 177, 215, 216, 217, 218, 219, 220, 227, 268, 285
'unbusinesslike' behaviour 109
unions 116, 271
Universal British Directory, The 82, 83, 231
Unprotected, or Facts in Dressmaking Life, The 199–201
Upper Brook Street 101, 108, 227, Plate 17

Vaughan, Ann 37
Vaughan, Mary 40
Vaughan, Miss 158
Ventnor 158
Verita, May 271
Versailles 58
Victoria, Queen 190
Vinck, C. 111
Viney, Richard 58
'Violet' 155

Vogue 104
Vyner family 11, Colour Plate I

Wage Boards 116, 271
wages 18, 39, 40, 42, 60, 92, 97, 105, 115, 116, 117, 118, 120, 126, 131, 132, 135, 137, 155, 163, 165, 166, 169, 171, 172, 184, 195, 200, 212, 265, 269, 270, 271, 272, 277
Wagland, Mary 214
Wakefield 17, 277
Wakes Colne 79
Walker, Mrs 120
Walkley, Mary Anne 96
Walkowitz, Judith 225, 285
Walsh, Claire 152
Walsingham, Augusta Lady 79
Walters of Chichester 165
Wanzer kilting machine 142–3, 181, Plate 21
War of the Spanish Succession 29
Ward, Mary 222
Ward, Mrs 112
Wardrope, Anne 214
Ware and Co, Davies Street 241
Warmingham, Mrs 17
Warndell, Mary 75
Warwick 8, 63, 66, 83, 277
washballs 51
'Water Police' 225
waterman 37
watershed of the 1870s 2, 139–167
Watson, Elizabeth Dorothy 47
Watson, Mrs 128
Watts, Alexander 144
Watts, George Frederick 202
Watts, S.J. and Co 107
Waugh, Norah 15, 274
Wayble, Ann 84
Weary 197, 202
Weatherill, Lorna 26, 275, 278
weaver 25, 235
Webb, Miss 239
Webb, Sydney 169
Webb, William 40
Webster 44, 117
Webster, Thomas and Co 117
Weeks and Fletcher 101
Weisner, Merry 16
Weldon, Christopher Edward 149

Weldon's Bazaar 187
Weldon's Dressmaker 187
Weldon's Ladies' Journal of Dress 149
Weldon's Needlework 187
Wells and Co, A.R. 184
Wells and Son of Wood Street 144
Wells-next-the-Sea 177
Welshpool 121, 132
Wendly, William 233
West End first rate establishment 100–101, 102–103
Westmoreland 8, 18
Weston, Emmeline and Clara 221
Weston-and-Wixhill-under-Red-Castle 241, 285
Weston-super-Mare 177
Wetley Rocks 248
Weymouth Assembly Rooms 31, Plate 6
Wharton, Mrs 51
Wheeler and Wilson 139, 141, 181
whisky 98, 112
Whissonsett 75
White, Florence 145, 187
White, John 15
White, W. E. of Ipswich 157–158
Whitehaven 95, 128
Whiteley's 254
Whittaker, Janea 68
White, Mrs of Drury Lane 37
Whiteley's 254
Why Dressmaking Does Not Pay 1, 120
Whyte, Mary 22
Wicker, Mrs 45
Wigmore Street 241, 251, 252, 253
Wigston 235
Wilcox, Margaret 14
Willcox and Gibbs 257
Willem, E. 84
William, Prince, Duke of Gloucester 52
Williams, Katherine 77
Williams, Mrs 17, 64, 78
Williamson, Ann Elizabeth and Lucy Williamson 219
Williamson, Christian and Edmond 52
Williamson, General Adam 78
Williamson, Mrs Ann (née Jones) 64, 78, 233–235, 258, 259
Willimott, Mrs Thomas 177
Wilson, J. 234

Wilson, Messrs 184
Wilson, Miss 199, 250
Wilson, Muriel 174
Wiltshire 8, 35, 80, 82, 229, 234
Winchelsea 47
Winchester 83, 84
Winder, Barb 84
Winn, Lady Sabine 53
Winstanley, Hilda 155, 212
Winter, Mrs Christian 176
Wolfe, Reverend Thomas of Howick 35–36, 214
Wolverhampton 157
women banned from working underground 1842,, 87
Women's Co-operative Guild, The 170
women's earnings 39–40, 47, 87, 116–118, 269, 270
Women's Industrial Council, The 170
Women's Labour League, The 170
Women's Protective and Provident League, The 169, 170
Wood, Isobel 11, 15
Wood, Mrs 112, 187
Wood, Mrs of Bowness 112
Wood Street 144, 146, 181
Wood, William – warehouse 70
Woodforde, Parson and Nancy 55, 278
Woollett, Mary 68
Worcester/Worcestershire 8, 20, 22, 40, 82, 83, 125, 275
Work and Wages 184, 277
working class housing 169
working class women unable to sew 135–136
Workshop Regulation Act of 1868, 150–152
Workwoman's Guide, The 13, 14
World of Fashion, The 147
Worthing 158
Worton, the Oswestry staymaker 241
Woutherington, Frances 110
Wright, Anne 76
Wright, Michael John 273
Wroughton staymaker 231
Wyches, Cyrill 36

X, Mrs 174–176
'XC' 226

Yarmouth, Countess of 126
Yeomans, Mary 16, 18, 213
Yeomans, Mrs Elizabeth 18
York/Yorkshire 8, 16, 17, 18, 19, 30, 36, 53, 54, 58, 59, 65, 77, 80, 82, 83, 107, 110, 129, 130, 131, 132, 133, 149, 170, 174, 213, 248, 269, 270, 274, 275, 276, 277, 278, 281

Young, Carola 214
Young Milliners, The 197
Young, Miss 127, 158
Young, Sarah 221
Young, Susannah 17
Young Woman's Guide, The 177

Colour Plate I *The Vyner Family* by John Michael Wright, *c.* 1673. Lady Vyner wears an early form of the mantua.

 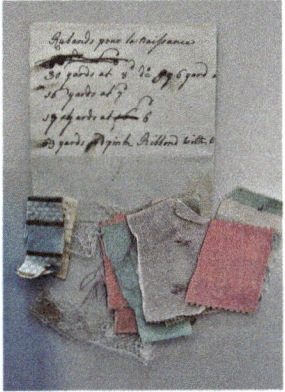

Colour Plate II Samples of printed calico and ribbon sent to Lady Winn at Nostell Priory in Yorkshire by Mrs Charlton, her London dressmaker.

Colour Plate III The Shrewsbury mantua, 1708–9.

Colour Plate IV Details of the construction and stitching of the mantua.

Colour Plate V 1770s dress of striped silk brocade with elaborate garniture. The stomacher is not original.

Colour Plate VI Detail of a printed muslin dress of 1835 showing the 'diamond' back and huge sleeves which were a feature of the period. The piping was to prevent the hand-stitched seams from gaping.

Colour Plate VII Detail of a dress purple ribbed silk made by Adderly's department store, Leicester, *c*. 1895. It is beautifully made and finished, with scalloped seams as recommended by Jeanette Davis in 1894.

Colour Plate VIII *The Song of the Shirt* by John Thomas Peele, 1849. It shows a young seamstress, her eyes red-rimmed with tiredness, in a bare attic room, and is typical of many paintings based on Thomas Hood's poem.

www.ingramcontent.com/pod-product-compliance
Lightning Source LLC
Chambersburg PA
CBHW072121290426
44111CB00012B/1736